STORM DOGS

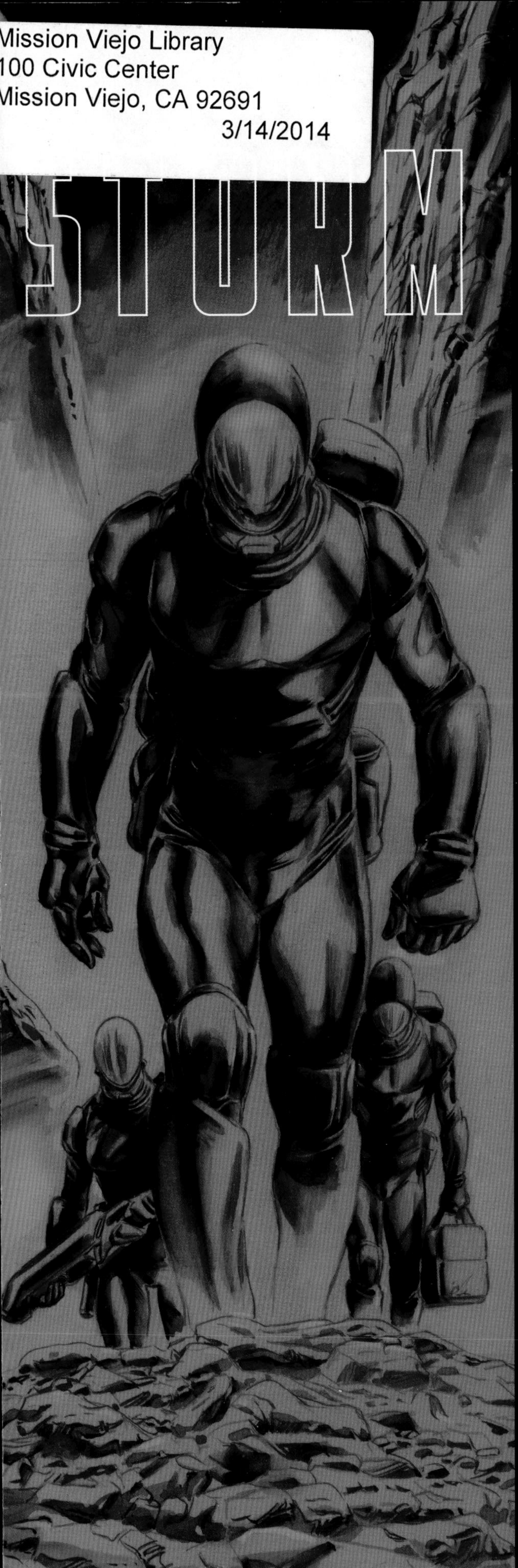

Script:
DAVID HINE
Art:
DOUG BRAITHWAITE
Colours:
ULISES ARREOLA
Lettering:
**RICHARD STARKINGS &
COMICRAFT'S JIMMY
BETANCOURT**
Design and Production:
JG ROSHELL OF COMICRAFT
Cover art::
DOUG & SUE BRAITHWAITE

IMAGE COMICS, INC.
Robert Kirkman - chief operating officer
Erik Larsen - chief financial officer
Todd McFarlane - president
Marc Silvestri - chief executive officer
Jim Valentino - vice-president

Eric Stephenson - publisher
Ron Richards - director of business development
Jennifer de Guzman - pr & marketing director
Branwyn Bigglestone - accounts manager
Emily Miller - accounting assistant
Jamie Parreno - marketing assistant
Emilio Bautista - sales assistant
Jaemie Dudas - administrative assistant
Jeremy Sullivan - digital rights coordinator
Tyler Shainline - events coordinator
David Brothers - content manager
Jonathan Chan - production manager
Drew Gill - art director
Monica Garcia - senior production artist
Vincent Kukua - production artist
Jenna Savage - production artist
Addison Duke - production artist
www.imagecomics.com

STORM DOGS VOL. 1. First Printing. Published by Image
Comics, Inc. Office of publication: 2001 Center St. Sixth Floor,
Berkeley, CA 94704. Copyright © 2013 David Hine and Doug
Braithwaite. Originally published in single magazine form as
STORM DOGS #1-6. All rights reserved. STORM DOGS™
(including all prominent characters featured herein), its logo
and all character likenesses are trademarks of David Hine and
Doug Braithwaite, unless otherwise noted. Image Comics®
and its logos are registered trademarks of Image Comics, Inc.
No part of this publication may be reproduced or transmitted,
in any form or by any means (except for short excerpts for
review purposes) without the express written permission of
Image Comics, Inc. All names, characters, events and locales
in this publication are entirely fictional. Any resemblance to
actual persons (living or dead), events or places, without satiric
intent, is coincidental. PRINTED IN SOUTH KOREA. ISBN: 978-
1-60706-825-9. International Rights / Foreign Licensing --
foreignlicensing@imagecomics.com

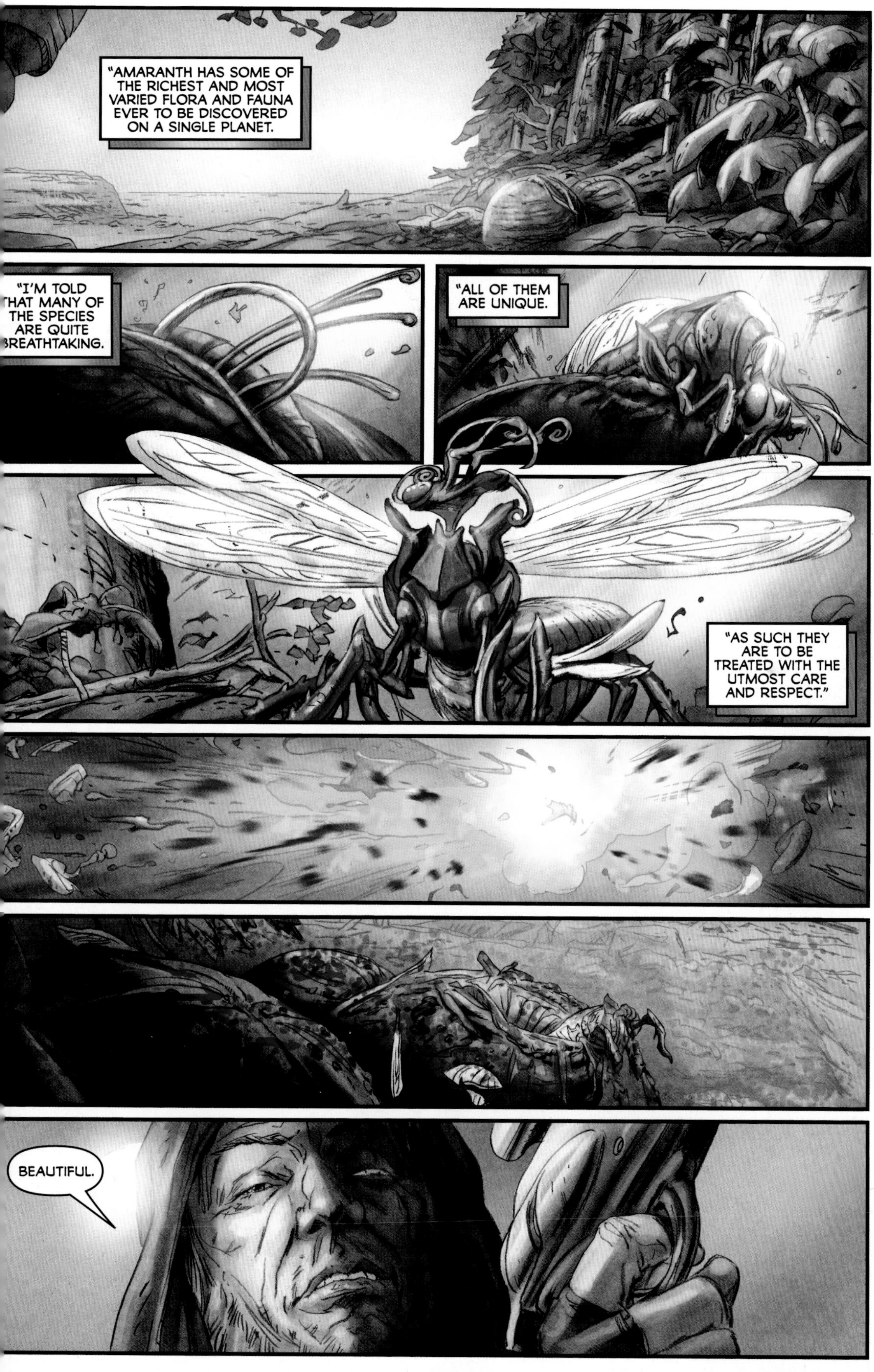
"AMARANTH HAS SOME OF THE RICHEST AND MOST VARIED FLORA AND FAUNA EVER TO BE DISCOVERED ON A SINGLE PLANET.
"I'M TOLD THAT MANY OF THE SPECIES ARE QUITE BREATHTAKING.
"ALL OF THEM ARE UNIQUE.
"AS SUCH THEY ARE TO BE TREATED WITH THE UTMOST CARE AND RESPECT."
BEAUTIFUL.

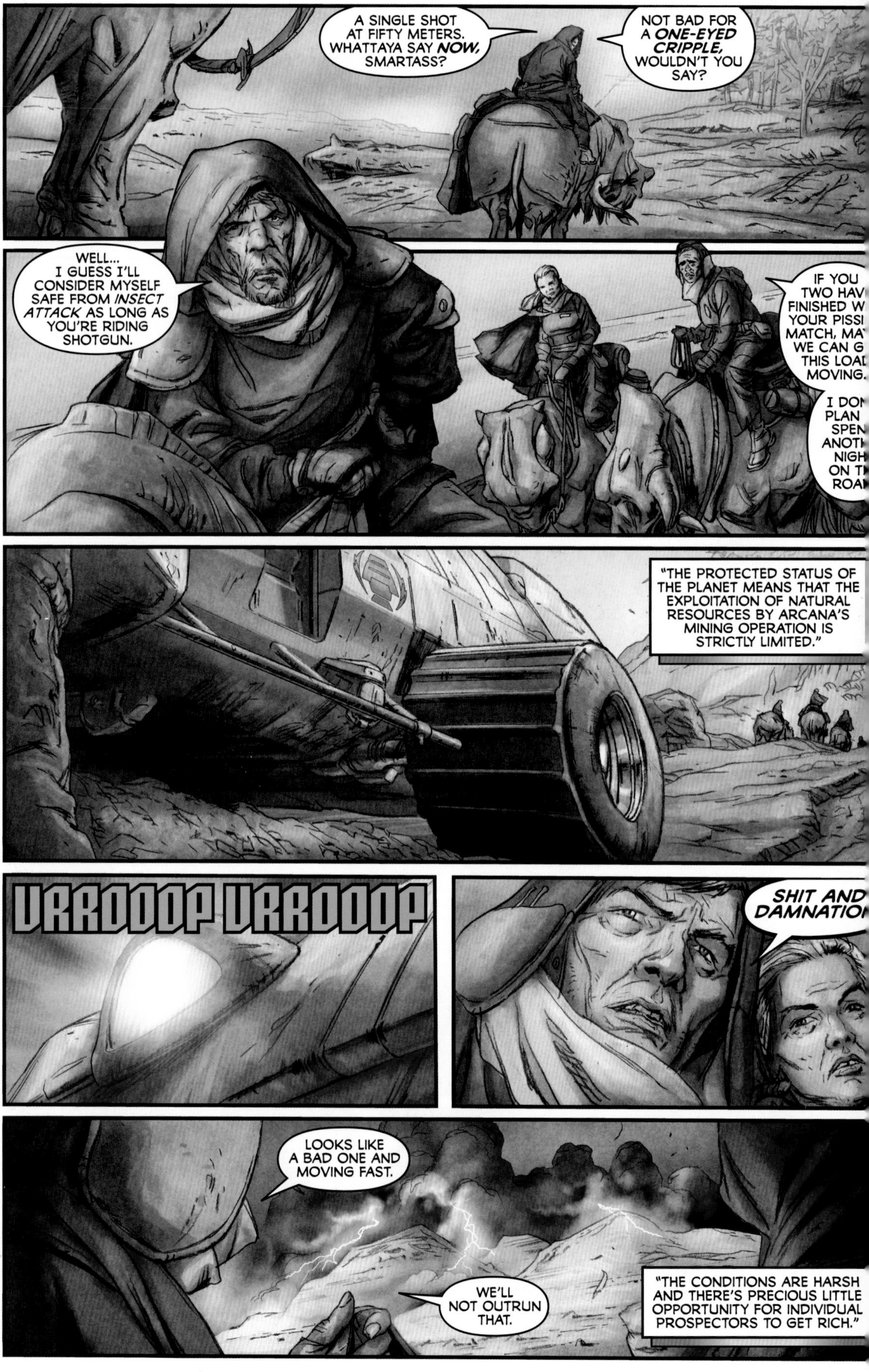
A SINGLE SHOT AT FIFTY METERS. WHATTAYA SAY *NOW,* SMARTASS?
NOT BAD FOR A ***ONE-EYED CRIPPLE,*** WOULDN'T YOU SAY?
WELL... I GUESS I'LL CONSIDER MYSELF SAFE FROM *INSECT ATTACK* AS LONG AS YOU'RE RIDING SHOTGUN.
"THE PROTECTED STATUS OF THE PLANET MEANS THAT THE EXPLOITATION OF NATURAL RESOURCES BY ARCANA'S MINING OPERATION IS STRICTLY LIMITED."
VRROOOP VRROOOP
LOOKS LIKE A BAD ONE AND MOVING FAST.
WE'LL NOT OUTRUN THAT.
"THE CONDITIONS ARE HARSH AND THERE'S PRECIOUS LITTLE OPPORTUNITY FOR INDIVIDUAL PROSPECTORS TO GET RICH."

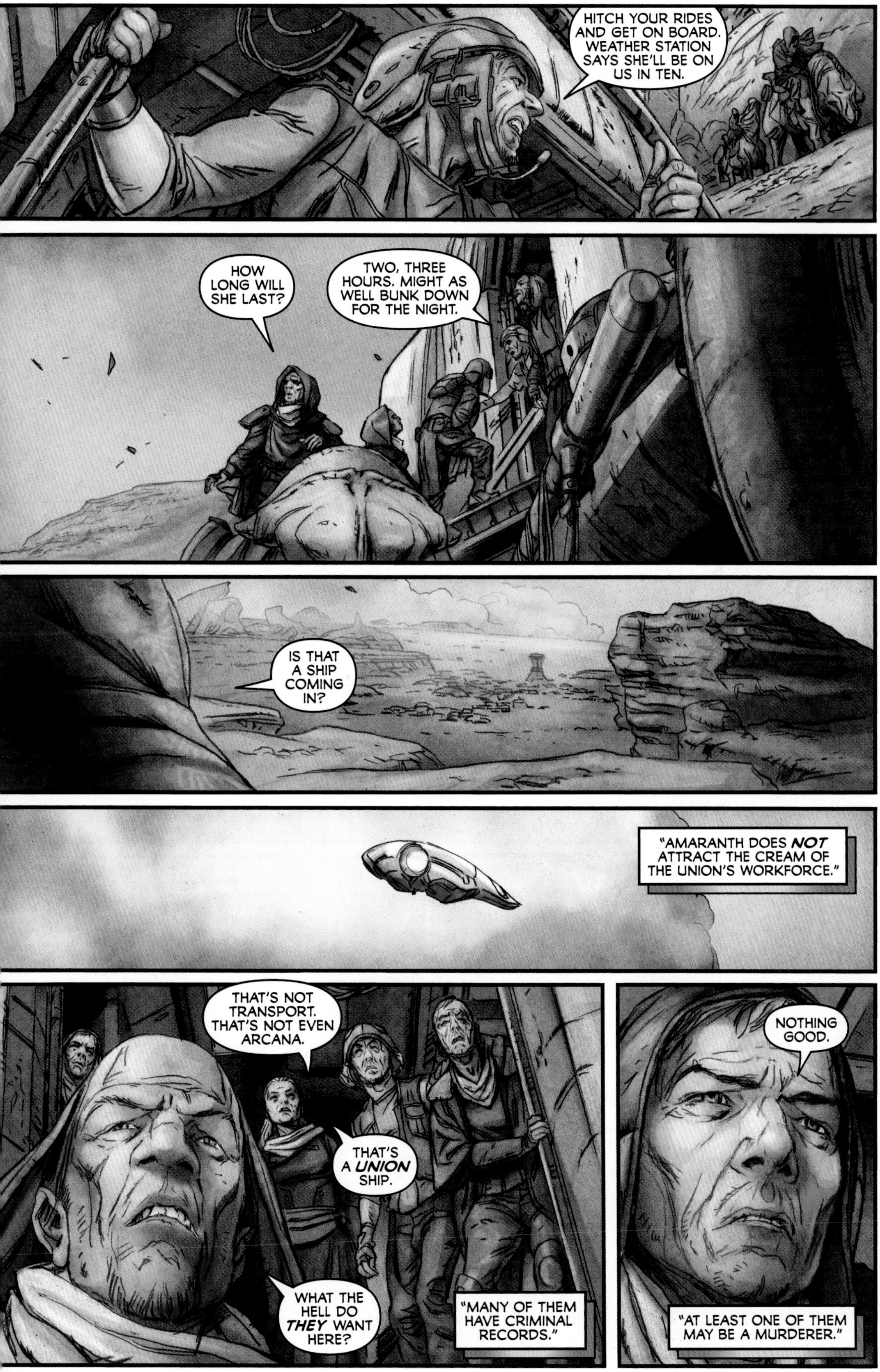
HITCH YOUR RIDES AND GET ON BOARD. WEATHER STATION SAYS SHE'LL BE ON US IN TEN.
HOW LONG WILL SHE LAST?
TWO, THREE HOURS. MIGHT AS WELL BUNK DOWN FOR THE NIGHT.
IS THAT A SHIP COMING IN?
"AMARANTH DOES *NOT* ATTRACT THE CREAM OF THE UNION'S WORKFORCE."
THAT'S NOT TRANSPORT. THAT'S NOT EVEN ARCANA.
THAT'S A *UNION* SHIP.
WHAT THE HELL DO *THEY* WANT HERE?
"MANY OF THEM HAVE CRIMINAL RECORDS."
NOTHING GOOD.
"AT LEAST ONE OF THEM MAY BE A MURDERER."

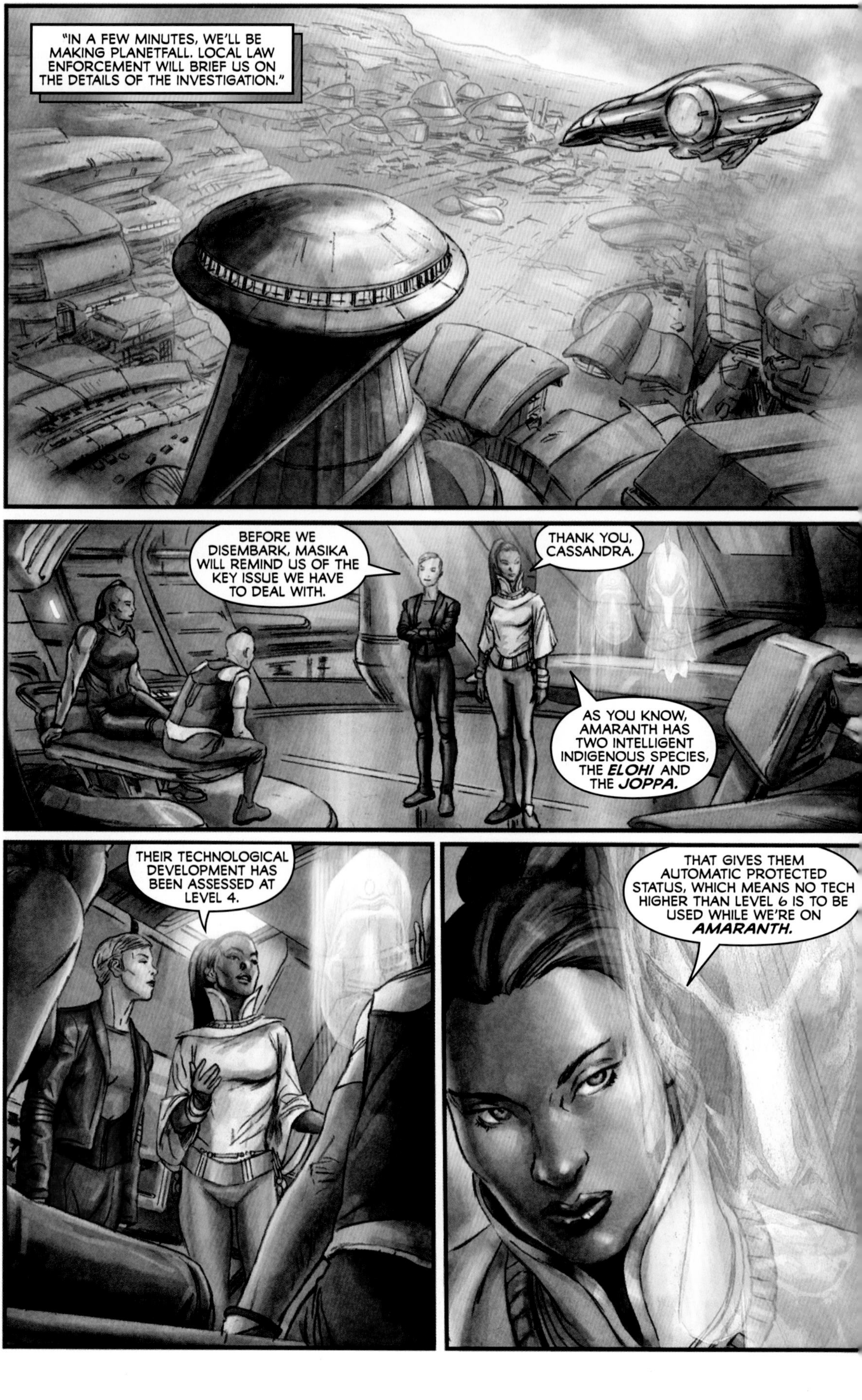
"IN A FEW MINUTES, WE'LL BE MAKING PLANETFALL. LOCAL LAW ENFORCEMENT WILL BRIEF US ON THE DETAILS OF THE INVESTIGATION."
BEFORE WE DISEMBARK, MASIKA WILL REMIND US OF THE KEY ISSUE WE HAVE TO DEAL WITH.
THANK YOU, CASSANDRA.
AS YOU KNOW, AMARANTH HAS TWO INTELLIGENT INDIGENOUS SPECIES, THE *ELOHI* AND THE *JOPPA.*
THEIR TECHNOLOGICAL DEVELOPMENT HAS BEEN ASSESSED AT LEVEL 4.
THAT GIVES THEM AUTOMATIC PROTECTED STATUS, WHICH MEANS NO TECH HIGHER THAN LEVEL 6 IS TO BE USED WHILE WE'RE ON *AMARANTH.*

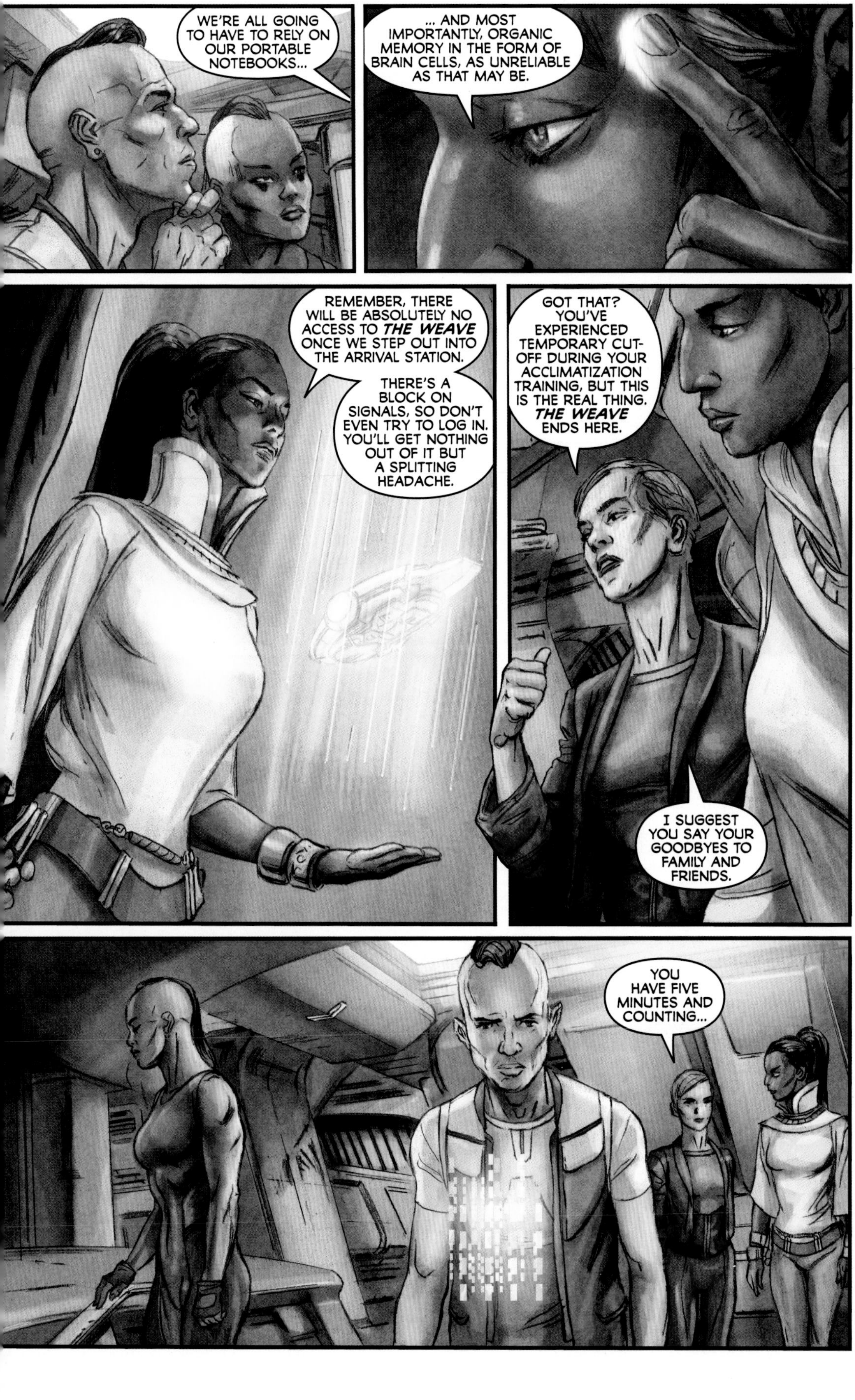
WE'RE ALL GOING TO HAVE TO RELY ON OUR PORTABLE NOTEBOOKS...
... AND MOST IMPORTANTLY, ORGANIC MEMORY IN THE FORM OF BRAIN CELLS, AS UNRELIABLE AS THAT MAY BE.
REMEMBER, THERE WILL BE ABSOLUTELY NO ACCESS TO *THE WEAVE* ONCE WE STEP OUT INTO THE ARRIVAL STATION.
THERE'S A BLOCK ON SIGNALS, SO DON'T EVEN TRY TO LOG IN. YOU'LL GET NOTHING OUT OF IT BUT A SPLITTING HEADACHE.
GOT THAT? YOU'VE EXPERIENCED TEMPORARY CUT-OFF DURING YOUR ACCLIMATIZATION TRAINING, BUT THIS IS THE REAL THING. *THE WEAVE* ENDS HERE.
I SUGGEST YOU SAY YOUR GOODBYES TO FAMILY AND FRIENDS.
YOU HAVE FIVE MINUTES AND COUNTING...

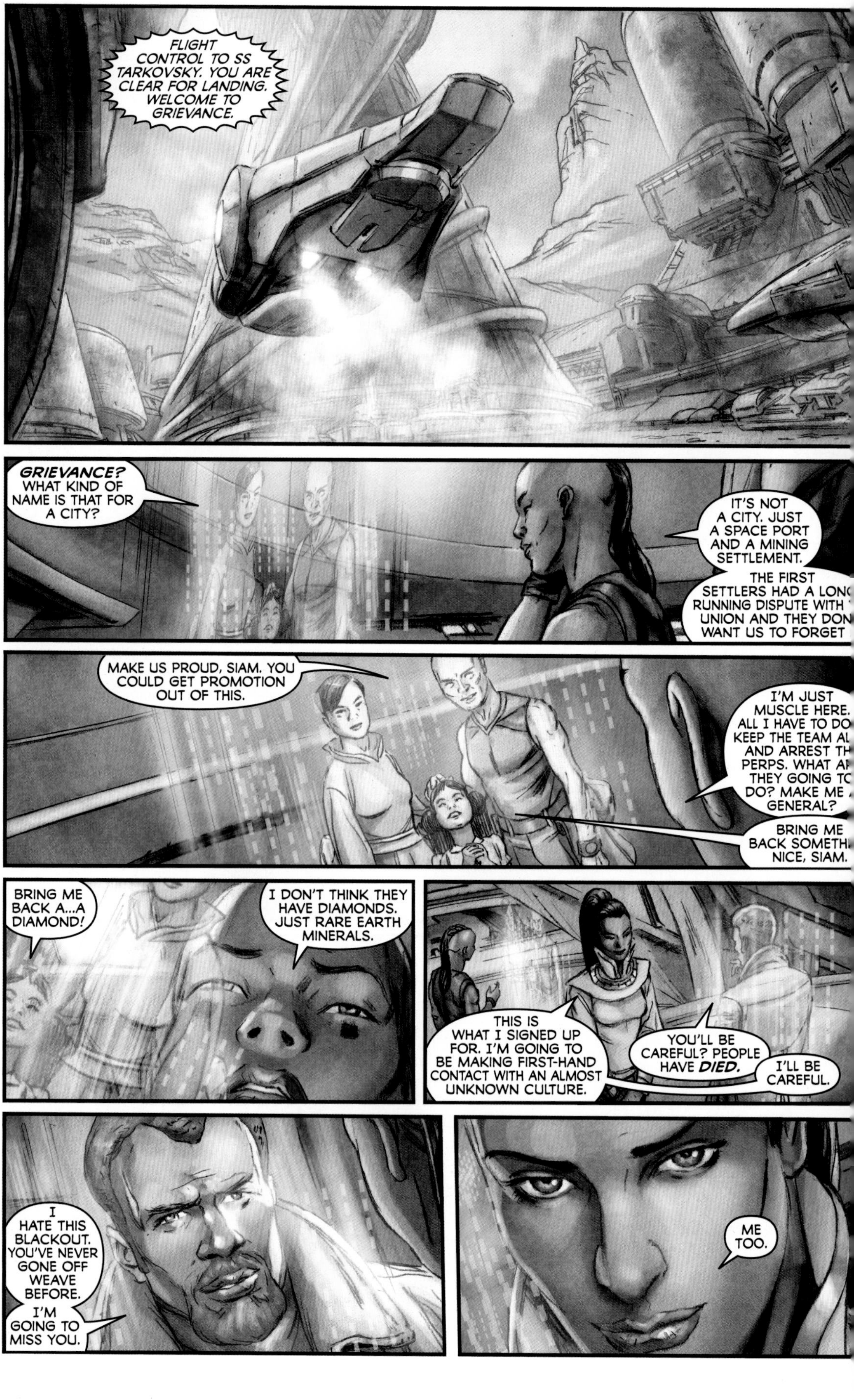

FLIGHT CONTROL TO SS TARKOVSKY. YOU ARE CLEAR FOR LANDING. WELCOME TO GRIEVANCE.
GRIEVANCE? WHAT KIND OF NAME IS THAT FOR A CITY?
IT'S NOT A CITY. JUST A SPACE PORT AND A MINING SETTLEMENT.
THE FIRST SETTLERS HAD A LON RUNNING DISPUTE WITH UNION AND THEY DON WANT US TO FORGET
MAKE US PROUD, SIAM. YOU COULD GET PROMOTION OUT OF THIS.
I'M JUST MUSCLE HERE. ALL I HAVE TO DO KEEP THE TEAM AL AND ARREST TH PERPS. WHAT AI THEY GOING TO DO? MAKE ME GENERAL?
BRING ME BACK SOMETH NICE, SIAM.
BRING ME BACK A...A DIAMOND!
I DON'T THINK THEY HAVE DIAMONDS. JUST RARE EARTH MINERALS.
THIS IS WHAT I SIGNED UP FOR. I'M GOING TO BE MAKING FIRST-HAND CONTACT WITH AN ALMOST UNKNOWN CULTURE.
YOU'LL BE CAREFUL? PEOPLE HAVE DIED.
I'LL BE CAREFUL.
I HATE THIS BLACKOUT. YOU'VE NEVER GONE OFF WEAVE BEFORE.
I'M GOING TO MISS YOU.
ME TOO.

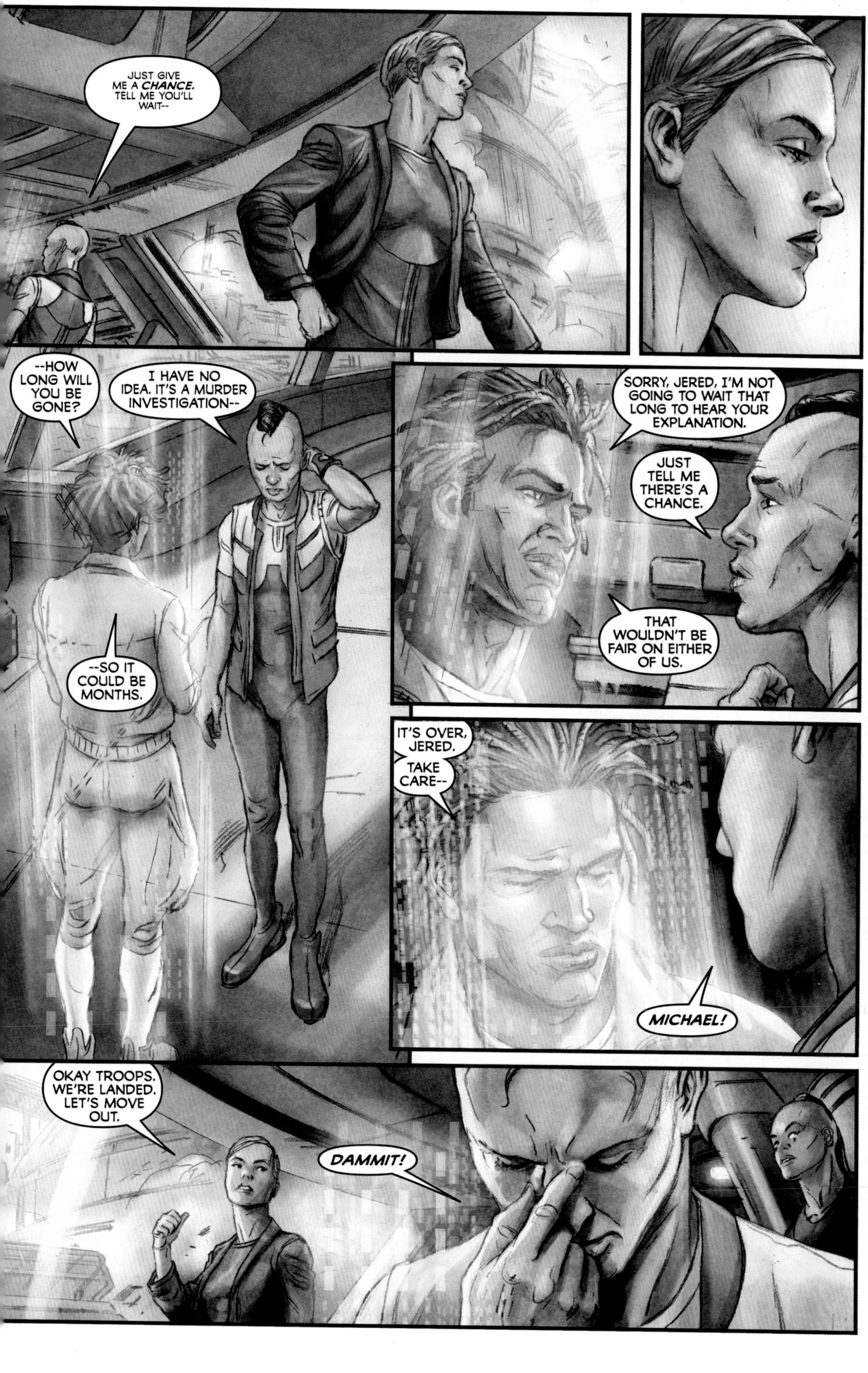
JUST GIVE ME A *CHANCE.* TELL ME YOU'LL WAIT--
--HOW LONG WILL YOU BE GONE?
I HAVE NO IDEA. IT'S A MURDER INVESTIGATION--
--SO IT COULD BE MONTHS.
SORRY, JERED, I'M NOT GOING TO WAIT THAT LONG TO HEAR YOUR EXPLANATION.
JUST TELL ME THERE'S A CHANCE.
THAT WOULDN'T BE FAIR ON EITHER OF US.
IT'S OVER, JERED.
TAKE CARE--
MICHAEL!
OKAY TROOPS. WE'RE LANDED. LET'S MOVE OUT.
DAMMIT!

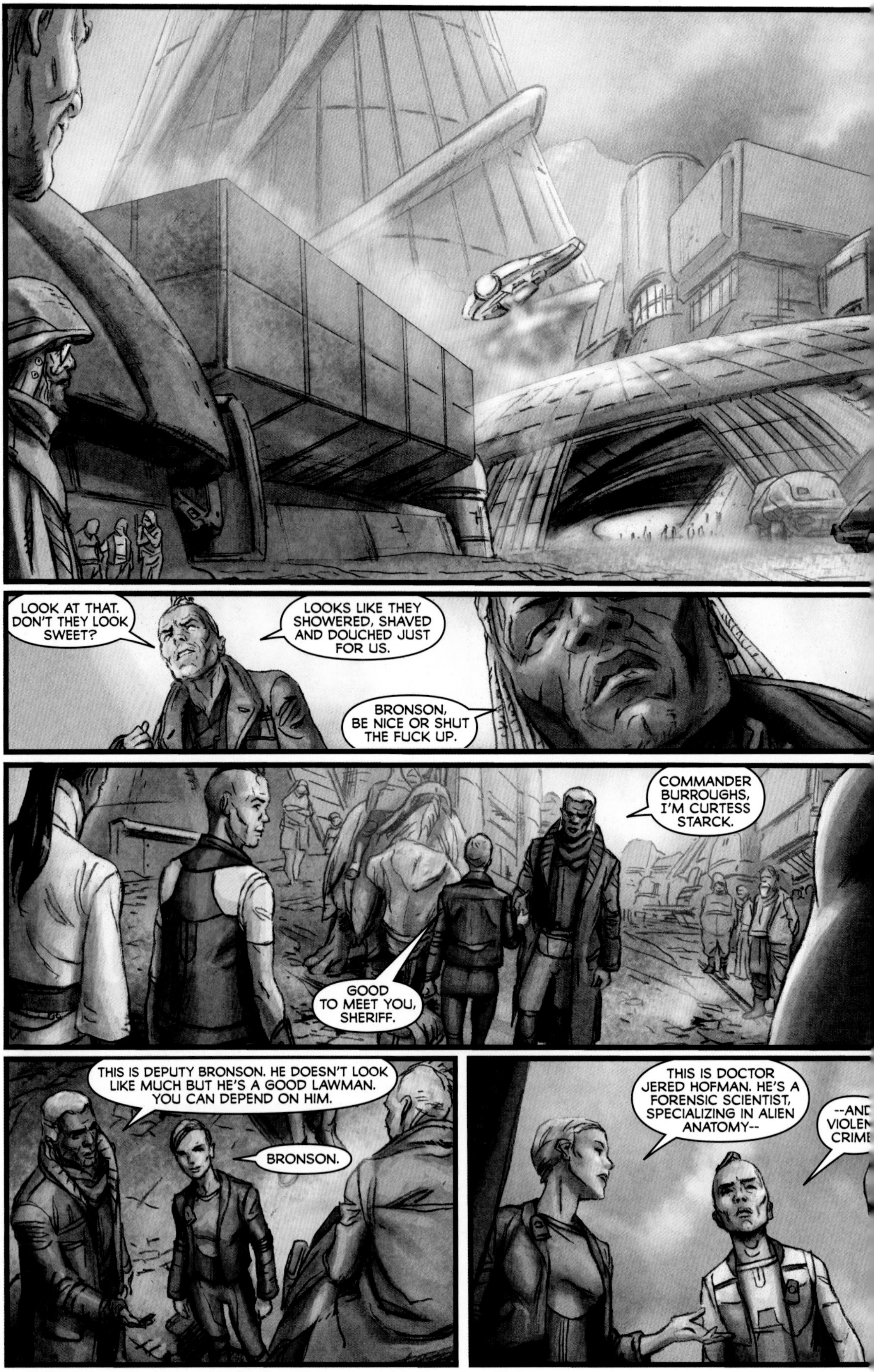
LOOK AT THAT. DON'T THEY LOOK SWEET?
LOOKS LIKE THEY SHOWERED, SHAVED AND DOUCHED JUST FOR US.
BRONSON, BE NICE OR SHUT THE FUCK UP.
COMMANDER BURROUGHS, I'M CURTESS STARCK.
GOOD TO MEET YOU, SHERIFF.
THIS IS DEPUTY BRONSON. HE DOESN'T LOOK LIKE MUCH BUT HE'S A GOOD LAWMAN. YOU CAN DEPEND ON HIM.
BRONSON.
THIS IS DOCTOR JERED HOFMAN. HE'S A FORENSIC SCIENTIST, SPECIALIZING IN ALIEN ANATOMY--

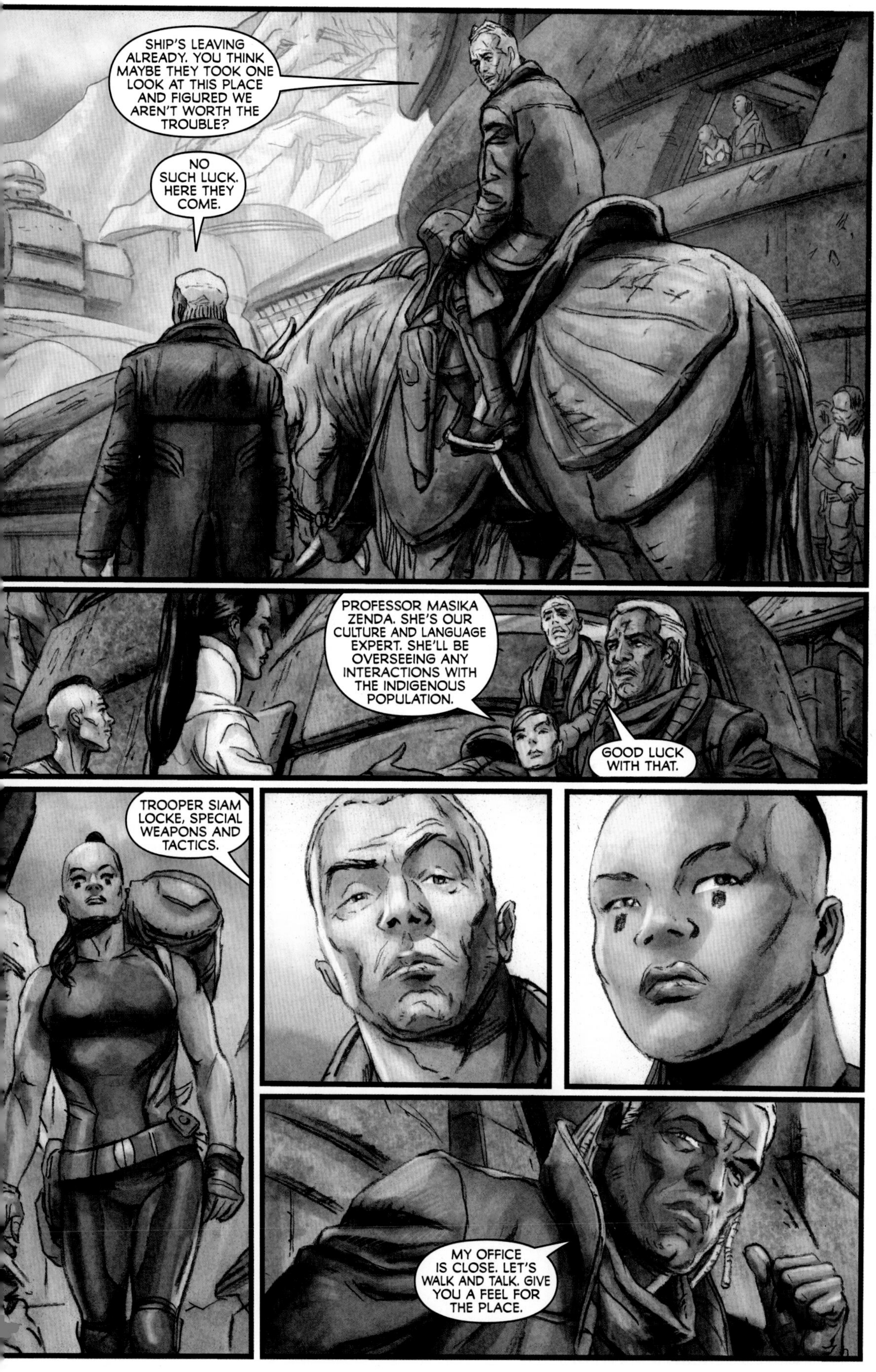
SHIP'S LEAVING ALREADY. YOU THINK MAYBE THEY TOOK ONE LOOK AT THIS PLACE AND FIGURED WE AREN'T WORTH THE TROUBLE?
NO SUCH LUCK. HERE THEY COME.
PROFESSOR MASIKA ZENDA. SHE'S OUR CULTURE AND LANGUAGE EXPERT. SHE'LL BE OVERSEEING ANY INTERACTIONS WITH THE INDIGENOUS POPULATION.
GOOD LUCK WITH THAT.
TROOPER SIAM LOCKE, SPECIAL WEAPONS AND TACTICS.
MY OFFICE IS CLOSE. LET'S WALK AND TALK. GIVE YOU A FEEL FOR THE PLACE.

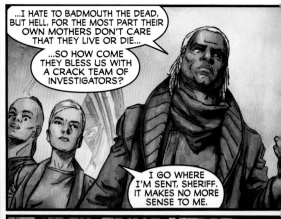

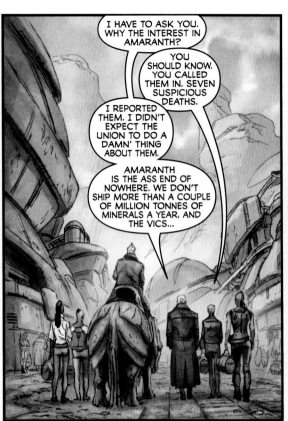

I HAVE TO ASK YOU. WHY THE INTEREST IN AMARANTH?

YOU SHOULD KNOW. YOU CALLED THEM IN. SEVEN SUSPICIOUS DEATHS.

I REPORTED THEM. I DIDN'T EXPECT THE UNION TO DO A DAMN' THING ABOUT THEM.

AMARANTH IS THE ASS END OF NOWHERE. WE DON'T SHIP MORE THAN A COUPLE OF MILLION TONNES OF MINERALS A YEAR, AND THE VICS...

...I HATE TO BADMOUTH THE DEAD, BUT HELL, FOR THE MOST PART THEIR OWN MOTHERS DON'T CARE THAT THEY LIVE OR DIE...

...SO HOW COME THEY BLESS US WITH A CRACK TEAM OF INVESTIGATORS?

I GO WHERE I'M SENT, SHERIFF. IT MAKES NO MORE SENSE TO ME.

STORM COMING.

BEEP

BEEP

BEEP

BEEP

TOLD YOU.

YEAH, YOU TOLD US.

ALL RIGHT, WEATHER TOWER SAYS WE HAVE ROLLING THUNDER HEADING THIS WAY. DUE IN FIFTEEN TO TWENTY MINUTES, SO LET'S GET THE HELL OFF THE STREET.

BEEP

YOUR FIRST STORM. YOU'RE IN FOR A TREAT.

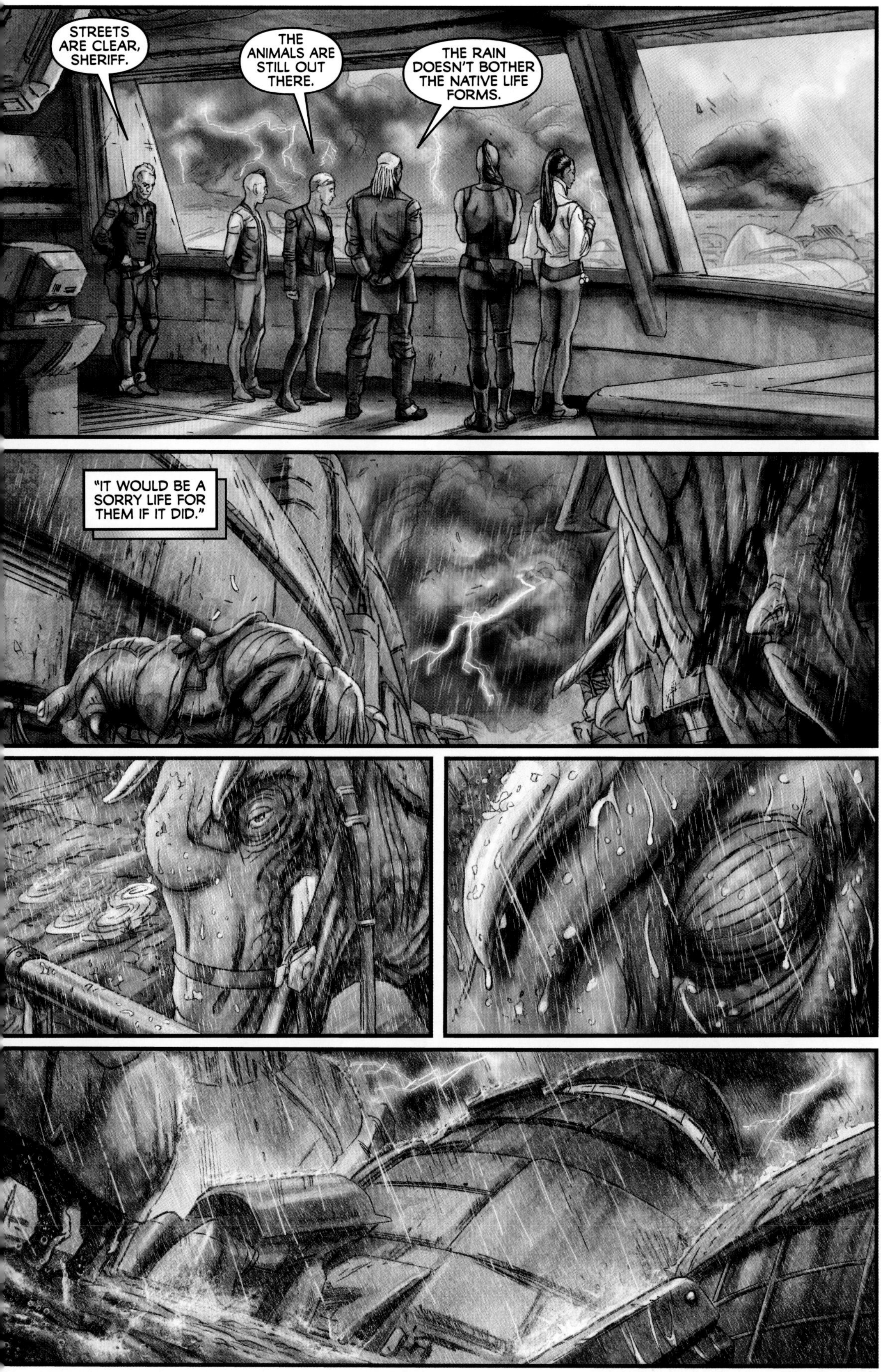
STREETS ARE CLEAR, SHERIFF.
THE ANIMALS ARE STILL OUT THERE.
THE RAIN DOESN'T BOTHER THE NATIVE LIFE FORMS.
"IT WOULD BE A SORRY LIFE FOR THEM IF IT DID."

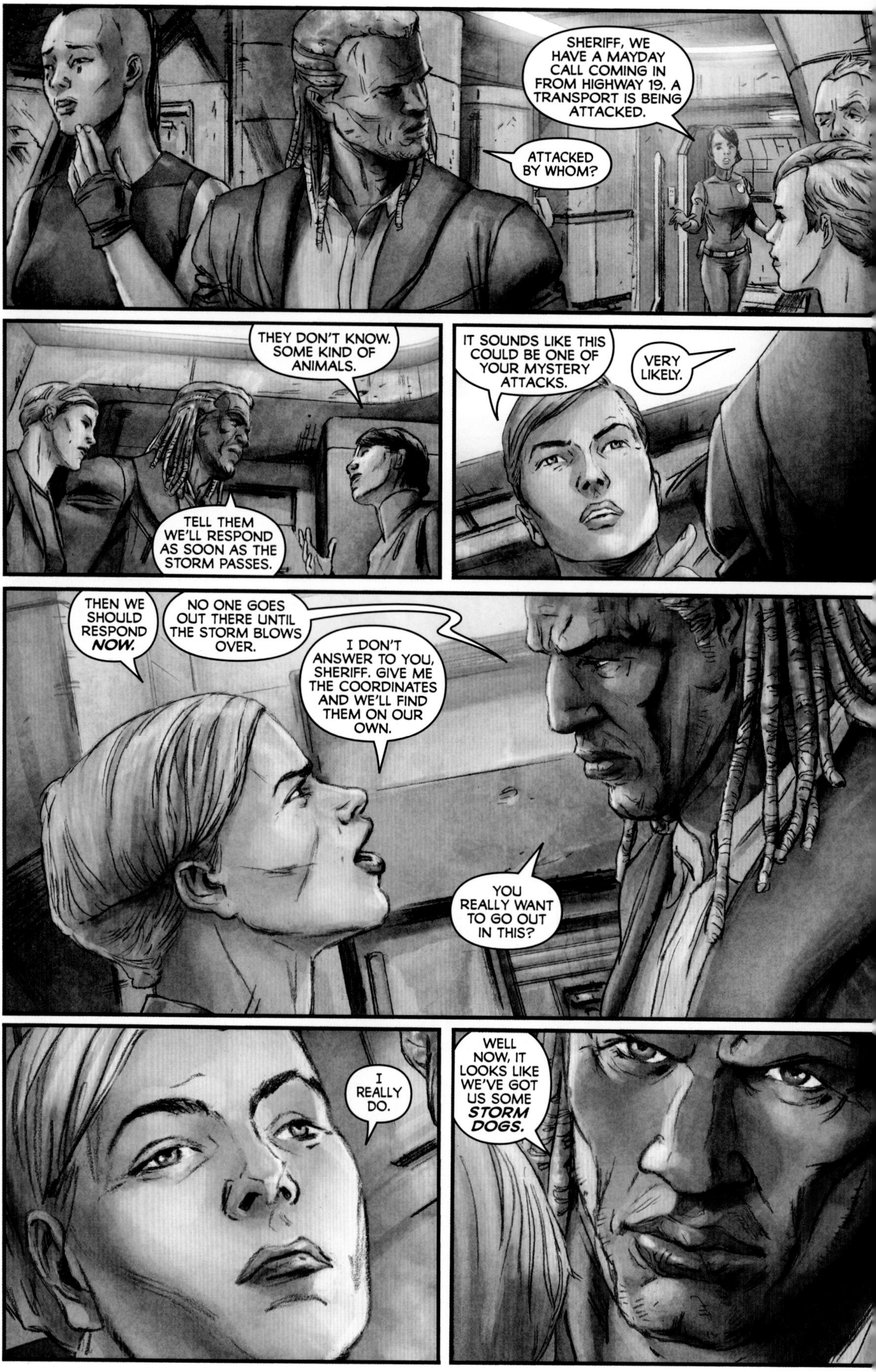
SHERIFF, WE HAVE A MAYDAY CALL COMING IN FROM HIGHWAY 19. A TRANSPORT IS BEING ATTACKED.
ATTACKED BY WHOM?
THEY DON'T KNOW. SOME KIND OF ANIMALS.
TELL THEM WE'LL RESPOND AS SOON AS THE STORM PASSES.
IT SOUNDS LIKE THIS COULD BE ONE OF YOUR MYSTERY ATTACKS.
VERY LIKELY.
THEN WE SHOULD RESPOND ***NOW.***
NO ONE GOES OUT THERE UNTIL THE STORM BLOWS OVER.
I DON'T ANSWER TO YOU, SHERIFF. GIVE ME THE COORDINATES AND WE'LL FIND THEM ON OUR OWN.
YOU REALLY WANT TO GO OUT IN THIS?
I REALLY DO.
WELL NOW, IT LOOKS LIKE WE'VE GOT US SOME ***STORM DOGS.***

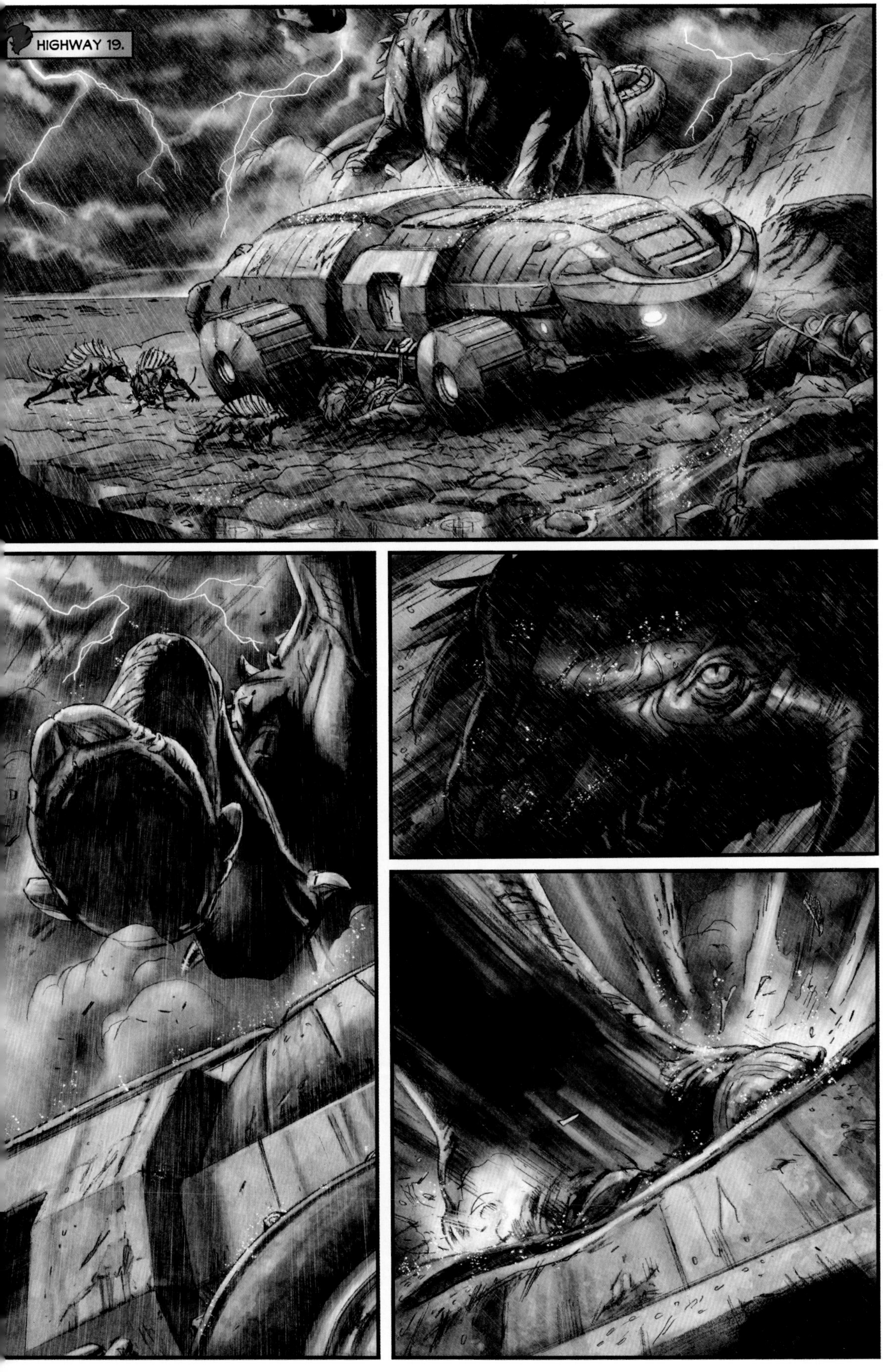
HIGHWAY 19.

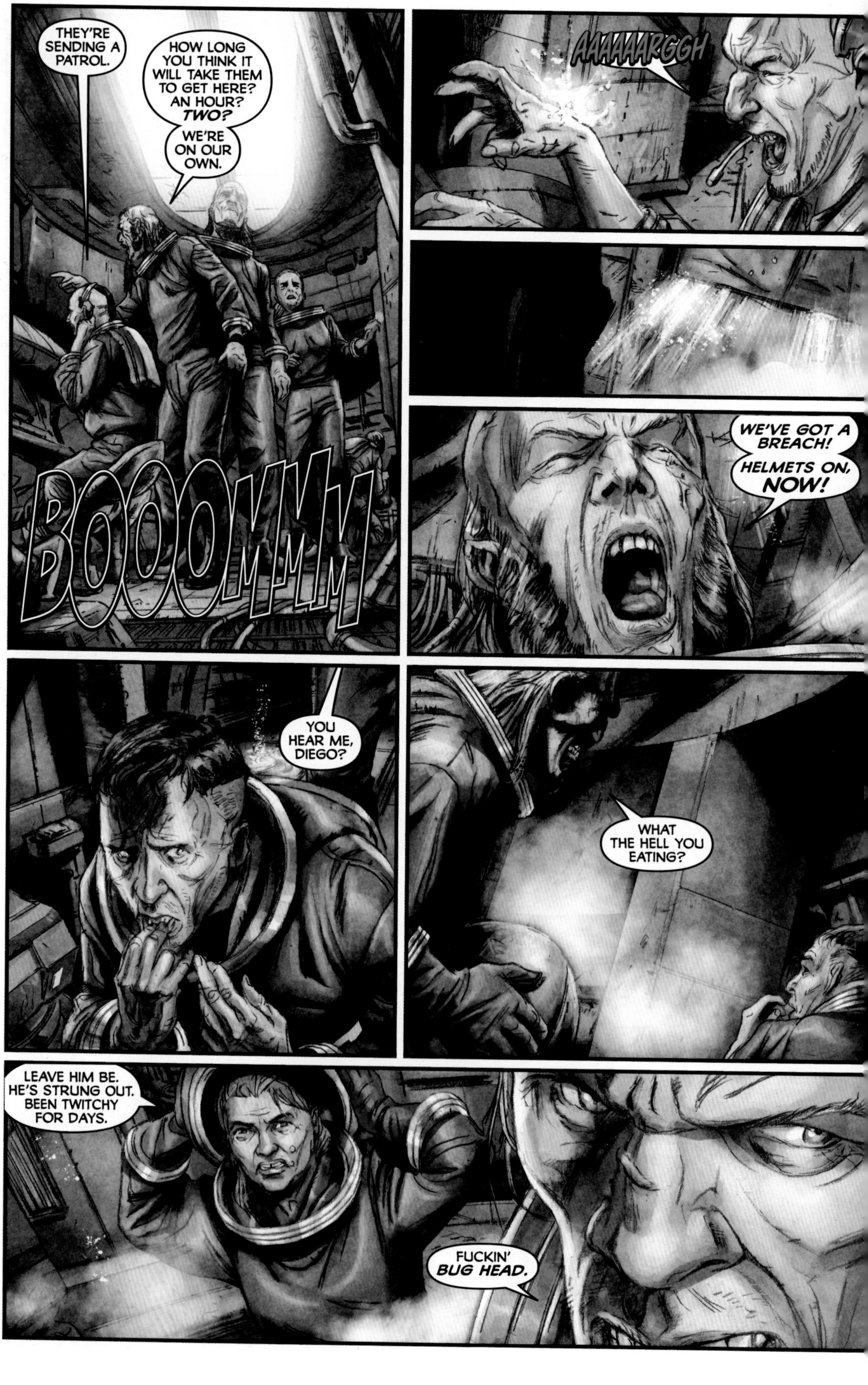
THEY'RE SENDING A PATROL.
HOW LONG YOU THINK IT WILL TAKE THEM TO GET HERE? AN HOUR? *TWO?*
WE'RE ON OUR OWN.
BOOOMMM
AAAAAARGGH
WE'VE GOT A BREACH!
HELMETS ON, NOW!
YOU HEAR ME, DIEGO?
WHAT THE HELL YOU EATING?
LEAVE HIM BE. HE'S STRUNG OUT. BEEN TWITCHY FOR DAYS.
FUCKIN' *BUG HEAD.*

BADOOOM

WHATEVER THAT IS OUT THERE, IT'S COMING IN!

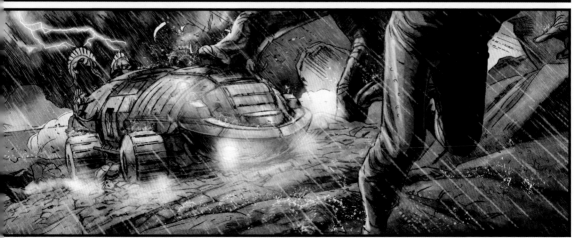

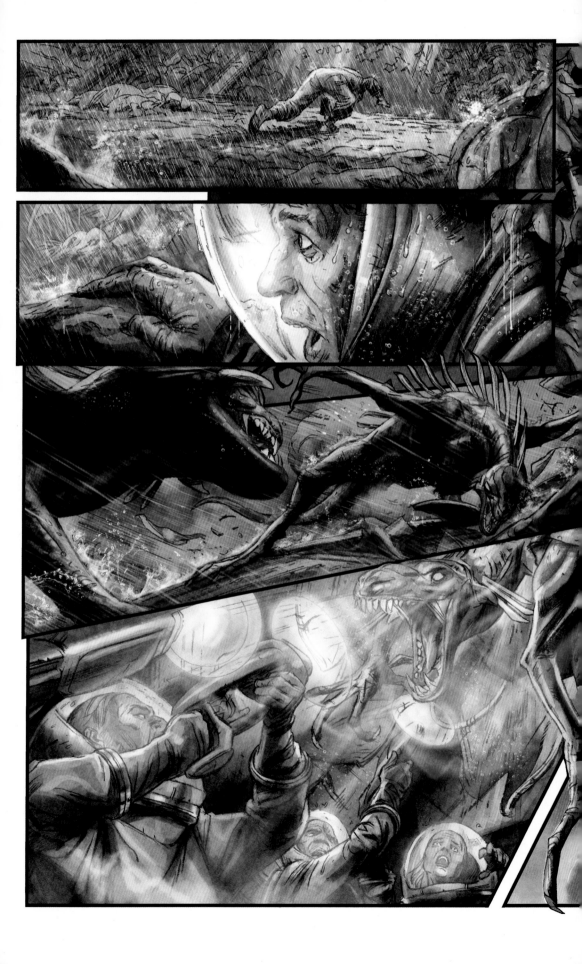

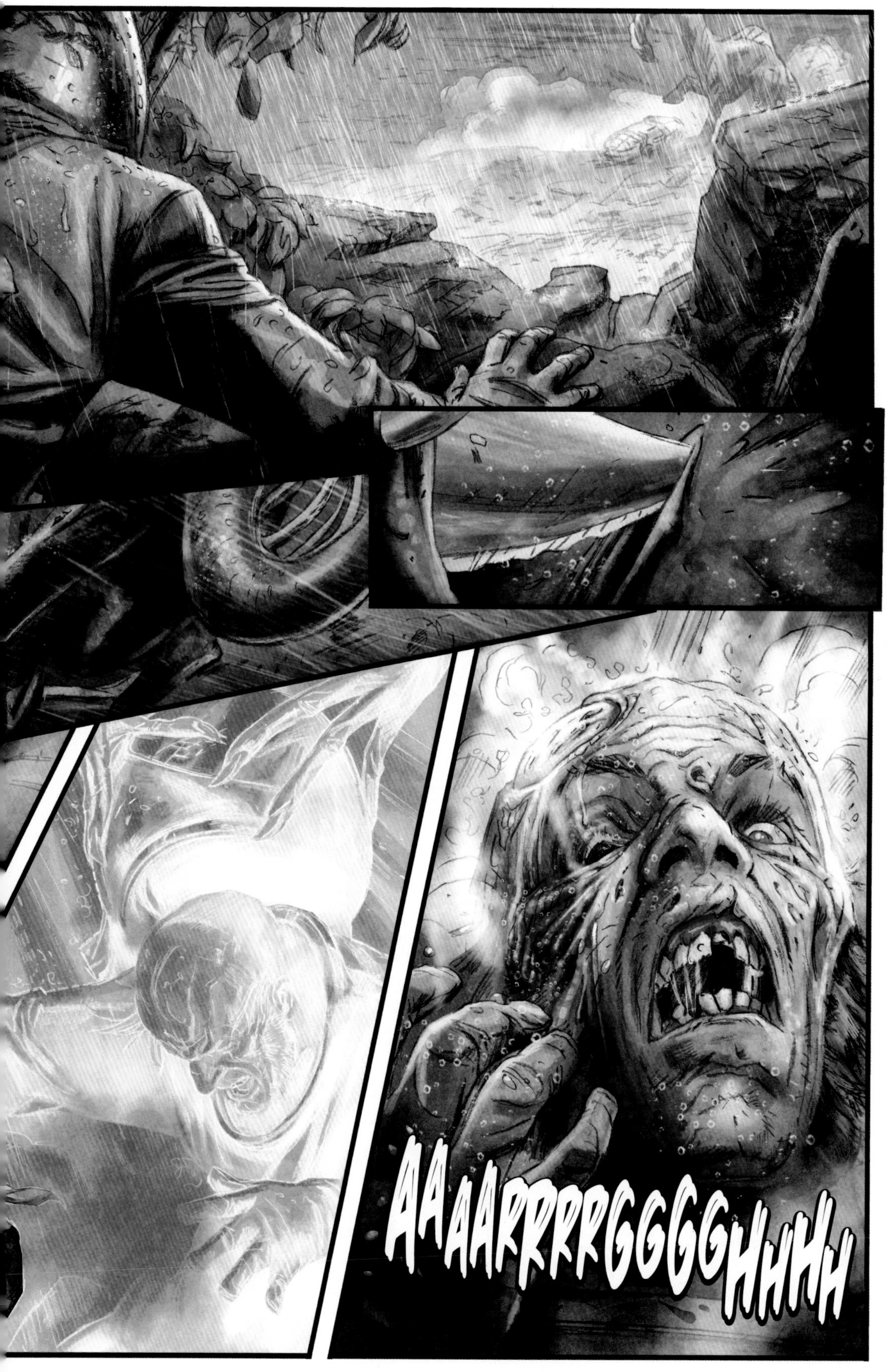
AAAARRRRGGGGHHHH

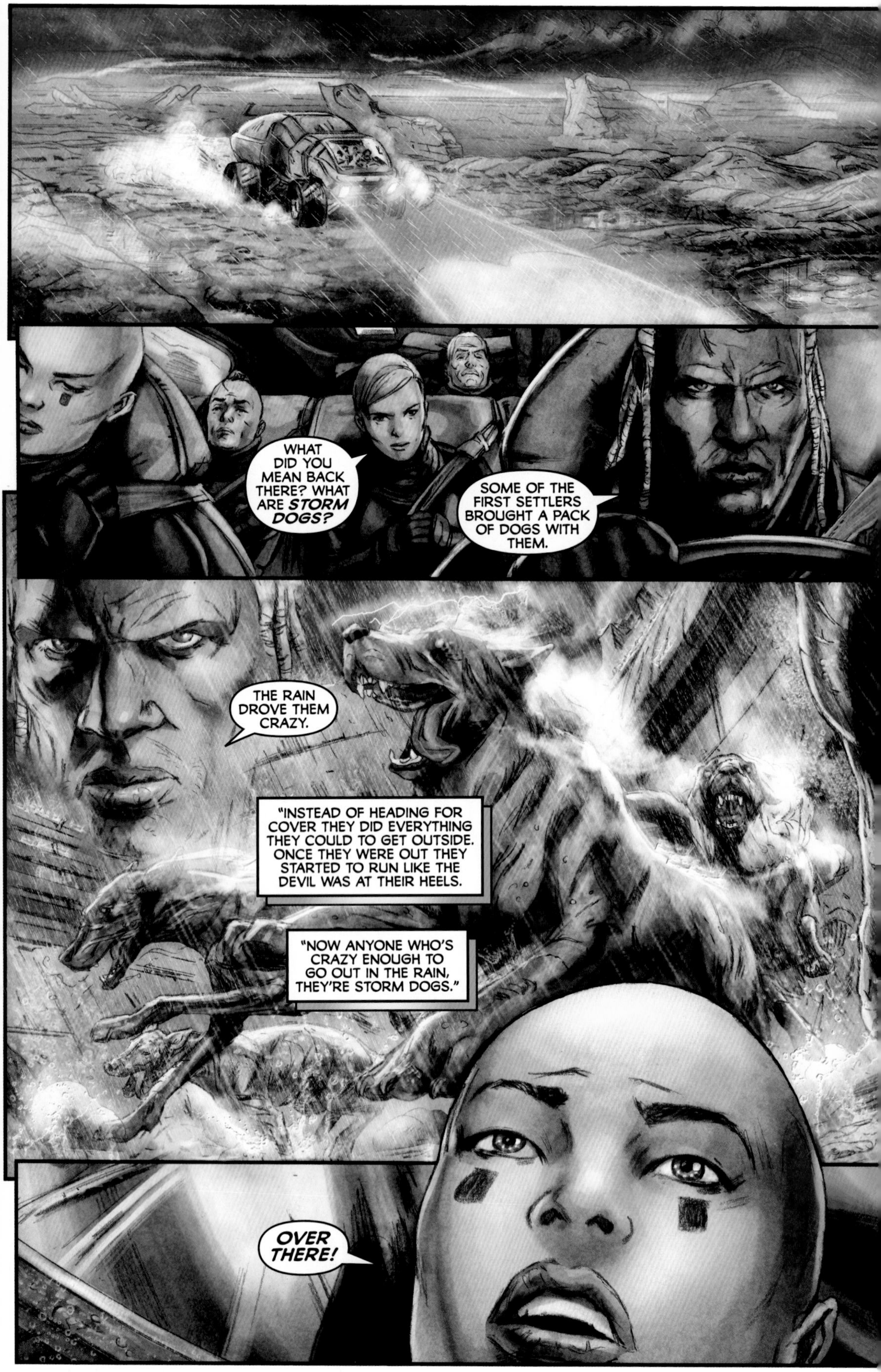
WHAT DID YOU MEAN BACK THERE? WHAT ARE STORM DOGS?
SOME OF THE FIRST SETTLERS BROUGHT A PACK OF DOGS WITH THEM.
THE RAIN DROVE THEM CRAZY.
"INSTEAD OF HEADING FOR COVER THEY DID EVERYTHING THEY COULD TO GET OUTSIDE. ONCE THEY WERE OUT THEY STARTED TO RUN LIKE THE DEVIL WAS AT THEIR HEELS.
"NOW ANYONE WHO'S CRAZY ENOUGH TO GO OUT IN THE RAIN, THEY'RE STORM DOGS."
OVER THERE!

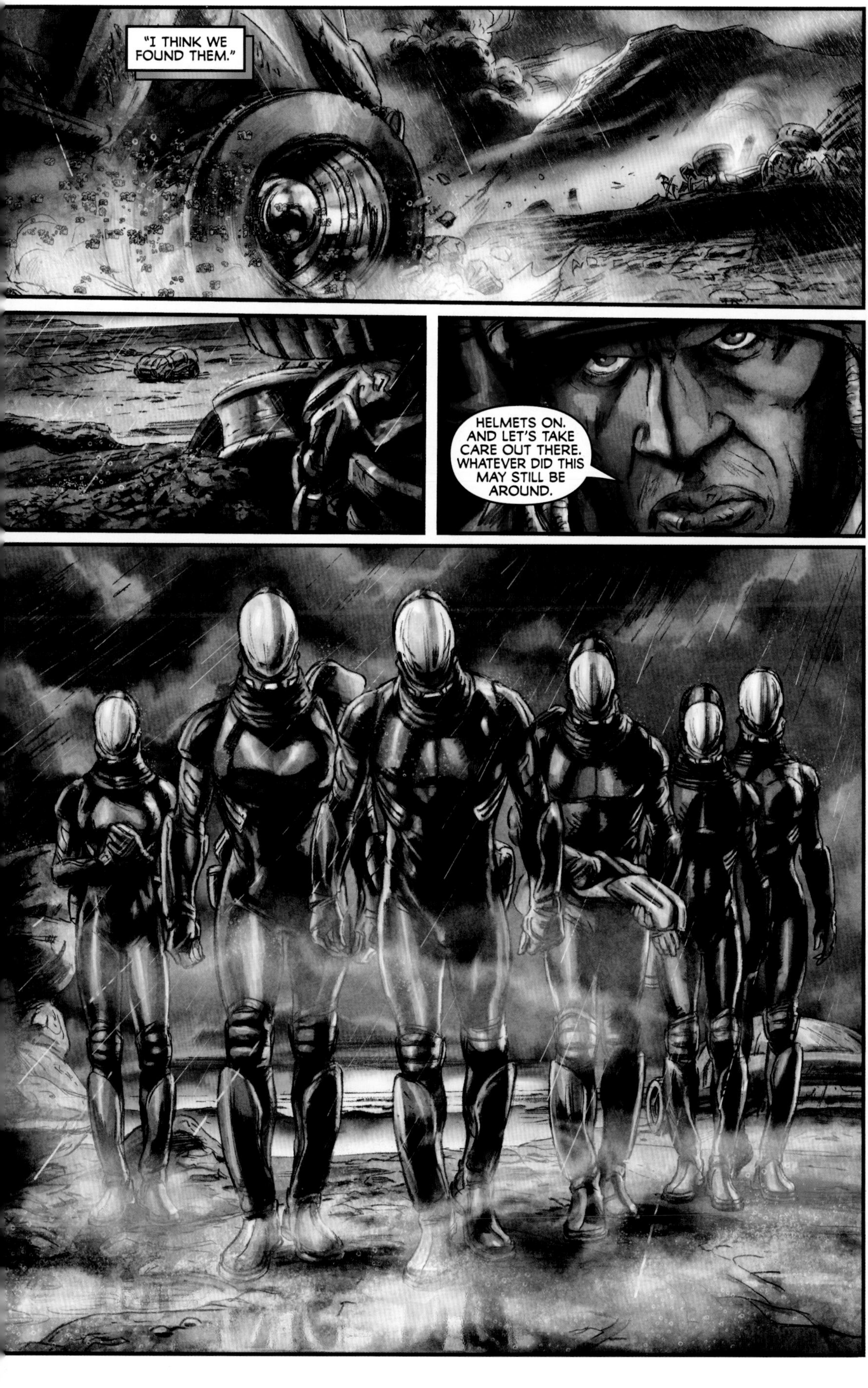
"I THINK WE FOUND THEM."
HELMETS ON. AND LET'S TAKE CARE OUT THERE. WHATEVER DID THIS MAY STILL BE AROUND.

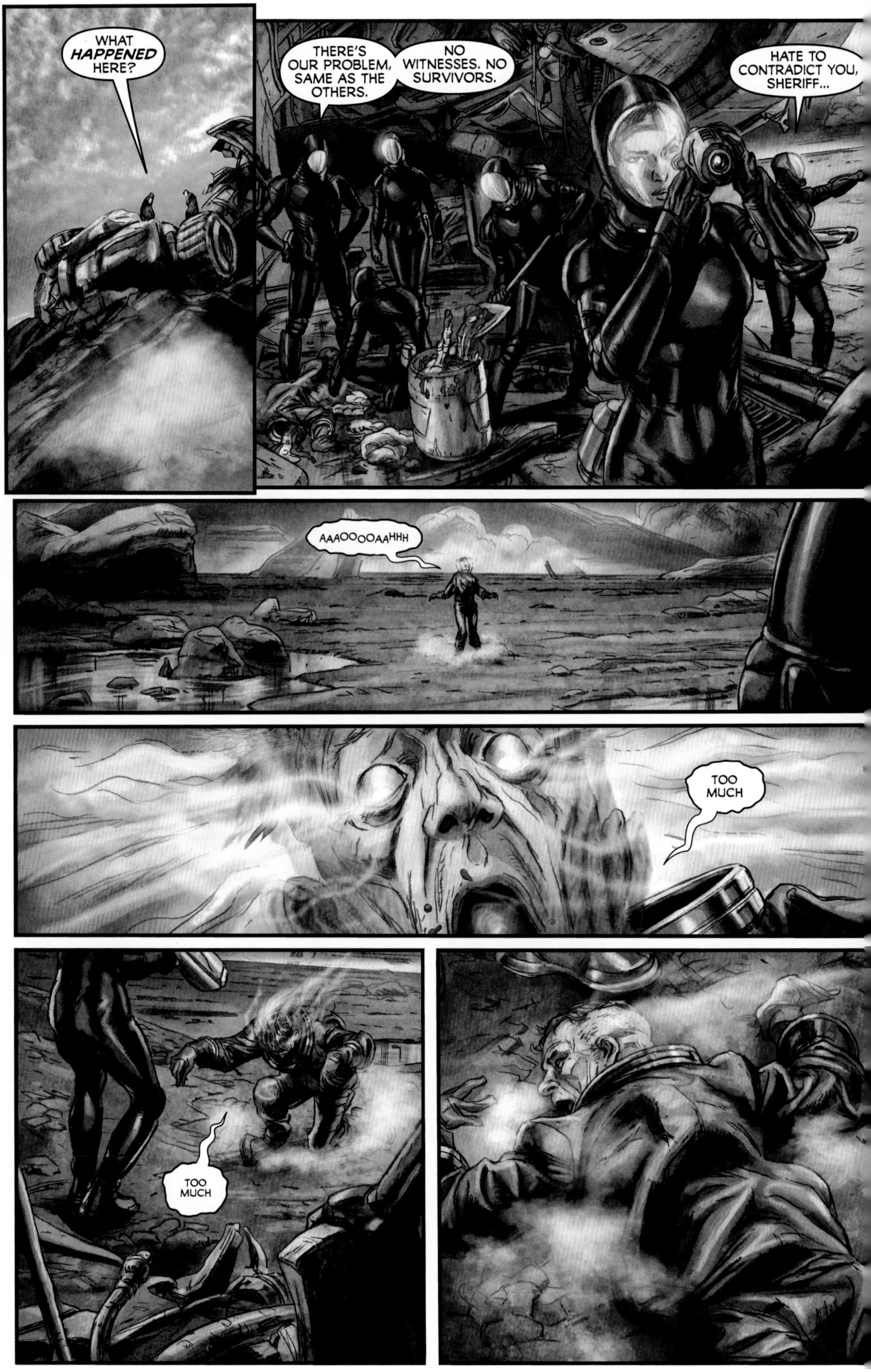
WHAT HAPPENED HERE?
THERE'S OUR PROBLEM, SAME AS THE OTHERS.
NO WITNESSES. NO SURVIVORS.
HATE TO CONTRADICT YOU, SHERIFF...
AAAOOOOAAHHH
TOO MUCH
TOO MUCH

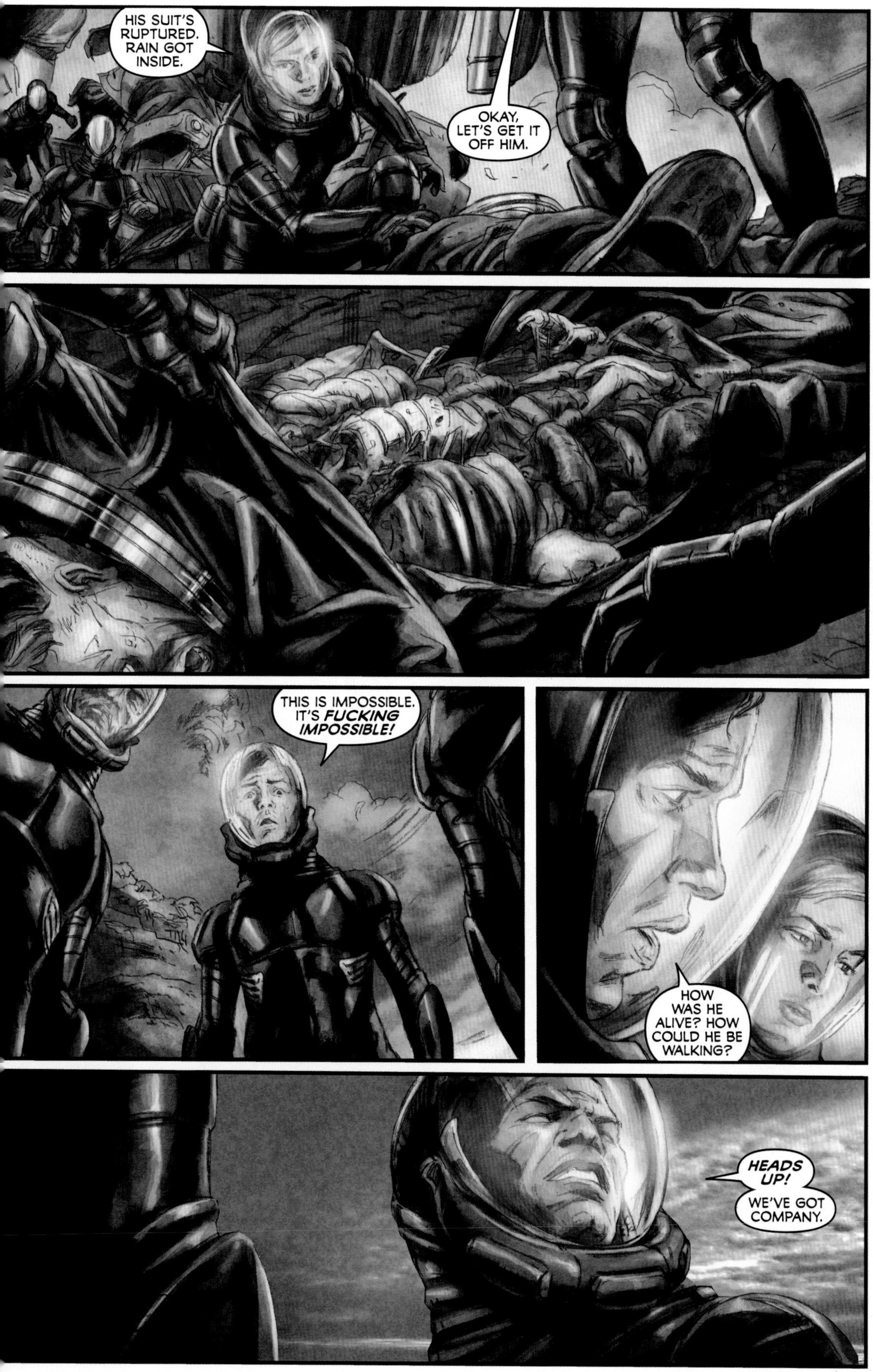
HIS SUIT'S RUPTURED. RAIN GOT INSIDE.
OKAY, LET'S GET IT OFF HIM.
THIS IS IMPOSSIBLE. IT'S *FUCKING IMPOSSIBLE!*
HOW WAS HE ALIVE? HOW COULD HE BE WALKING?
HEADS UP!
WE'VE GOT COMPANY.

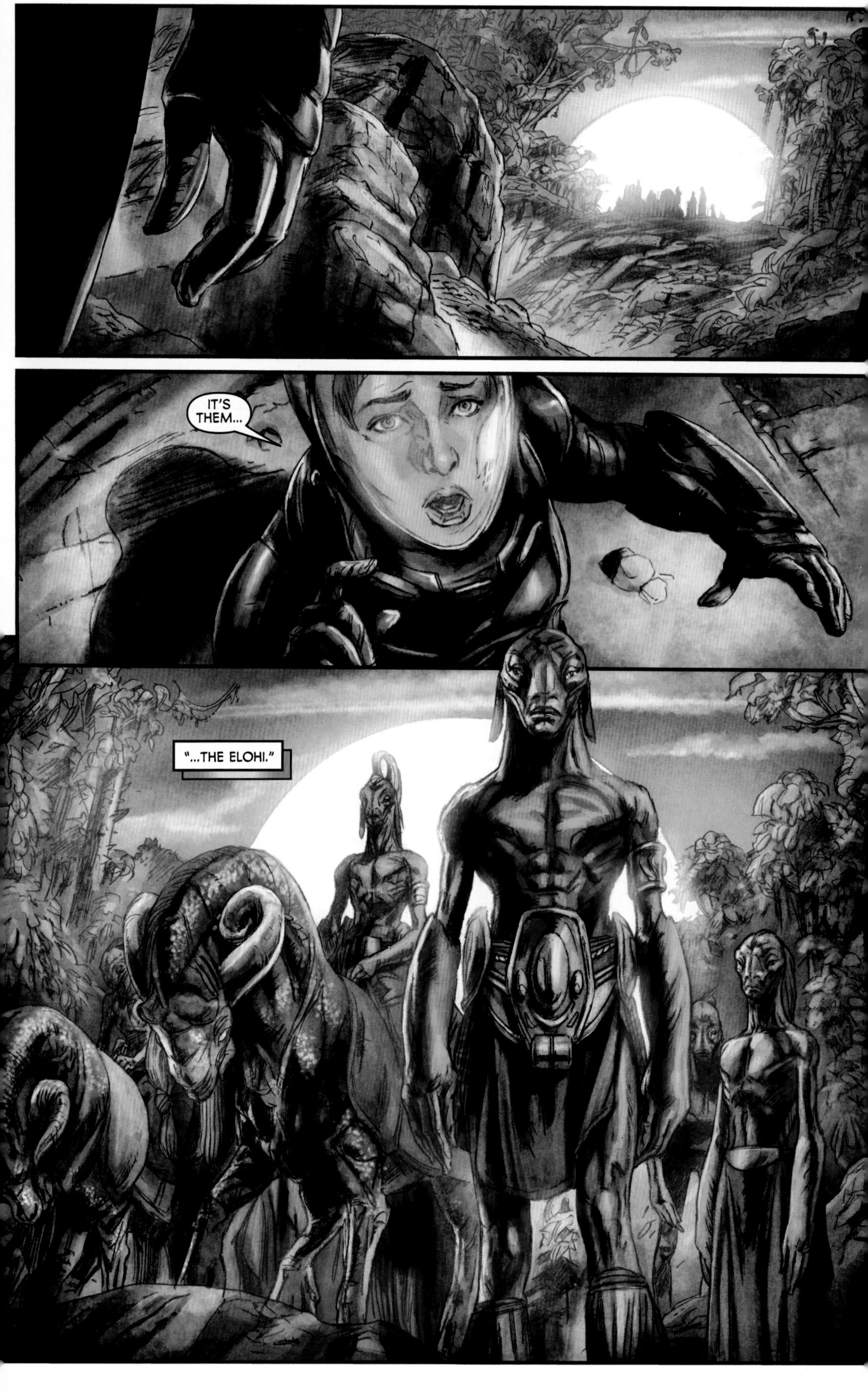
IT'S THEM...
"...THE ELOHI."

JERED HOFMAN, FORENSIC PATHOLOGIST. FIRST REPORT AT 27.15 HOURS, LOCAL TIME.

THERE ARE EVEN CADAVERS FROM PREVIOUS INCIDENTS. ELIMINARY AUTOPSIES BY SIDENT SURGEON INDICATE CAUSES OF DEATH AS FOLLOWS...

"SURGEON!"...HIS NOTES READ LIKE A FIRST YEAR MED STUDENT.

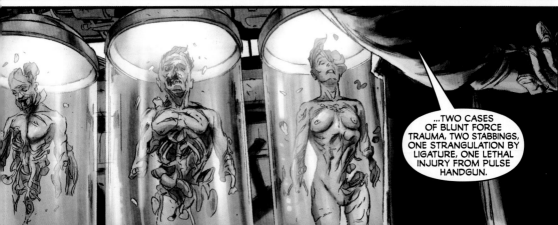

...TWO CASES OF BLUNT FORCE TRAUMA, TWO STABBINGS, ONE STRANGULATION BY LIGATURE, ONE LETHAL INJURY FROM PULSE HANDGUN.

THESE FINDINGS ARE INCONCLUSIVE AS ALL THE BODIES HAVE SUFFERED ACCELERATED DECOMPOSITION AFTER EXPOSURE TO ACID RAIN, INCLUDING THE EARLIEST REPORTED VICTIM, WHO WAS APPARENTLY ATTACKED BY ANIMALS.

WHY WOULD AN ANIMAL ATTACK BE CLASSIFIED AS A 'SUSPICIOUS DEATH'? THERE'S SOMETHING HERE THAT STARCK HASN'T TOLD US YET. SOMETHING THAT CONNECTS THESE DEATHS.

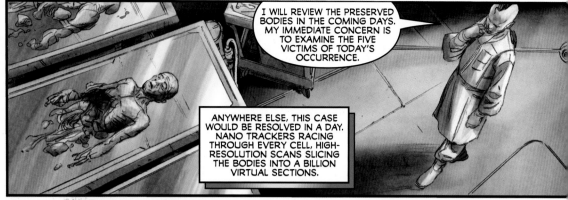

I WILL REVIEW THE PRESERVED BODIES IN THE COMING DAYS. MY IMMEDIATE CONCERN IS TO EXAMINE THE FIVE VICTIMS OF TODAY'S OCCURRENCE.

ANYWHERE ELSE, THIS CASE WOULD BE RESOLVED IN A DAY. NANO TRACKERS RACING THROUGH EVERY CELL, HIGH-RESOLUTION SCANS SLICING THE BODIES INTO A BILLION VIRTUAL SECTIONS.

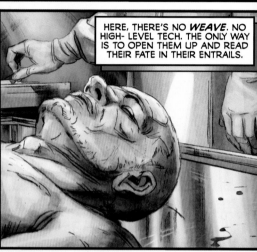

HERE, THERE'S NO *WEAVE*. NO HIGH- LEVEL TECH. THE ONLY WAY IS TO OPEN THEM UP AND READ THEIR FATE IN THEIR ENTRAILS.

WE WOULD KNOW HOW AND WHEN THEY DIED AND THE *WEAVE* WOULD TELL US WHO KILLED THEM AND WHY.

MURDER IS NO CHALLENGE ANY MORE, EXCEPT ON A PLANET LIKE AMARANTH.

MICHAEL THINKS I'M OBSESSED WITH DEATH. HE'S WRONG. SEEING THIS...THE FRAGILITY OF THE FLESH...IT MAKES ME AWARE OF MY MORTALITY...

VVVRRRREEE

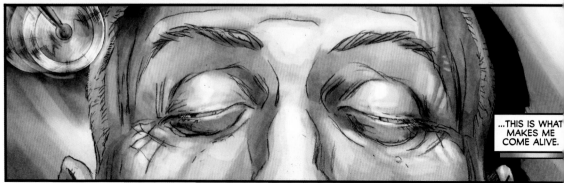

...THIS IS WHAT MAKES ME COME ALIVE.

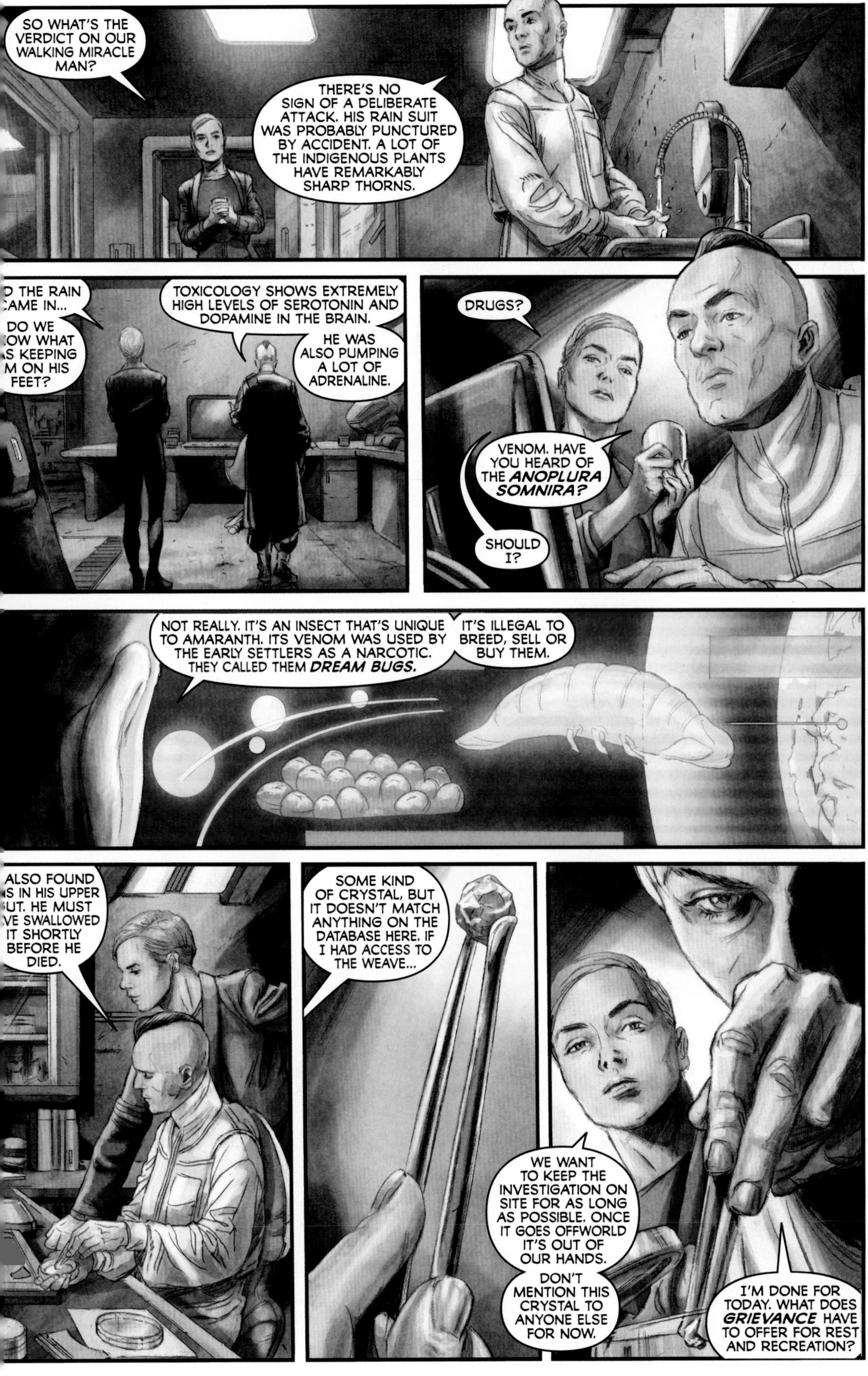
SO WHAT'S THE VERDICT ON OUR WALKING MIRACLE MAN?
THERE'S NO SIGN OF A DELIBERATE ATTACK. HIS RAIN SUIT WAS PROBABLY PUNCTURED BY ACCIDENT. A LOT OF THE INDIGENOUS PLANTS HAVE REMARKABLY SHARP THORNS.
D THE RAIN CAME IN...
DO WE OW WHAT S KEEPING M ON HIS FEET?
TOXICOLOGY SHOWS EXTREMELY HIGH LEVELS OF SEROTONIN AND DOPAMINE IN THE BRAIN.
HE WAS ALSO PUMPING A LOT OF ADRENALINE.
DRUGS?
VENOM. HAVE YOU HEARD OF THE ANOPLURA SOMNIRA?
SHOULD I?
NOT REALLY. IT'S AN INSECT THAT'S UNIQUE TO AMARANTH. ITS VENOM WAS USED BY THE EARLY SETTLERS AS A NARCOTIC. THEY CALLED THEM DREAM BUGS.
IT'S ILLEGAL TO BREED, SELL OR BUY THEM.
ALSO FOUND S IN HIS UPPER UT. HE MUST VE SWALLOWED IT SHORTLY BEFORE HE DIED.
SOME KIND OF CRYSTAL, BUT IT DOESN'T MATCH ANYTHING ON THE DATABASE HERE. IF I HAD ACCESS TO THE WEAVE...
WE WANT TO KEEP THE INVESTIGATION ON SITE FOR AS LONG AS POSSIBLE. ONCE IT GOES OFFWORLD IT'S OUT OF OUR HANDS.
DON'T MENTION THIS CRYSTAL TO ANYONE ELSE FOR NOW.
I'M DONE FOR TODAY. WHAT DOES GRIEVANCE HAVE TO OFFER FOR REST AND RECREATION?

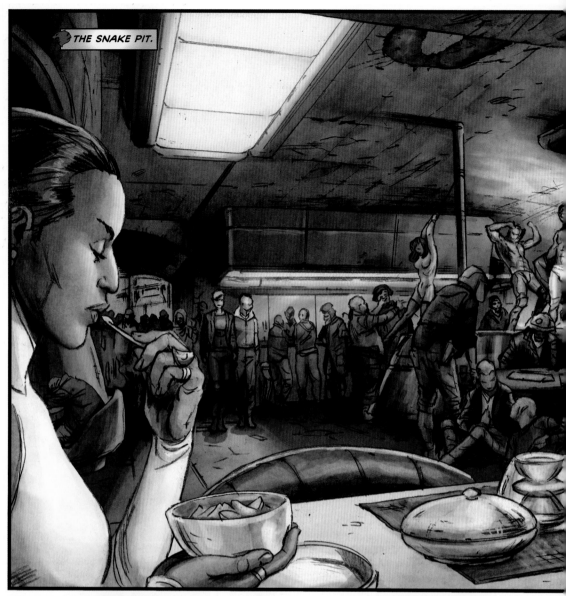

THE SNAKE PIT.

HOW DID YOUR AUTOPSY GO? HAVE WE GOT ANY ANSWERS?

WE DO HAVE A WHOLE NEW LIST OF QUESTIONS.

THE BIG ONE IS HOW COME OUR WALKING DEAD MAN HAD *DREAM BUG* VENOM RUNNING AROUND HIS VEINS?

I'M HOPING YOU CAN HELP ME OUT WITH THAT ONE, SHERIFF.

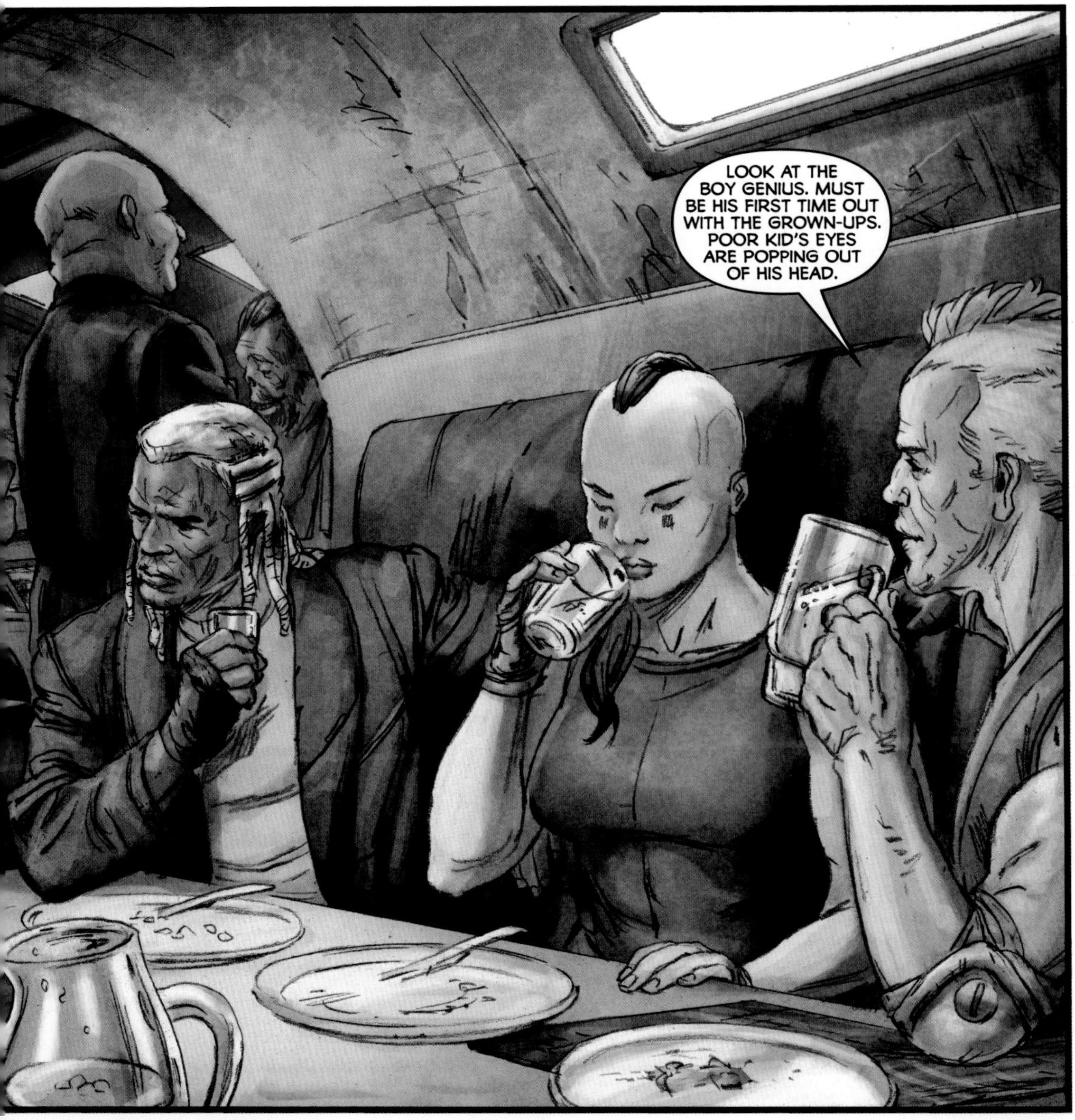
LOOK AT THE BOY GENIUS. MUST BE HIS FIRST TIME OUT WITH THE GROWN-UPS. POOR KID'S EYES ARE POPPING OUT OF HIS HEAD.

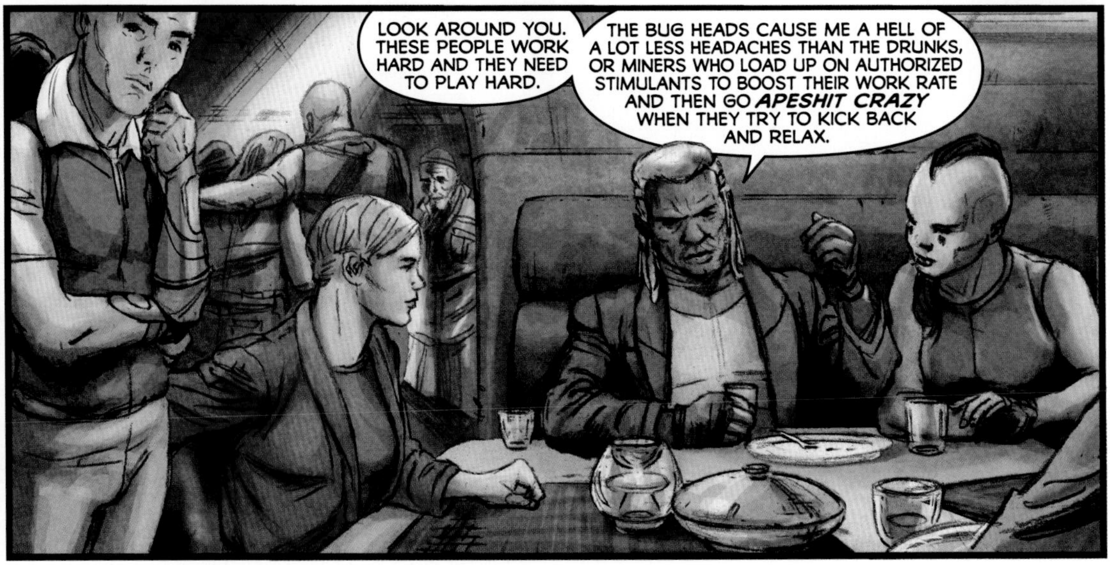
LOOK AROUND YOU. THESE PEOPLE WORK HARD AND THEY NEED TO PLAY HARD.
THE BUG HEADS CAUSE ME A HELL OF A LOT LESS HEADACHES THAN THE DRUNKS, OR MINERS WHO LOAD UP ON AUTHORIZED STIMULANTS TO BOOST THEIR WORK RATE AND THEN GO ***APESHIT CRAZY*** WHEN THEY TRY TO KICK BACK AND RELAX.

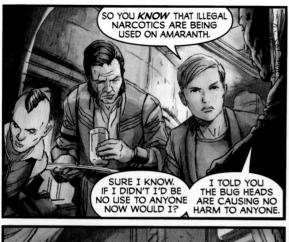

SO YOU *KNOW* THAT ILLEGAL NARCOTICS ARE BEING USED ON AMARANTH.

SURE I KNOW. IF I DIDN'T I'D BE NO USE TO ANYONE NOW WOULD I?

I TOLD YOU THE BUG HEADS ARE CAUSING NO HARM TO ANYONE.

CHECK OUT THE BIG GUY OVER THERE WITH THE BUG SUCKING ON HIS ARM.

ISN'T HE ONE SWEET-NATURED SONOFABITCH?

HE LOOKS HAPPY ENOUGH.

HE'S GOT A CHARGE SHEET AS LONG AS MY DICK FOR ASSAULT AND BATTERY ON A DOZEN PLANETS.

TAKE THE BUGS AWAY AND IN TWO DAYS HE'LL BE PAINTING THESE WALLS WITH *BLOOD* BECAUSE SOMEONE SPILLED HIS BEER.

YOU THINKING ABOUT THE SIZE OF THAT CHARGE SHEE COMMANDER?

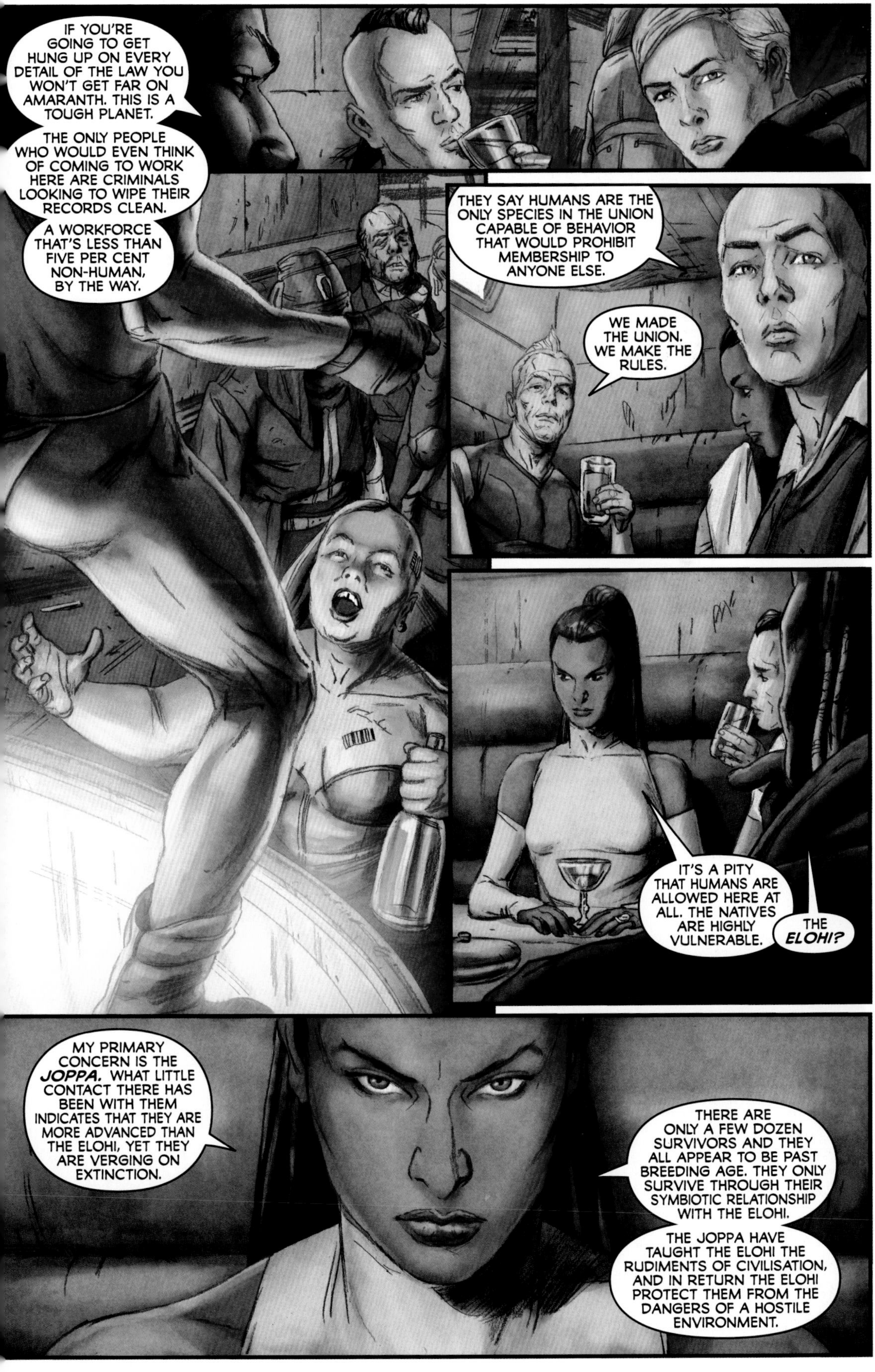
IF YOU'RE GOING TO GET HUNG UP ON EVERY DETAIL OF THE LAW YOU WON'T GET FAR ON AMARANTH. THIS IS A TOUGH PLANET.
THE ONLY PEOPLE WHO WOULD EVEN THINK OF COMING TO WORK HERE ARE CRIMINALS LOOKING TO WIPE THEIR RECORDS CLEAN.
A WORKFORCE THAT'S LESS THAN FIVE PER CENT NON-HUMAN, BY THE WAY.
THEY SAY HUMANS ARE THE ONLY SPECIES IN THE UNION CAPABLE OF BEHAVIOR THAT WOULD PROHIBIT MEMBERSHIP TO ANYONE ELSE.
WE MADE THE UNION. WE MAKE THE RULES.
IT'S A PITY THAT HUMANS ARE ALLOWED HERE AT ALL. THE NATIVES ARE HIGHLY VULNERABLE.
THE *ELOHI?*
MY PRIMARY CONCERN IS THE *JOPPA.* WHAT LITTLE CONTACT THERE HAS BEEN WITH THEM INDICATES THAT THEY ARE MORE ADVANCED THAN THE ELOHI, YET THEY ARE VERGING ON EXTINCTION.
THERE ARE ONLY A FEW DOZEN SURVIVORS AND THEY ALL APPEAR TO BE PAST BREEDING AGE. THEY ONLY SURVIVE THROUGH THEIR SYMBIOTIC RELATIONSHIP WITH THE ELOHI.
THE JOPPA HAVE TAUGHT THE ELOHI THE RUDIMENTS OF CIVILISATION, AND IN RETURN THE ELOHI PROTECT THEM FROM THE DANGERS OF A HOSTILE ENVIRONMENT.

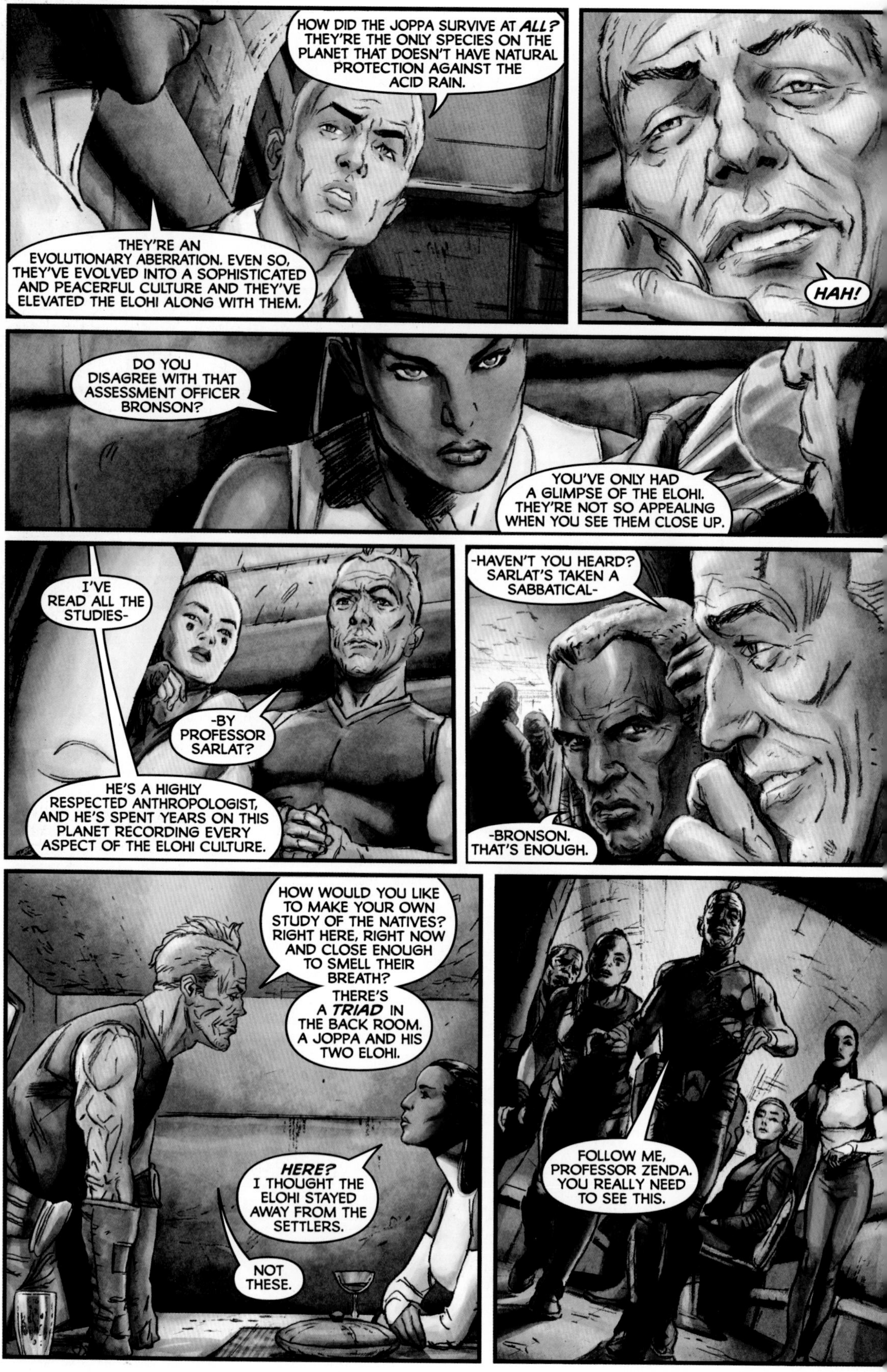
HOW DID THE JOPPA SURVIVE AT *ALL?* THEY'RE THE ONLY SPECIES ON THE PLANET THAT DOESN'T HAVE NATURAL PROTECTION AGAINST THE ACID RAIN.
THEY'RE AN EVOLUTIONARY ABERRATION. EVEN SO, THEY'VE EVOLVED INTO A SOPHISTICATED AND PEACEFUL CULTURE AND THEY'VE ELEVATED THE ELOHI ALONG WITH THEM.
HAH!
DO YOU DISAGREE WITH THAT ASSESSMENT OFFICER BRONSON?
YOU'VE ONLY HAD A GLIMPSE OF THE ELOHI. THEY'RE NOT SO APPEALING WHEN YOU SEE THEM CLOSE UP.
I'VE READ ALL THE STUDIES-
-BY PROFESSOR SARLAT?
HE'S A HIGHLY RESPECTED ANTHROPOLOGIST, AND HE'S SPENT YEARS ON THIS PLANET RECORDING EVERY ASPECT OF THE ELOHI CULTURE.
-HAVEN'T YOU HEARD? SARLAT'S TAKEN A SABBATICAL-
-BRONSON. THAT'S ENOUGH.
HOW WOULD YOU LIKE TO MAKE YOUR OWN STUDY OF THE NATIVES? RIGHT HERE, RIGHT NOW AND CLOSE ENOUGH TO SMELL THEIR BREATH?
THERE'S A *TRIAD* IN THE BACK ROOM. A JOPPA AND HIS TWO ELOHI.
HERE? I THOUGHT THE ELOHI STAYED AWAY FROM THE SETTLERS.
NOT THESE.
FOLLOW ME, PROFESSOR ZENDA. YOU REALLY NEED TO SEE THIS.

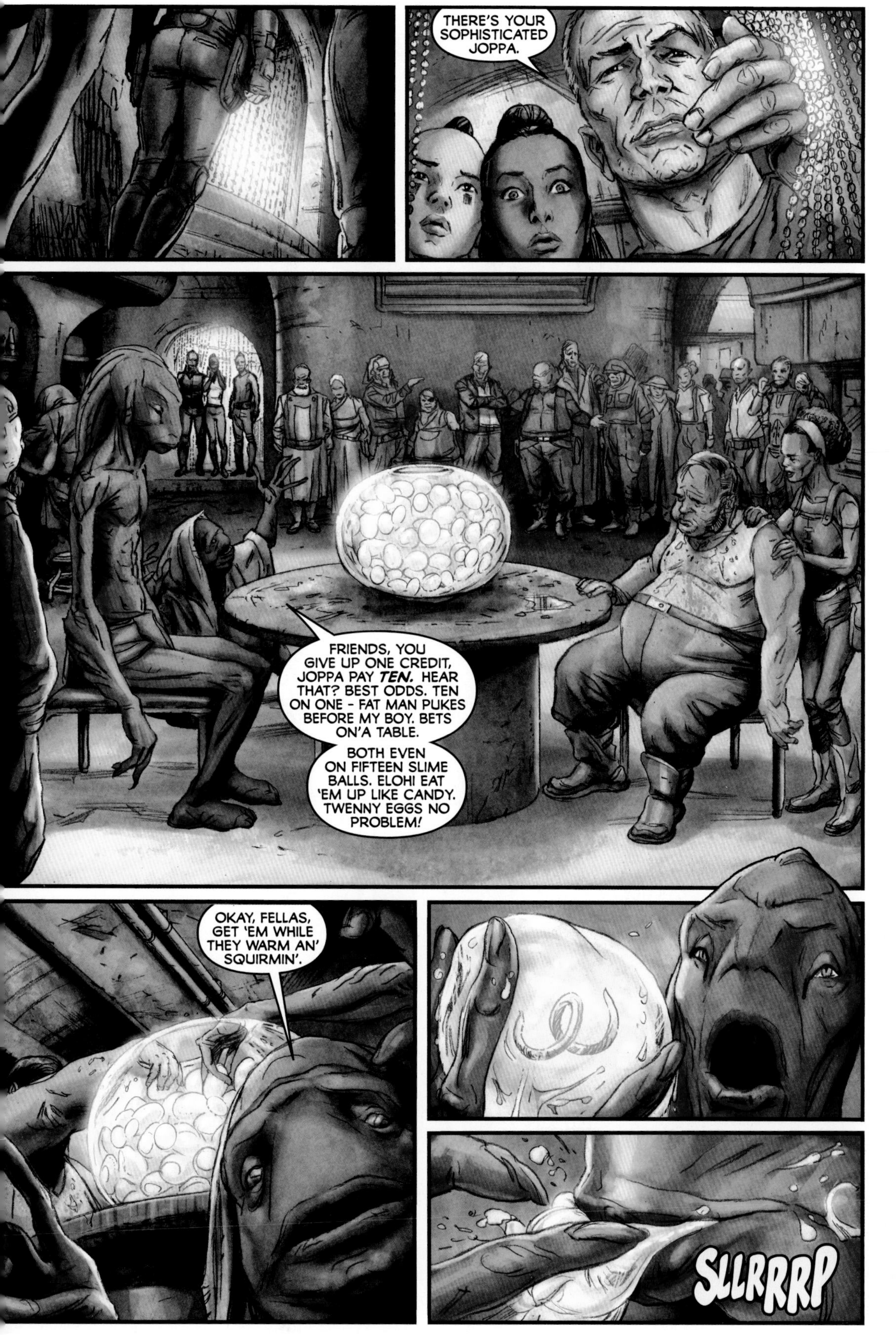
THERE'S YOUR SOPHISTICATED JOPPA.
FRIENDS, YOU GIVE UP ONE CREDIT, JOPPA PAY *TEN.* HEAR THAT? BEST ODDS. TEN ON ONE - FAT MAN PUKES BEFORE MY BOY. BETS ON'A TABLE.
BOTH EVEN ON FIFTEEN SLIME BALLS. ELOHI EAT 'EM UP LIKE CANDY. TWENNY EGGS NO PROBLEM!
OKAY, FELLAS, GET 'EM WHILE THEY WARM AN' SQUIRMIN'.
SLLRRRP

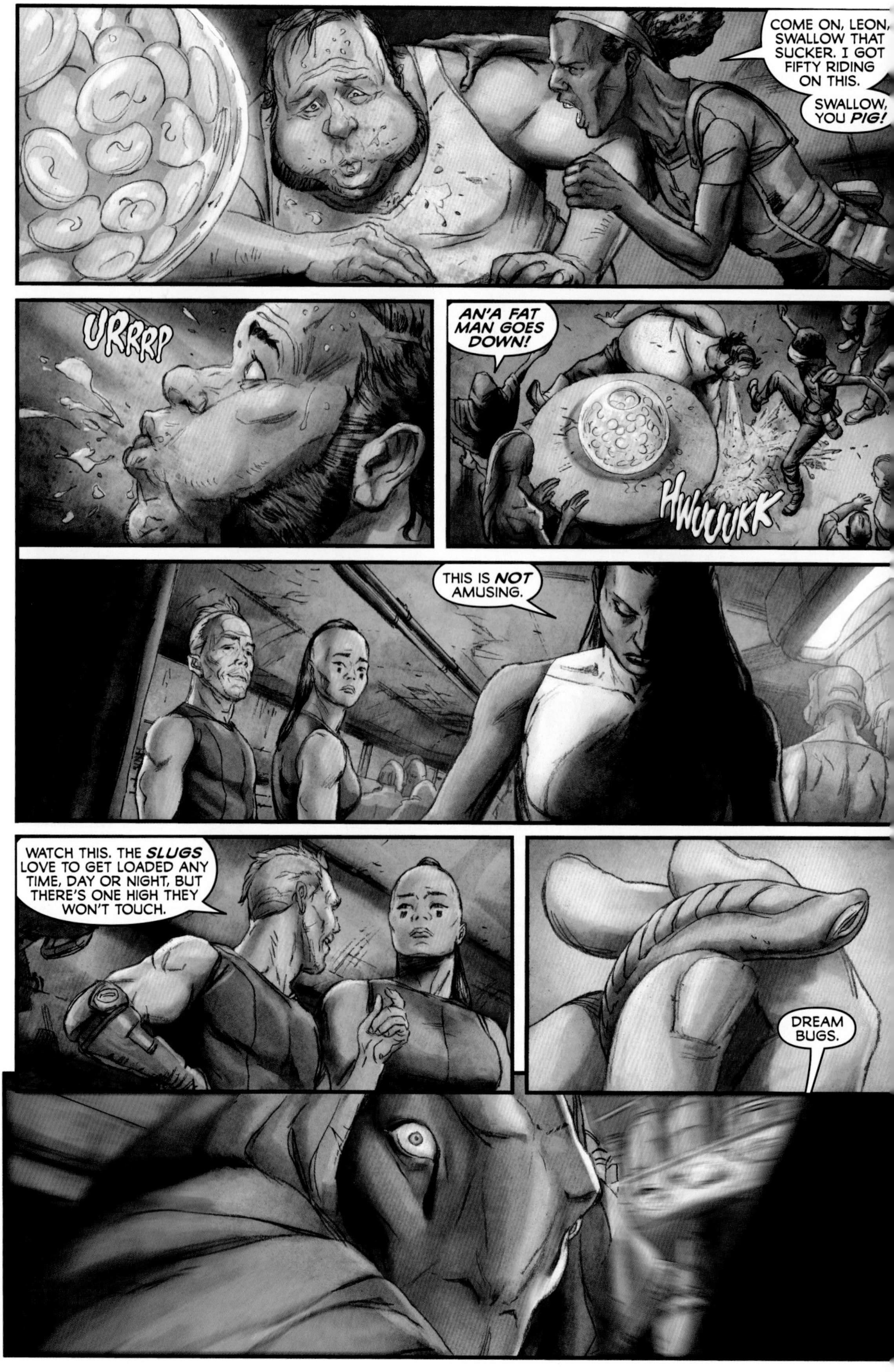
COME ON, LEON, SWALLOW THAT SUCKER. I GOT FIFTY RIDING ON THIS.
SWALLOW, YOU PIG!
URRRP
AN'A FAT MAN GOES DOWN!
HWUUUUKK
THIS IS NOT AMUSING.
WATCH THIS. THE SLUGS LOVE TO GET LOADED ANY TIME, DAY OR NIGHT, BUT THERE'S ONE HIGH THEY WON'T TOUCH.
DREAM BUGS.

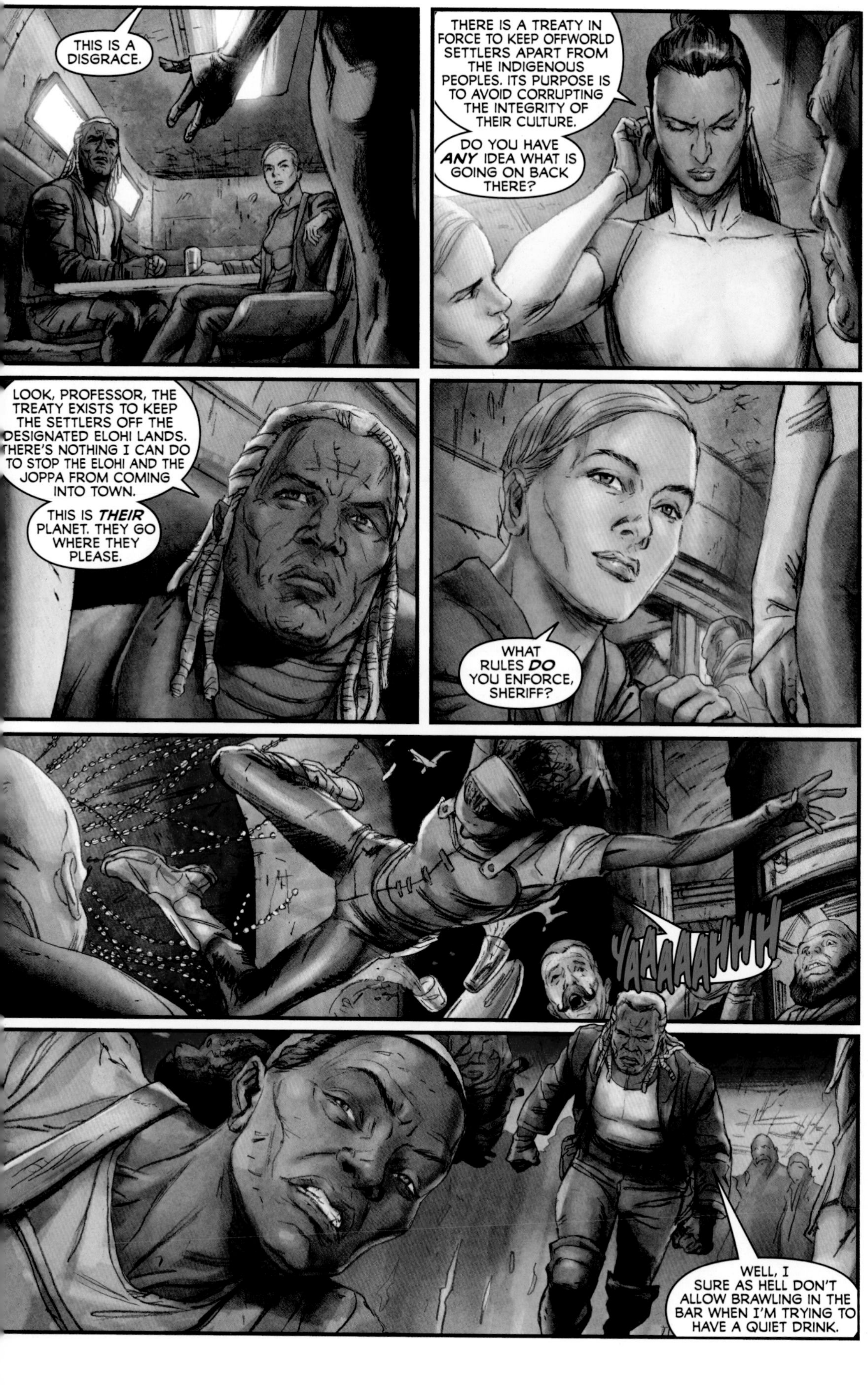
THIS IS A DISGRACE.
THERE IS A TREATY IN FORCE TO KEEP OFFWORLD SETTLERS APART FROM THE INDIGENOUS PEOPLES. ITS PURPOSE IS TO AVOID CORRUPTING THE INTEGRITY OF THEIR CULTURE.
DO YOU HAVE ANY IDEA WHAT IS GOING ON BACK THERE?
LOOK, PROFESSOR, THE TREATY EXISTS TO KEEP THE SETTLERS OFF THE DESIGNATED ELOHI LANDS. THERE'S NOTHING I CAN DO TO STOP THE ELOHI AND THE JOPPA FROM COMING INTO TOWN.
THIS IS THEIR PLANET. THEY GO WHERE THEY PLEASE.
WHAT RULES DO YOU ENFORCE, SHERIFF?
YAAAAAHHH
WELL, I SURE AS HELL DON'T ALLOW BRAWLING IN THE BAR WHEN I'M TRYING TO HAVE A QUIET DRINK.

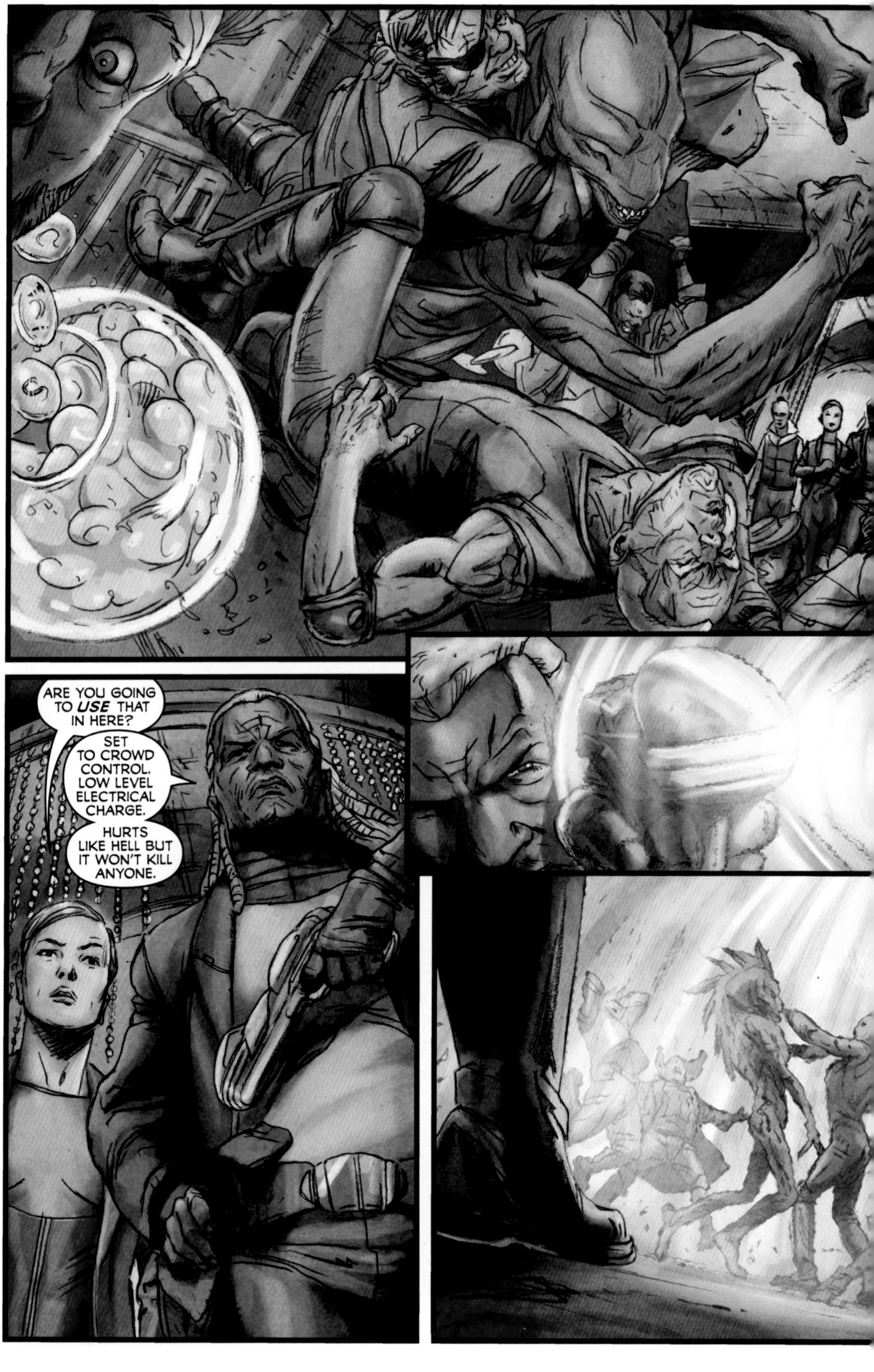
ARE YOU GOING TO USE THAT IN HERE?
SET TO CROWD CONTROL. LOW LEVEL ELECTRICAL CHARGE.
HURTS LIKE HELL BUT IT WON'T KILL ANYONE.

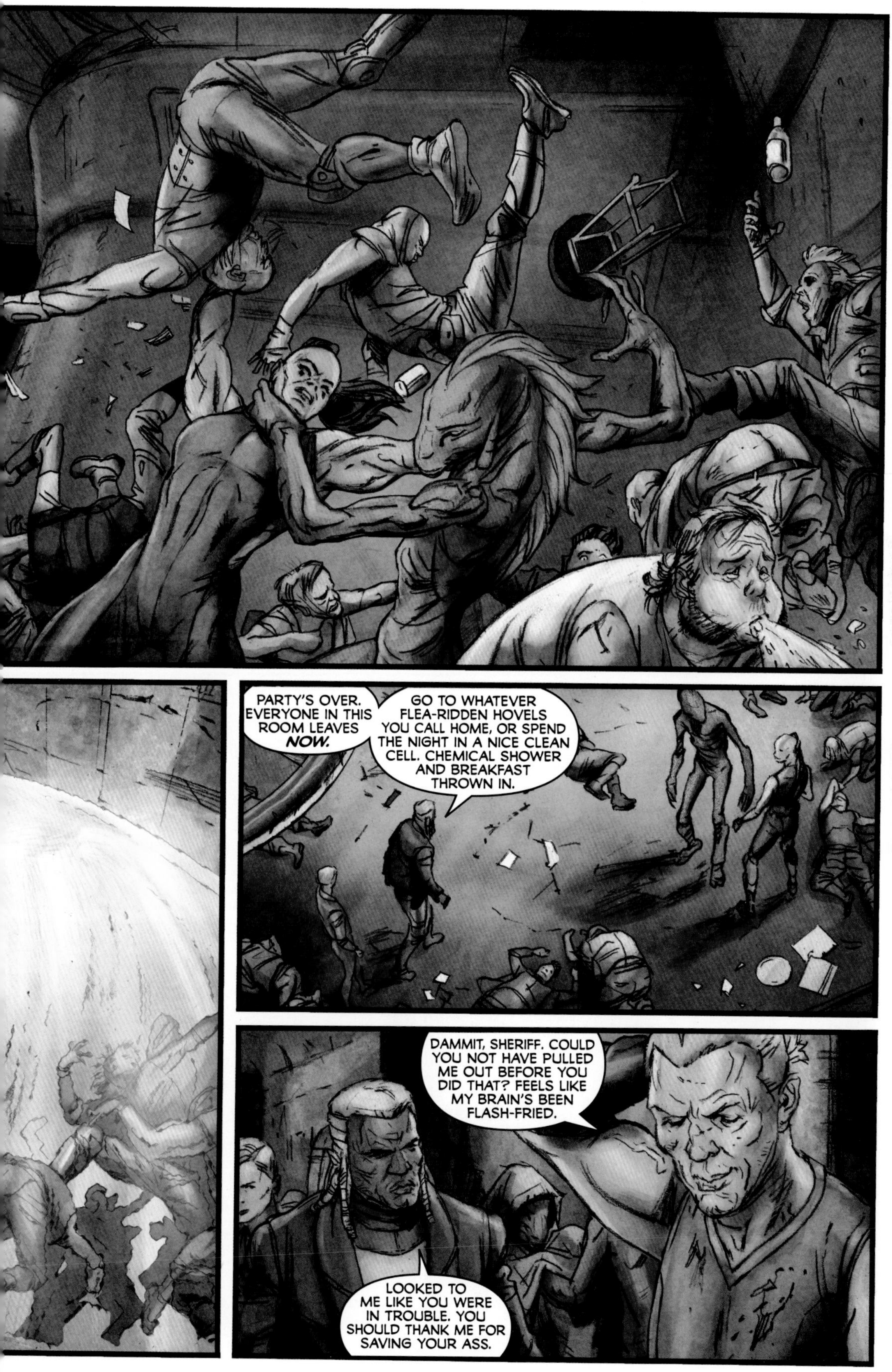
PARTY'S OVER. EVERYONE IN THIS ROOM LEAVES *NOW.*
GO TO WHATEVER FLEA-RIDDEN HOVELS YOU CALL HOME, OR SPEND THE NIGHT IN A NICE CLEAN CELL. CHEMICAL SHOWER AND BREAKFAST THROWN IN.
DAMMIT, SHERIFF. COULD YOU NOT HAVE PULLED ME OUT BEFORE YOU DID THAT? FEELS LIKE MY BRAIN'S BEEN FLASH-FRIED.
LOOKED TO ME LIKE YOU WERE IN TROUBLE. YOU SHOULD THANK ME FOR SAVING YOUR ASS.

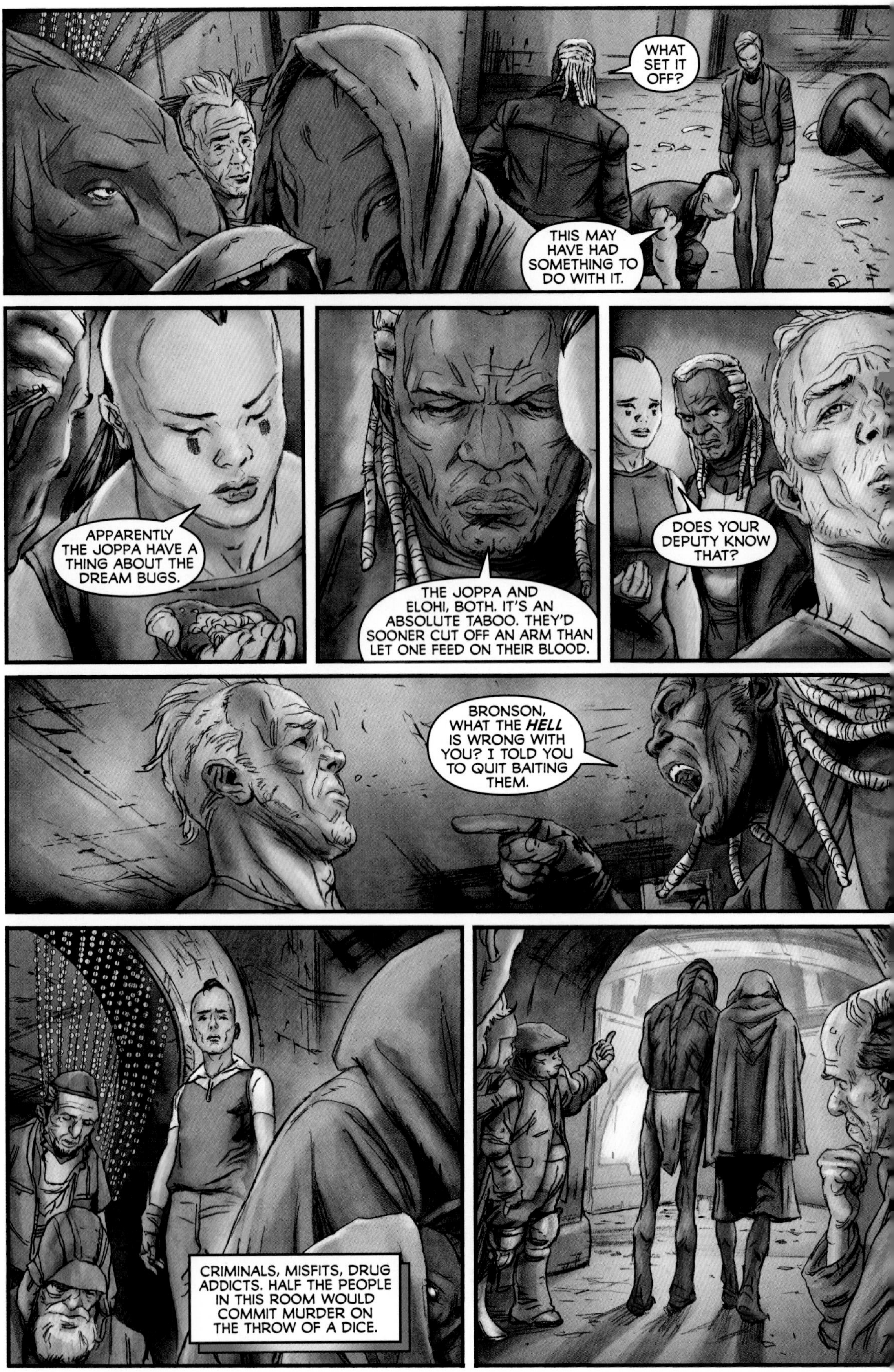
WHAT SET IT OFF?
THIS MAY HAVE HAD SOMETHING TO DO WITH IT.
APPARENTLY THE JOPPA HAVE A THING ABOUT THE DREAM BUGS.
THE JOPPA AND ELOHI, BOTH. IT'S AN ABSOLUTE TABOO. THEY'D SOONER CUT OFF AN ARM THAN LET ONE FEED ON THEIR BLOOD.
DOES YOUR DEPUTY KNOW THAT?
BRONSON, WHAT THE *HELL* IS WRONG WITH YOU? I TOLD YOU TO QUIT BAITING THEM.
CRIMINALS, MISFITS, DRUG ADDICTS. HALF THE PEOPLE IN THIS ROOM WOULD COMMIT MURDER ON THE THROW OF A DICE.

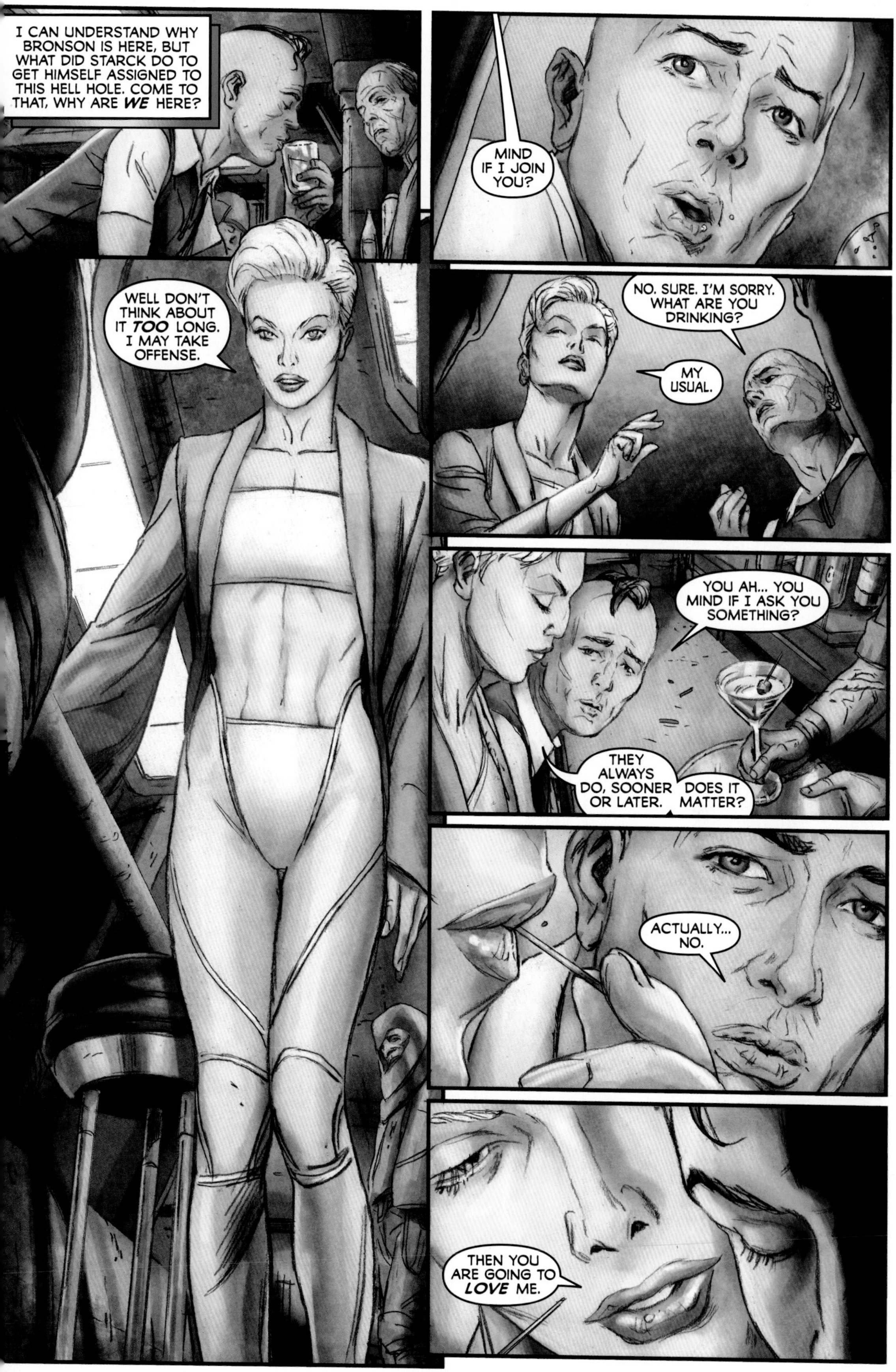
I CAN UNDERSTAND WHY BRONSON IS HERE, BUT WHAT DID STARCK DO TO GET HIMSELF ASSIGNED TO THIS HELL HOLE. COME TO THAT, WHY ARE *WE* HERE?
MIND IF I JOIN YOU?
WELL DON'T THINK ABOUT IT *TOO* LONG. I MAY TAKE OFFENSE.
NO. SURE. I'M SORRY. WHAT ARE YOU DRINKING?
MY USUAL.
YOU AH... YOU MIND IF I ASK YOU SOMETHING?
THEY ALWAYS DO, SOONER OR LATER.
DOES IT MATTER?
ACTUALLY... NO.
THEN YOU ARE GOING TO *LOVE* ME.

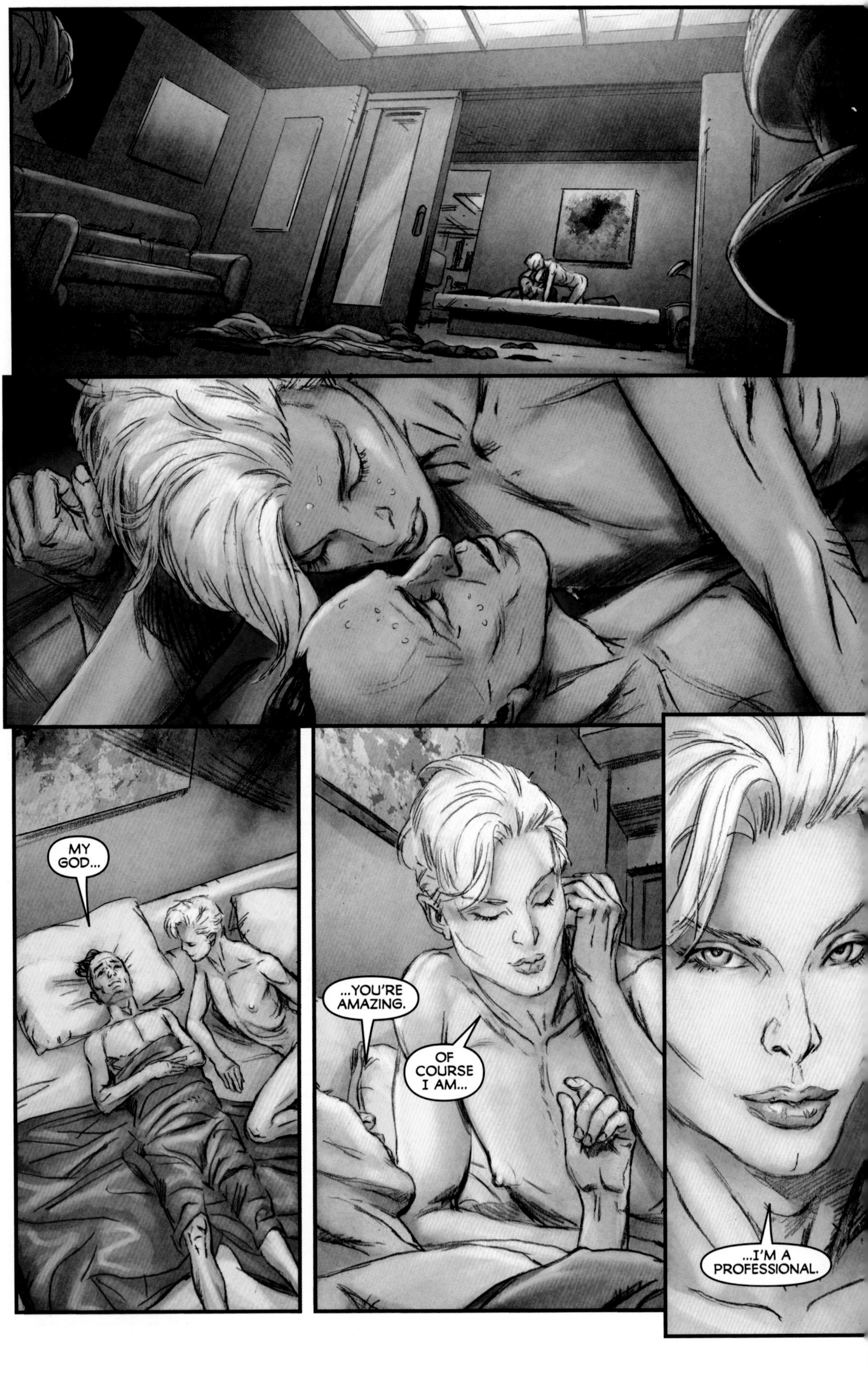
MY GOD...
...YOU'RE AMAZING.
OF COURSE I AM...
...I'M A PROFESSIONAL.

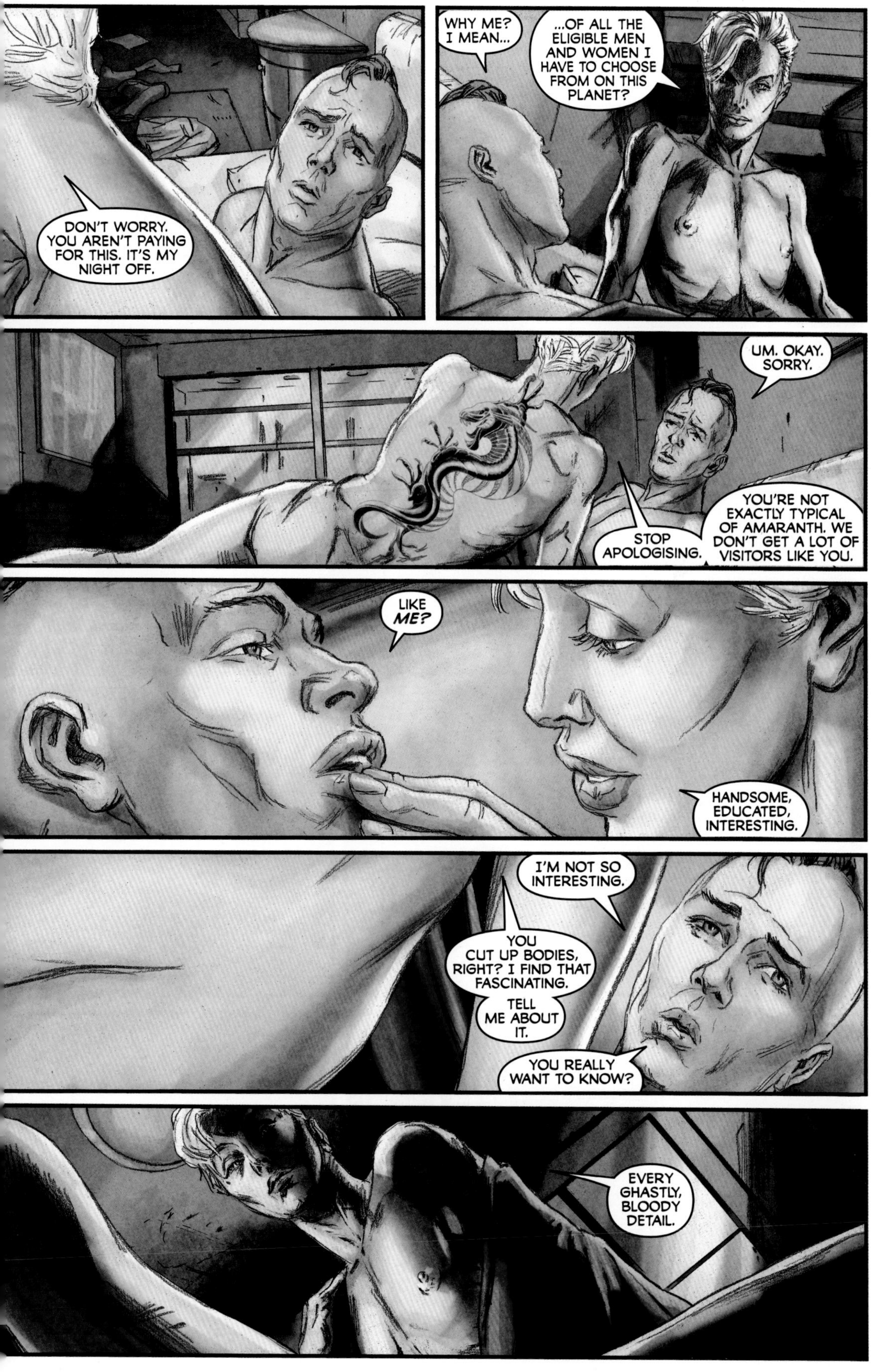
DON'T WORRY. YOU AREN'T PAYING FOR THIS. IT'S MY NIGHT OFF.
WHY ME? I MEAN...
...OF ALL THE ELIGIBLE MEN AND WOMEN I HAVE TO CHOOSE FROM ON THIS PLANET?
UM. OKAY. SORRY.
STOP APOLOGISING.
YOU'RE NOT EXACTLY TYPICAL OF AMARANTH. WE DON'T GET A LOT OF VISITORS LIKE YOU.
LIKE *ME?*
HANDSOME, EDUCATED, INTERESTING.
I'M NOT SO INTERESTING.
YOU CUT UP BODIES, RIGHT? I FIND THAT FASCINATING.
TELL ME ABOUT IT.
YOU REALLY WANT TO KNOW?
EVERY GHASTLY, BLOODY DETAIL.

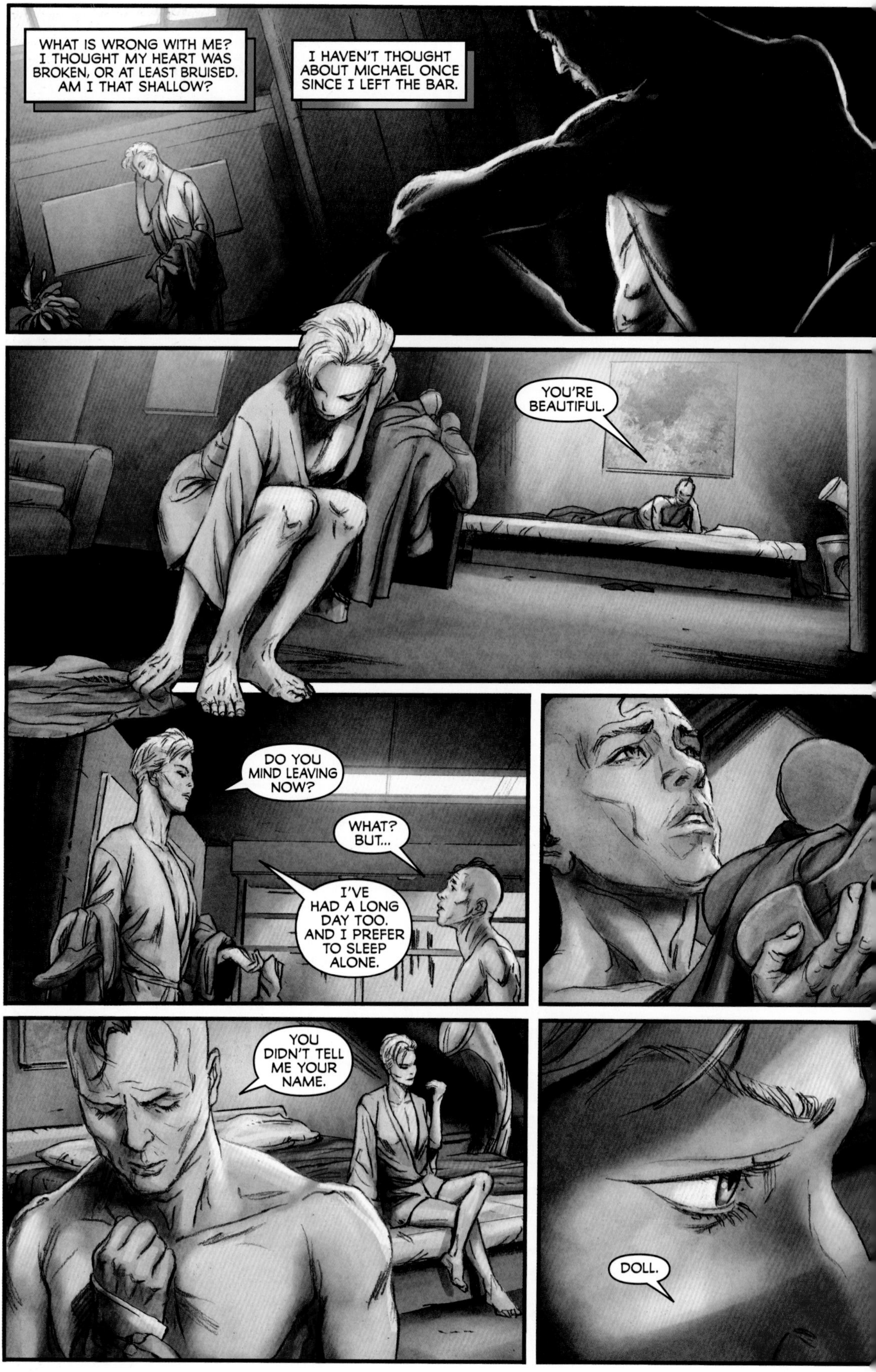
WHAT IS WRONG WITH ME? I THOUGHT MY HEART WAS BROKEN, OR AT LEAST BRUISED. AM I THAT SHALLOW?
I HAVEN'T THOUGHT ABOUT MICHAEL ONCE SINCE I LEFT THE BAR.
YOU'RE BEAUTIFUL.
DO YOU MIND LEAVING NOW?
WHAT? BUT...
I'VE HAD A LONG DAY TOO. AND I PREFER TO SLEEP ALONE.
YOU DIDN'T TELL ME YOUR NAME.
DOLL.

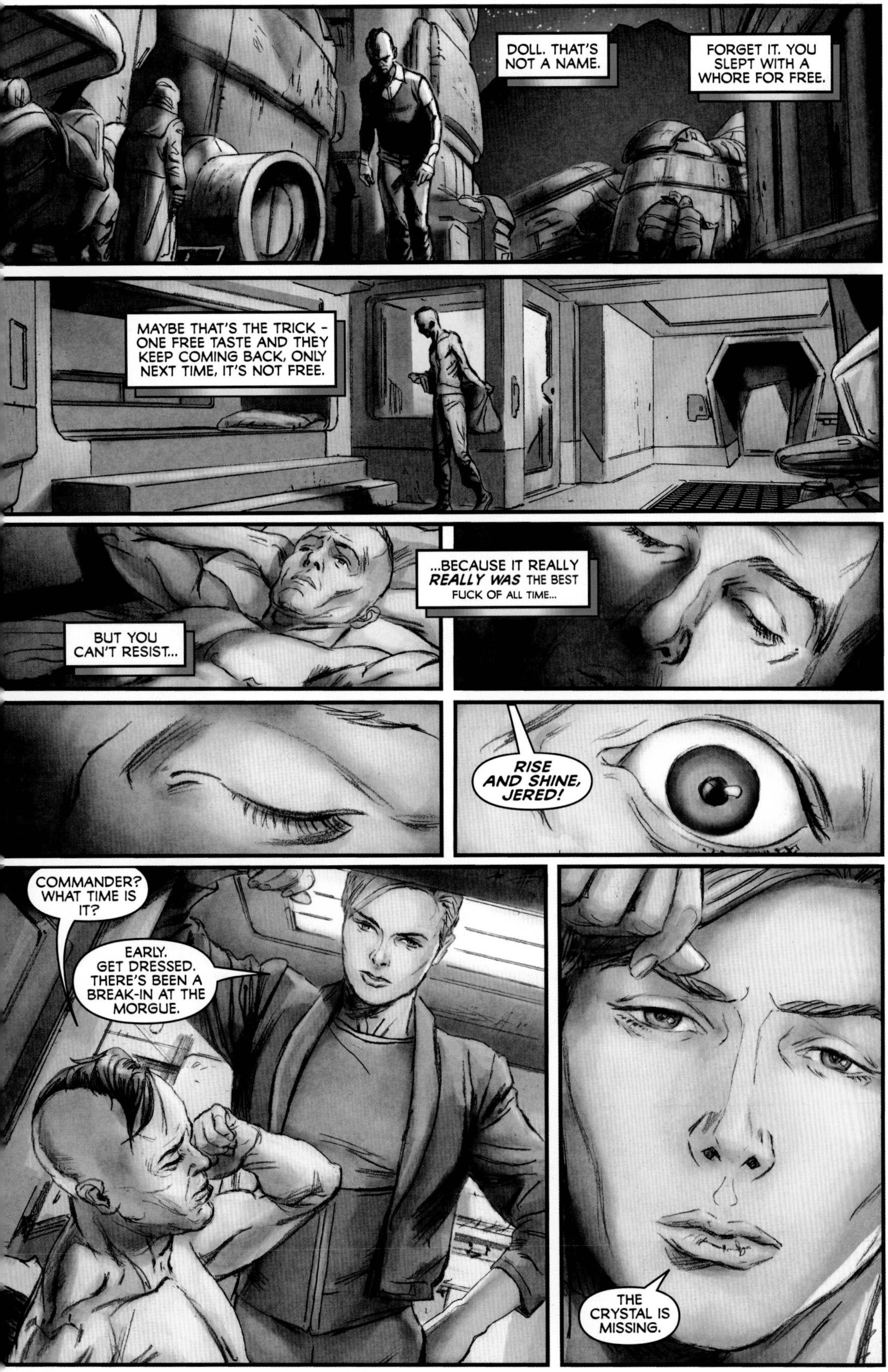
DOLL. THAT'S NOT A NAME.
FORGET IT. YOU SLEPT WITH A WHORE FOR FREE.
MAYBE THAT'S THE TRICK - ONE FREE TASTE AND THEY KEEP COMING BACK, ONLY NEXT TIME, IT'S NOT FREE.
BUT YOU CAN'T RESIST...
...BECAUSE IT REALLY *REALLY WAS* THE BEST FUCK OF ALL TIME...
RISE AND SHINE, JERED!
COMMANDER? WHAT TIME IS IT?
EARLY. GET DRESSED. THERE'S BEEN A BREAK-IN AT THE MORGUE.
THE CRYSTAL IS MISSING.

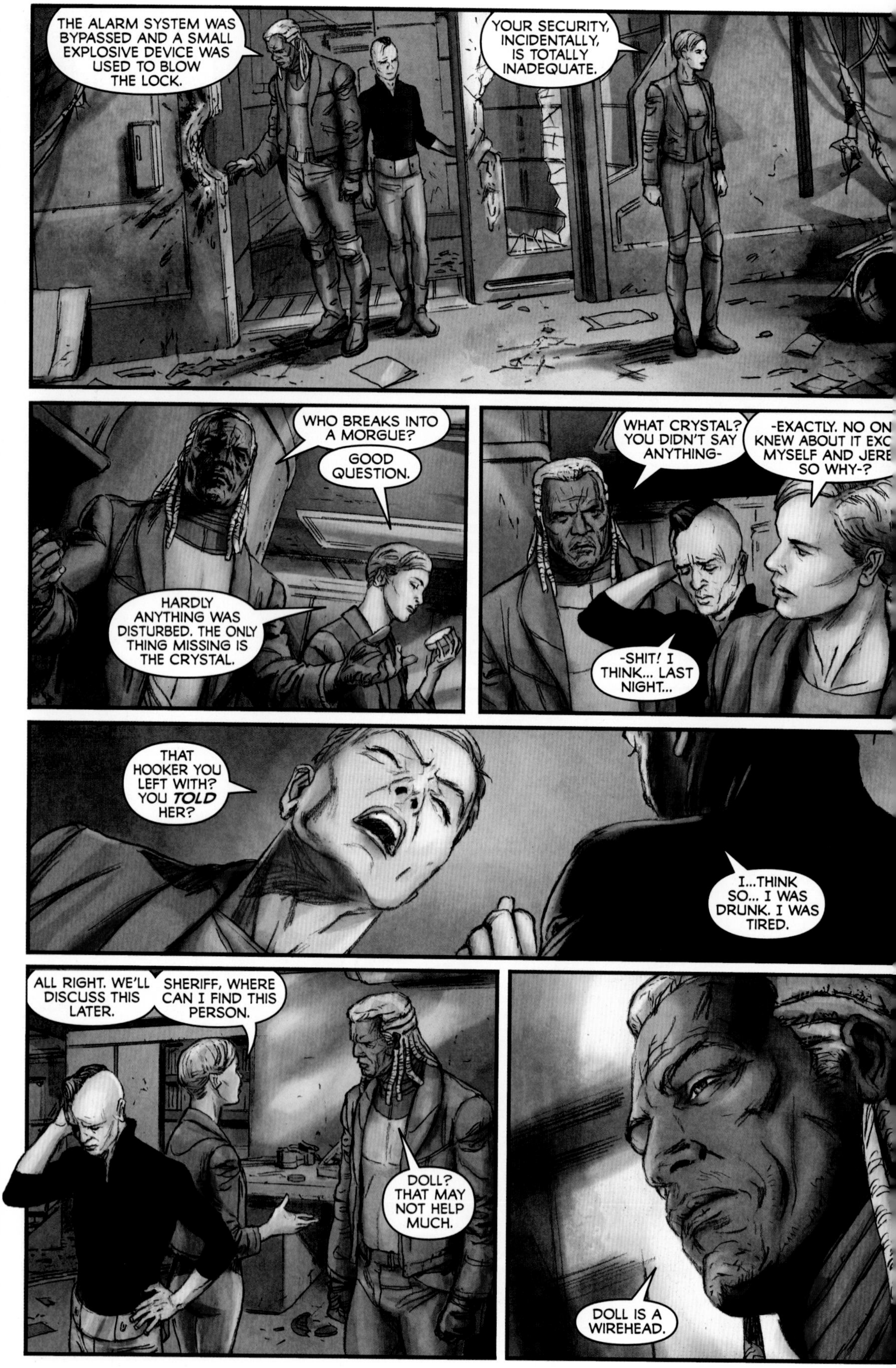
THE ALARM SYSTEM WAS BYPASSED AND A SMALL EXPLOSIVE DEVICE WAS USED TO BLOW THE LOCK.
YOUR SECURITY, INCIDENTALLY, IS TOTALLY INADEQUATE.
WHO BREAKS INTO A MORGUE?
GOOD QUESTION.
HARDLY ANYTHING WAS DISTURBED. THE ONLY THING MISSING IS THE CRYSTAL.
WHAT CRYSTAL? YOU DIDN'T SAY ANYTHING-
-EXACTLY. NO ON KNEW ABOUT IT EXC MYSELF AND JERE SO WHY-?
-SHIT! I THINK... LAST NIGHT...
THAT HOOKER YOU LEFT WITH? YOU ***TOLD*** HER?
I...THINK SO... I WAS DRUNK. I WAS TIRED.
ALL RIGHT. WE'LL DISCUSS THIS LATER.
SHERIFF, WHERE CAN I FIND THIS PERSON.
DOLL? THAT MAY NOT HELP MUCH.
DOLL IS A WIREHEAD.

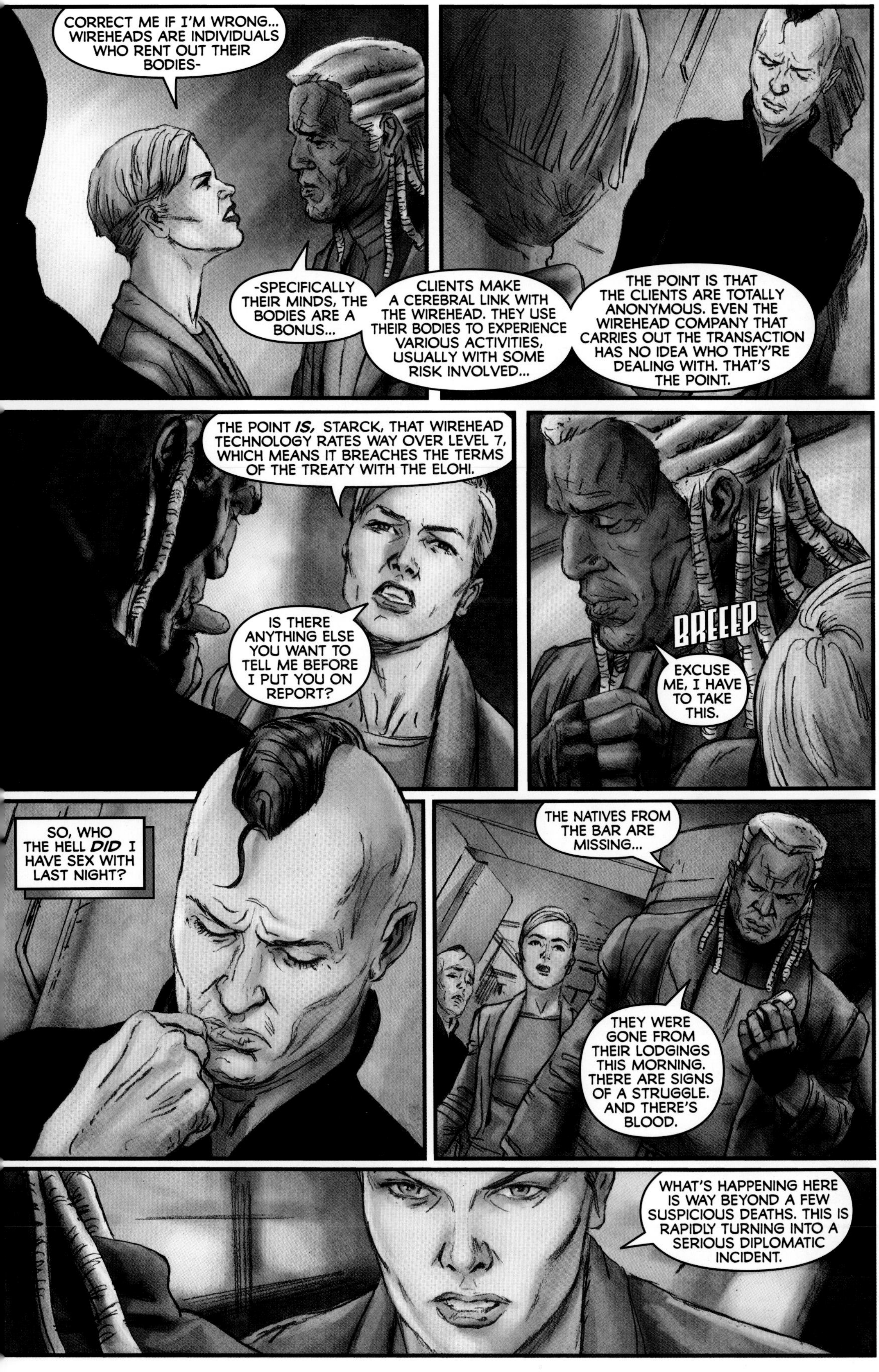
CORRECT ME IF I'M WRONG... WIREHEADS ARE INDIVIDUALS WHO RENT OUT THEIR BODIES-
-SPECIFICALLY THEIR MINDS, THE BODIES ARE A BONUS...
CLIENTS MAKE A CEREBRAL LINK WITH THE WIREHEAD. THEY USE THEIR BODIES TO EXPERIENCE VARIOUS ACTIVITIES, USUALLY WITH SOME RISK INVOLVED...
THE POINT IS THAT THE CLIENTS ARE TOTALLY ANONYMOUS. EVEN THE WIREHEAD COMPANY THAT CARRIES OUT THE TRANSACTION HAS NO IDEA WHO THEY'RE DEALING WITH. THAT'S THE POINT.
THE POINT *IS,* STARCK, THAT WIREHEAD TECHNOLOGY RATES WAY OVER LEVEL 7, WHICH MEANS IT BREACHES THE TERMS OF THE TREATY WITH THE ELOHI.
IS THERE ANYTHING ELSE YOU WANT TO TELL ME BEFORE I PUT YOU ON REPORT?
BREEEP
EXCUSE ME, I HAVE TO TAKE THIS.
SO, WHO THE HELL *DID* I HAVE SEX WITH LAST NIGHT?
THE NATIVES FROM THE BAR ARE MISSING...
THEY WERE GONE FROM THEIR LODGINGS THIS MORNING. THERE ARE SIGNS OF A STRUGGLE. AND THERE'S BLOOD.
WHAT'S HAPPENING HERE IS WAY BEYOND A FEW SUSPICIOUS DEATHS. THIS IS RAPIDLY TURNING INTO A SERIOUS DIPLOMATIC INCIDENT.

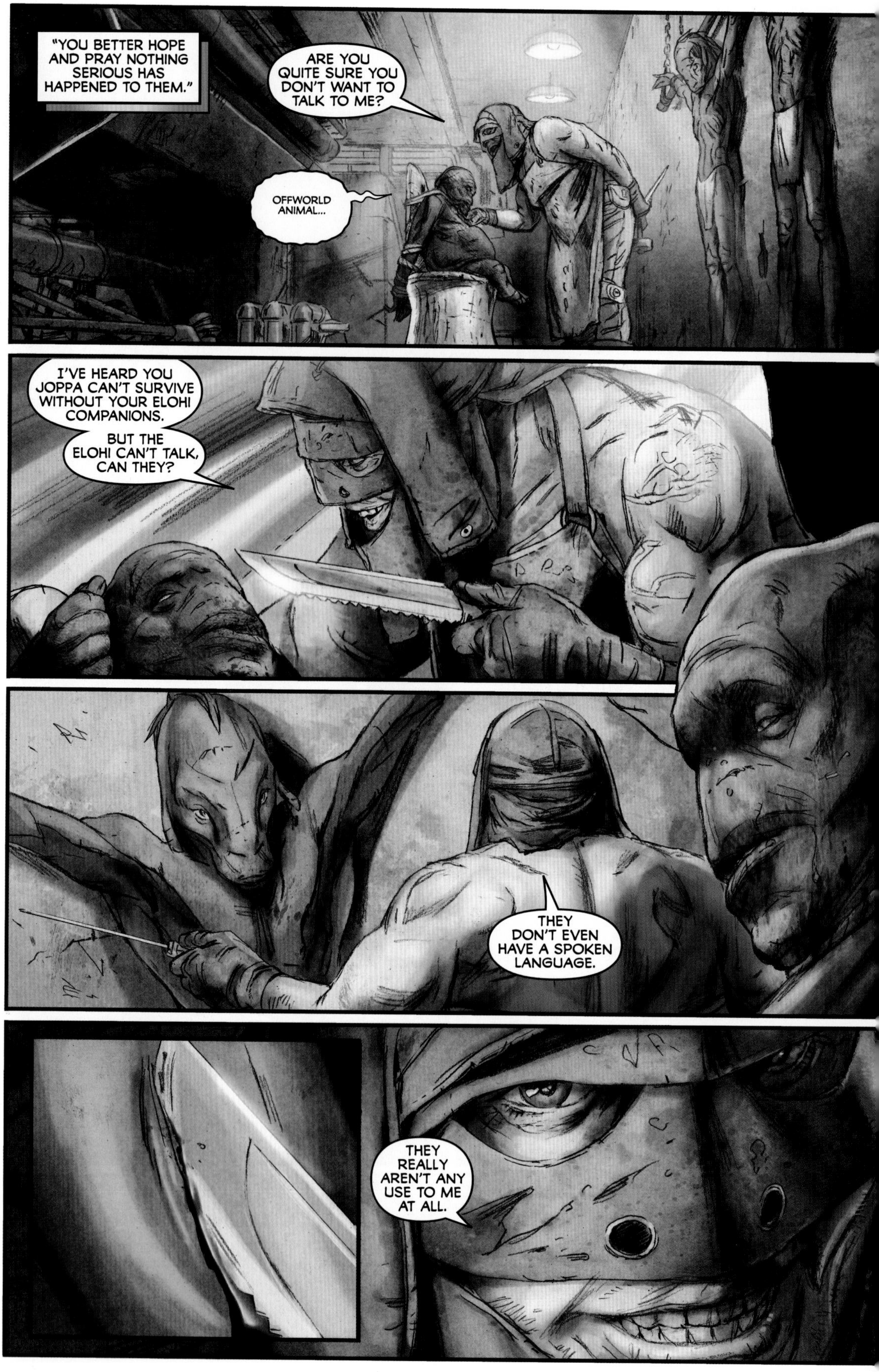
"YOU BETTER HOPE AND PRAY NOTHING SERIOUS HAS HAPPENED TO THEM."
ARE YOU QUITE SURE YOU DON'T WANT TO TALK TO ME?
OFFWORLD ANIMAL...
I'VE HEARD YOU JOPPA CAN'T SURVIVE WITHOUT YOUR ELOHI COMPANIONS.
BUT THE ELOHI CAN'T TALK, CAN THEY?
THEY DON'T EVEN HAVE A SPOKEN LANGUAGE.
THEY REALLY AREN'T ANY USE TO ME AT ALL.

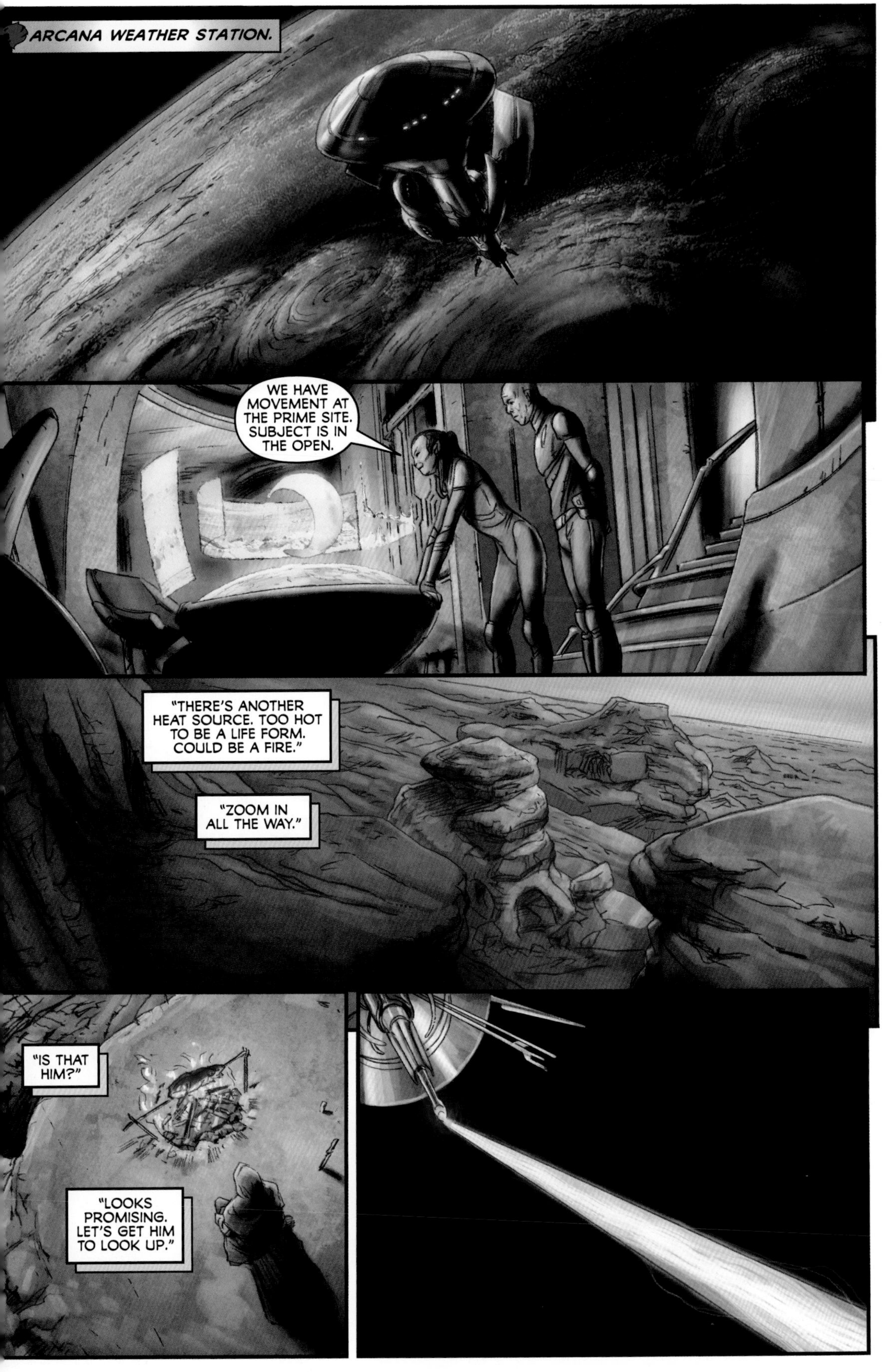
ARCANA WEATHER STATION.
WE HAVE MOVEMENT AT THE PRIME SITE. SUBJECT IS IN THE OPEN.
"THERE'S ANOTHER HEAT SOURCE. TOO HOT TO BE A LIFE FORM. COULD BE A FIRE."
"ZOOM IN ALL THE WAY."
"IS THAT HIM?"
"LOOKS PROMISING. LET'S GET HIM TO LOOK UP."

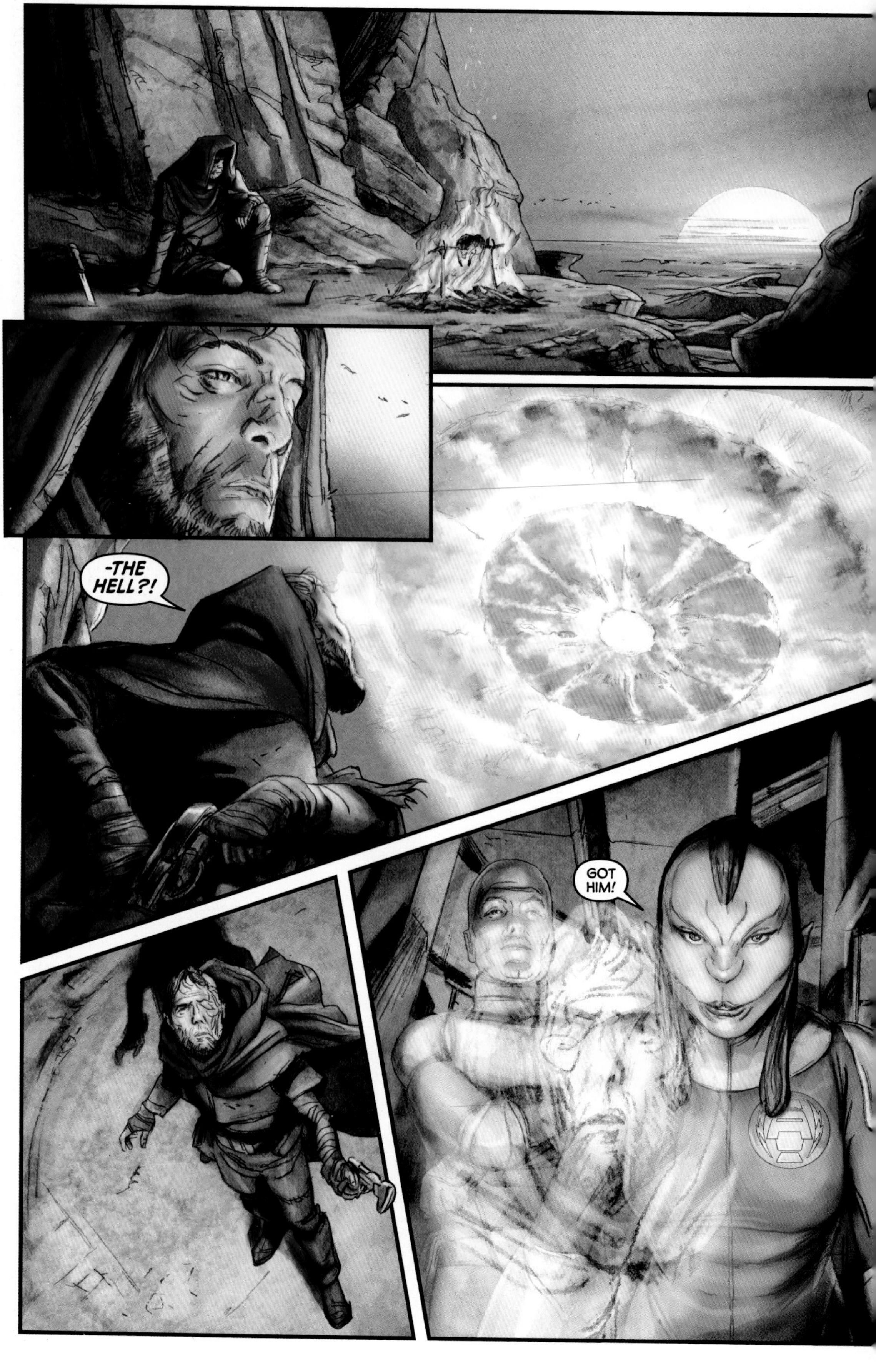
-THE HELL?!
GOT HIM!

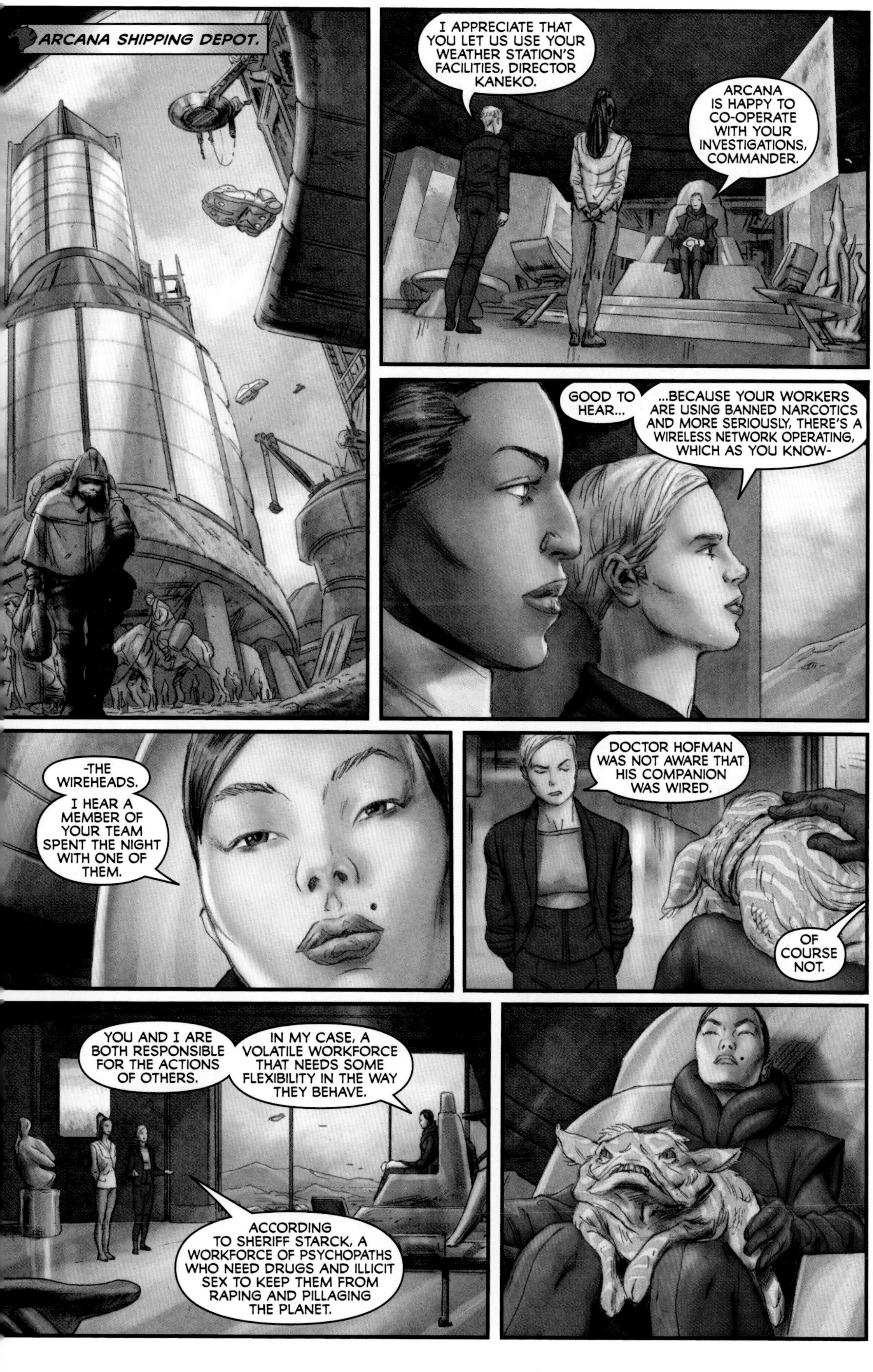
ARCANA SHIPPING DEPOT.
I APPRECIATE THAT YOU LET US USE YOUR WEATHER STATION'S FACILITIES, DIRECTOR KANEKO.
ARCANA IS HAPPY TO CO-OPERATE WITH YOUR INVESTIGATIONS, COMMANDER.
GOOD TO HEAR...
...BECAUSE YOUR WORKERS ARE USING BANNED NARCOTICS AND MORE SERIOUSLY, THERE'S A WIRELESS NETWORK OPERATING, WHICH AS YOU KNOW-
-THE WIREHEADS.
I HEAR A MEMBER OF YOUR TEAM SPENT THE NIGHT WITH ONE OF THEM.
DOCTOR HOFMAN WAS NOT AWARE THAT HIS COMPANION WAS WIRED.
OF COURSE NOT.
YOU AND I ARE BOTH RESPONSIBLE FOR THE ACTIONS OF OTHERS.
IN MY CASE, A VOLATILE WORKFORCE THAT NEEDS SOME FLEXIBILITY IN THE WAY THEY BEHAVE.
ACCORDING TO SHERIFF STARCK, A WORKFORCE OF PSYCHOPATHS WHO NEED DRUGS AND ILLICIT SEX TO KEEP THEM FROM RAPING AND PILLAGING THE PLANET.

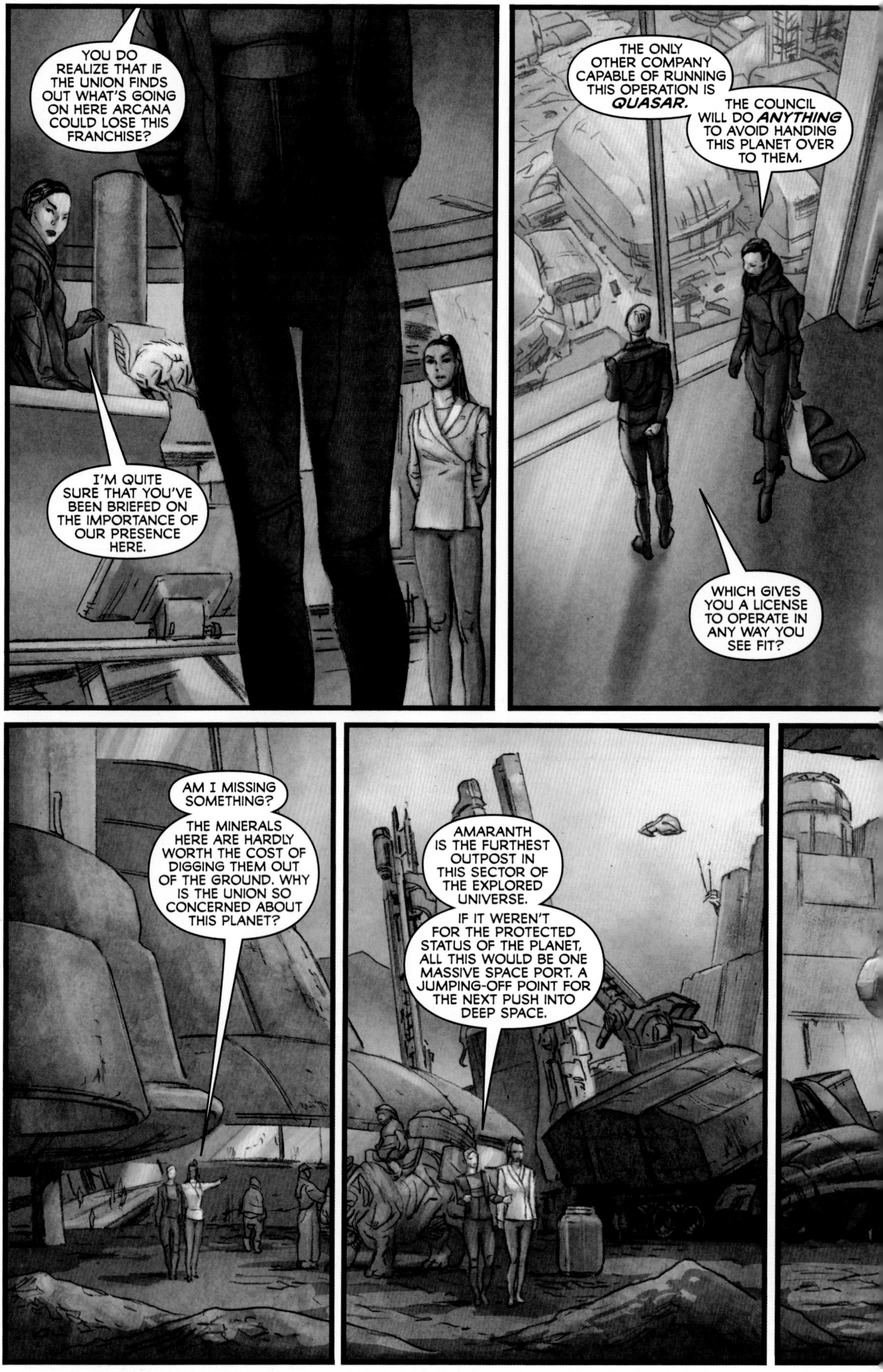
YOU DO REALIZE THAT IF THE UNION FINDS OUT WHAT'S GOING ON HERE ARCANA COULD LOSE THIS FRANCHISE?
I'M QUITE SURE THAT YOU'VE BEEN BRIEFED ON THE IMPORTANCE OF OUR PRESENCE HERE.
THE ONLY OTHER COMPANY CAPABLE OF RUNNING THIS OPERATION IS QUASAR.
THE COUNCIL WILL DO ANYTHING TO AVOID HANDING THIS PLANET OVER TO THEM.
WHICH GIVES YOU A LICENSE TO OPERATE IN ANY WAY YOU SEE FIT?
AM I MISSING SOMETHING?
THE MINERALS HERE ARE HARDLY WORTH THE COST OF DIGGING THEM OUT OF THE GROUND. WHY IS THE UNION SO CONCERNED ABOUT THIS PLANET?
AMARANTH IS THE FURTHEST OUTPOST IN THIS SECTOR OF THE EXPLORED UNIVERSE.
IF IT WEREN'T FOR THE PROTECTED STATUS OF THE PLANET, ALL THIS WOULD BE ONE MASSIVE SPACE PORT. A JUMPING-OFF POINT FOR THE NEXT PUSH INTO DEEP SPACE.

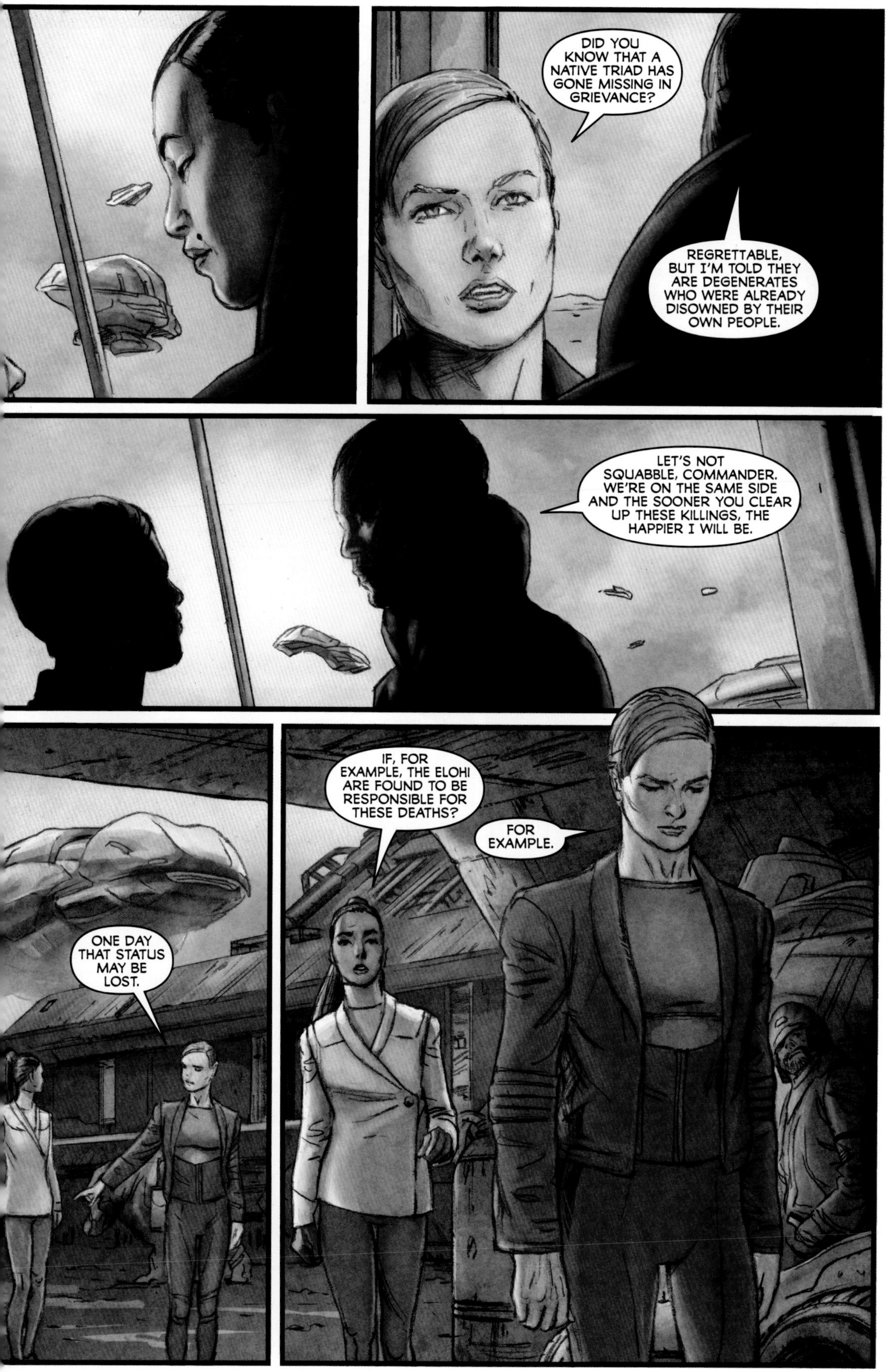

DID YOU KNOW THAT A NATIVE TRIAD HAS GONE MISSING IN GRIEVANCE?
REGRETTABLE, BUT I'M TOLD THEY ARE DEGENERATES WHO WERE ALREADY DISOWNED BY THEIR OWN PEOPLE.
LET'S NOT SQUABBLE, COMMANDER. WE'RE ON THE SAME SIDE AND THE SOONER YOU CLEAR UP THESE KILLINGS, THE HAPPIER I WILL BE.
ONE DAY THAT STATUS MAY BE LOST.
IF, FOR EXAMPLE, THE ELOHI ARE FOUND TO BE RESPONSIBLE FOR THESE DEATHS?
FOR EXAMPLE.

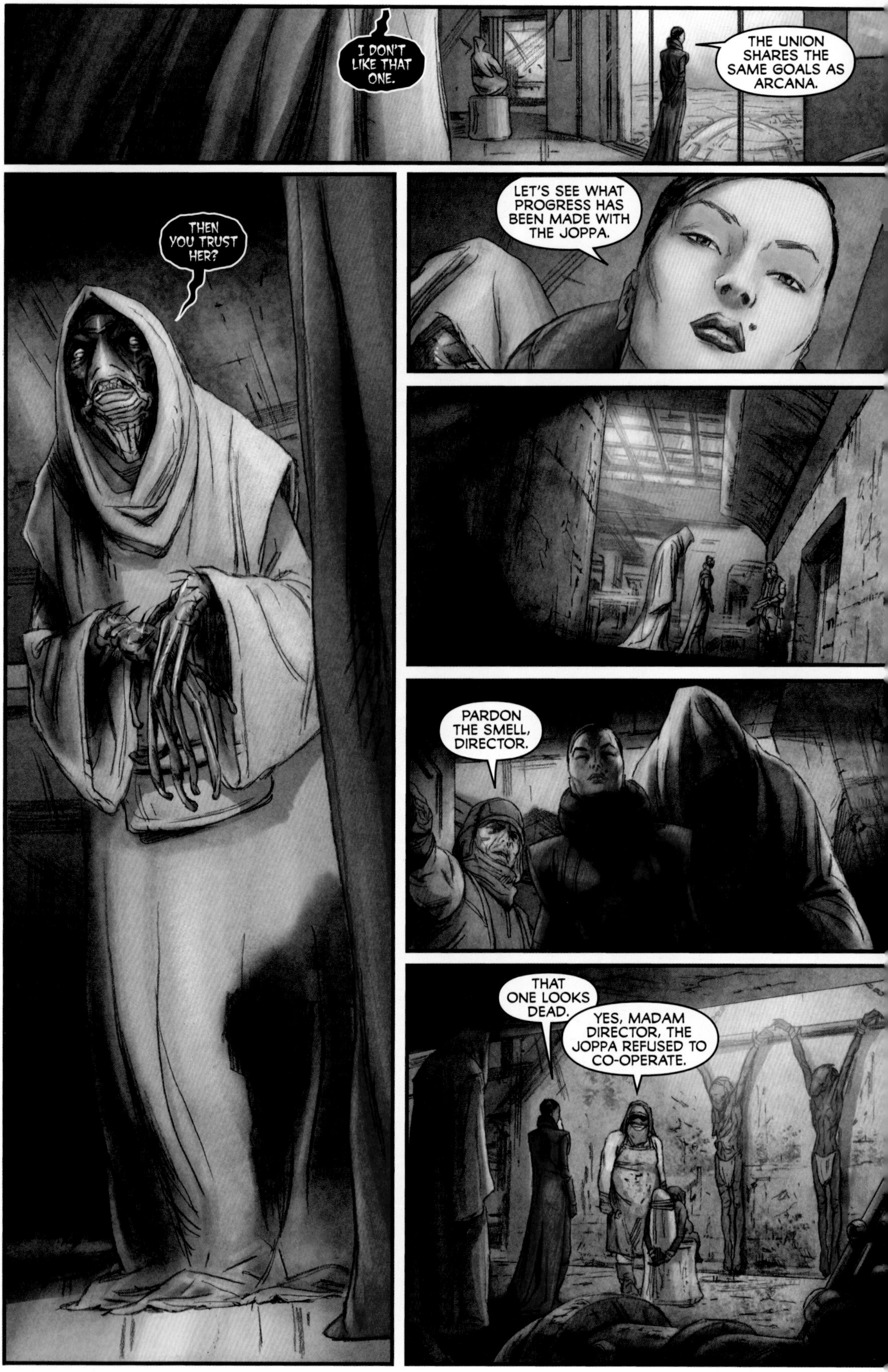
I DON'T LIKE THAT ONE.
THE UNION SHARES THE SAME GOALS AS ARCANA.
THEN YOU TRUST HER?
LET'S SEE WHAT PROGRESS HAS BEEN MADE WITH THE JOPPA.
PARDON THE SMELL, DIRECTOR.
THAT ONE LOOKS DEAD.
YES, MADAM DIRECTOR, THE JOPPA REFUSED TO CO-OPERATE.

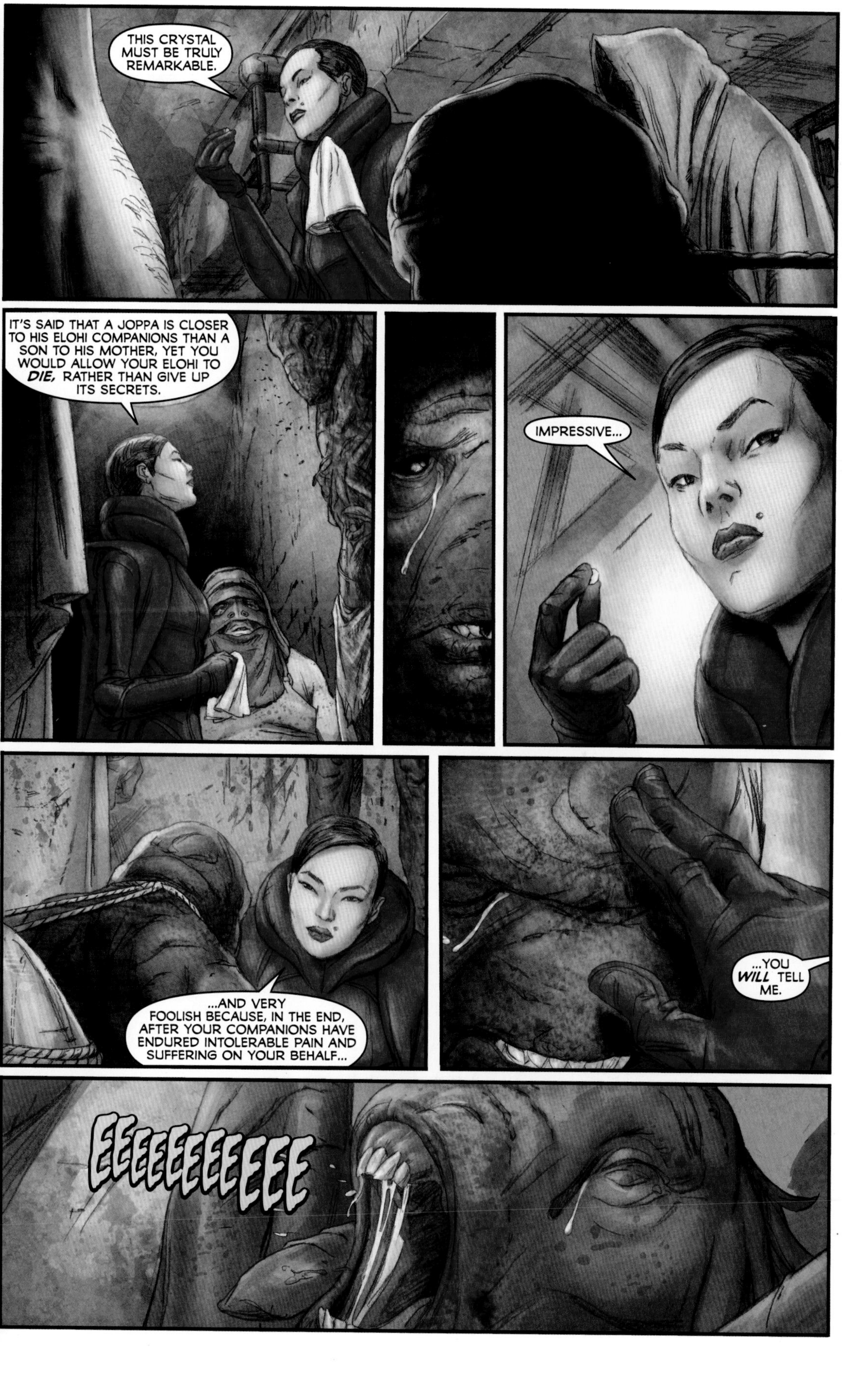
THIS CRYSTAL MUST BE TRULY REMARKABLE.
IT'S SAID THAT A JOPPA IS CLOSER TO HIS ELOHI COMPANIONS THAN A SON TO HIS MOTHER, YET YOU WOULD ALLOW YOUR ELOHI TO *DIE,* RATHER THAN GIVE UP ITS SECRETS.
IMPRESSIVE...
...AND VERY FOOLISH BECAUSE, IN THE END, AFTER YOUR COMPANIONS HAVE ENDURED INTOLERABLE PAIN AND SUFFERING ON YOUR BEHALF...
...YOU *WILL* TELL ME.
EEEEEEEEEEEE

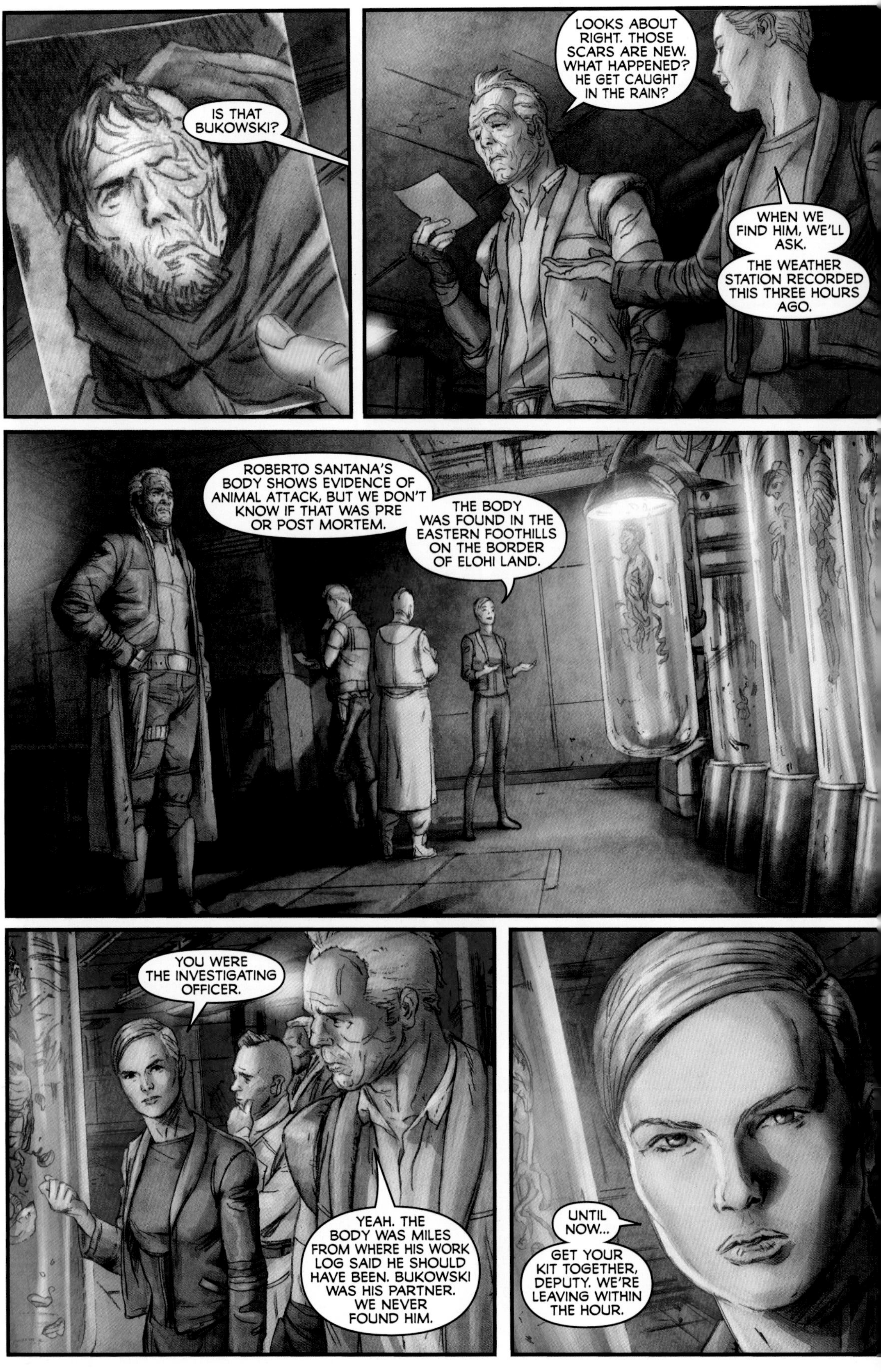
IS THAT BUKOWSKI?
LOOKS ABOUT RIGHT. THOSE SCARS ARE NEW. WHAT HAPPENED? HE GET CAUGHT IN THE RAIN?
WHEN WE FIND HIM, WE'LL ASK.
THE WEATHER STATION RECORDED THIS THREE HOURS AGO.
ROBERTO SANTANA'S BODY SHOWS EVIDENCE OF ANIMAL ATTACK, BUT WE DON'T KNOW IF THAT WAS PRE OR POST MORTEM.
THE BODY WAS FOUND IN THE EASTERN FOOTHILLS ON THE BORDER OF ELOHI LAND.
YOU WERE THE INVESTIGATING OFFICER.
YEAH. THE BODY WAS MILES FROM WHERE HIS WORK LOG SAID HE SHOULD HAVE BEEN. BUKOWSKI WAS HIS PARTNER. WE NEVER FOUND HIM.
UNTIL NOW...
GET YOUR KIT TOGETHER, DEPUTY. WE'RE LEAVING WITHIN THE HOUR.

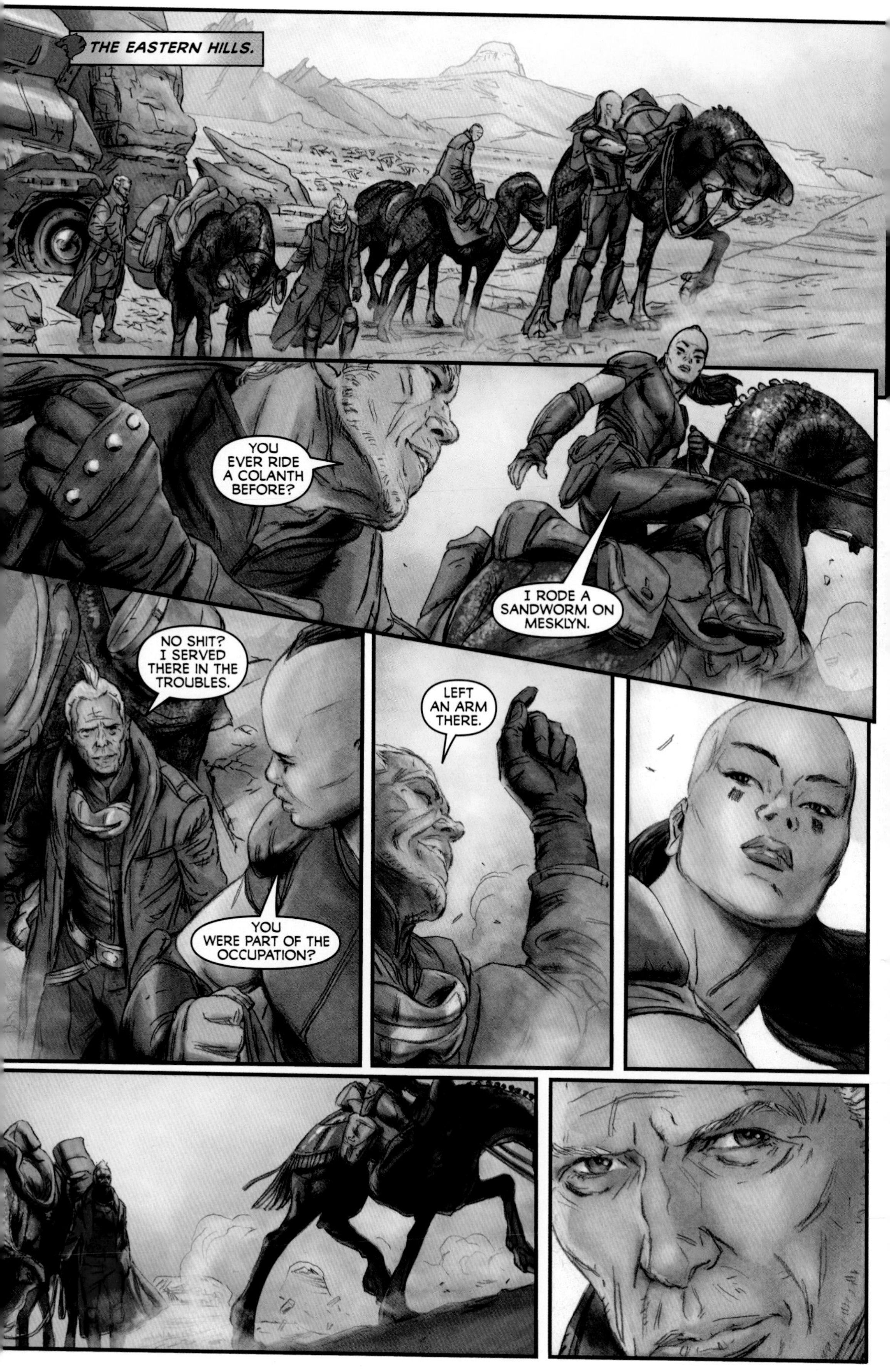
THE EASTERN HILLS.
YOU EVER RIDE A COLANTH BEFORE?
I RODE A SANDWORM ON MESKLYN.
NO SHIT? I SERVED THERE IN THE TROUBLES.
YOU WERE PART OF THE OCCUPATION?
LEFT AN ARM THERE.

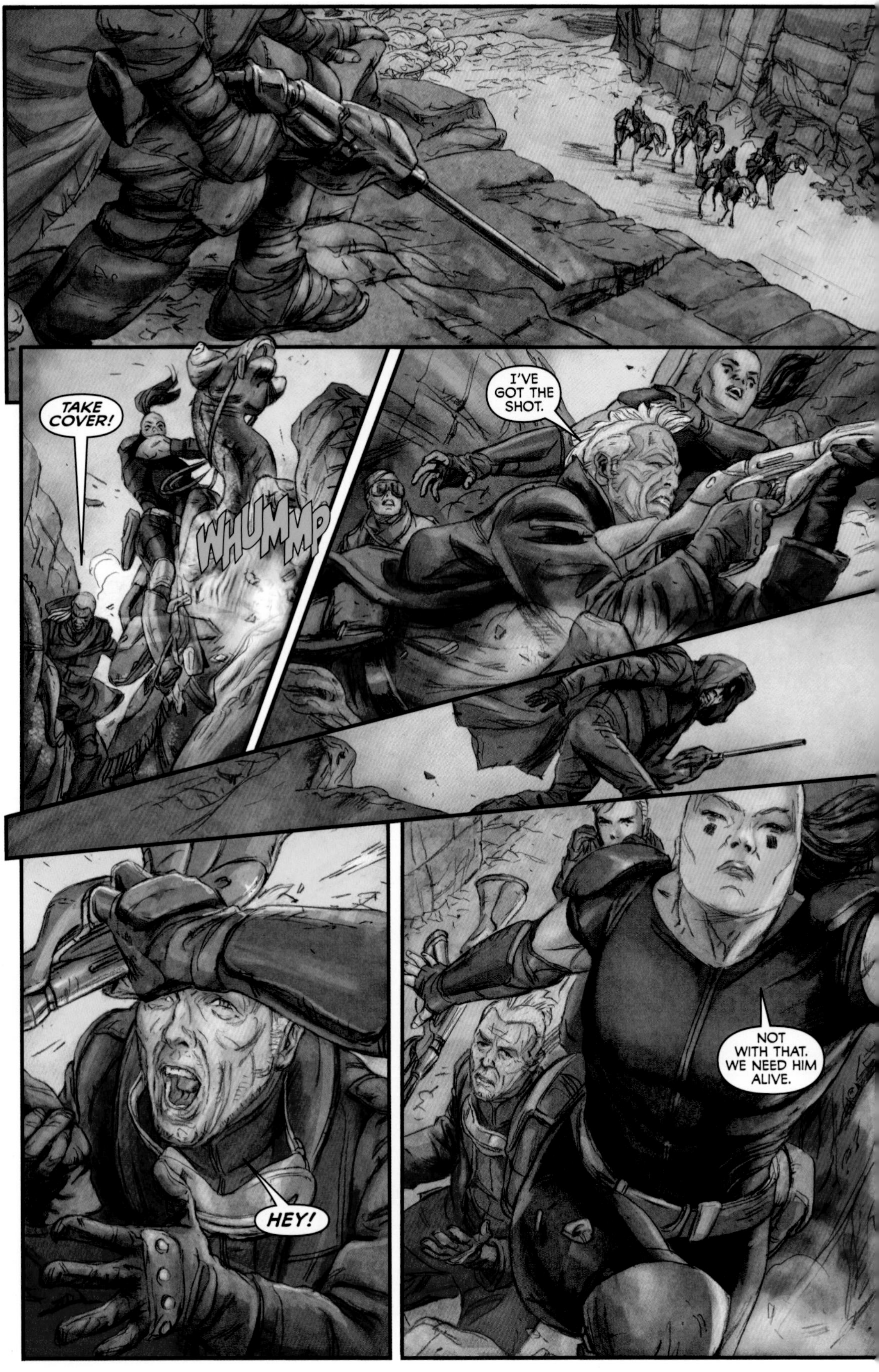
TAKE COVER!
WHUMMMP
I'VE GOT THE SHOT.
HEY!
NOT WITH THAT. WE NEED HIM ALIVE.

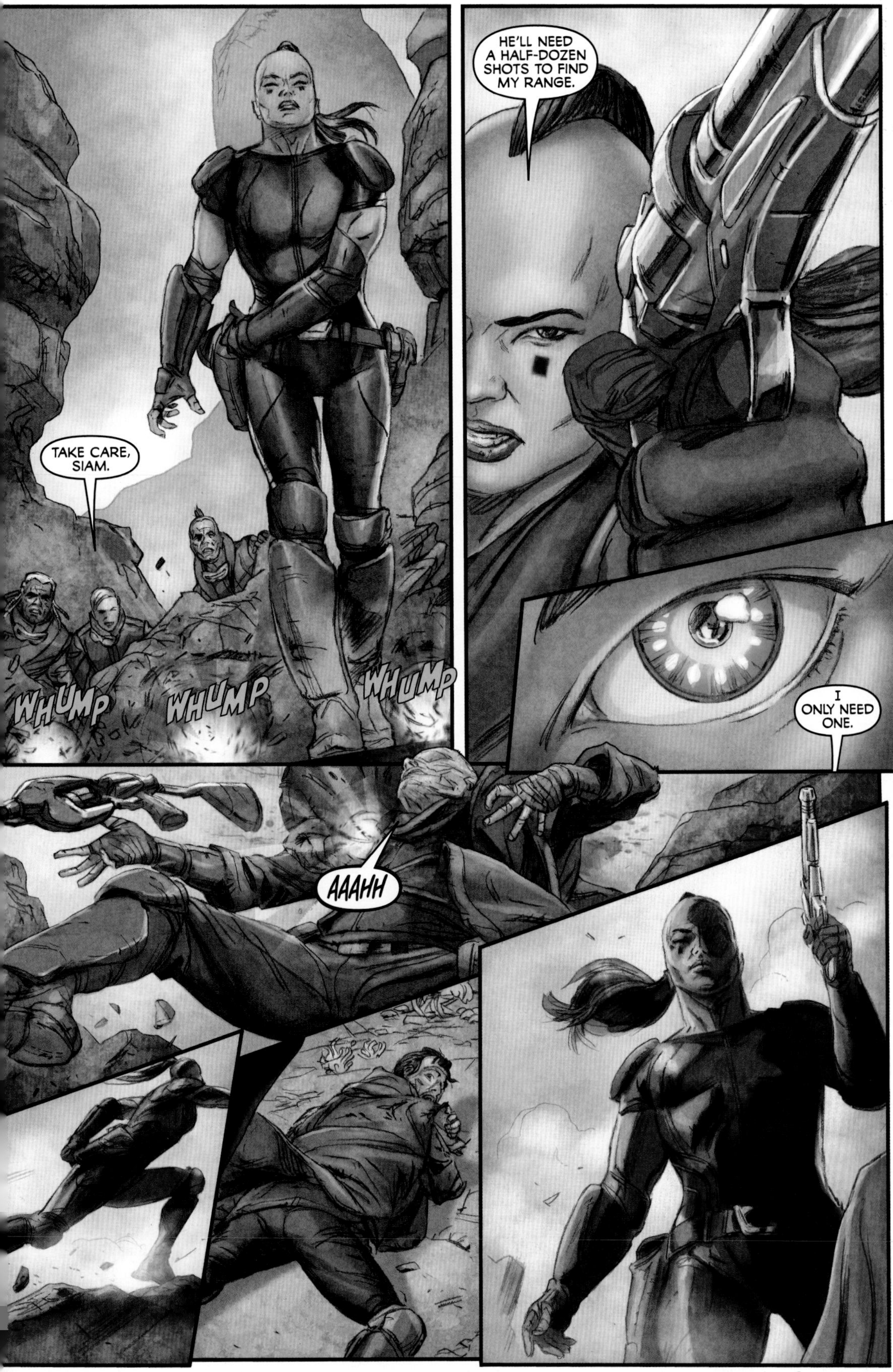
TAKE CARE, SIAM.
WHUMP
WHUMP
WHUMP
HE'LL NEED A HALF-DOZEN SHOTS TO FIND MY RANGE.
I ONLY NEED ONE.
AAAHH

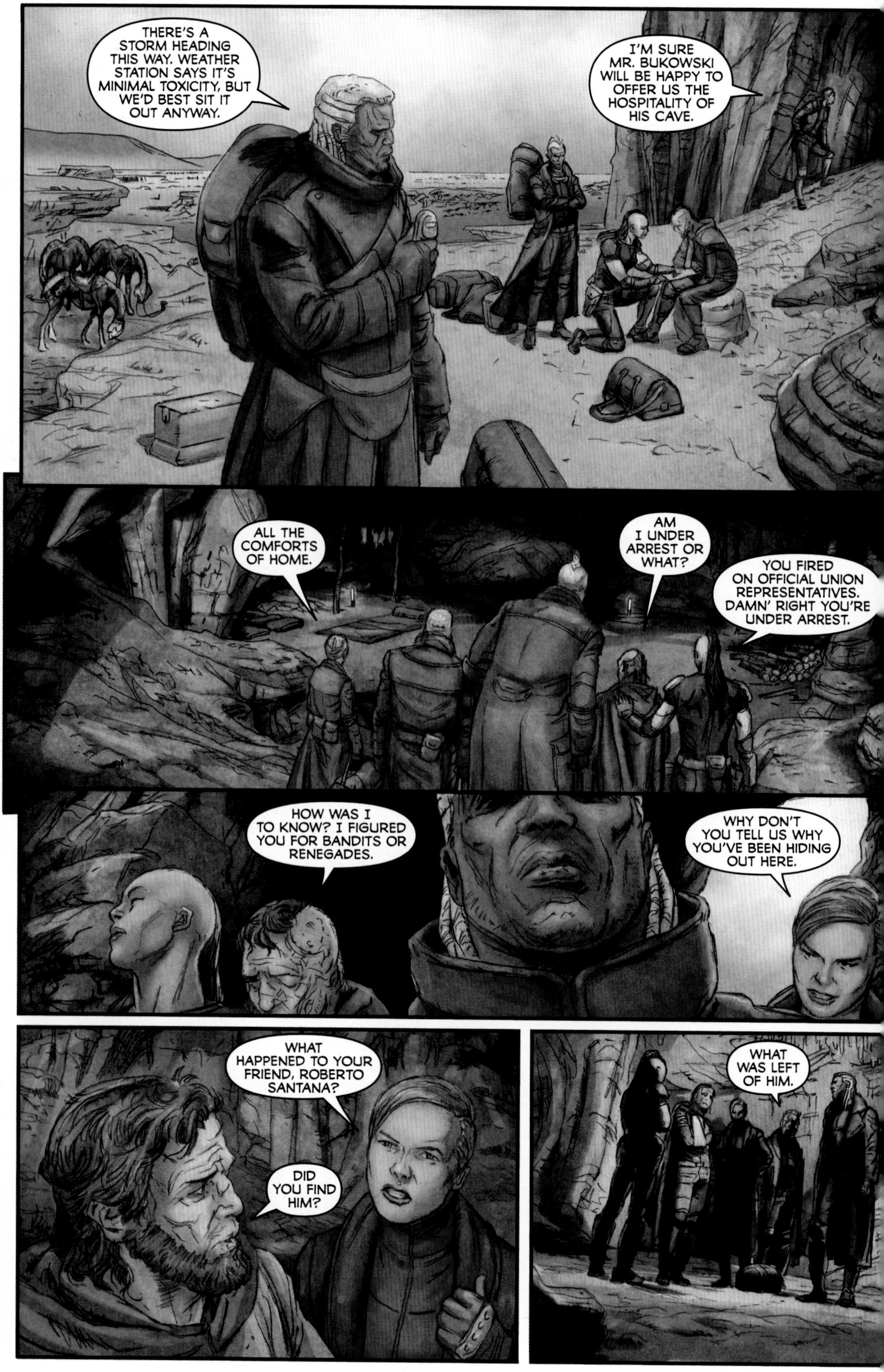
THERE'S A STORM HEADING THIS WAY. WEATHER STATION SAYS IT'S MINIMAL TOXICITY, BUT WE'D BEST SIT IT OUT ANYWAY.
I'M SURE MR. BUKOWSKI WILL BE HAPPY TO OFFER US THE HOSPITALITY OF HIS CAVE.
ALL THE COMFORTS OF HOME.
AM I UNDER ARREST OR WHAT?
YOU FIRED ON OFFICIAL UNION REPRESENTATIVES. DAMN' RIGHT YOU'RE UNDER ARREST.
HOW WAS I TO KNOW? I FIGURED YOU FOR BANDITS OR RENEGADES.
WHY DON'T YOU TELL US WHY YOU'VE BEEN HIDING OUT HERE.
WHAT HAPPENED TO YOUR FRIEND, ROBERTO SANTANA?
DID YOU FIND HIM?
WHAT WAS LEFT OF HIM.

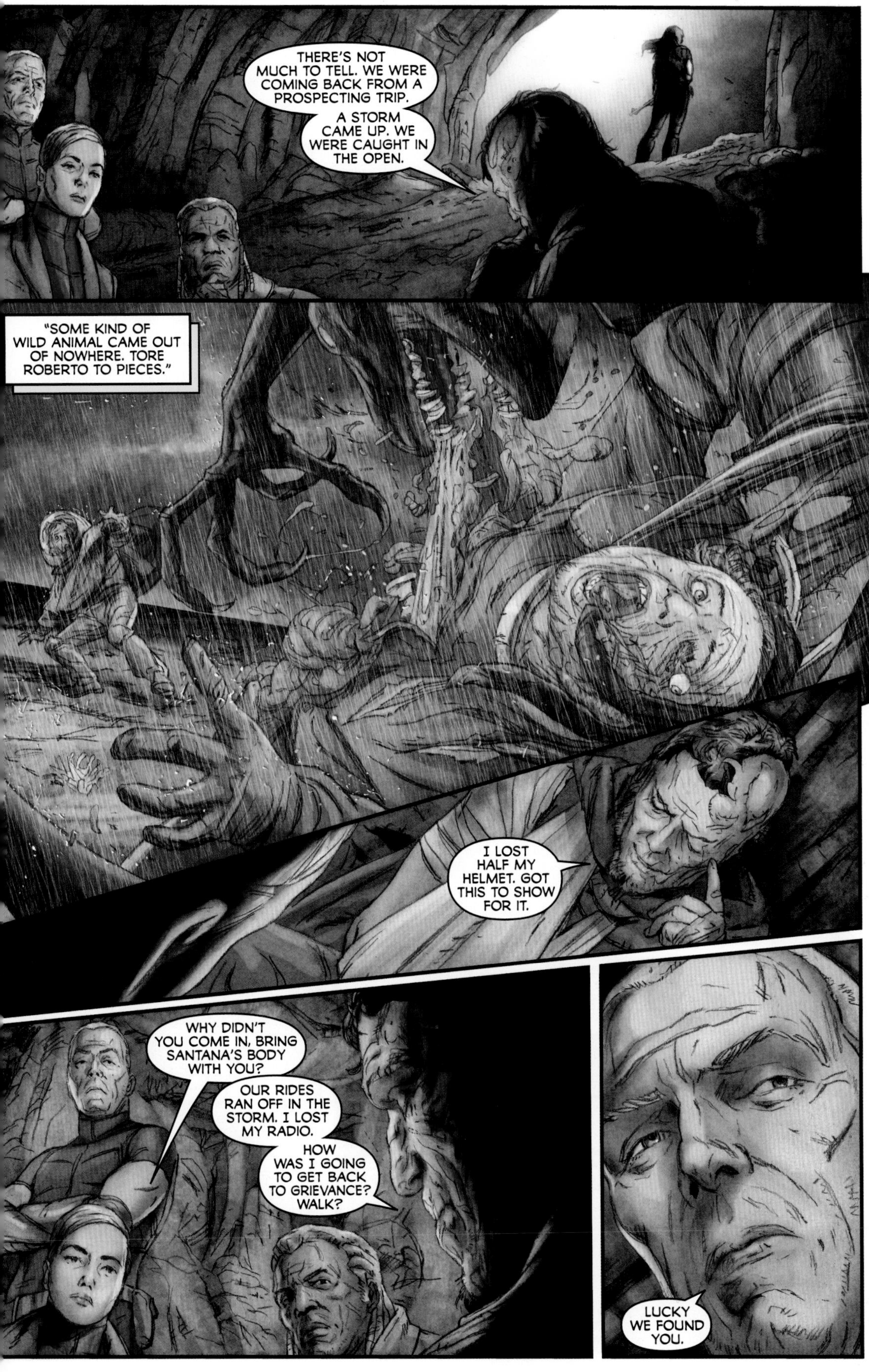
THERE'S NOT MUCH TO TELL. WE WERE COMING BACK FROM A PROSPECTING TRIP.
A STORM CAME UP. WE WERE CAUGHT IN THE OPEN.
"SOME KIND OF WILD ANIMAL CAME OUT OF NOWHERE. TORE ROBERTO TO PIECES."
I LOST HALF MY HELMET. GOT THIS TO SHOW FOR IT.
WHY DIDN'T YOU COME IN, BRING SANTANA'S BODY WITH YOU?
OUR RIDES RAN OFF IN THE STORM. I LOST MY RADIO.
HOW WAS I GOING TO GET BACK TO GRIEVANCE? WALK?
LUCKY WE FOUND YOU.

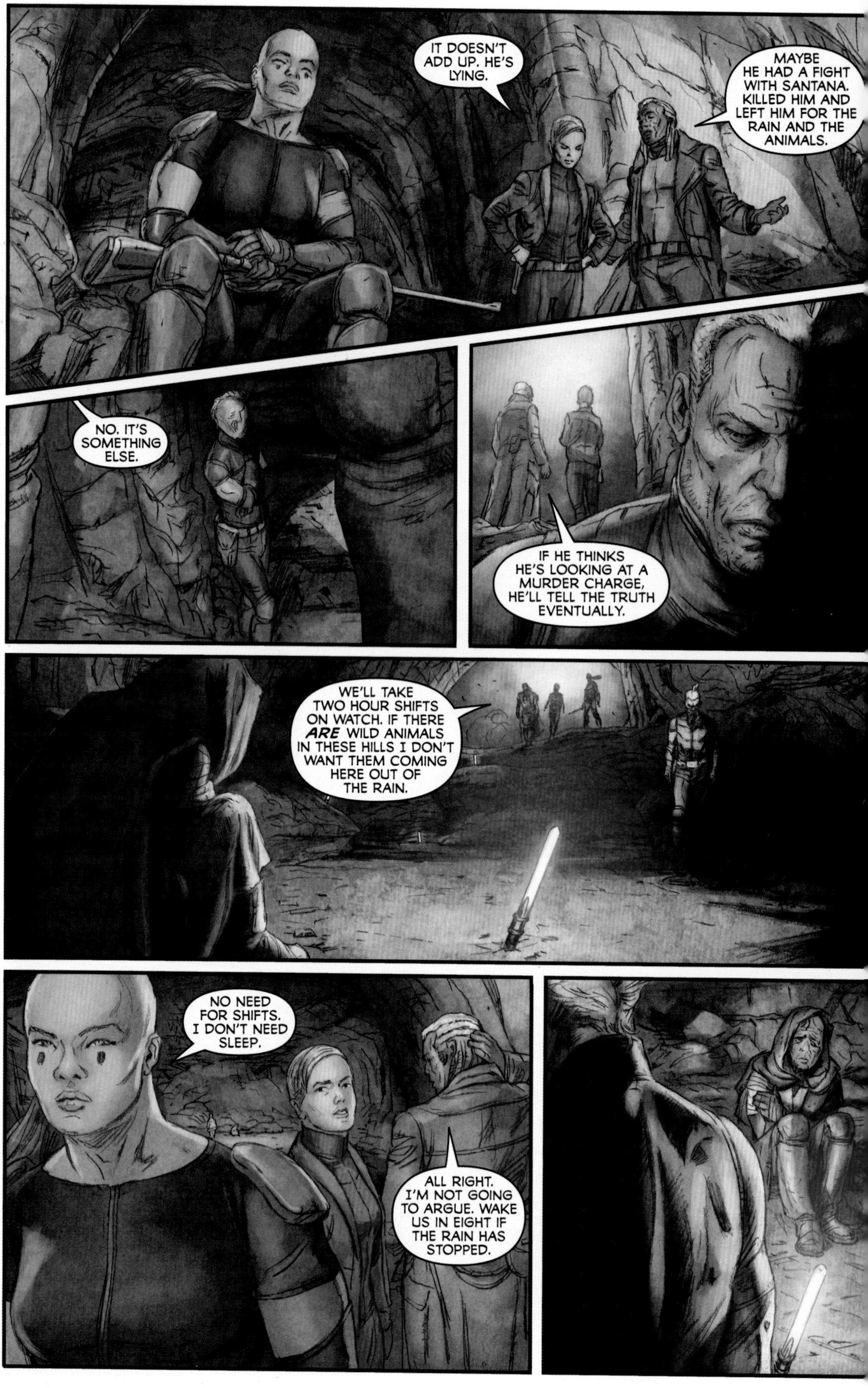
IT DOESN'T ADD UP. HE'S LYING.
MAYBE HE HAD A FIGHT WITH SANTANA. KILLED HIM AND LEFT HIM FOR THE RAIN AND THE ANIMALS.
NO. IT'S SOMETHING ELSE.
IF HE THINKS HE'S LOOKING AT A MURDER CHARGE, HE'LL TELL THE TRUTH EVENTUALLY.
WE'LL TAKE TWO HOUR SHIFTS ON WATCH. IF THERE *ARE* WILD ANIMALS IN THESE HILLS I DON'T WANT THEM COMING HERE OUT OF THE RAIN.
NO NEED FOR SHIFTS. I DON'T NEED SLEEP.
ALL RIGHT. I'M NOT GOING TO ARGUE. WAKE US IN EIGHT IF THE RAIN HAS STOPPED.

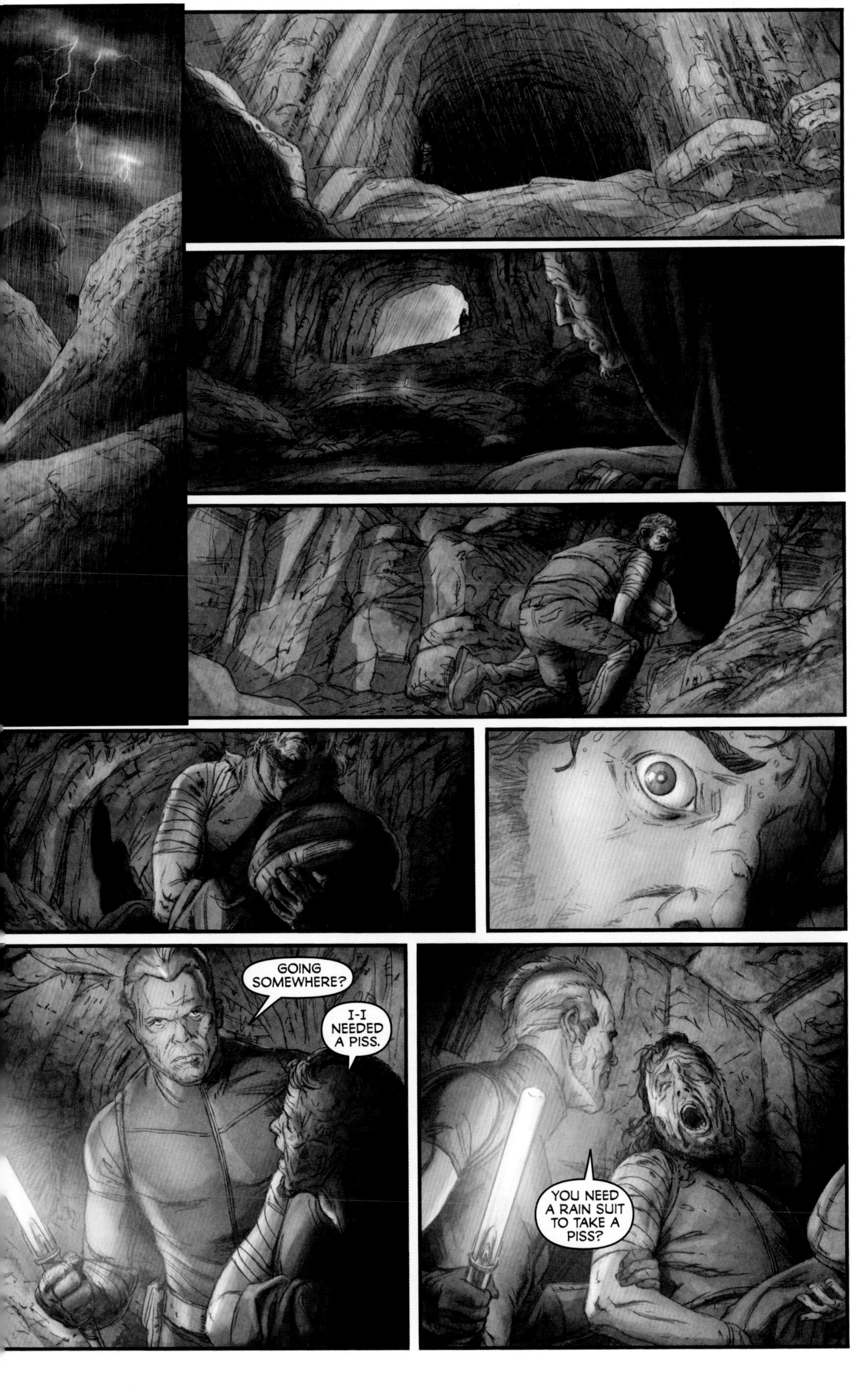
GOING SOMEWHERE?
I-I NEEDED A PISS.
YOU NEED A RAIN SUIT TO TAKE A PISS?

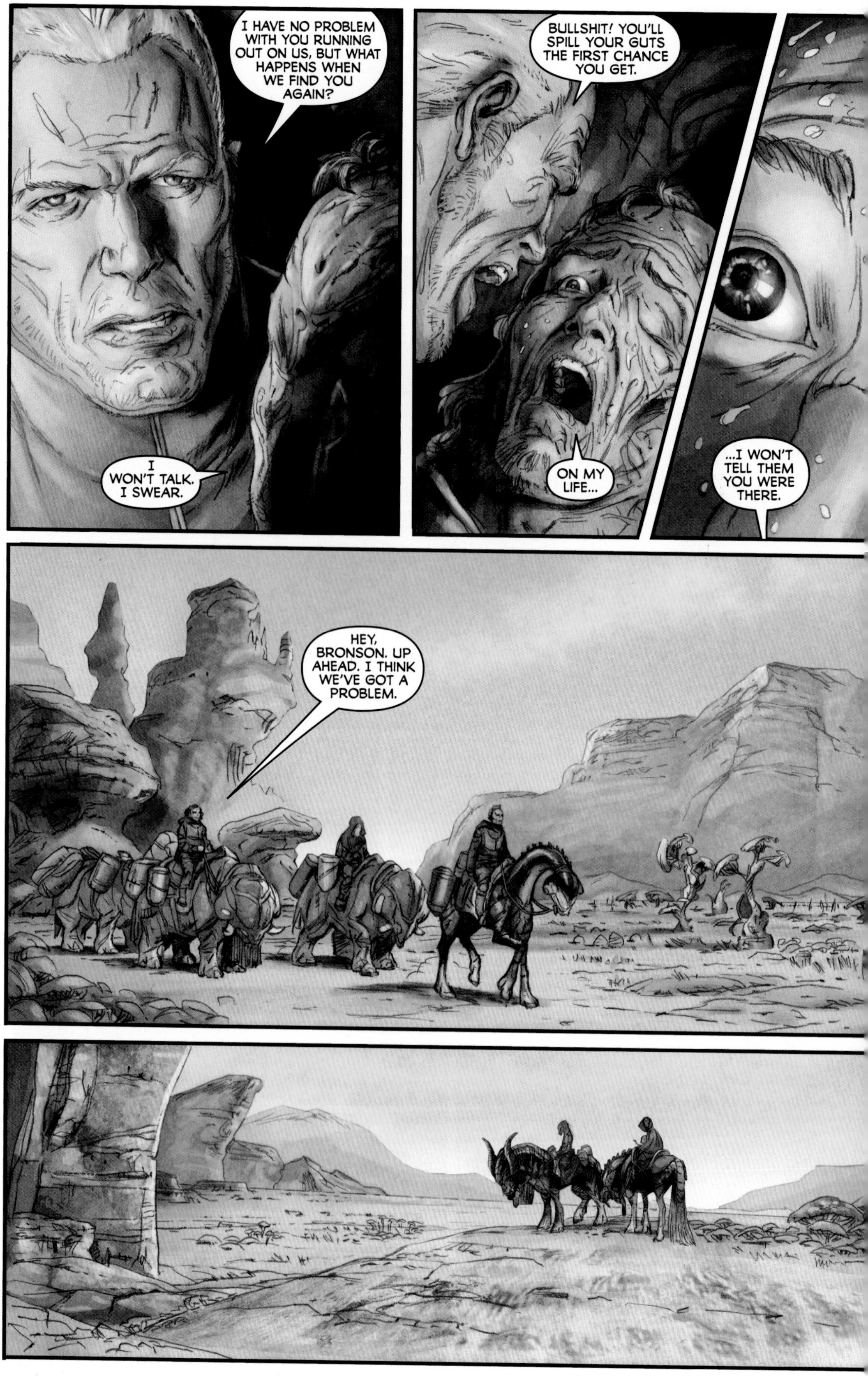
I HAVE NO PROBLEM WITH YOU RUNNING OUT ON US, BUT WHAT HAPPENS WHEN WE FIND YOU AGAIN?
I WON'T TALK. I SWEAR.
BULLSHIT! YOU'LL SPILL YOUR GUTS THE FIRST CHANCE YOU GET.
ON MY LIFE...
...I WON'T TELL THEM YOU WERE THERE.
HEY, BRONSON. UP AHEAD. I THINK WE'VE GOT A PROBLEM.

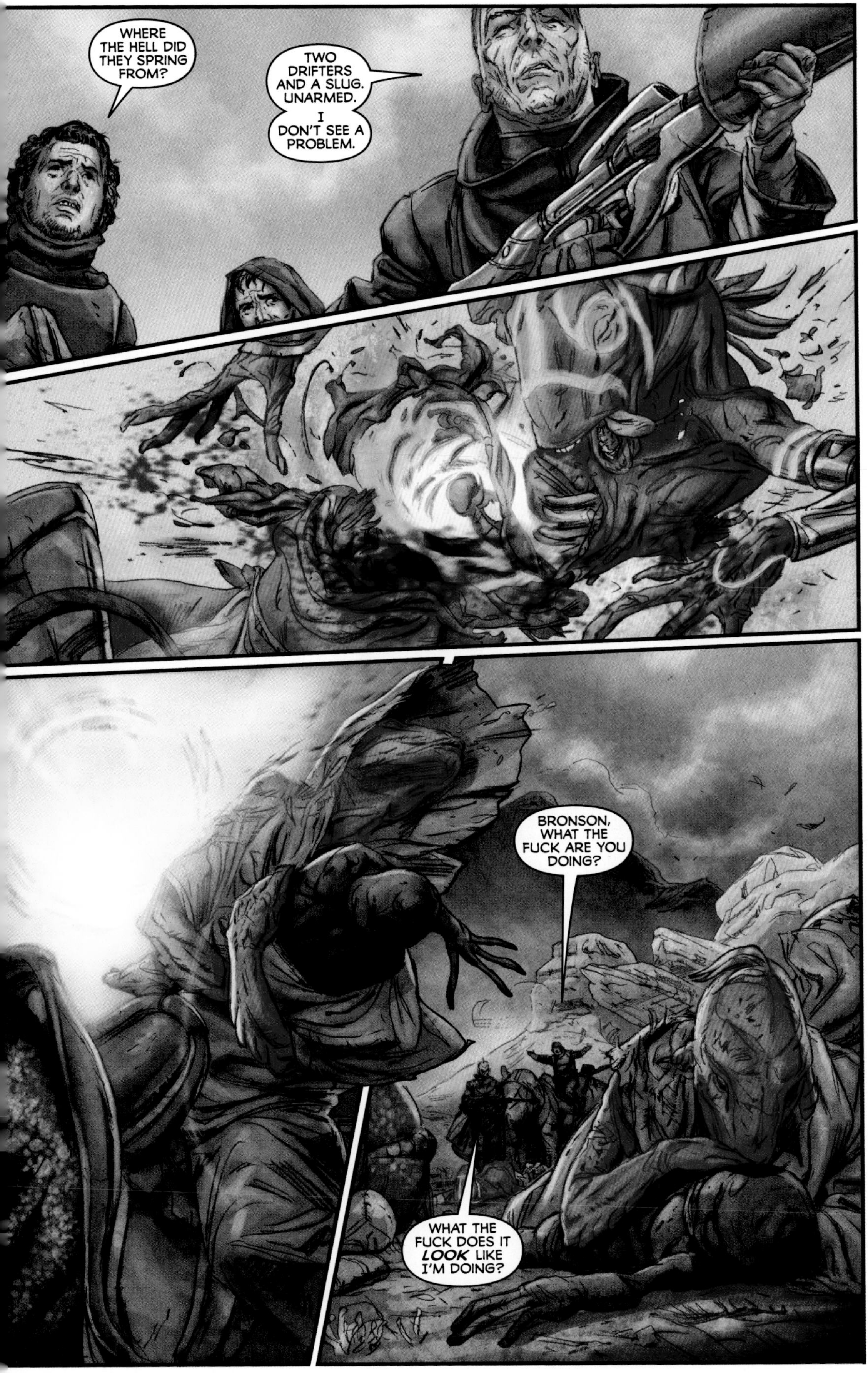
WHERE THE HELL DID THEY SPRING FROM?
TWO DRIFTERS AND A SLUG. UNARMED.
I DON'T SEE A PROBLEM.
BRONSON, WHAT THE FUCK ARE YOU DOING?
WHAT THE FUCK DOES IT LOOK LIKE I'M DOING?

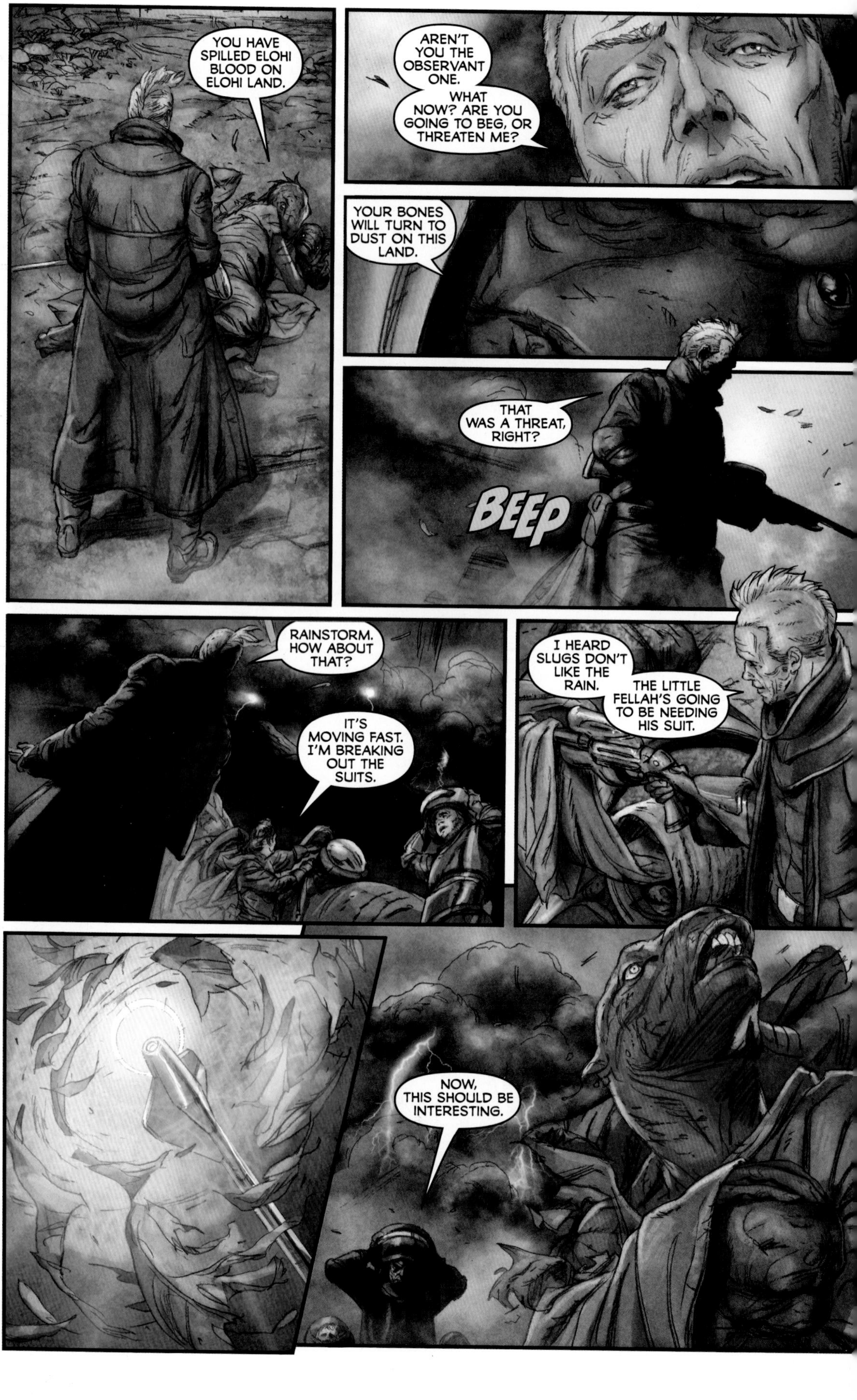
YOU HAVE SPILLED ELOHI BLOOD ON ELOHI LAND.
AREN'T YOU THE OBSERVANT ONE.
WHAT NOW? ARE YOU GOING TO BEG, OR THREATEN ME?
YOUR BONES WILL TURN TO DUST ON THIS LAND.
THAT WAS A THREAT, RIGHT?
BEEP
RAINSTORM. HOW ABOUT THAT?
IT'S MOVING FAST. I'M BREAKING OUT THE SUITS.
I HEARD SLUGS DON'T LIKE THE RAIN.
THE LITTLE FELLAH'S GOING TO BE NEEDING HIS SUIT.
NOW, THIS SHOULD BE INTERESTING.

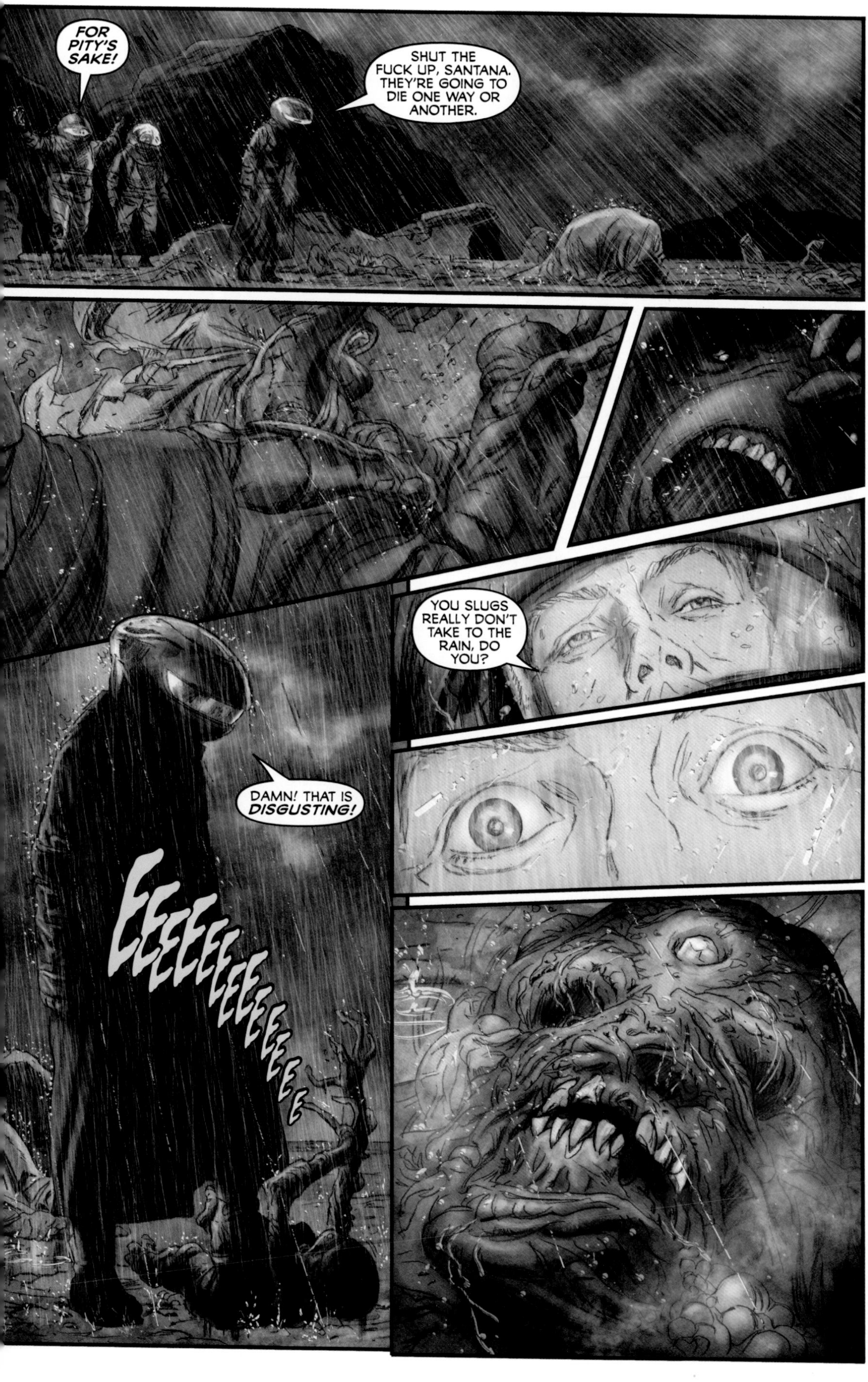
FOR PITY'S SAKE!
SHUT THE FUCK UP, SANTANA. THEY'RE GOING TO DIE ONE WAY OR ANOTHER.
YOU SLUGS REALLY DON'T TAKE TO THE RAIN, DO YOU?
DAMN! THAT IS *DISGUSTING!*
EEEEEEEEEEEEEEEEE

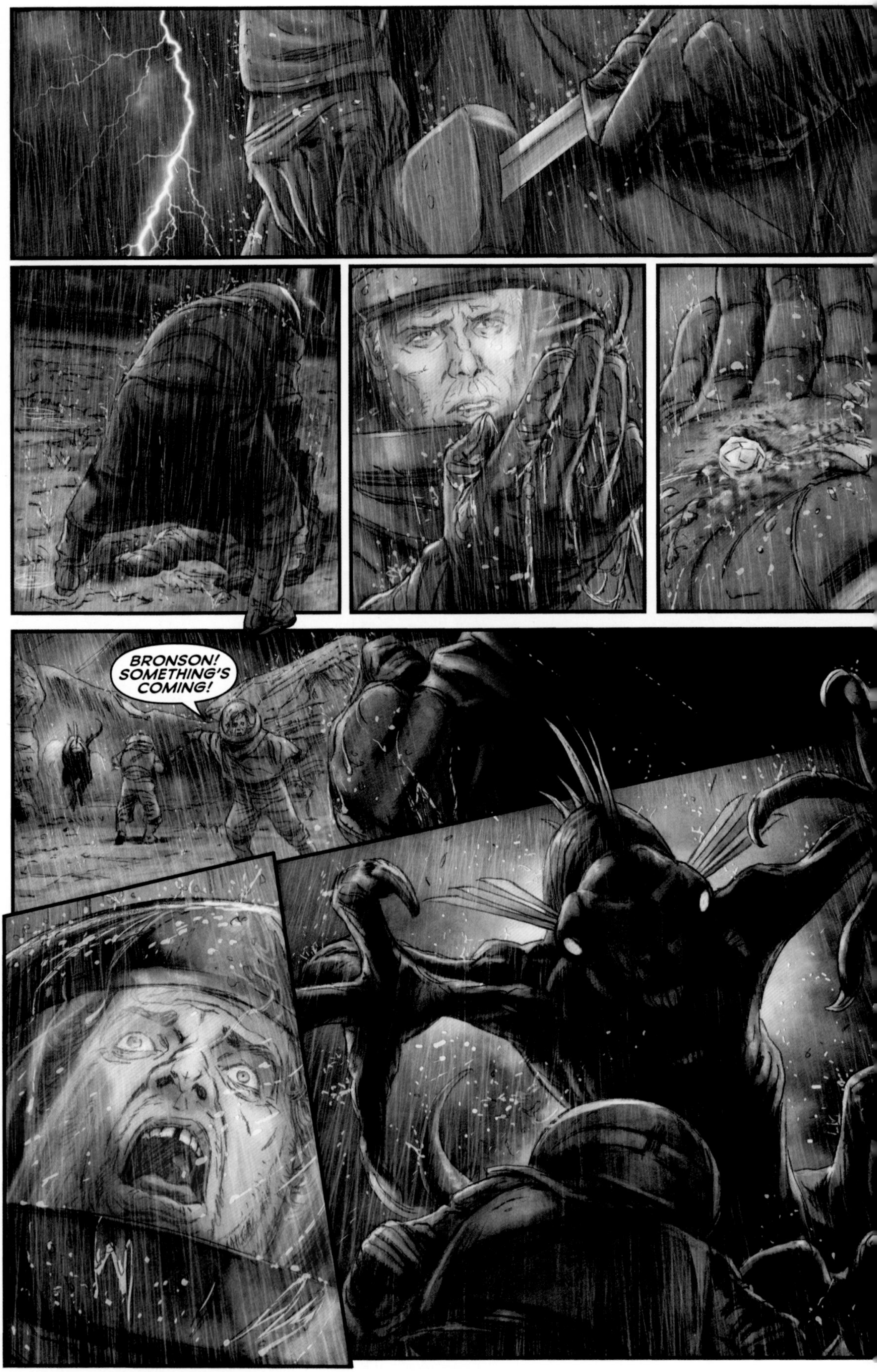
BRONSON! SOMETHING'S COMING!

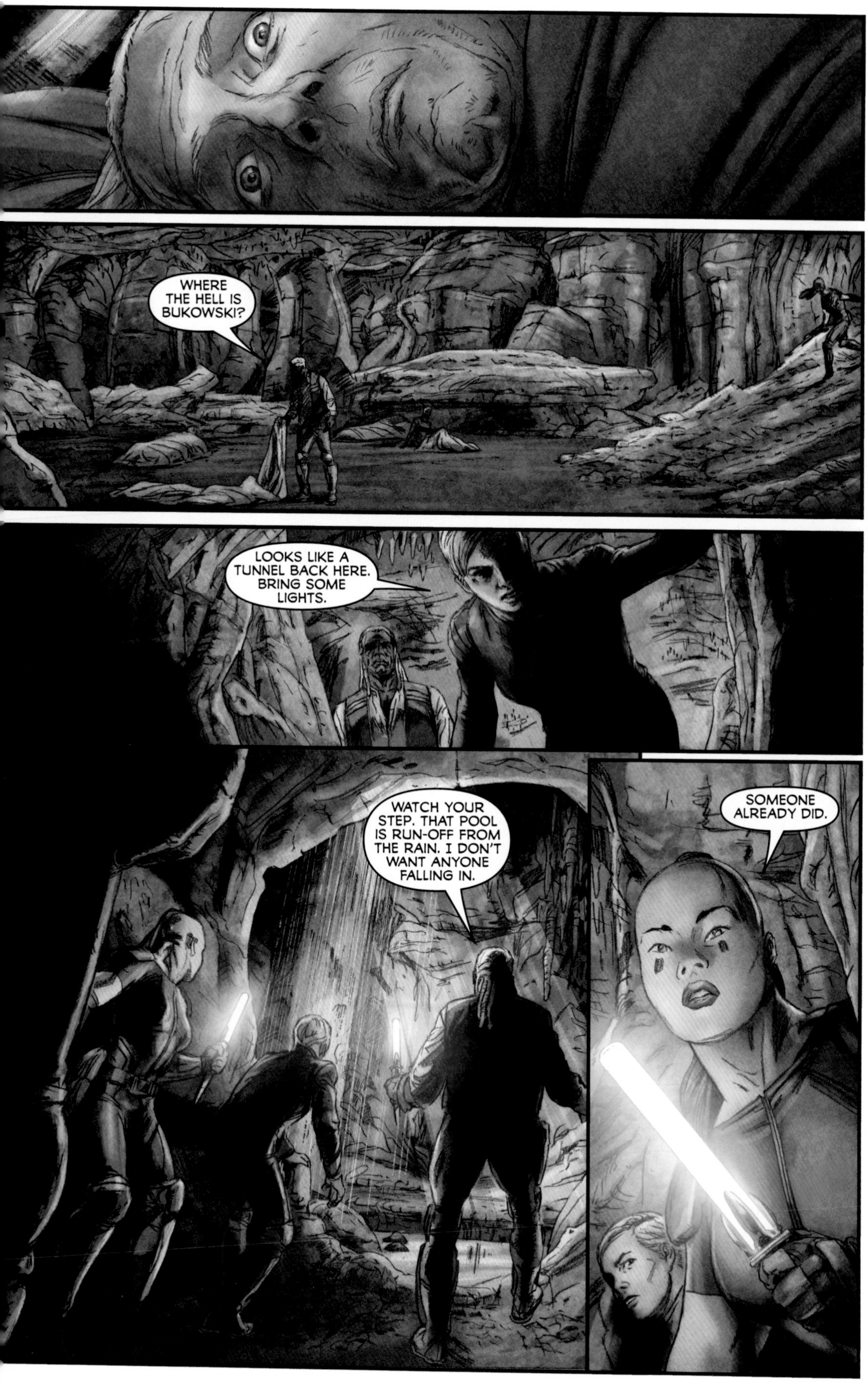
WHERE THE HELL IS BUKOWSKI?
LOOKS LIKE A TUNNEL BACK HERE. BRING SOME LIGHTS.
WATCH YOUR STEP. THAT POOL IS RUN-OFF FROM THE RAIN. I DON'T WANT ANYONE FALLING IN.
SOMEONE ALREADY DID.

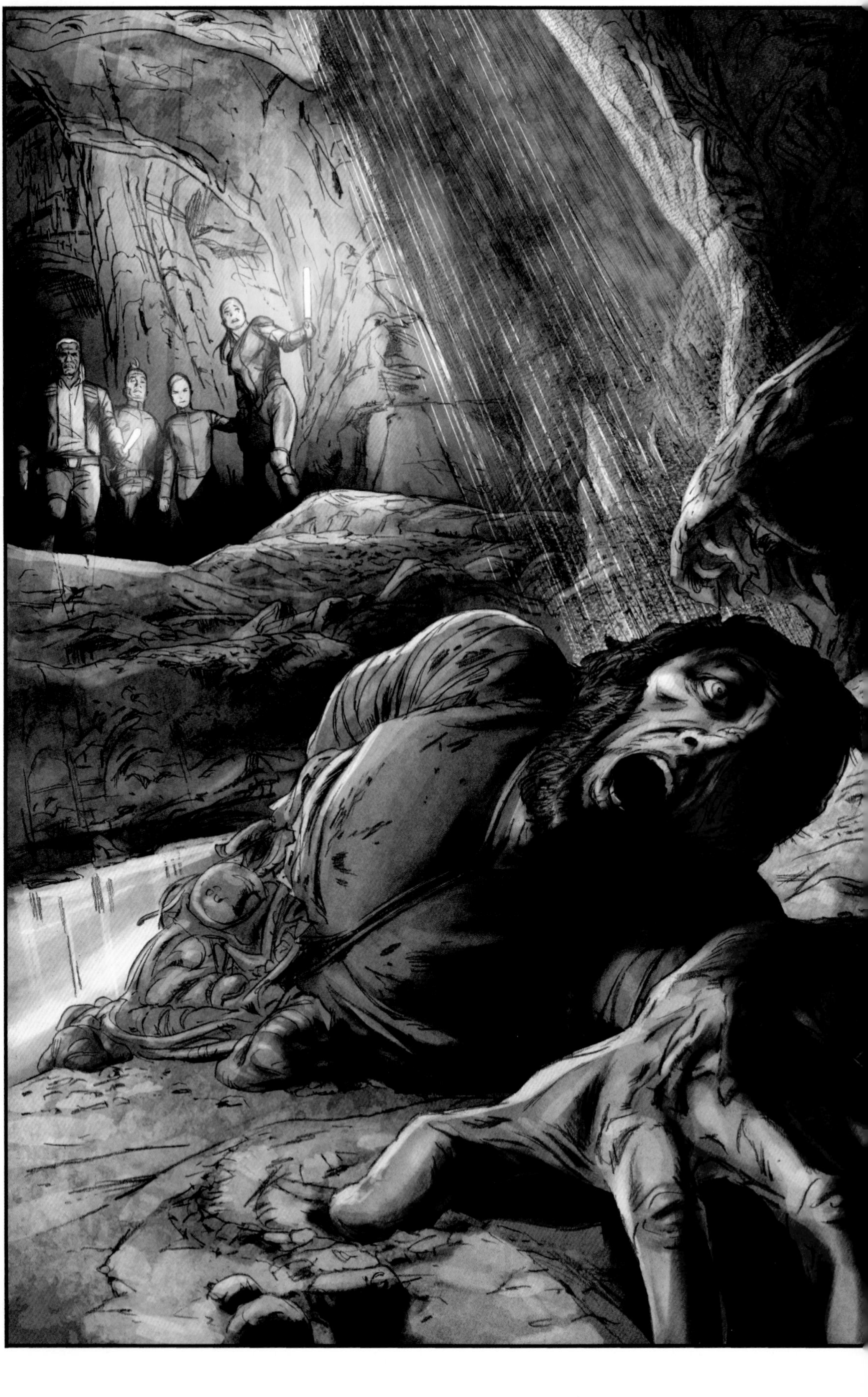

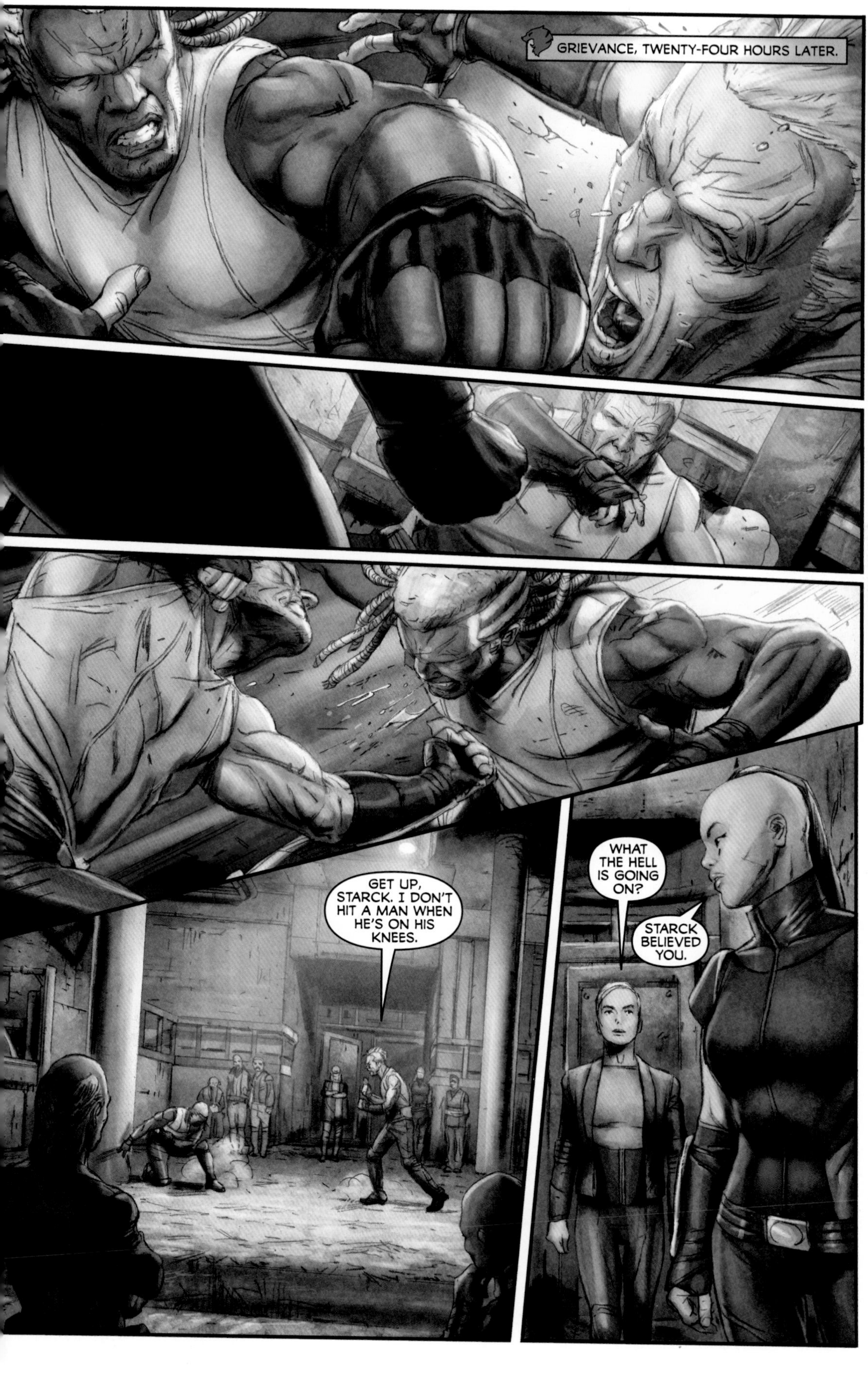
GRIEVANCE, TWENTY-FOUR HOURS LATER.
GET UP, STARCK. I DON'T HIT A MAN WHEN HE'S ON HIS KNEES.
WHAT THE HELL IS GOING ON?
STARCK BELIEVED YOU.

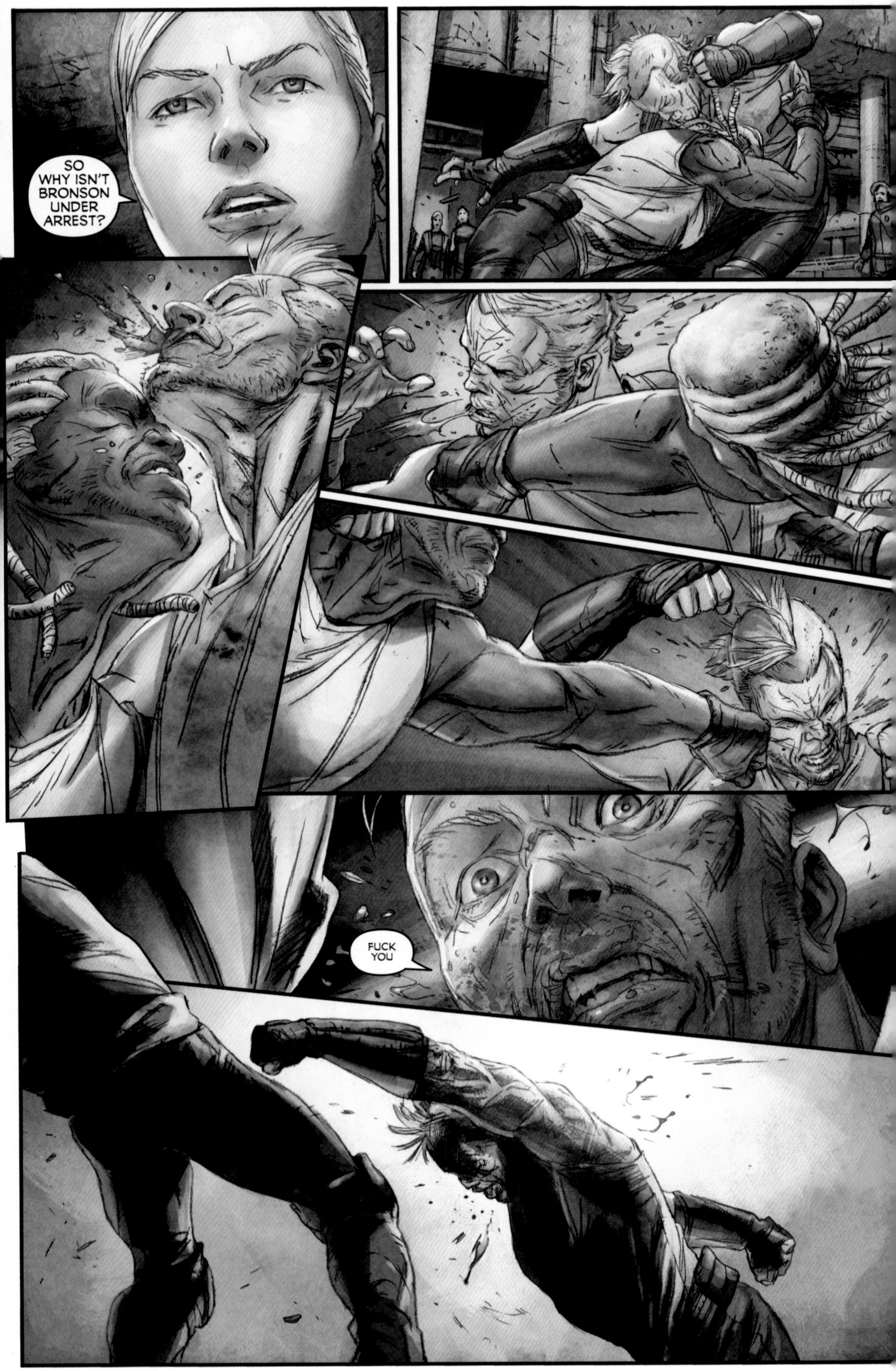
SO WHY ISN'T BRONSON UNDER ARREST?
FUCK YOU

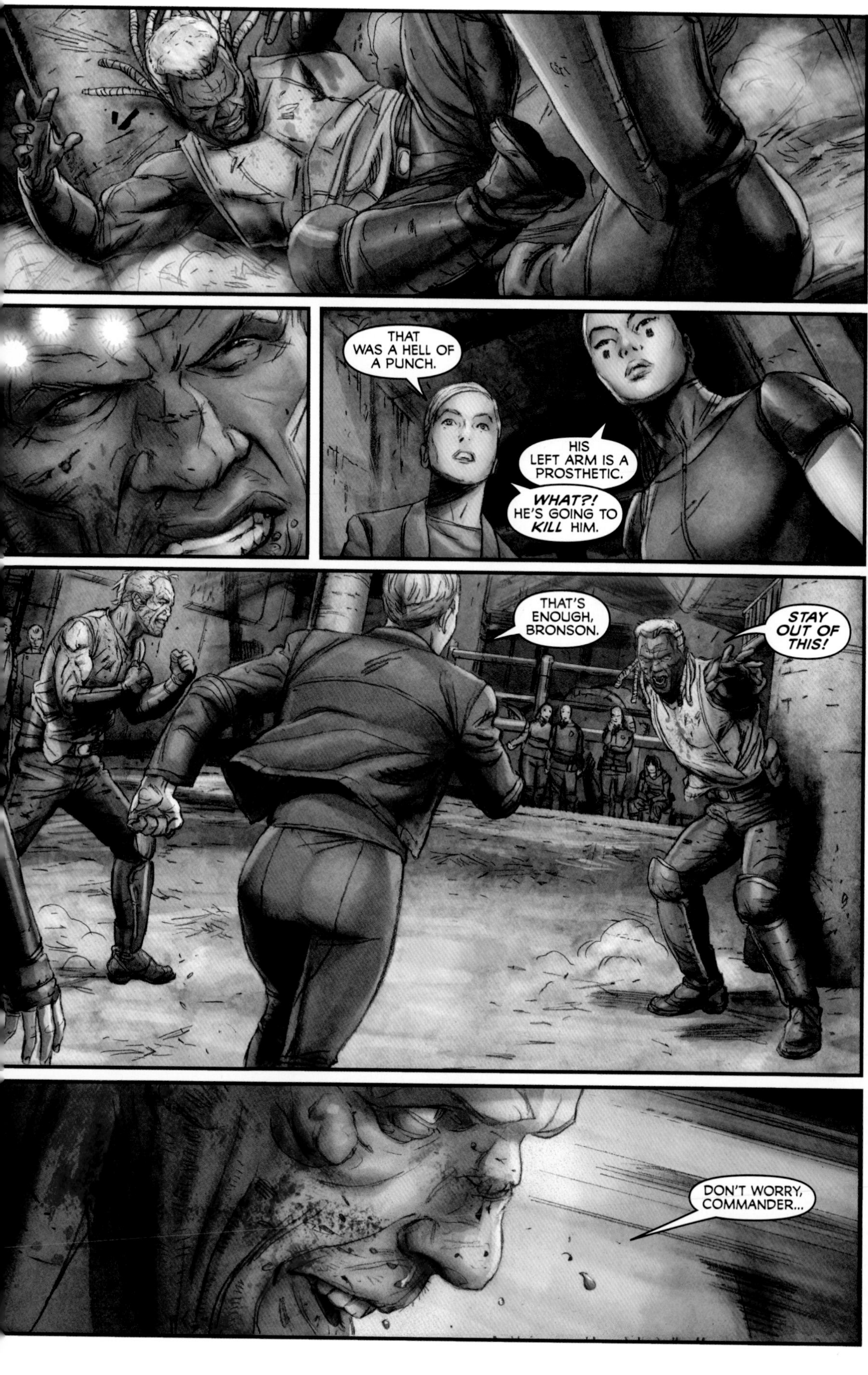
THAT WAS A HELL OF A PUNCH.
HIS LEFT ARM IS A PROSTHETIC.
WHAT?! HE'S GOING TO KILL HIM.
THAT'S ENOUGH, BRONSON.
STAY OUT OF THIS!
DON'T WORRY, COMMANDER...

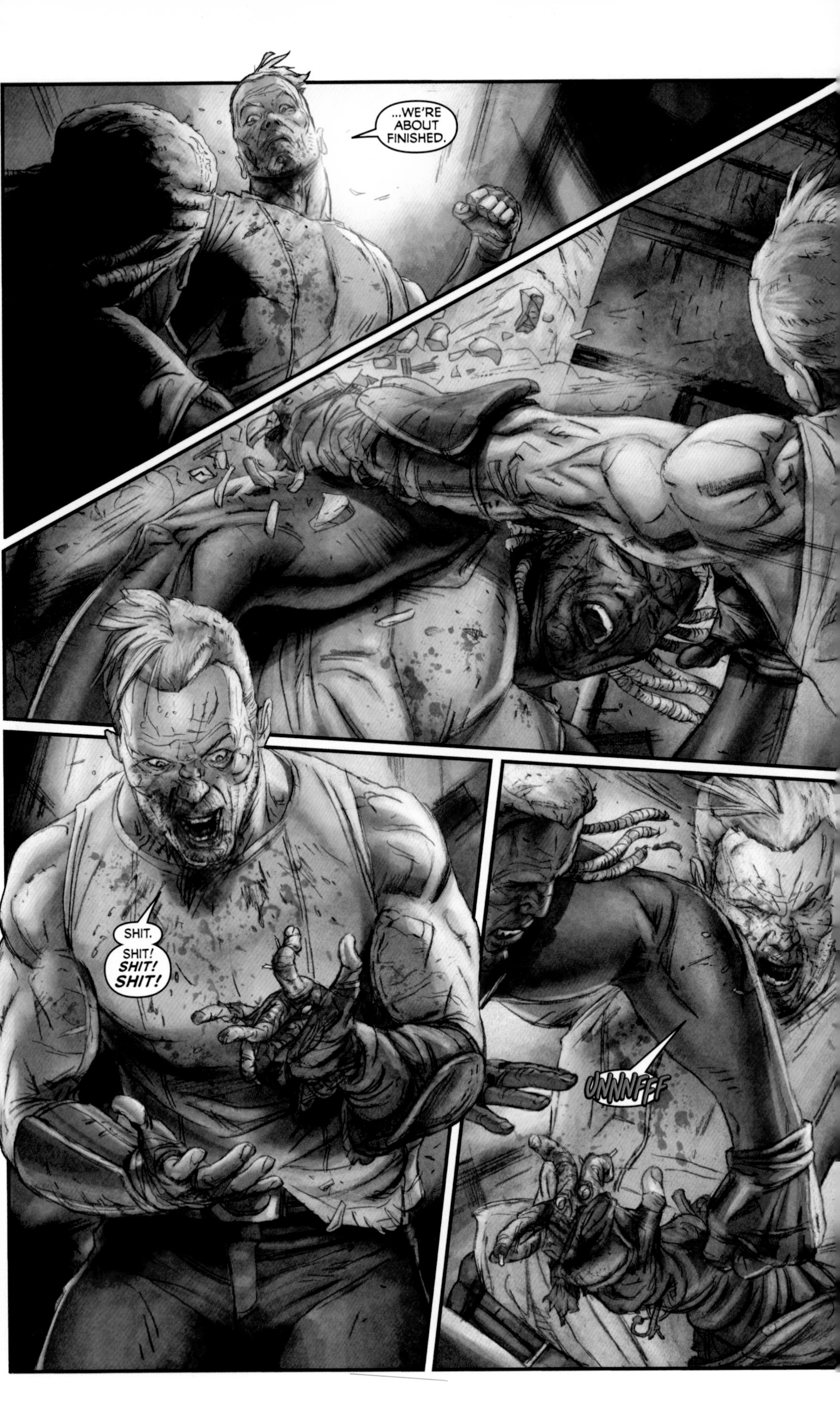
...WE'RE ABOUT FINISHED.
SHIT. SHIT! SHIT! SHIT!
UNNNFFF

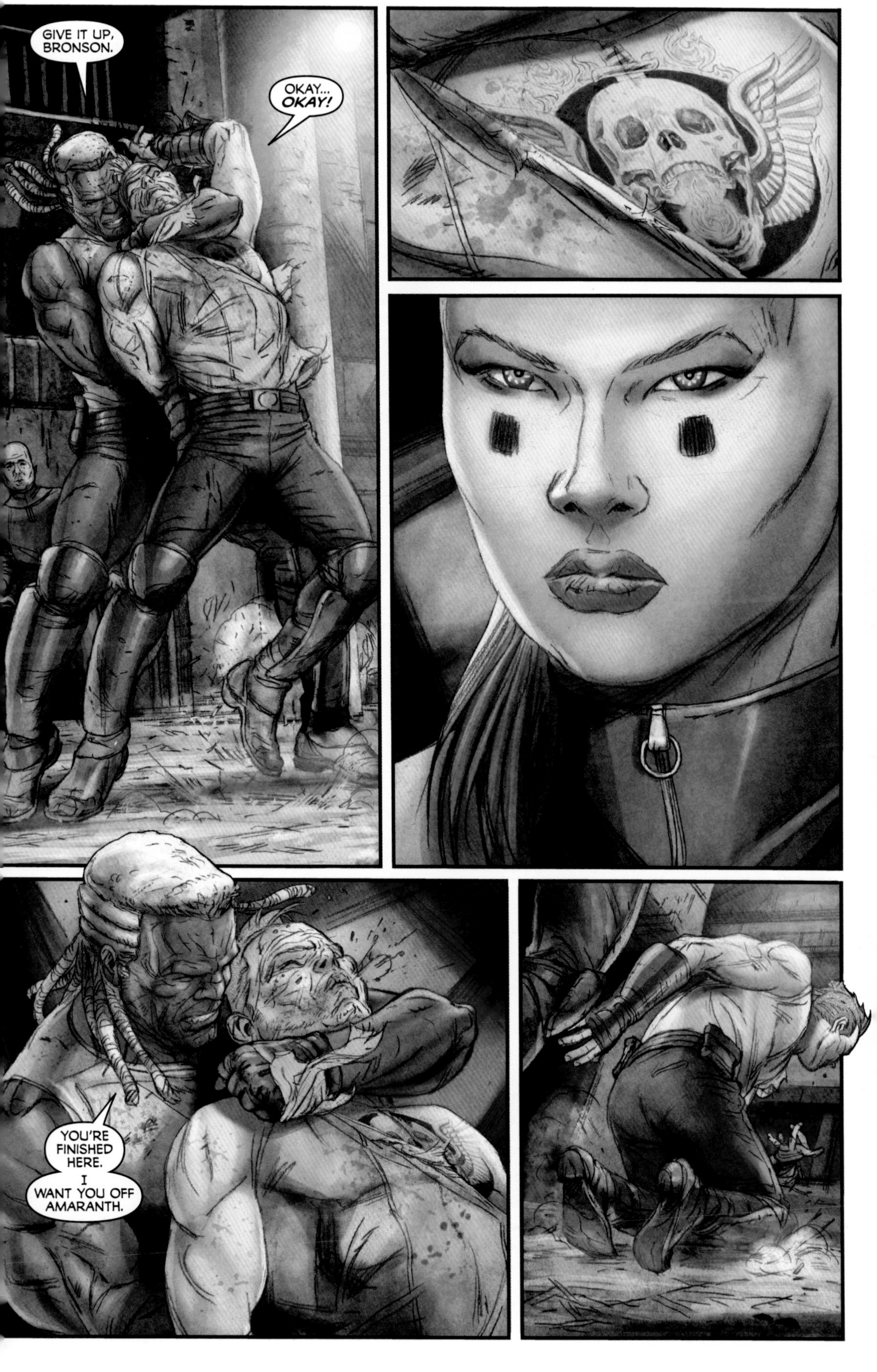
GIVE IT UP, BRONSON.
OKAY... *OKAY!*
YOU'RE FINISHED HERE. I WANT YOU OFF AMARANTH.

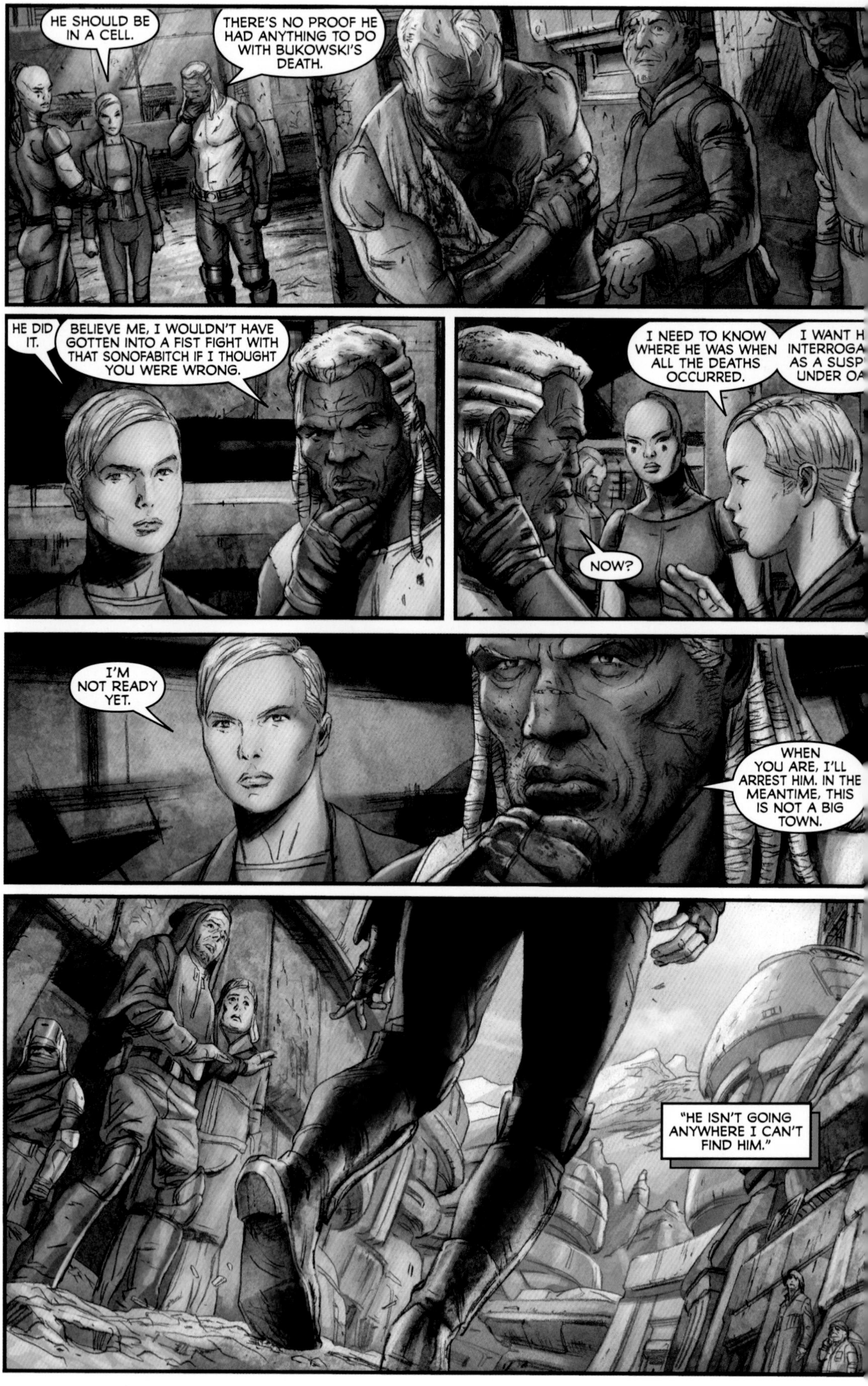
HE SHOULD BE IN A CELL.
THERE'S NO PROOF HE HAD ANYTHING TO DO WITH BUKOWSKI'S DEATH.
HE DID IT.
BELIEVE ME, I WOULDN'T HAVE GOTTEN INTO A FIST FIGHT WITH THAT SONOFABITCH IF I THOUGHT YOU WERE WRONG.
I NEED TO KNOW WHERE HE WAS WHEN ALL THE DEATHS OCCURRED.
I WANT H INTERROGA AS A SUSP UNDER OA
NOW?
I'M NOT READY YET.
WHEN YOU ARE, I'LL ARREST HIM. IN THE MEANTIME, THIS IS NOT A BIG TOWN.
"HE ISN'T GOING ANYWHERE I CAN'T FIND HIM."

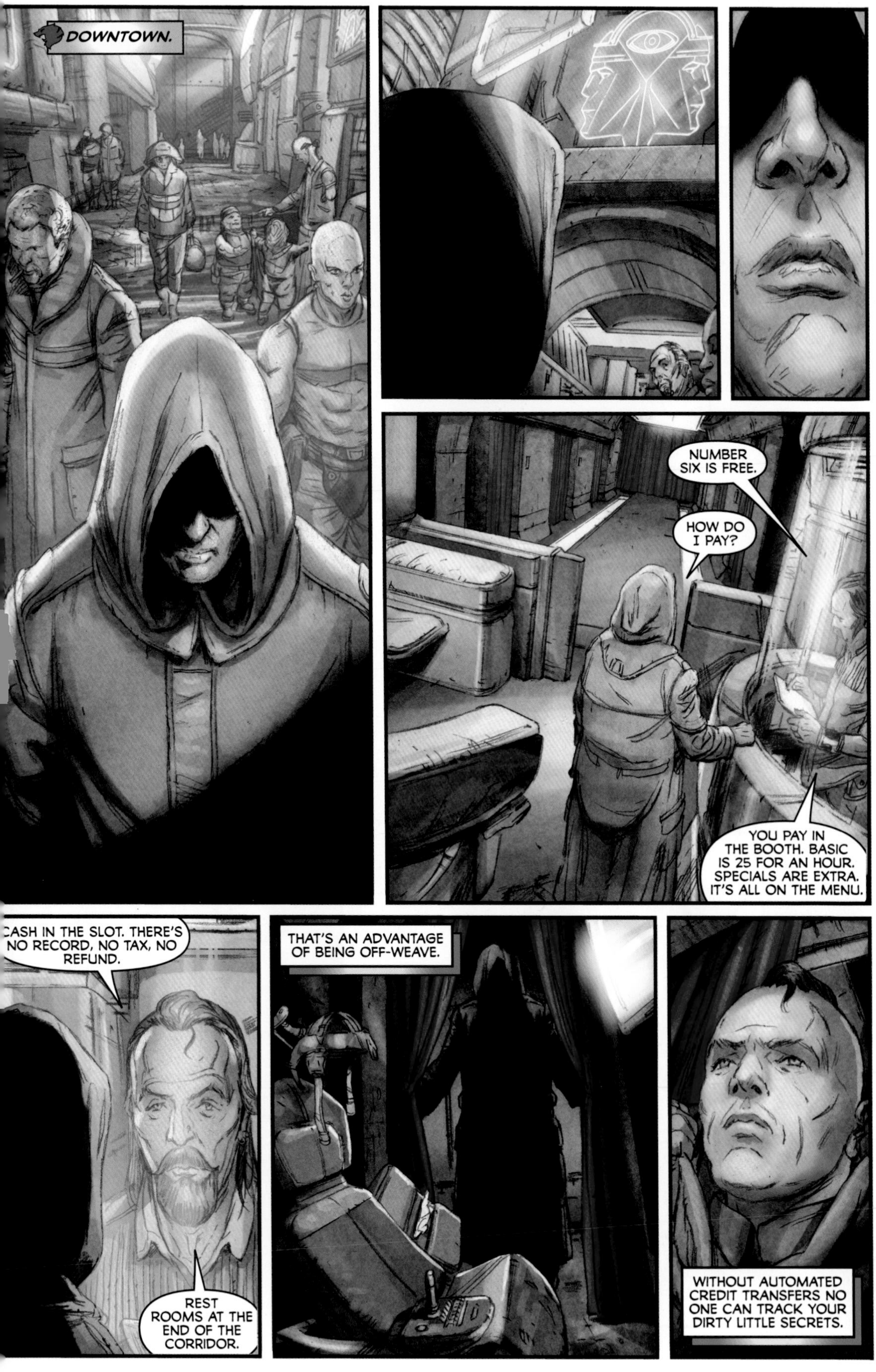
DOWNTOWN.
NUMBER SIX IS FREE.
HOW DO I PAY?
YOU PAY IN THE BOOTH. BASIC IS 25 FOR AN HOUR. SPECIALS ARE EXTRA. IT'S ALL ON THE MENU.
CASH IN THE SLOT. THERE'S NO RECORD, NO TAX, NO REFUND.
REST ROOMS AT THE END OF THE CORRIDOR.
THAT'S AN ADVANTAGE OF BEING OFF-WEAVE.
WITHOUT AUTOMATED CREDIT TRANSFERS NO ONE CAN TRACK YOUR DIRTY LITTLE SECRETS.

WELCOME TO *HEAD TRIP*. PLEASE SELECT MENU FOR A LIST OF HOSTS. ONCE YOU HAVE MADE YOUR CHOICE, PAY AS INDICATED.

WE HOPE YOU ENJOY YOUR TIME WITH US TODAY.

EATER'S OLFACTORY AND TASTE SENSORS ARE HEIGHTENED FOR MAXIMUM APRECIATION OF EXQUISITE GOURMET PREPARATIONS. EATER IS ABLE TO CONSUME BOTH SOLIDS AND LIQUIDS ALMOST WITHOUT LIMIT AND, AS A BONUS, CAN INGEST SUBSTANCES THAT ARE NORMALLY TOXIC TO HUMAN CONSUMERS.

SELECT 'E' FOR 'EATER.'

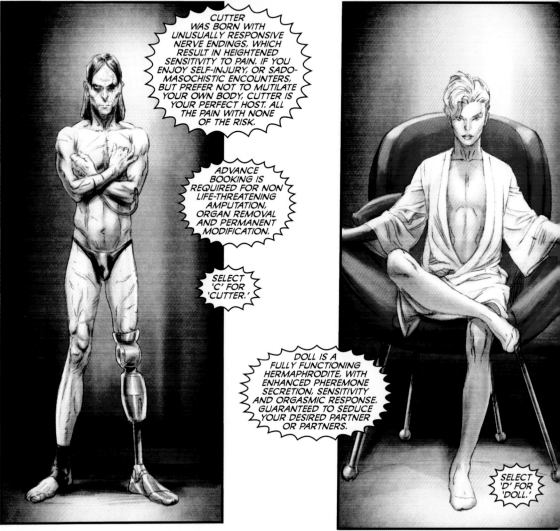

CUTTER WAS BORN WITH UNUSUALLY RESPONSIVE NERVE ENDINGS, WHICH RESULT IN HEIGHTENED SENSITIVITY TO PAIN. IF YOU ENJOY SELF-INJURY, OR SADO-MASOCHISTIC ENCOUNTERS, BUT PREFER NOT TO MUTILATE YOUR OWN BODY, CUTTER IS YOUR PERFECT HOST. ALL THE PAIN WITH NONE OF THE RISK.

ADVANCE BOOKING IS REQUIRED FOR NON LIFE-THREATENING AMPUTATION, ORGAN REMOVAL AND PERMANENT MODIFICATION.

SELECT 'C' FOR 'CUTTER.'

DOLL IS A FULLY FUNCTIONING HERMAPHRODITE, WITH ENHANCED PHEREMONE SECRETION, SENSITIVITY AND ORGASMIC RESPONSE. GUARANTEED TO SEDUCE YOUR DESIRED PARTNER OR PARTNERS.

SELECT 'D' FOR 'DOLL.'

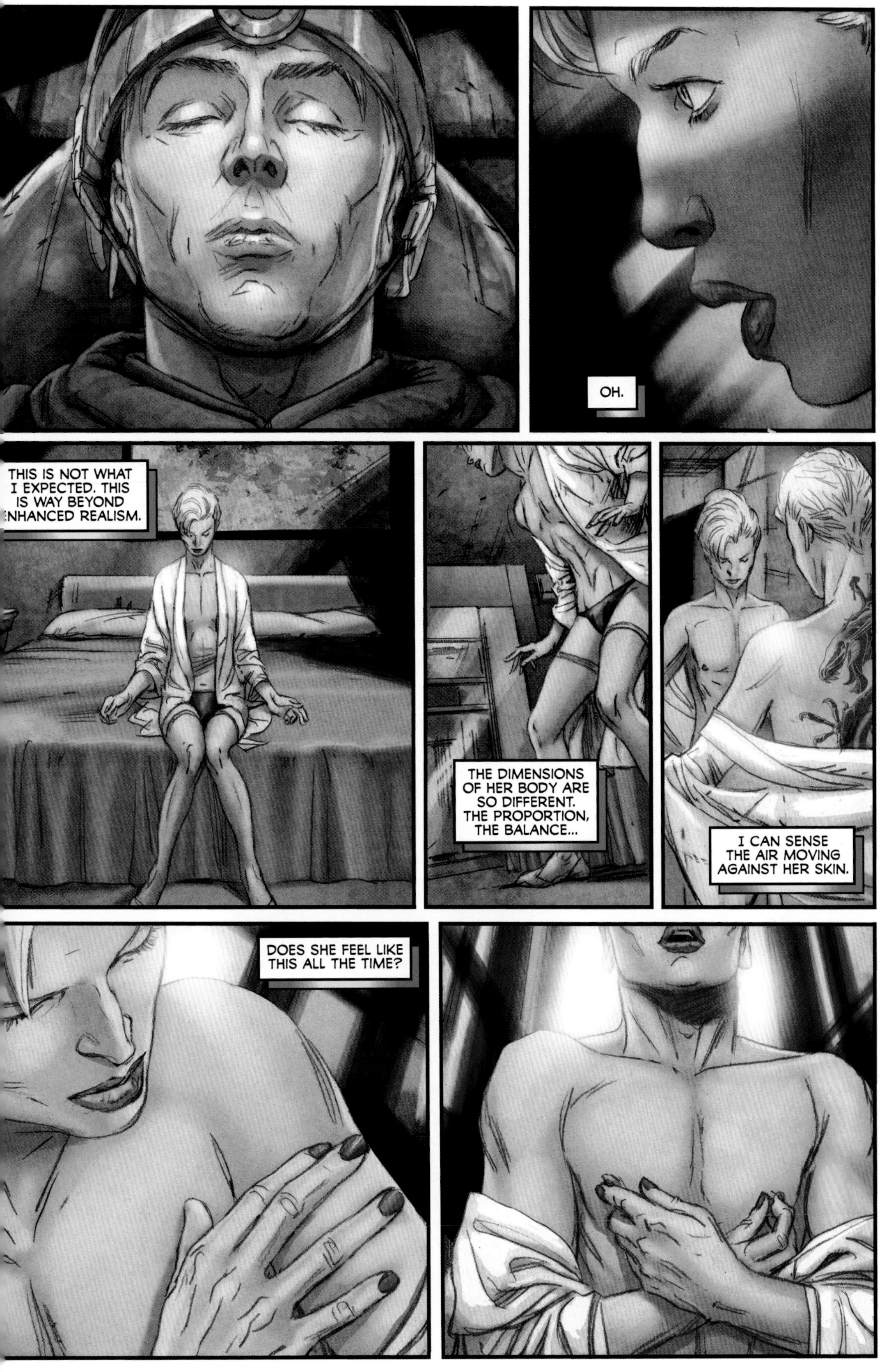
OH.
THIS IS NOT WHAT I EXPECTED. THIS IS WAY BEYOND ENHANCED REALISM.
THE DIMENSIONS OF HER BODY ARE SO DIFFERENT. THE PROPORTION, THE BALANCE...
I CAN SENSE THE AIR MOVING AGAINST HER SKIN.
DOES SHE FEEL LIKE THIS ALL THE TIME?

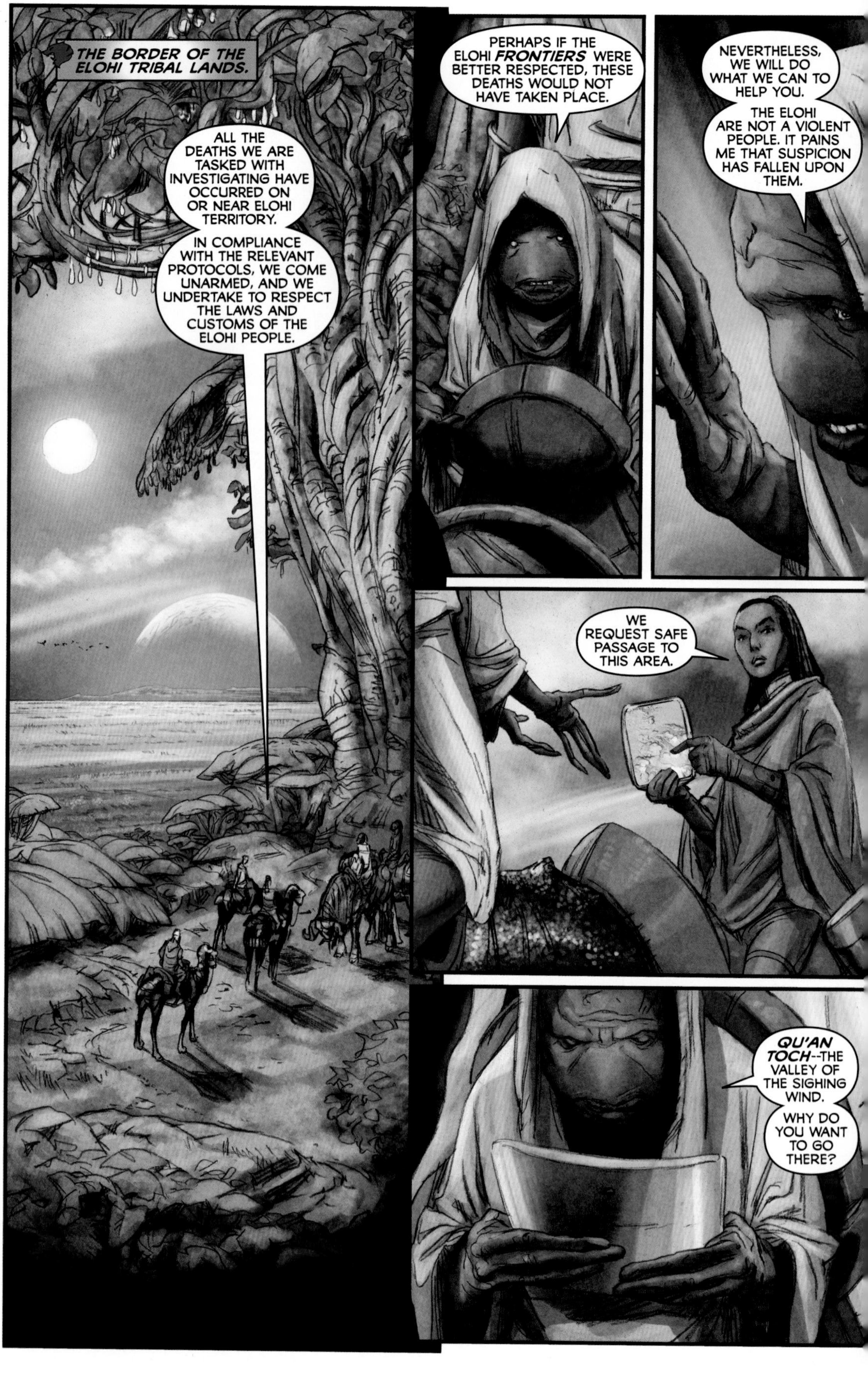
THE BORDER OF THE ELOHI TRIBAL LANDS.
ALL THE DEATHS WE ARE TASKED WITH INVESTIGATING HAVE OCCURRED ON OR NEAR ELOHI TERRITORY.
IN COMPLIANCE WITH THE RELEVANT PROTOCOLS, WE COME UNARMED, AND WE UNDERTAKE TO RESPECT THE LAWS AND CUSTOMS OF THE ELOHI PEOPLE.
PERHAPS IF THE ELOHI FRONTIERS WERE BETTER RESPECTED, THESE DEATHS WOULD NOT HAVE TAKEN PLACE.
NEVERTHELESS, WE WILL DO WHAT WE CAN TO HELP YOU.
THE ELOHI ARE NOT A VIOLENT PEOPLE. IT PAINS ME THAT SUSPICION HAS FALLEN UPON THEM.
WE REQUEST SAFE PASSAGE TO THIS AREA.
QU'AN TOCH--THE VALLEY OF THE SIGHING WIND.
WHY DO YOU WANT TO GO THERE?

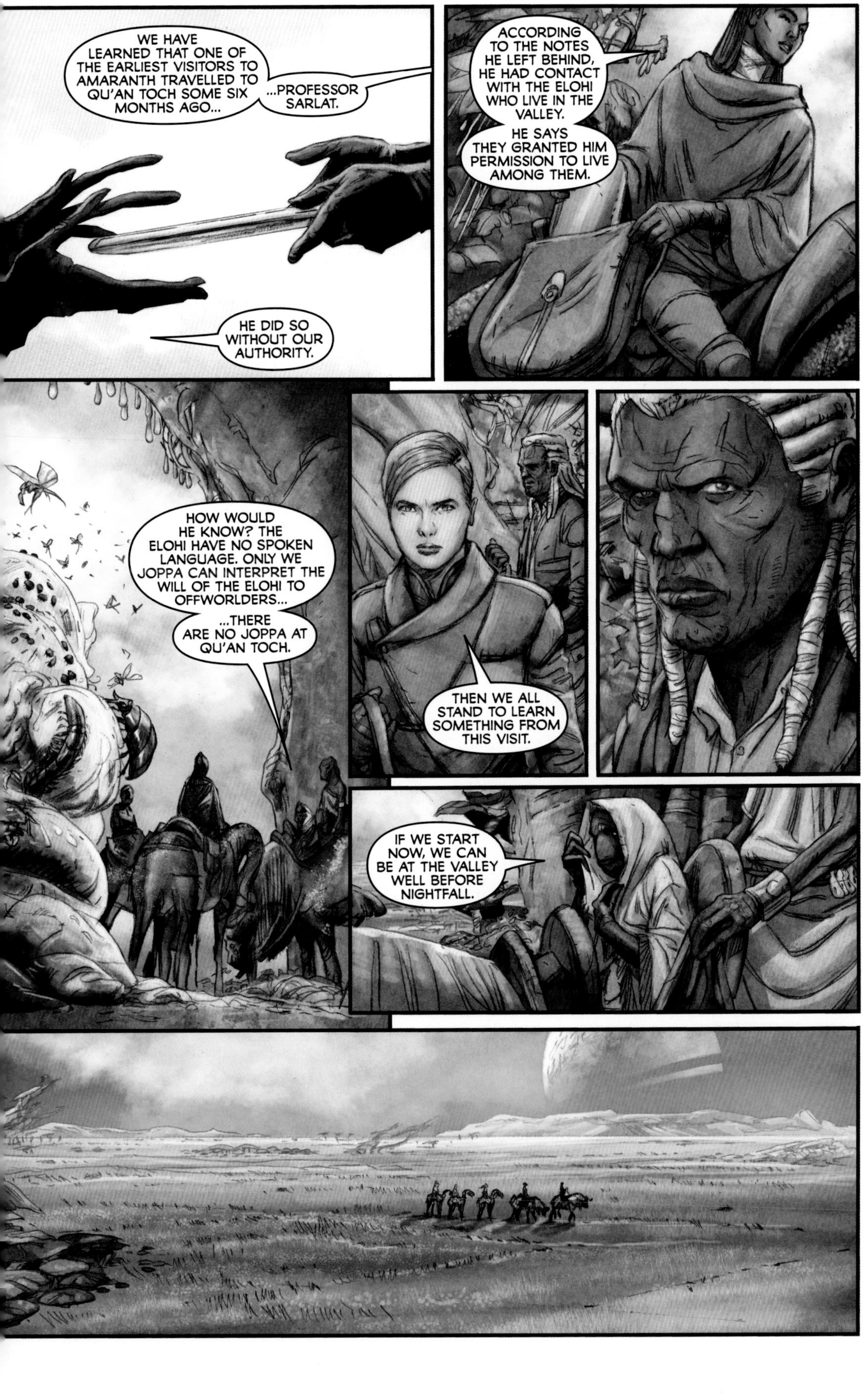
WE HAVE LEARNED THAT ONE OF THE EARLIEST VISITORS TO AMARANTH TRAVELLED TO QU'AN TOCH SOME SIX MONTHS AGO...
...PROFESSOR SARLAT.
HE DID SO WITHOUT OUR AUTHORITY.
ACCORDING TO THE NOTES HE LEFT BEHIND, HE HAD CONTACT WITH THE ELOHI WHO LIVE IN THE VALLEY.
HE SAYS THEY GRANTED HIM PERMISSION TO LIVE AMONG THEM.
HOW WOULD HE KNOW? THE ELOHI HAVE NO SPOKEN LANGUAGE. ONLY WE JOPPA CAN INTERPRET THE WILL OF THE ELOHI TO OFFWORLDERS...
...THERE ARE NO JOPPA AT QU'AN TOCH.
THEN WE ALL STAND TO LEARN SOMETHING FROM THIS VISIT.
IF WE START NOW, WE CAN BE AT THE VALLEY WELL BEFORE NIGHTFALL.

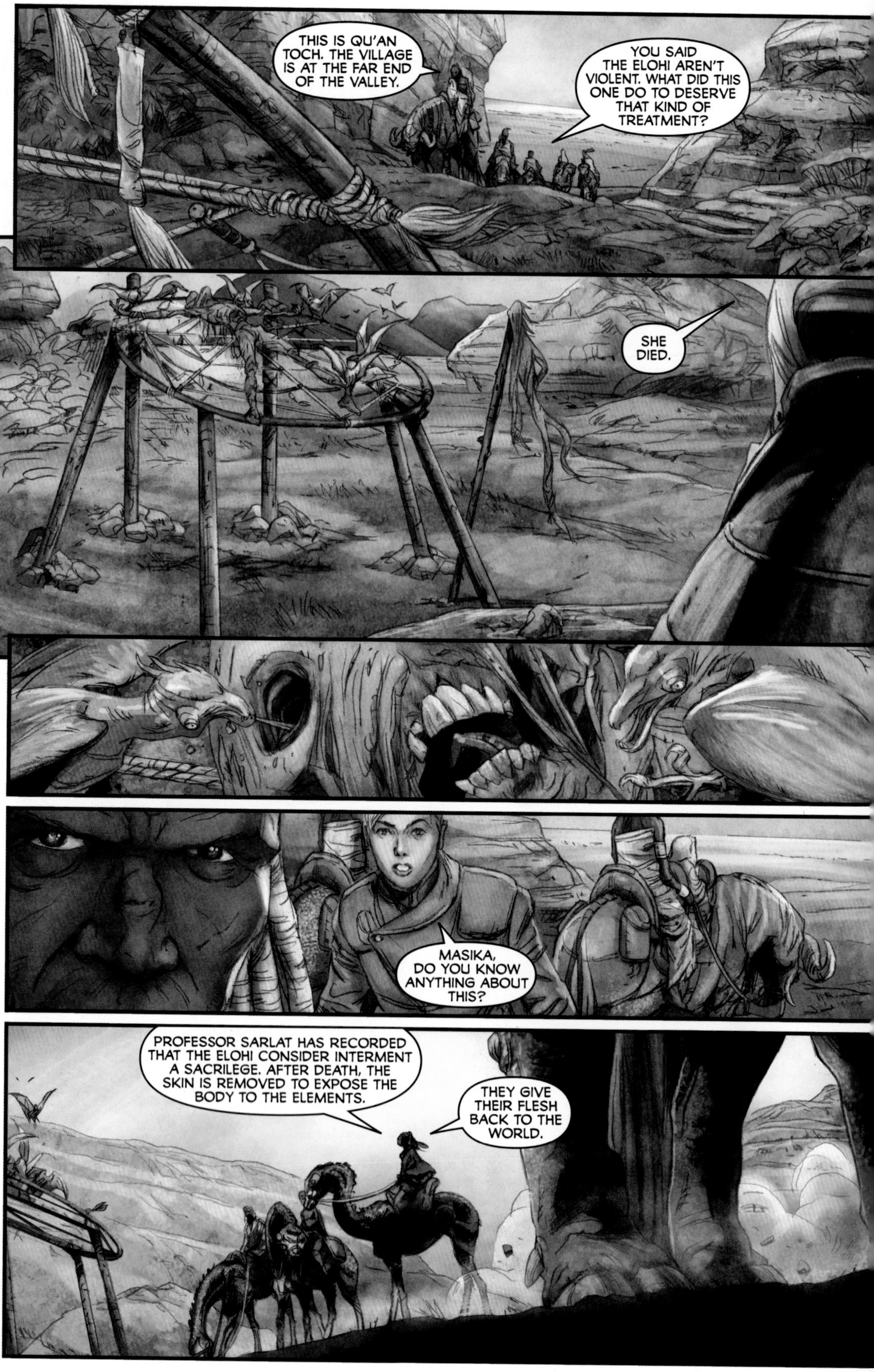
THIS IS QU'AN TOCH. THE VILLAGE IS AT THE FAR END OF THE VALLEY.
YOU SAID THE ELOHI AREN'T VIOLENT. WHAT DID THIS ONE DO TO DESERVE THAT KIND OF TREATMENT?
SHE DIED.
MASIKA, DO YOU KNOW ANYTHING ABOUT THIS?
PROFESSOR SARLAT HAS RECORDED THAT THE ELOHI CONSIDER INTERMENT A SACRILEGE. AFTER DEATH, THE SKIN IS REMOVED TO EXPOSE THE BODY TO THE ELEMENTS.
THEY GIVE THEIR FLESH BACK TO THE WORLD.

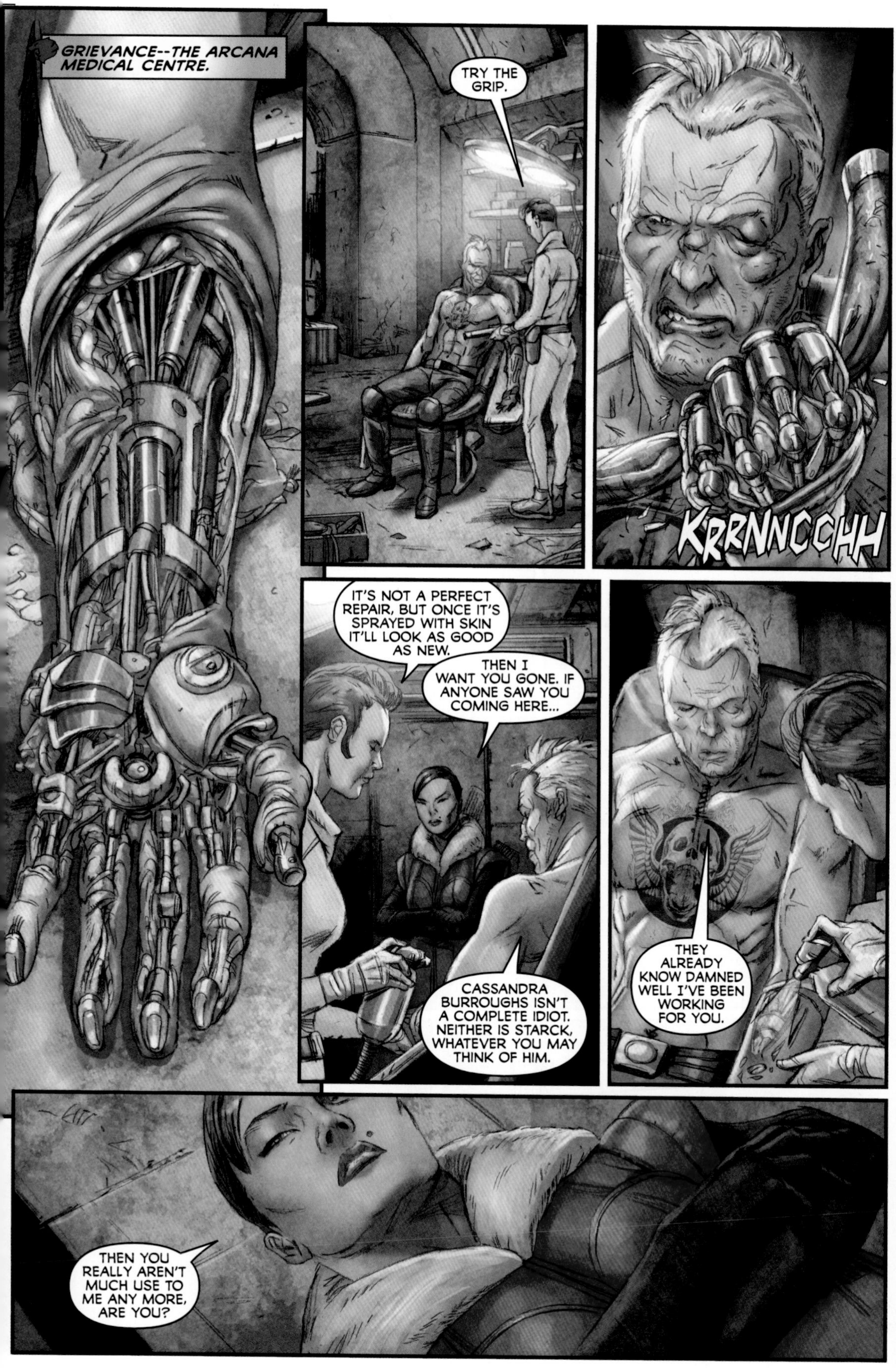
GRIEVANCE--THE ARCANA MEDICAL CENTRE.
TRY THE GRIP.
KRRNNCCHH
IT'S NOT A PERFECT REPAIR, BUT ONCE IT'S SPRAYED WITH SKIN IT'LL LOOK AS GOOD AS NEW.
THEN I WANT YOU GONE. IF ANYONE SAW YOU COMING HERE...
CASSANDRA BURROUGHS ISN'T A COMPLETE IDIOT. NEITHER IS STARCK, WHATEVER YOU MAY THINK OF HIM.
THEY ALREADY KNOW DAMNED WELL I'VE BEEN WORKING FOR YOU.
THEN YOU REALLY AREN'T MUCH USE TO ME ANY MORE, ARE YOU?

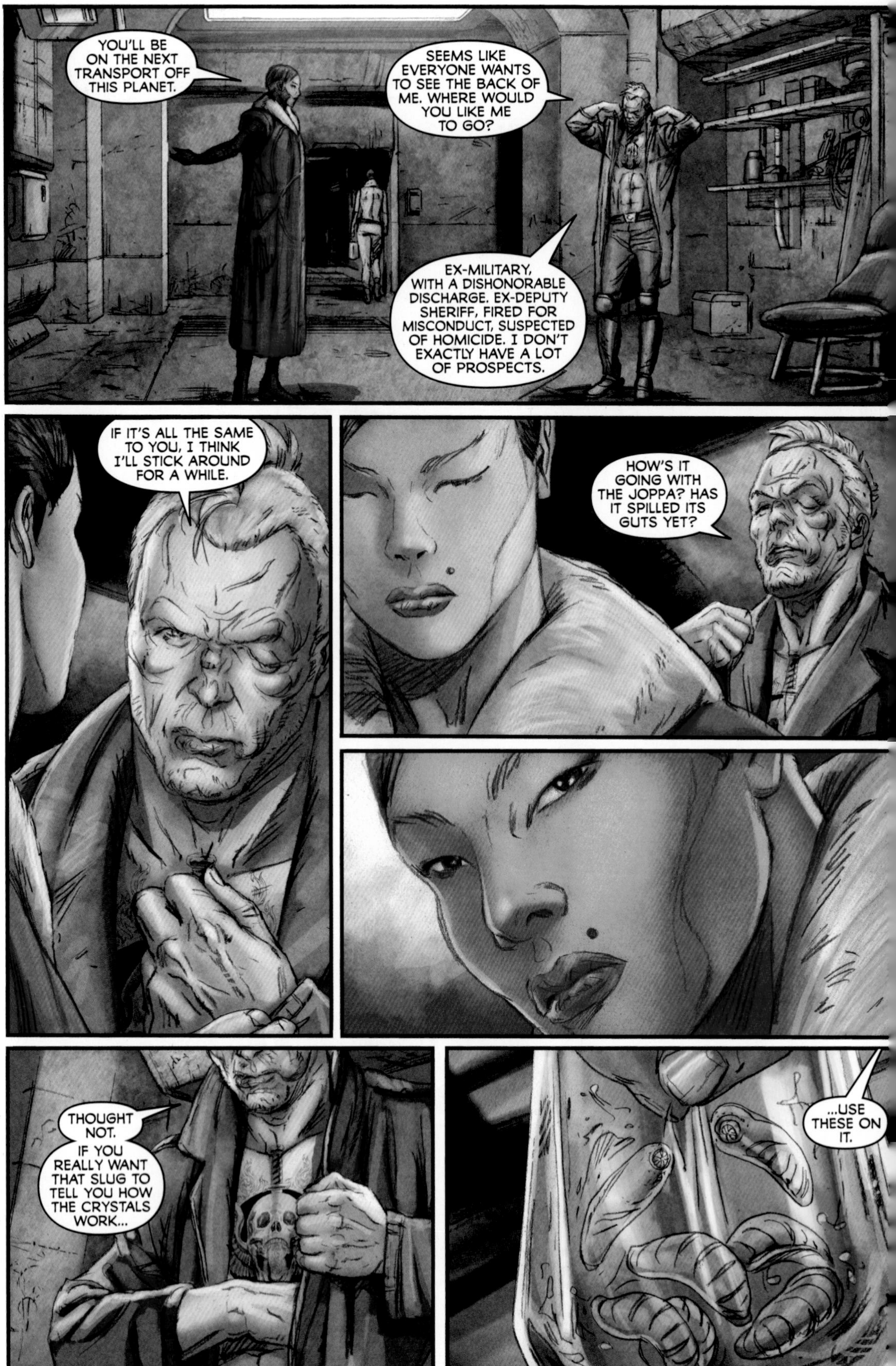
YOU'LL BE ON THE NEXT TRANSPORT OFF THIS PLANET.
SEEMS LIKE EVERYONE WANTS TO SEE THE BACK OF ME. WHERE WOULD YOU LIKE ME TO GO?
EX-MILITARY, WITH A DISHONORABLE DISCHARGE. EX-DEPUTY SHERIFF, FIRED FOR MISCONDUCT, SUSPECTED OF HOMICIDE. I DON'T EXACTLY HAVE A LOT OF PROSPECTS.
IF IT'S ALL THE SAME TO YOU, I THINK I'LL STICK AROUND FOR A WHILE.
HOW'S IT GOING WITH THE JOPPA? HAS IT SPILLED ITS GUTS YET?
THOUGHT NOT.
IF YOU REALLY WANT THAT SLUG TO TELL YOU HOW THE CRYSTALS WORK...
...USE THESE ON IT.

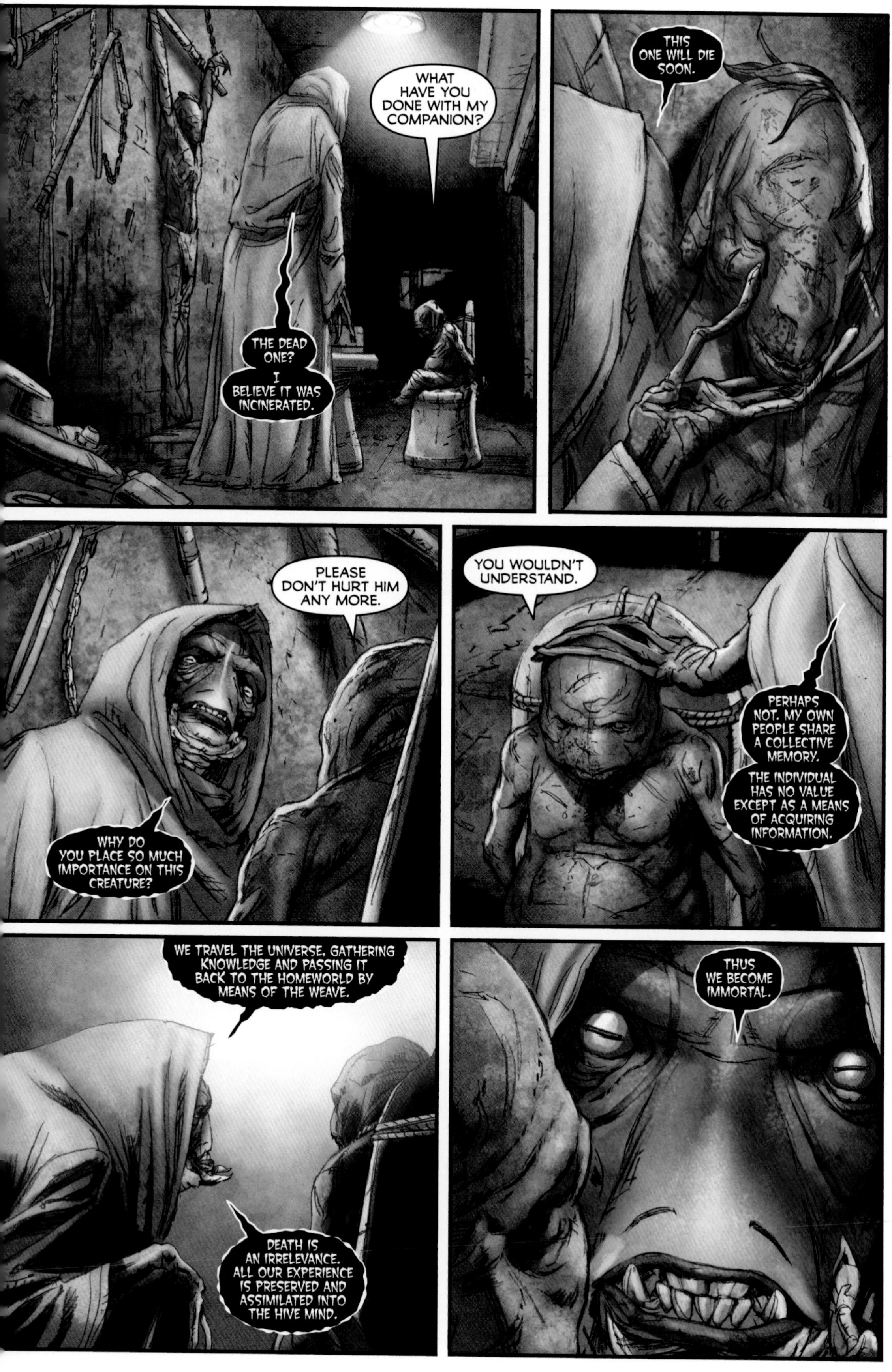
WHAT HAVE YOU DONE WITH MY COMPANION?
THE DEAD ONE?
I BELIEVE IT WAS INCINERATED.
THIS ONE WILL DIE SOON.
PLEASE DON'T HURT HIM ANY MORE.
WHY DO YOU PLACE SO MUCH IMPORTANCE ON THIS CREATURE?
YOU WOULDN'T UNDERSTAND.
PERHAPS NOT. MY OWN PEOPLE SHARE A COLLECTIVE MEMORY.
THE INDIVIDUAL HAS NO VALUE EXCEPT AS A MEANS OF ACQUIRING INFORMATION.
WE TRAVEL THE UNIVERSE, GATHERING KNOWLEDGE AND PASSING IT BACK TO THE HOMEWORLD BY MEANS OF THE WEAVE.
DEATH IS AN IRRELEVANCE. ALL OUR EXPERIENCE IS PRESERVED AND ASSIMILATED INTO THE HIVE MIND.
THUS WE BECOME IMMORTAL.

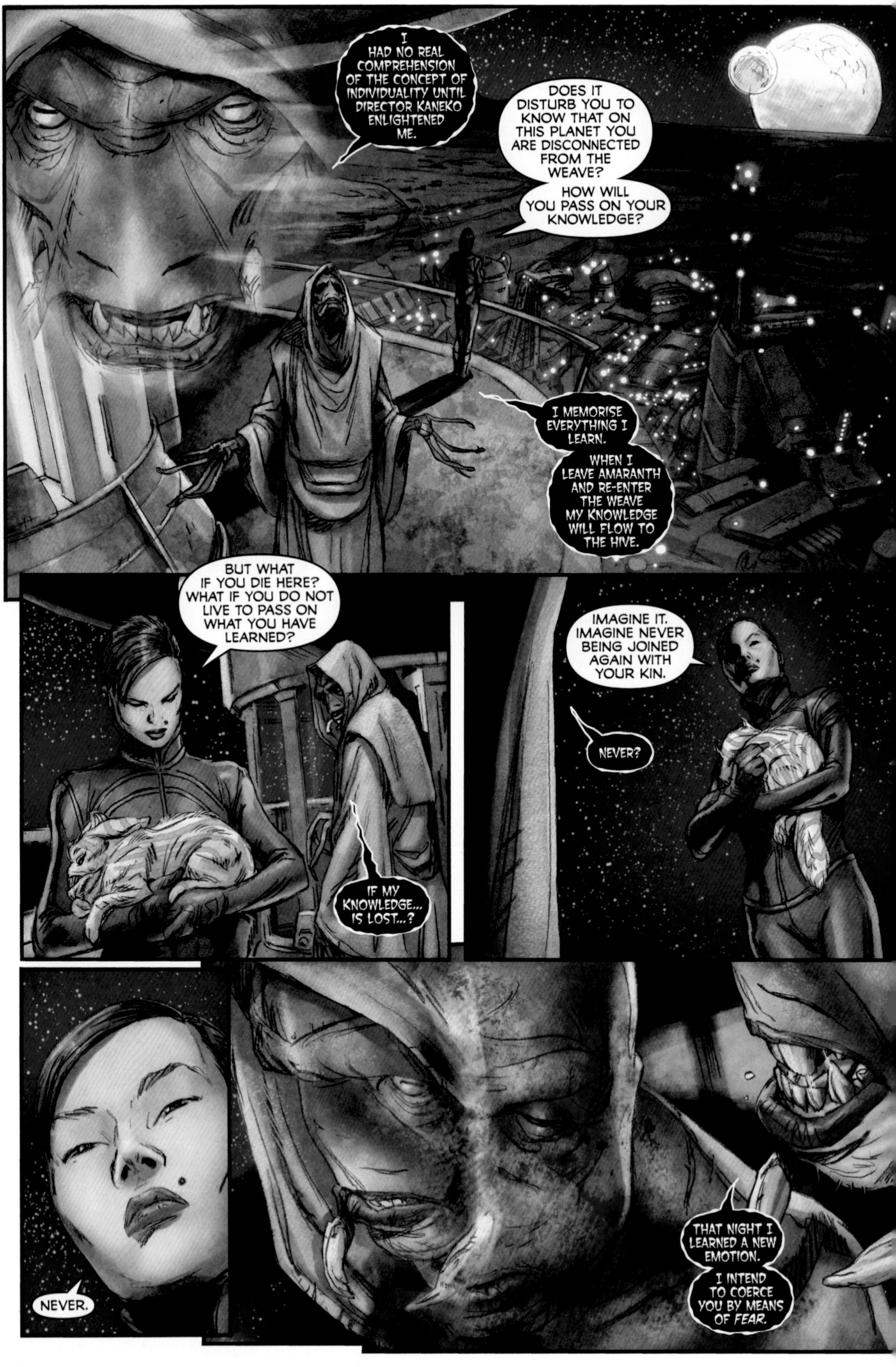
I HAD NO REAL COMPREHENSION OF THE CONCEPT OF INDIVIDUALITY UNTIL DIRECTOR KANEKO ENLIGHTENED ME.
DOES IT DISTURB YOU TO KNOW THAT ON THIS PLANET YOU ARE DISCONNECTED FROM THE WEAVE?
HOW WILL YOU PASS ON YOUR KNOWLEDGE?
I MEMORISE EVERYTHING I LEARN.
WHEN I LEAVE AMARANTH AND RE-ENTER THE WEAVE MY KNOWLEDGE WILL FLOW TO THE HIVE.
BUT WHAT IF YOU DIE HERE? WHAT IF YOU DO NOT LIVE TO PASS ON WHAT YOU HAVE LEARNED?
IF MY KNOWLEDGE... IS LOST...?
IMAGINE IT. IMAGINE NEVER BEING JOINED AGAIN WITH YOUR KIN.
NEVER?
NEVER.
THAT NIGHT I LEARNED A NEW EMOTION.
I INTEND TO COERCE YOU BY MEANS OF *FEAR*.

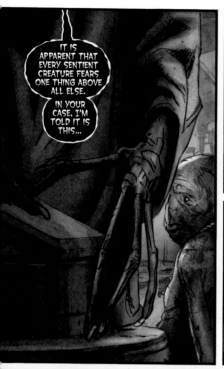

IT IS APPARENT THAT EVERY SENTIENT CREATURE FEARS ONE THING ABOVE ALL ELSE.

IN YOUR CASE, I'M TOLD IT IS THIS...

NO! YOU DON'T KNOW WHAT YOU'RE DOING!

YOU DO FEAR IT THEN.

TAKE IT AWAY! I'LL TELL YOU WHAT YOU WANT TO KNOW!

MY CURIOSITY IS AROUSED. I WISH TO KNOW WHY YOU ARE SO AFRAID.

AHHHH.

STOP THIS! GET IT OFF ME!

GET IT OFF BEFORE IT'S TOO LATE!

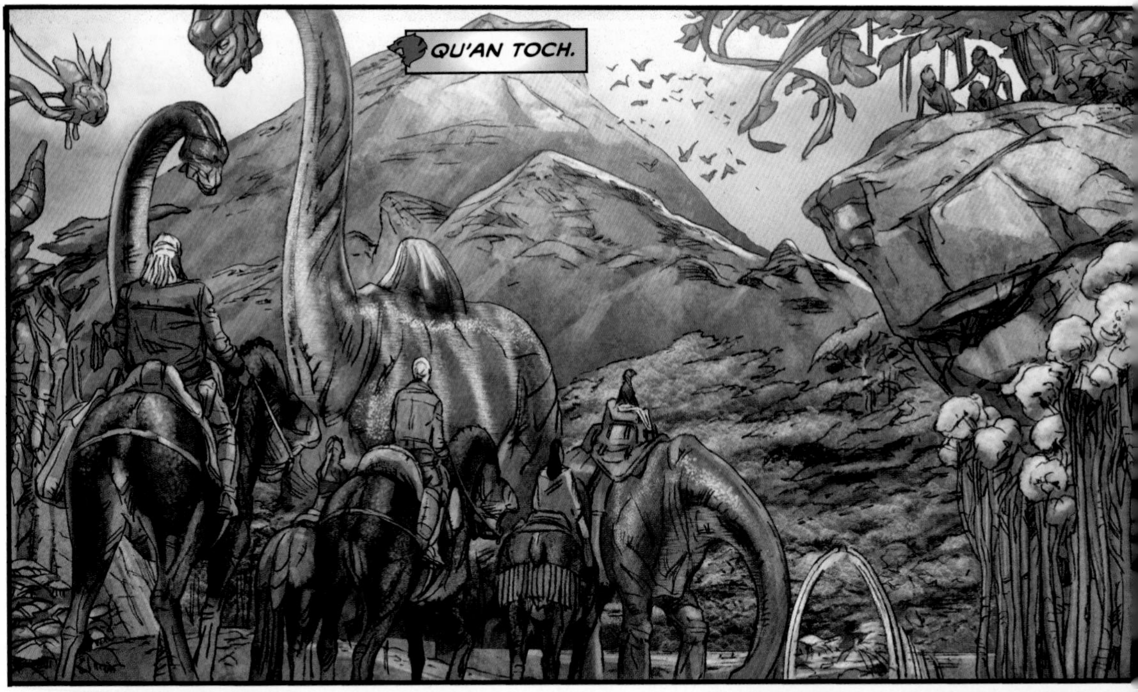
QU'AN TOCH.
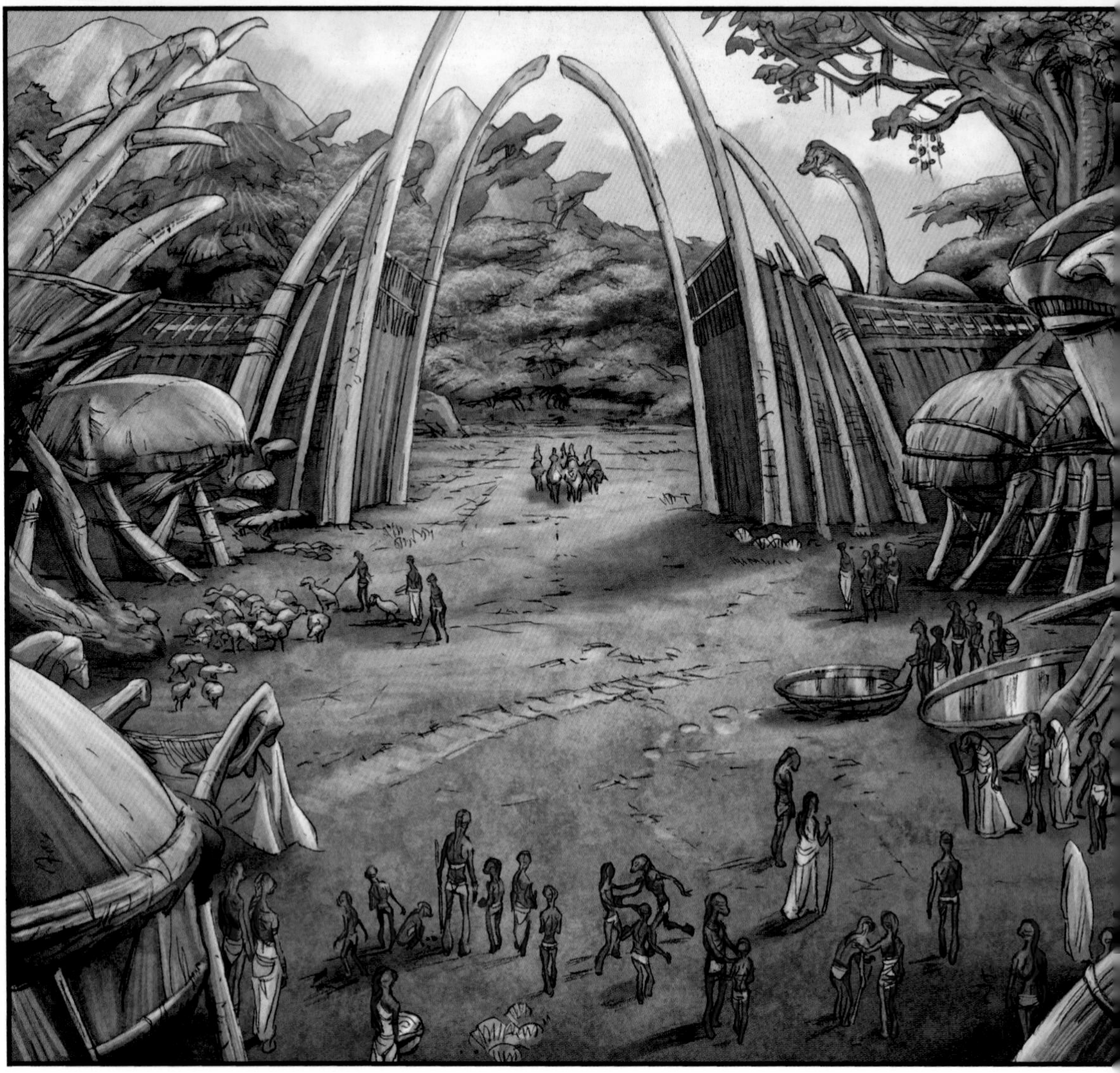

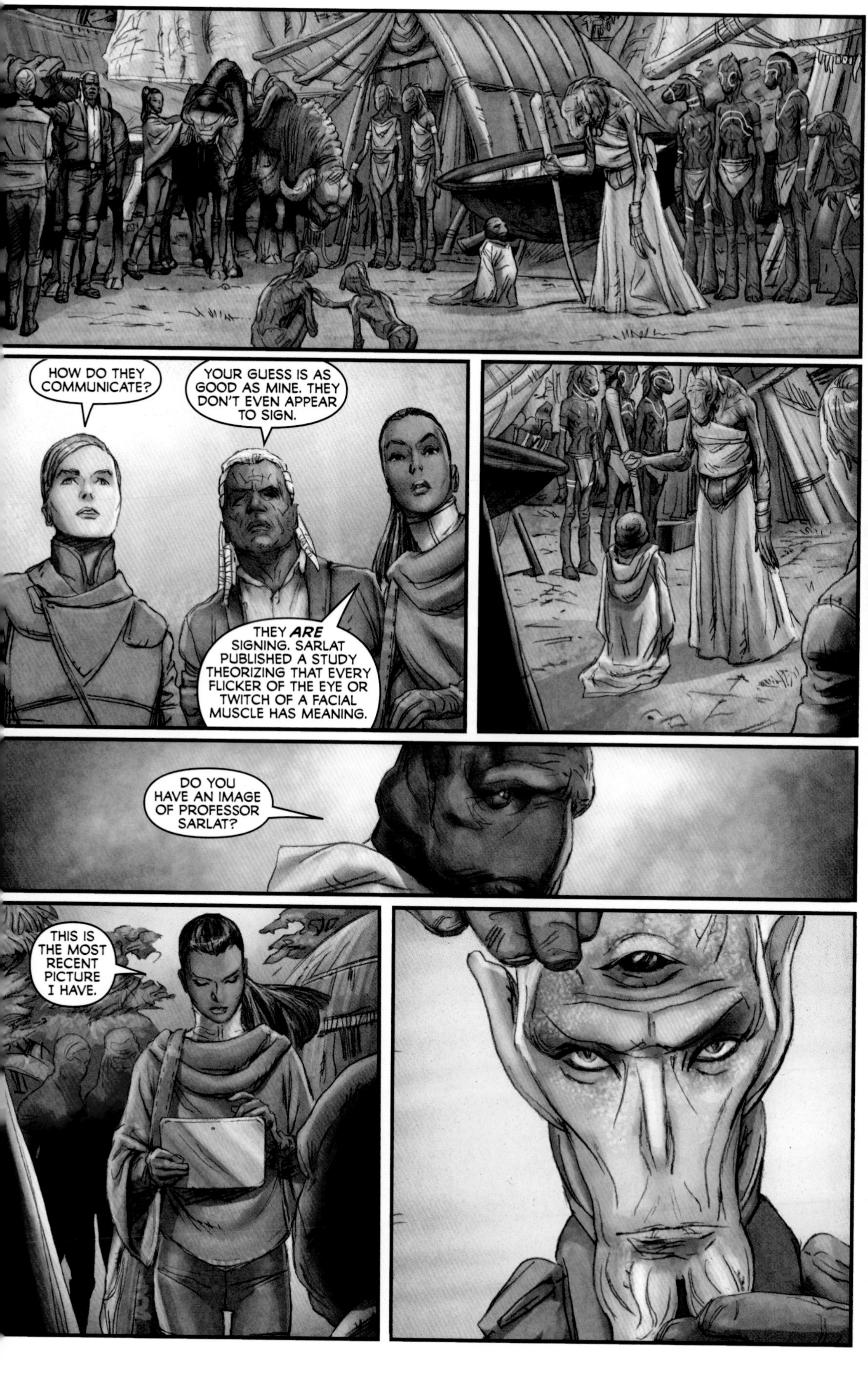
HOW DO THEY COMMUNICATE?
YOUR GUESS IS AS GOOD AS MINE. THEY DON'T EVEN APPEAR TO SIGN.
THEY ***ARE*** SIGNING. SARLAT PUBLISHED A STUDY THEORIZING THAT EVERY FLICKER OF THE EYE OR TWITCH OF A FACIAL MUSCLE HAS MEANING.
DO YOU HAVE AN IMAGE OF PROFESSOR SARLAT?
THIS IS THE MOST RECENT PICTURE I HAVE.

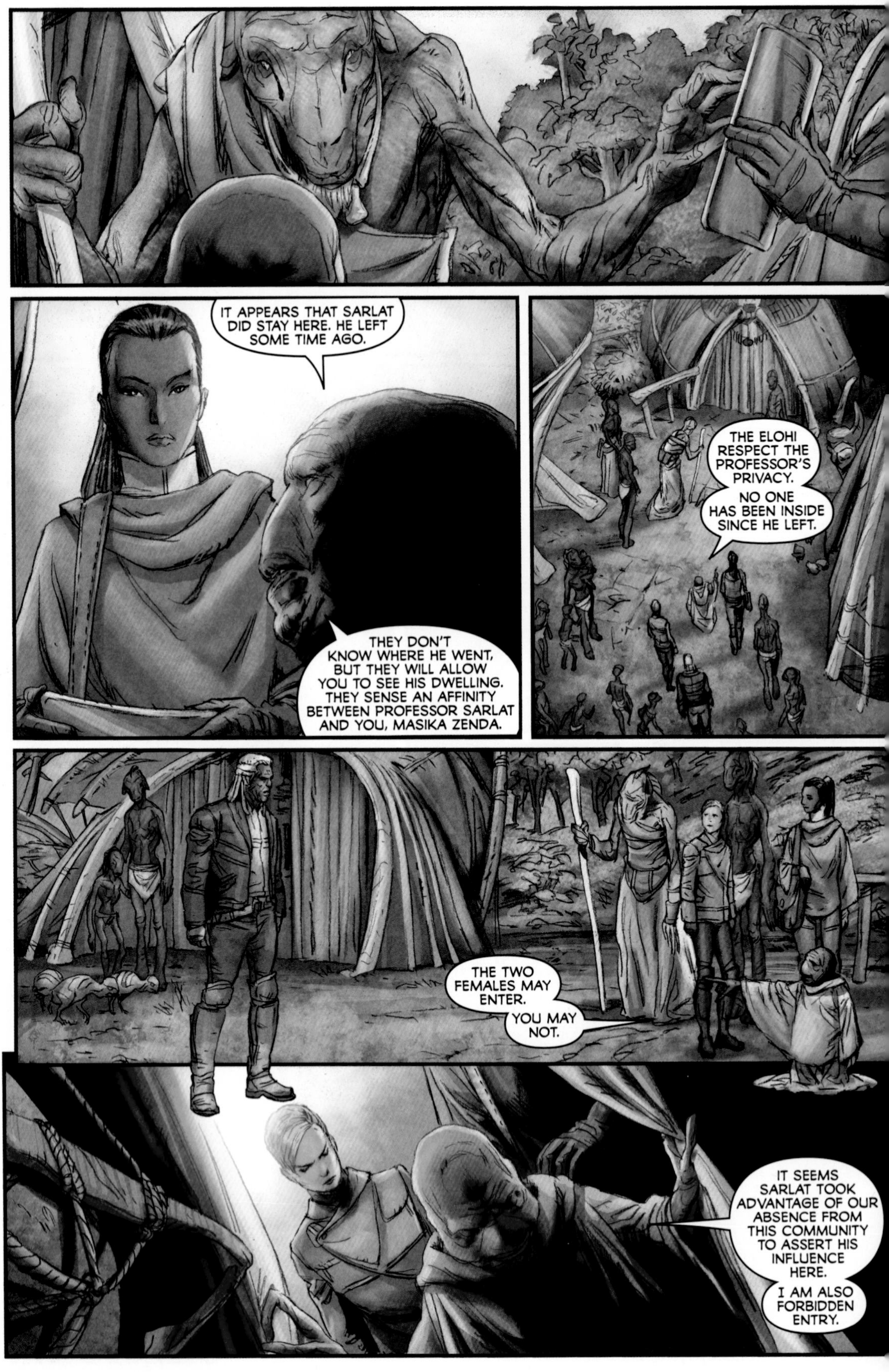
IT APPEARS THAT SARLAT DID STAY HERE. HE LEFT SOME TIME AGO.
THEY DON'T KNOW WHERE HE WENT, BUT THEY WILL ALLOW YOU TO SEE HIS DWELLING. THEY SENSE AN AFFINITY BETWEEN PROFESSOR SARLAT AND YOU, MASIKA ZENDA.
THE ELOHI RESPECT THE PROFESSOR'S PRIVACY.
NO ONE HAS BEEN INSIDE SINCE HE LEFT.
THE TWO FEMALES MAY ENTER.
YOU MAY NOT.
IT SEEMS SARLAT TOOK ADVANTAGE OF OUR ABSENCE FROM THIS COMMUNITY TO ASSERT HIS INFLUENCE HERE.
I AM ALSO FORBIDDEN ENTRY.

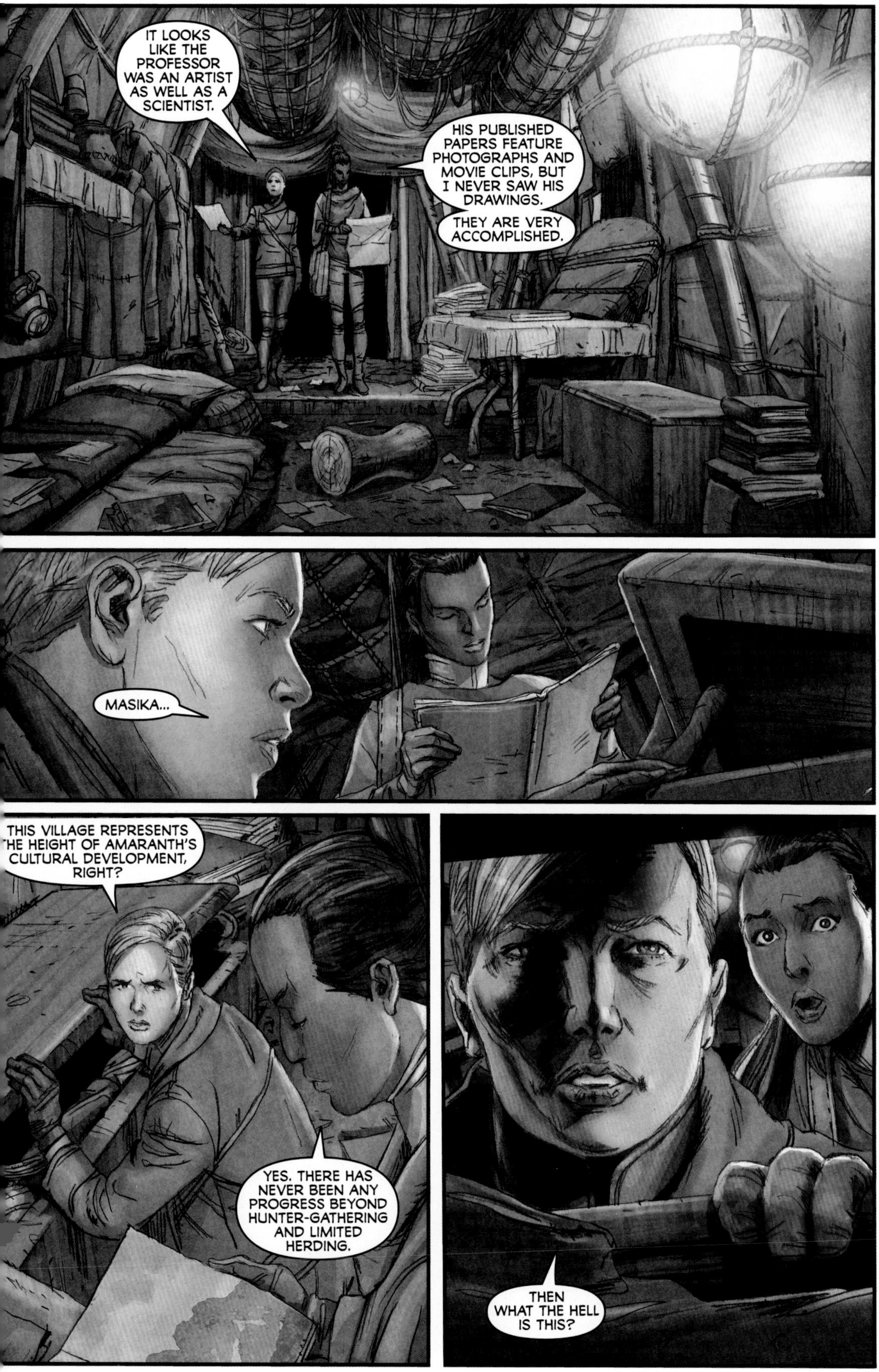
IT LOOKS LIKE THE PROFESSOR WAS AN ARTIST AS WELL AS A SCIENTIST.
HIS PUBLISHED PAPERS FEATURE PHOTOGRAPHS AND MOVIE CLIPS, BUT I NEVER SAW HIS DRAWINGS.
THEY ARE VERY ACCOMPLISHED.
MASIKA...
THIS VILLAGE REPRESENTS THE HEIGHT OF AMARANTH'S CULTURAL DEVELOPMENT, RIGHT?
YES. THERE HAS NEVER BEEN ANY PROGRESS BEYOND HUNTER-GATHERING AND LIMITED HERDING.
THEN WHAT THE HELL IS THIS?

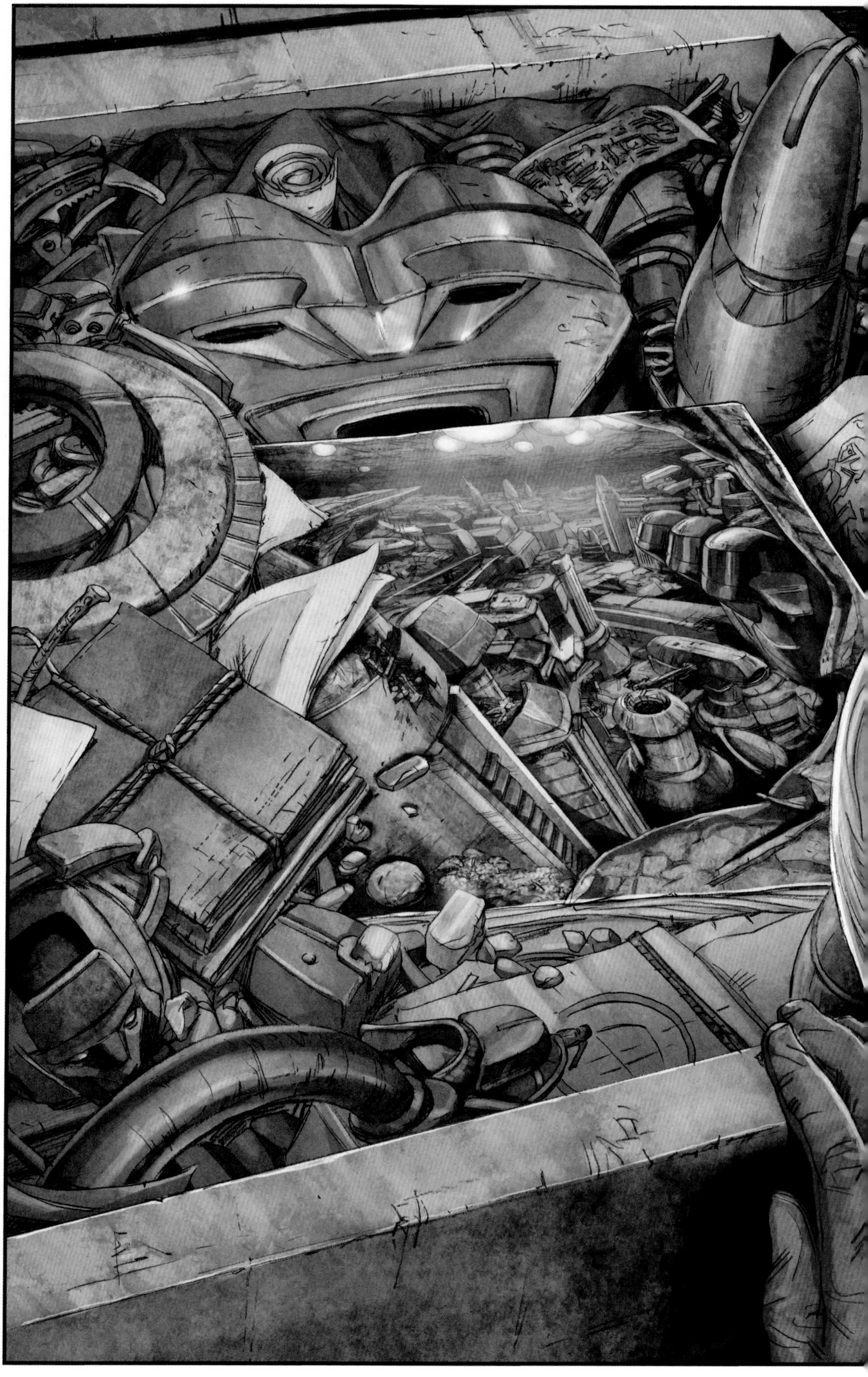

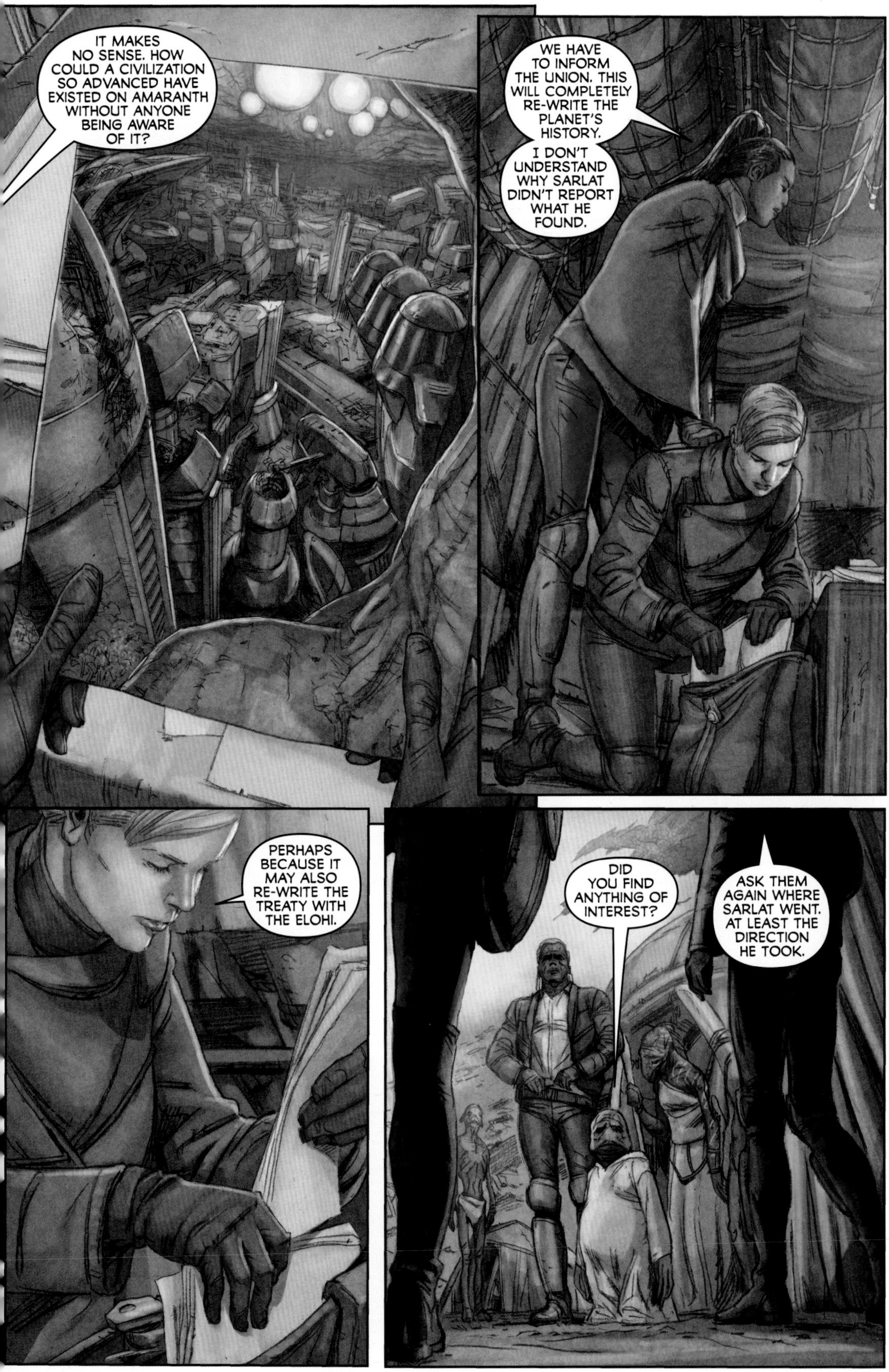
IT MAKES NO SENSE. HOW COULD A CIVILIZATION SO ADVANCED HAVE EXISTED ON AMARANTH WITHOUT ANYONE BEING AWARE OF IT?
WE HAVE TO INFORM THE UNION. THIS WILL COMPLETELY RE-WRITE THE PLANET'S HISTORY.
I DON'T UNDERSTAND WHY SARLAT DIDN'T REPORT WHAT HE FOUND.
PERHAPS BECAUSE IT MAY ALSO RE-WRITE THE TREATY WITH THE ELOHI.
DID YOU FIND ANYTHING OF INTEREST?
ASK THEM AGAIN WHERE SARLAT WENT. AT LEAST THE DIRECTION HE TOOK.

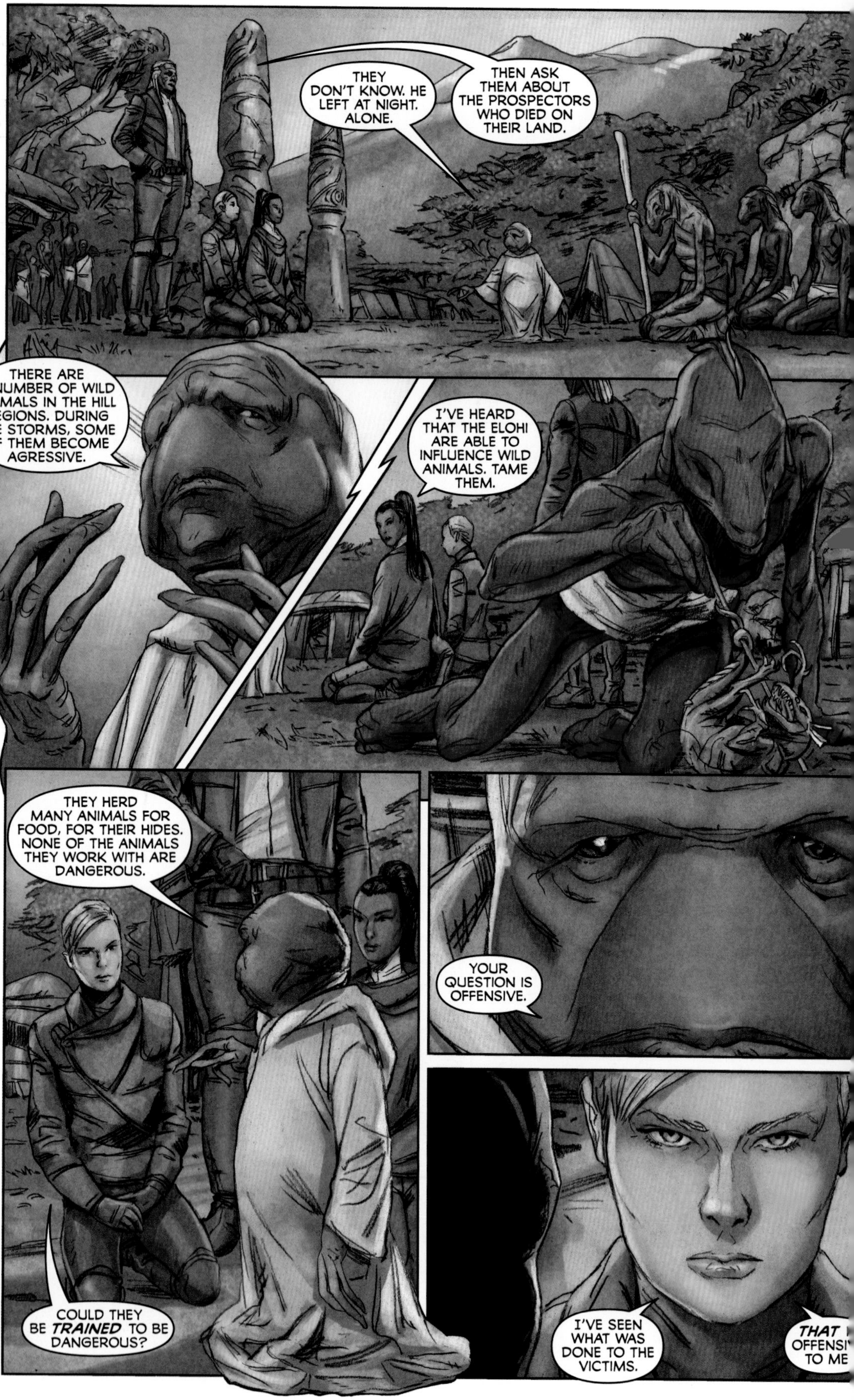

THEY DON'T KNOW. HE LEFT AT NIGHT. ALONE.
THEN ASK THEM ABOUT THE PROSPECTORS WHO DIED ON THEIR LAND.
THERE ARE A NUMBER OF WILD ANIMALS IN THE HILL REGIONS. DURING THE STORMS, SOME OF THEM BECOME AGRESSIVE.
I'VE HEARD THAT THE ELOHI ARE ABLE TO INFLUENCE WILD ANIMALS. TAME THEM.
THEY HERD MANY ANIMALS FOR FOOD, FOR THEIR HIDES. NONE OF THE ANIMALS THEY WORK WITH ARE DANGEROUS.
COULD THEY BE ***TRAINED*** TO BE DANGEROUS?
YOUR QUESTION IS OFFENSIVE.
I'VE SEEN WHAT WAS DONE TO THE VICTIMS.
THAT OFFENSI TO ME

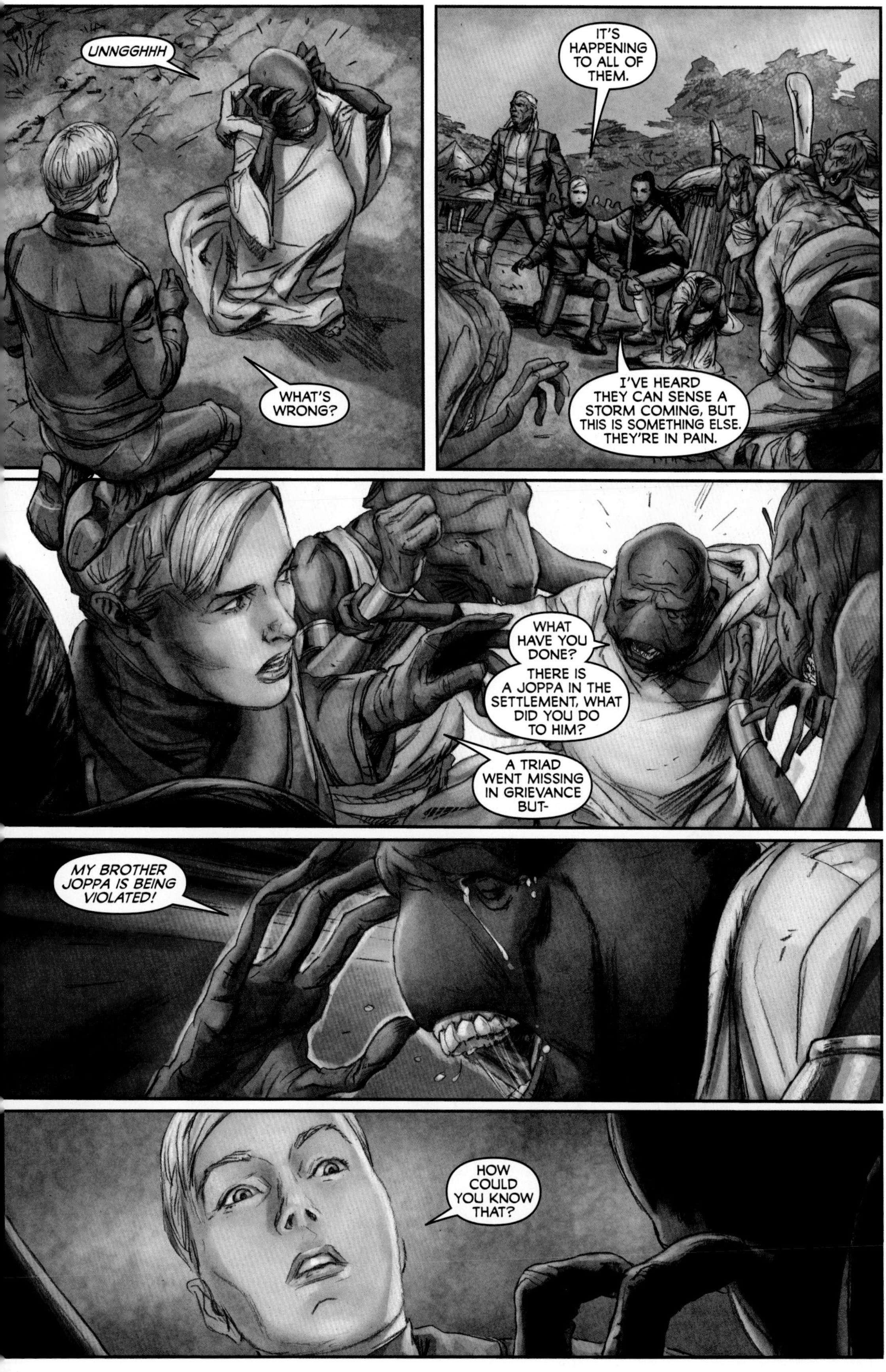
UNNGGHHH
WHAT'S WRONG?
IT'S HAPPENING TO ALL OF THEM.
I'VE HEARD THEY CAN SENSE A STORM COMING, BUT THIS IS SOMETHING ELSE. THEY'RE IN PAIN.
WHAT HAVE YOU DONE?
THERE IS A JOPPA IN THE SETTLEMENT, WHAT DID YOU DO TO HIM?
A TRIAD WENT MISSING IN GRIEVANCE BUT-
MY BROTHER JOPPA IS BEING VIOLATED!
HOW COULD YOU KNOW THAT?

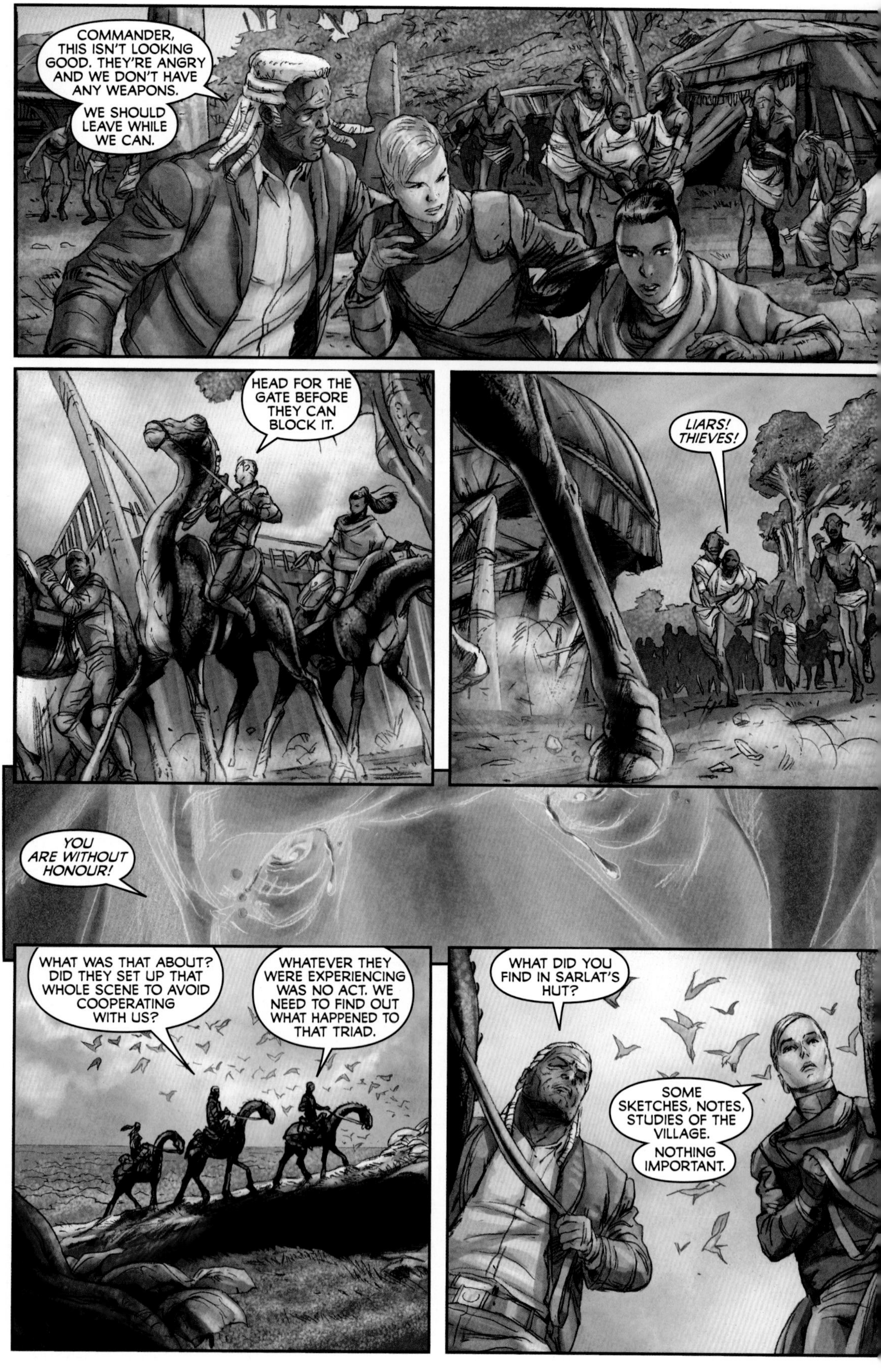
COMMANDER, THIS ISN'T LOOKING GOOD. THEY'RE ANGRY AND WE DON'T HAVE ANY WEAPONS.
WE SHOULD LEAVE WHILE WE CAN.
HEAD FOR THE GATE BEFORE THEY CAN BLOCK IT.
LIARS! THIEVES!
YOU ARE WITHOUT HONOUR!
WHAT WAS THAT ABOUT? DID THEY SET UP THAT WHOLE SCENE TO AVOID COOPERATING WITH US?
WHATEVER THEY WERE EXPERIENCING WAS NO ACT. WE NEED TO FIND OUT WHAT HAPPENED TO THAT TRIAD.
WHAT DID YOU FIND IN SARLAT'S HUT?
SOME SKETCHES, NOTES, STUDIES OF THE VILLAGE.
NOTHING IMPORTANT.

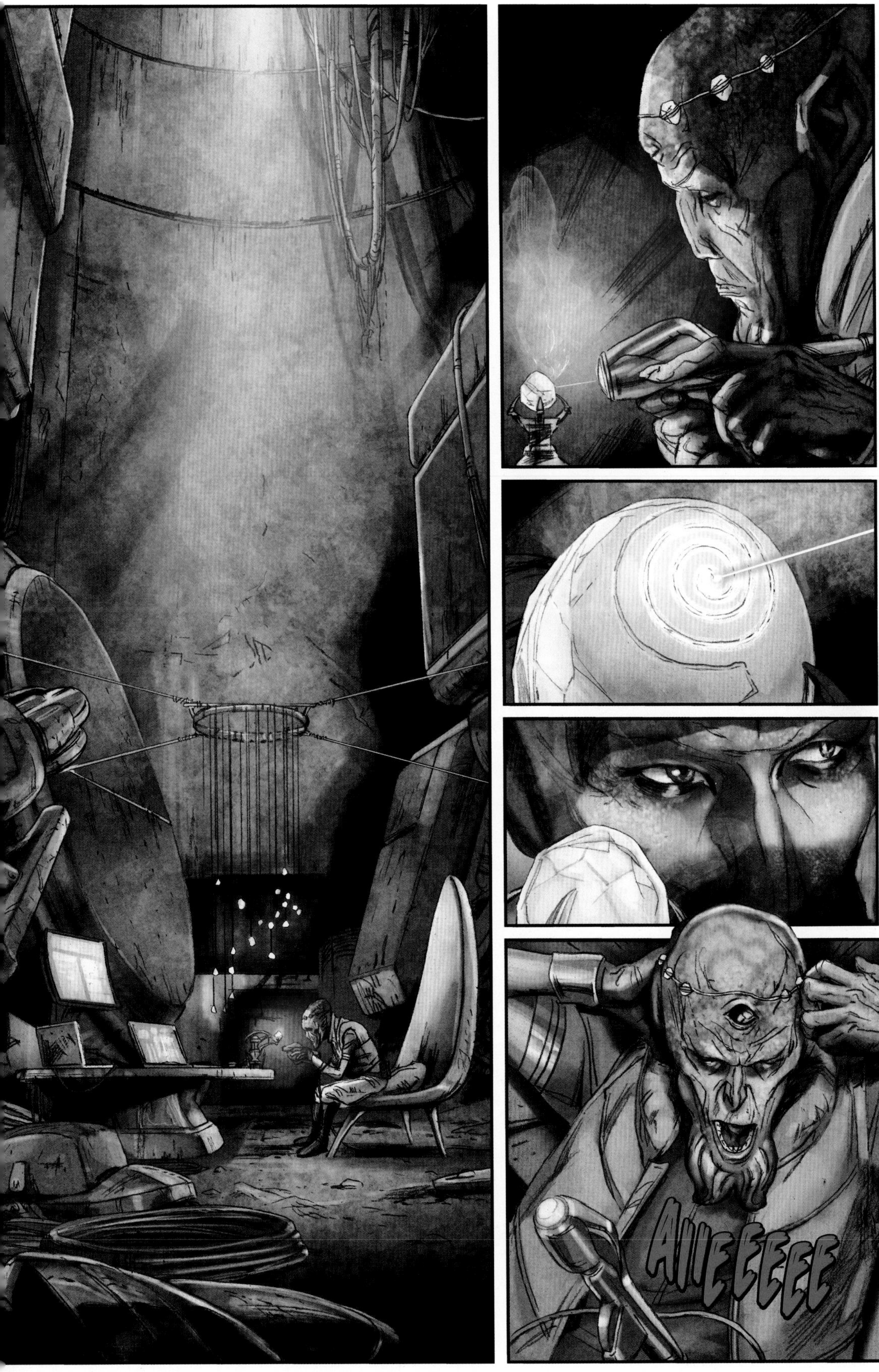
AIIEEEEE

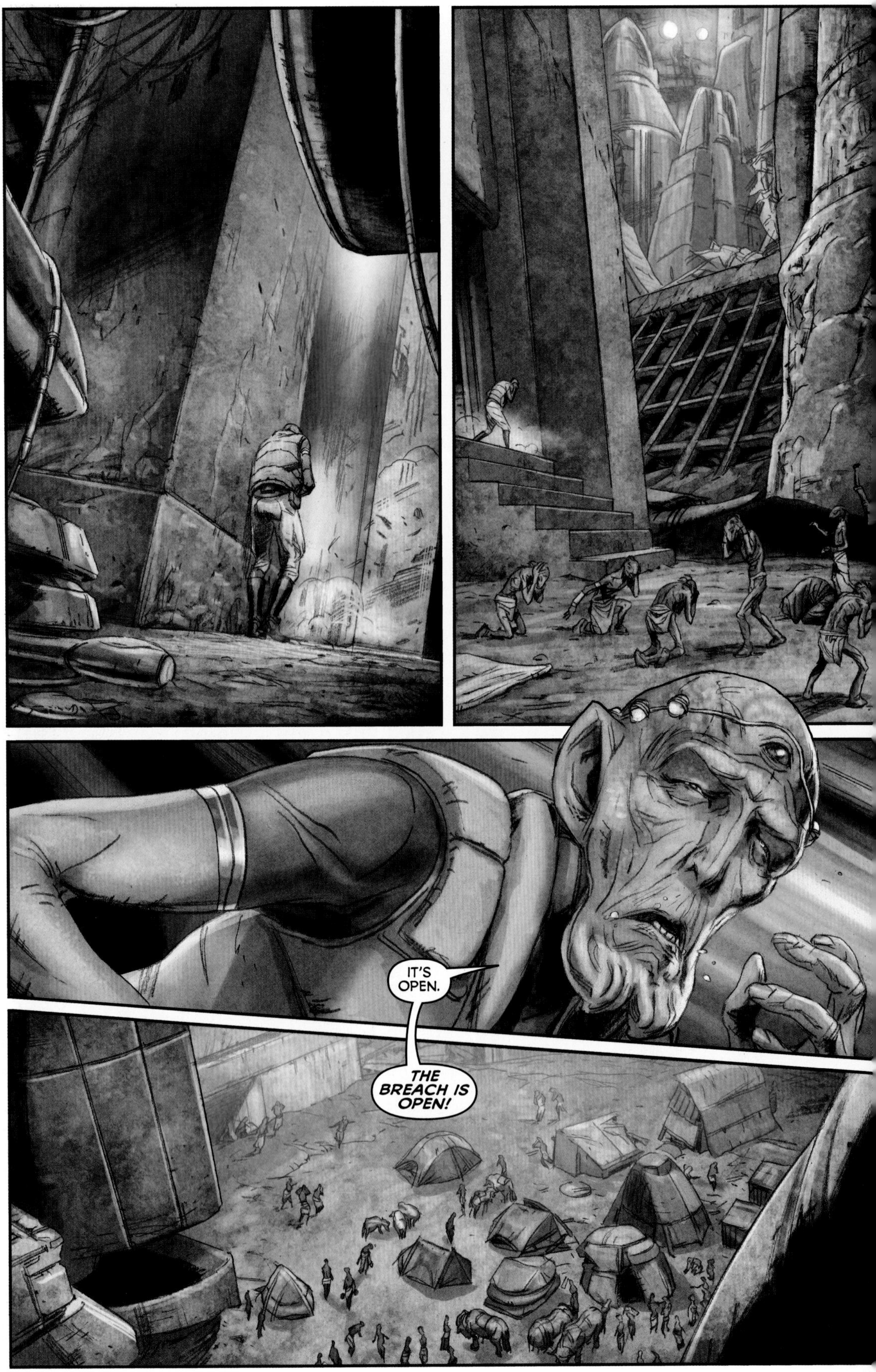
IT'S OPEN.
THE BREACH IS OPEN!

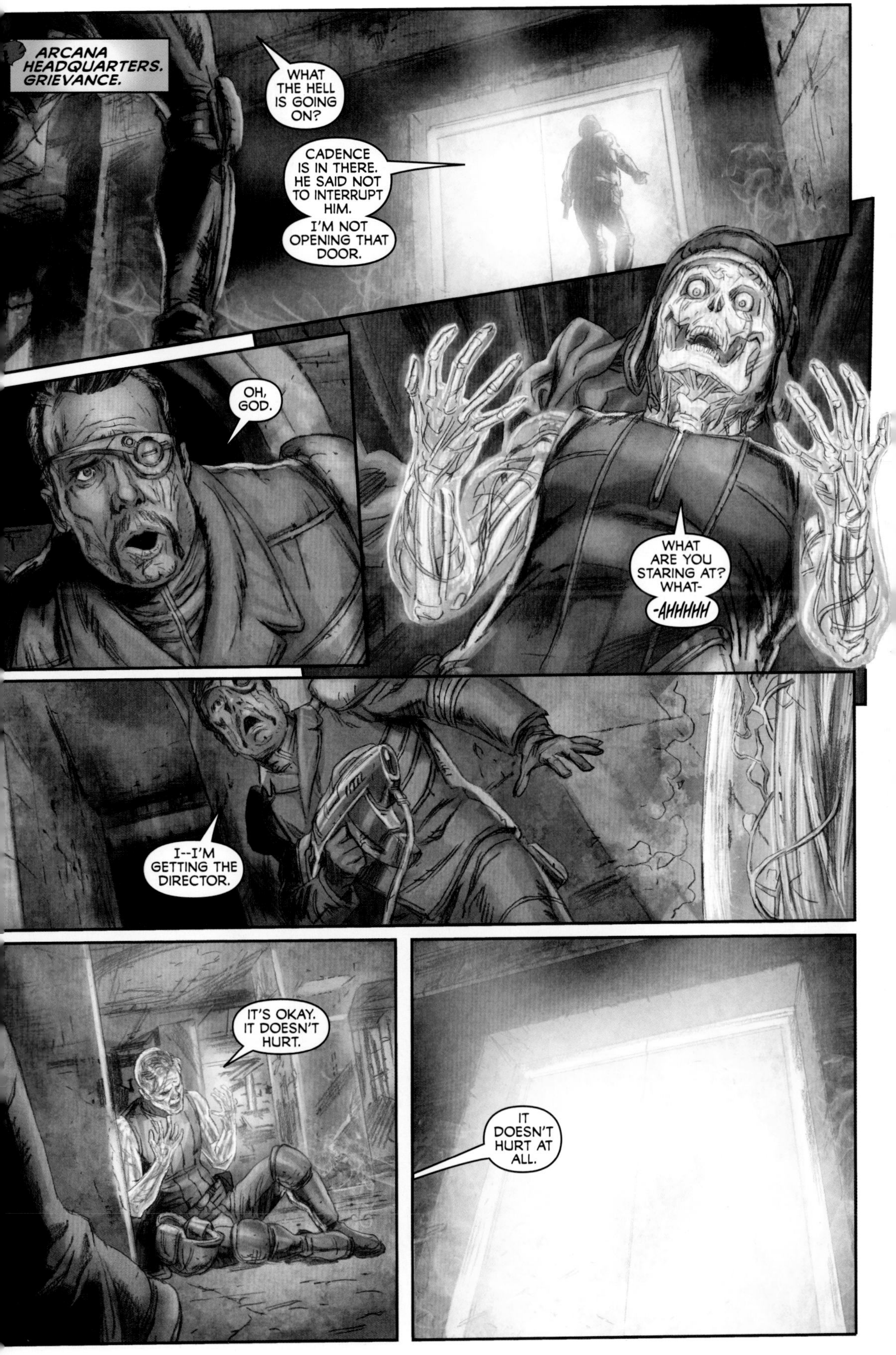
ARCANA HEADQUARTERS. GRIEVANCE.
WHAT THE HELL IS GOING ON?
CADENCE IS IN THERE. HE SAID NOT TO INTERRUPT HIM.
I'M NOT OPENING THAT DOOR.
OH, GOD.
WHAT ARE YOU STARING AT? WHAT-
-AHHHHH
I--I'M GETTING THE DIRECTOR.
IT'S OKAY. IT DOESN'T HURT.
IT DOESN'T HURT AT ALL.

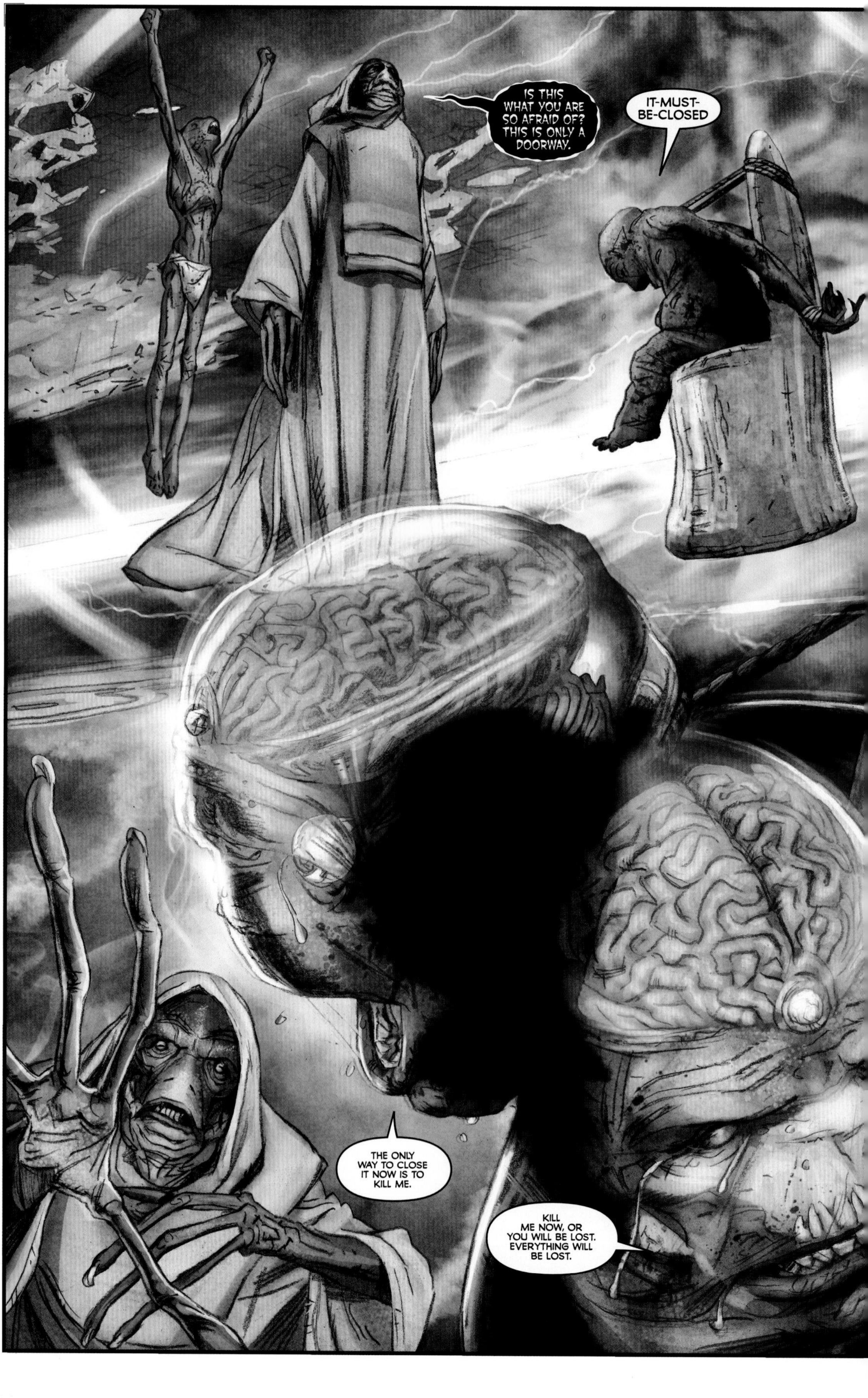
IS THIS WHAT YOU ARE SO AFRAID OF? THIS IS ONLY A DOORWAY.
IT-MUST-BE-CLOSED
THE ONLY WAY TO CLOSE IT NOW IS TO KILL ME.
KILL ME NOW, OR YOU WILL BE LOST. EVERYTHING WILL BE LOST.

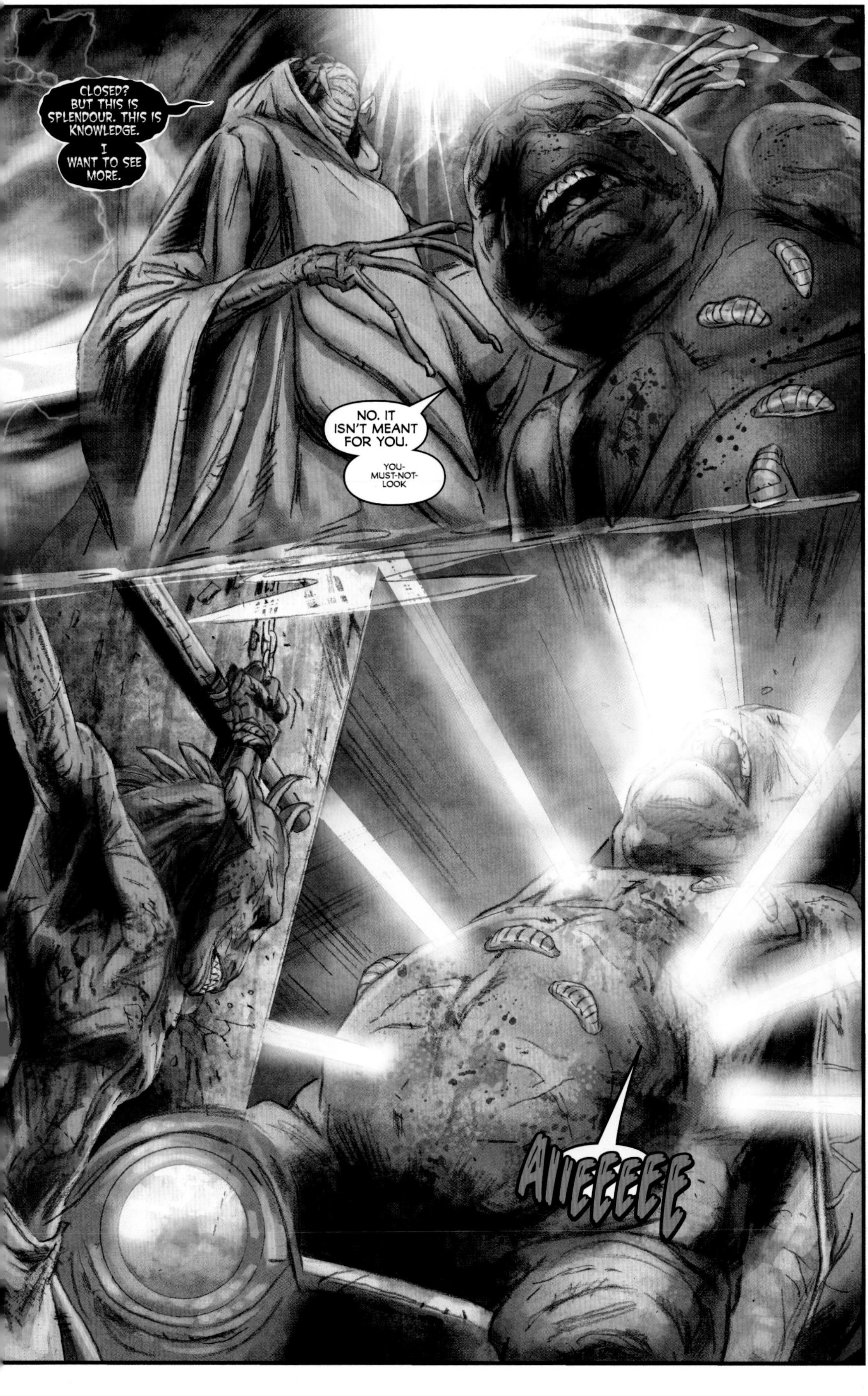
CLOSED? BUT THIS IS SPLENDOUR. THIS IS KNOWLEDGE.
I WANT TO SEE MORE.
NO. IT ISN'T MEANT FOR YOU.
YOU-MUST-NOT-LOOK
AIIEEEEE

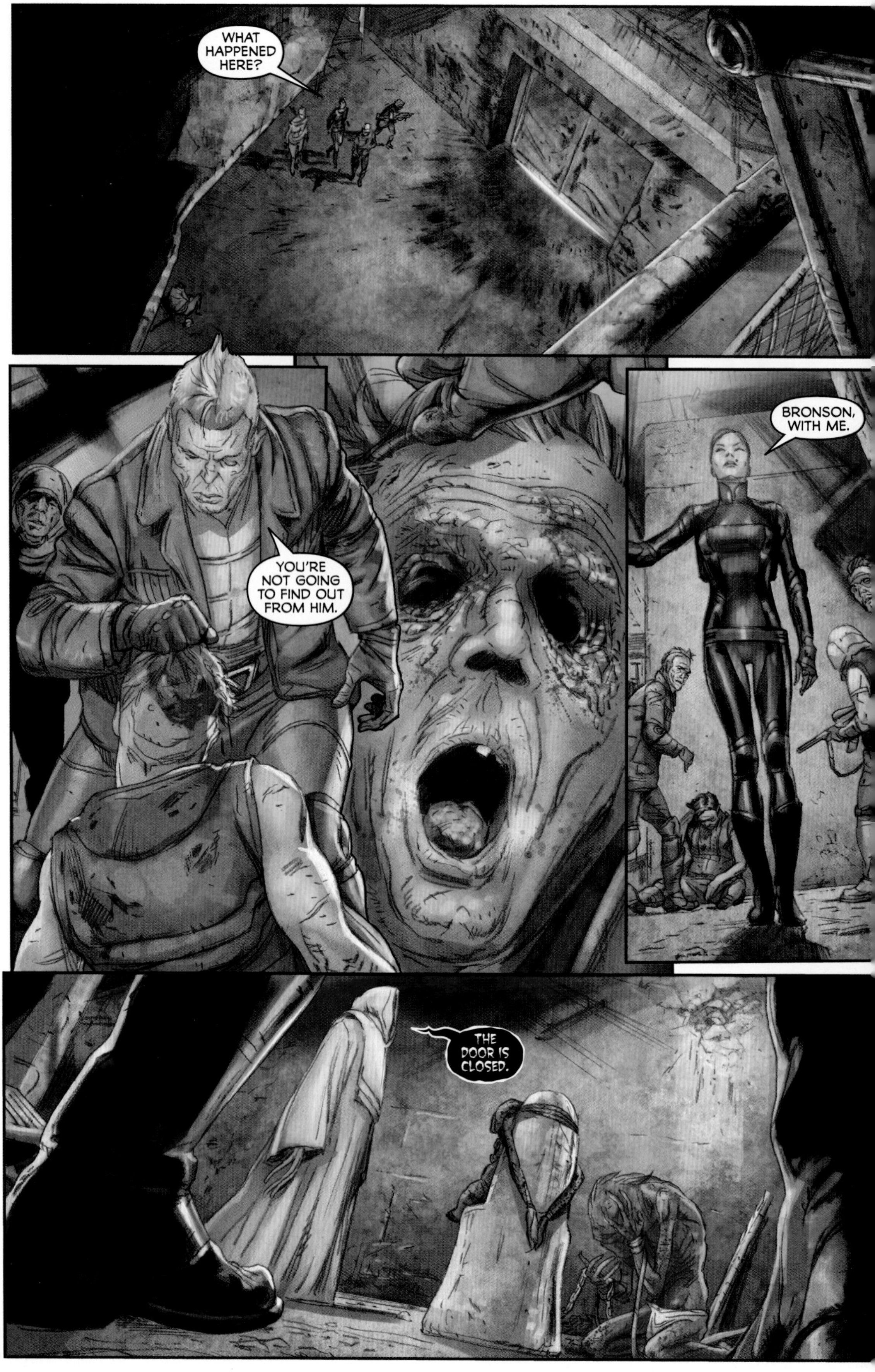
WHAT HAPPENED HERE?
YOU'RE NOT GOING TO FIND OUT FROM HIM.
BRONSON, WITH ME.
THE DOOR IS CLOSED.

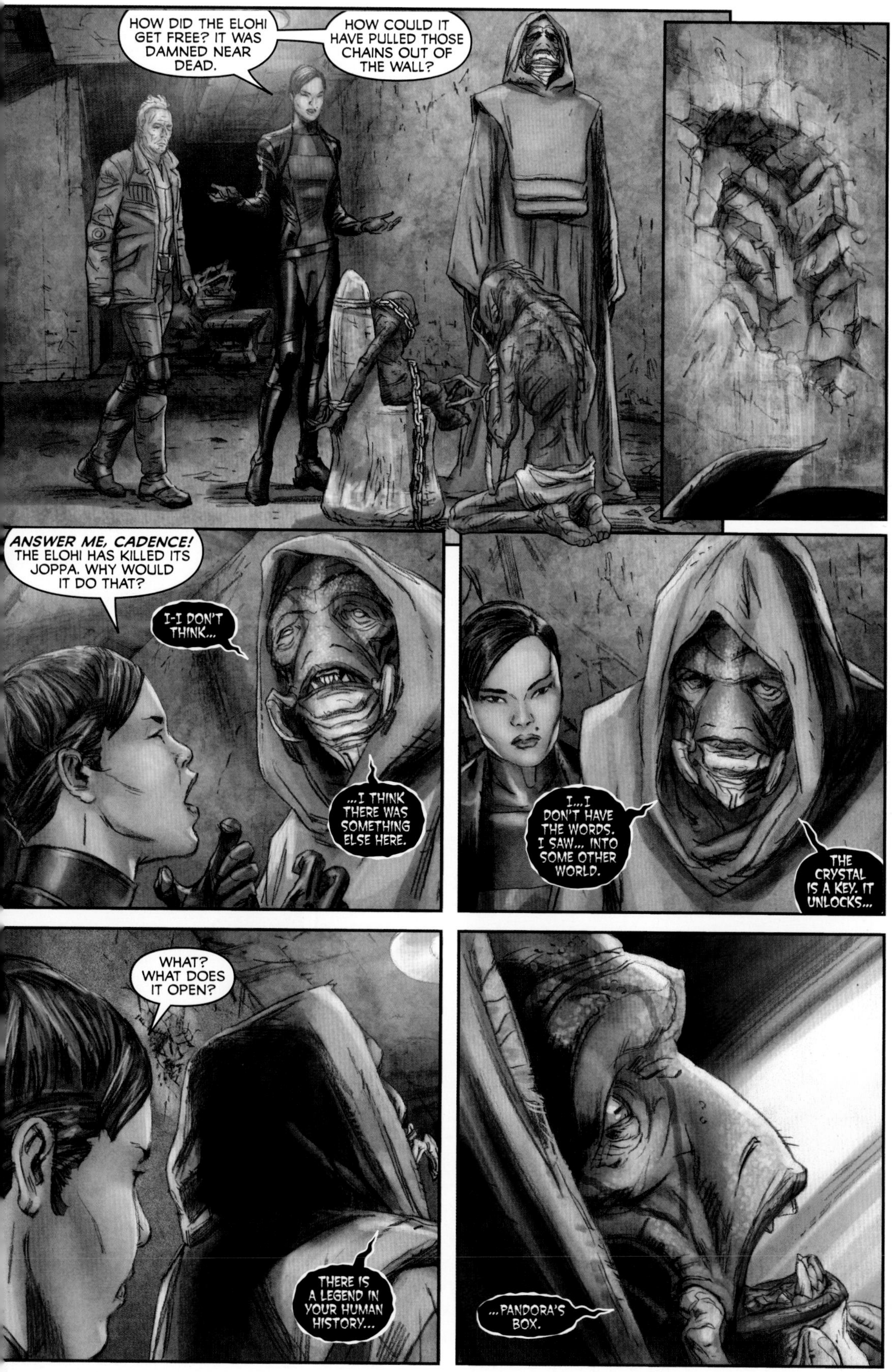
HOW DID THE ELOHI GET FREE? IT WAS DAMNED NEAR DEAD.
HOW COULD IT HAVE PULLED THOSE CHAINS OUT OF THE WALL?
ANSWER ME, CADENCE! THE ELOHI HAS KILLED ITS JOPPA. WHY WOULD IT DO THAT?
I-I DON'T THINK...
...I THINK THERE WAS SOMETHING ELSE HERE.
I...I DON'T HAVE THE WORDS. I SAW... INTO SOME OTHER WORLD.
THE CRYSTAL IS A KEY. IT UNLOCKS...
WHAT? WHAT DOES IT OPEN?
THERE IS A LEGEND IN YOUR HUMAN HISTORY...
...PANDORA'S BOX.

IS THAT ALL YOU HAVE TO SAY?

FOR THE MOMENT.

I HAVE TO PUT MY MIND IN ORDER.

TAKE THAT CREATURE TO ANOTHER CELL.

YOU KNOW WHAT TO DO. BRING IT TO ME IN MY OFFICE.

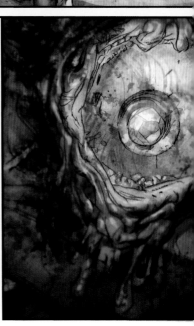

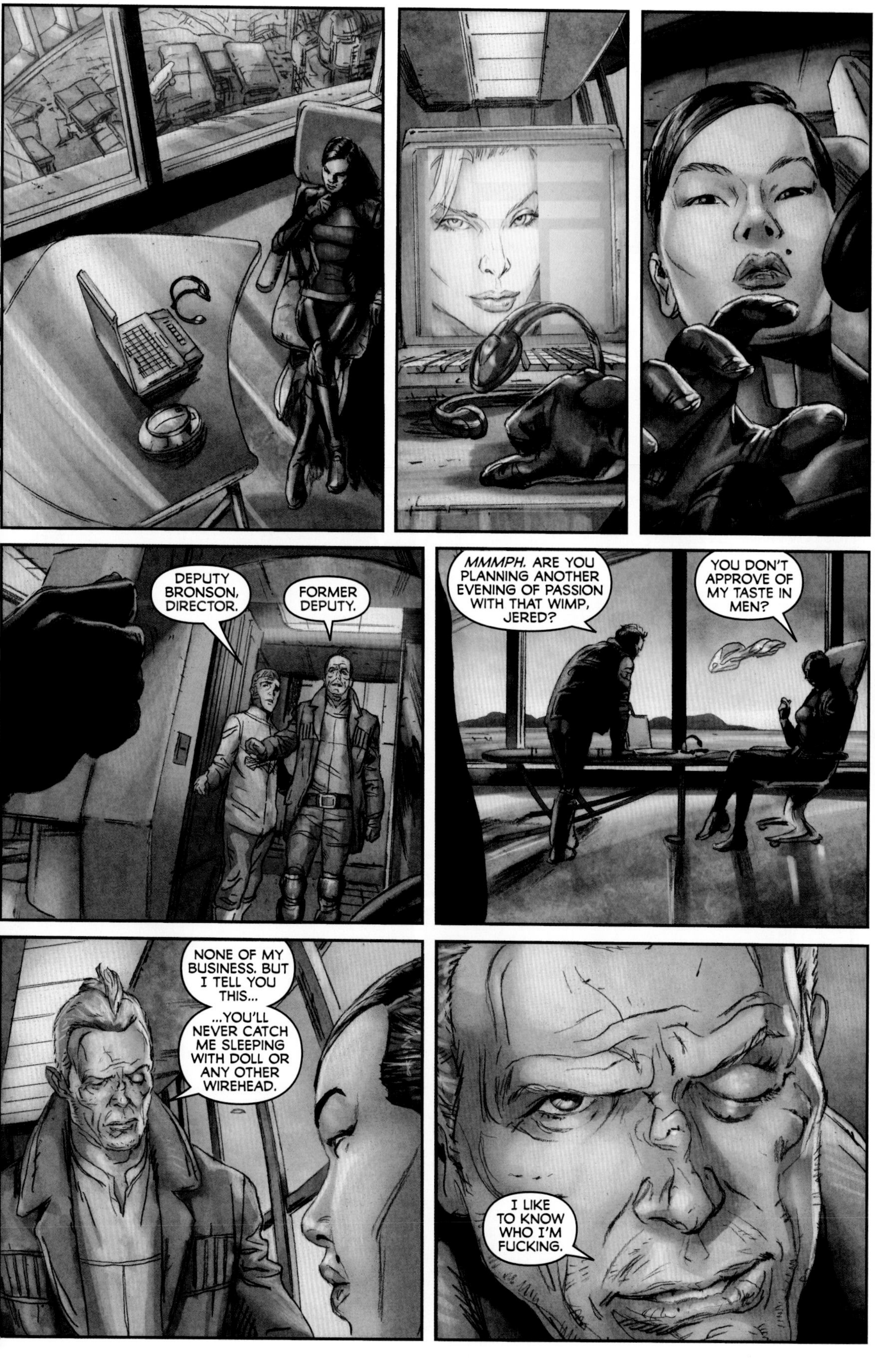
DEPUTY BRONSON, DIRECTOR.
FORMER DEPUTY.
MMMPH. ARE YOU PLANNING ANOTHER EVENING OF PASSION WITH THAT WIMP, JERED?
YOU DON'T APPROVE OF MY TASTE IN MEN?
NONE OF MY BUSINESS. BUT I TELL YOU THIS...
...YOU'LL NEVER CATCH ME SLEEPING WITH DOLL OR ANY OTHER WIREHEAD.
I LIKE TO KNOW WHO I'M FUCKING.

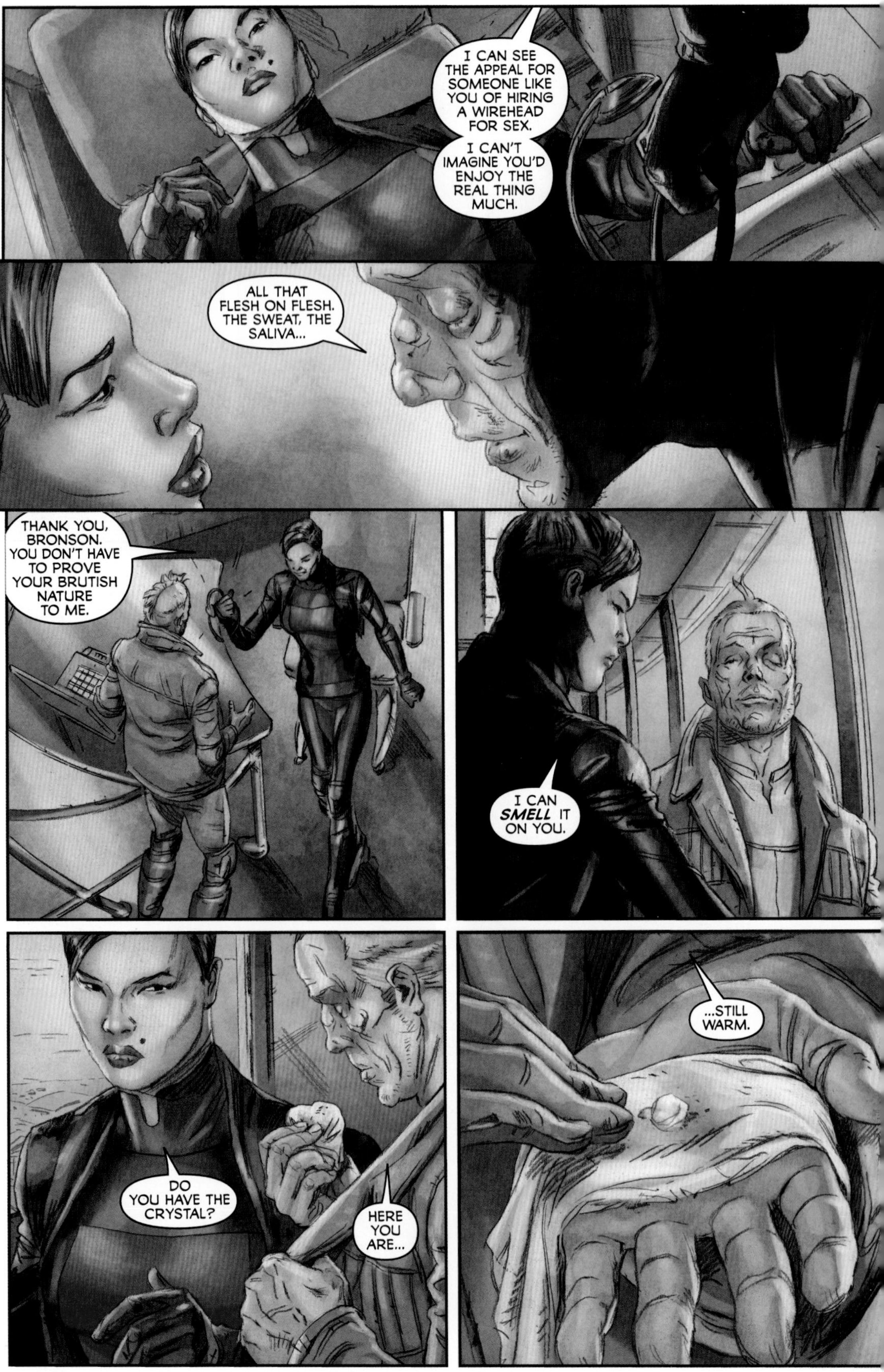

I CAN SEE THE APPEAL FOR SOMEONE LIKE YOU OF HIRING A WIREHEAD FOR SEX.
I CAN'T IMAGINE YOU'D ENJOY THE REAL THING MUCH.
ALL THAT FLESH ON FLESH. THE SWEAT, THE SALIVA...
THANK YOU, BRONSON. YOU DON'T HAVE TO PROVE YOUR BRUTISH NATURE TO ME.
I CAN *SMELL* IT ON YOU.
DO YOU HAVE THE CRYSTAL?
HERE YOU ARE...
...STILL WARM.

WILL YOU SEND IT TO YOUR PAYMASTERS AT ARCANA?

THEY DON'T KNOW DO THEY?

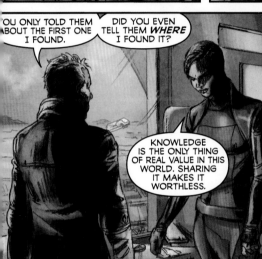

YOU ONLY TOLD THEM ABOUT THE FIRST ONE I FOUND.

DID YOU EVEN TELL THEM *WHERE* I FOUND IT?

KNOWLEDGE IS THE ONLY THING OF REAL VALUE IN THIS WORLD. SHARING IT MAKES IT WORTHLESS.

AND I KNOW FAR TOO MUCH.

I SUPPOSE YOU'LL *KILL* ME ONE OF THESE DAYS, WON'T YOU?

DO YOU EVEN CARE?

KARIS, SEND MY SURGEON UP.

IT'S TIME I FOUND OUT HOW THIS THING WORKS.

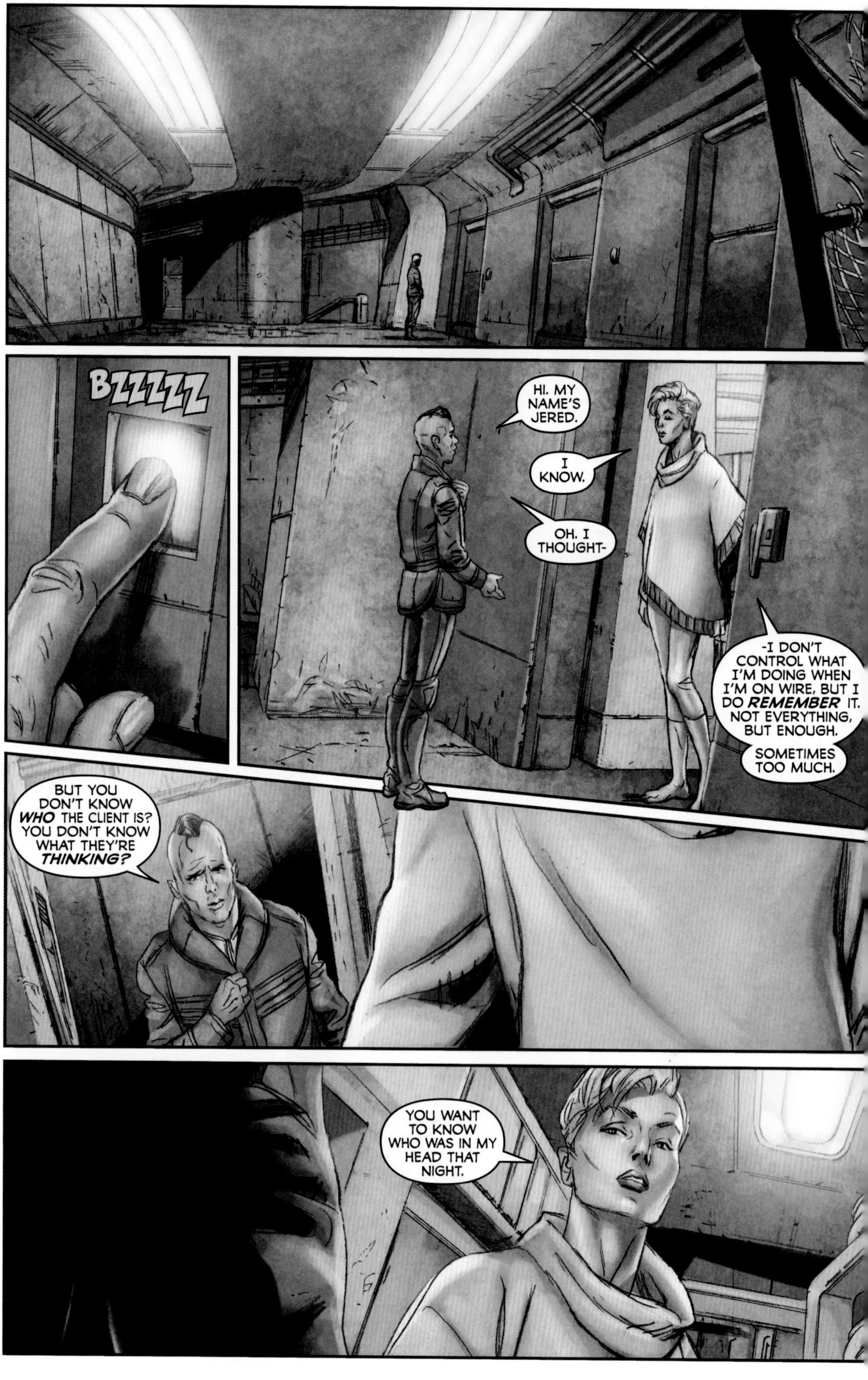
BZZZZZ
HI. MY NAME'S JERED.
I KNOW.
OH. I THOUGHT-
-I DON'T CONTROL WHAT I'M DOING WHEN I'M ON WIRE, BUT I DO *REMEMBER* IT. NOT EVERYTHING, BUT ENOUGH.
SOMETIMES TOO MUCH.
BUT YOU DON'T KNOW *WHO* THE CLIENT IS? YOU DON'T KNOW WHAT THEY'RE *THINKING?*
YOU WANT TO KNOW WHO WAS IN MY HEAD THAT NIGHT.

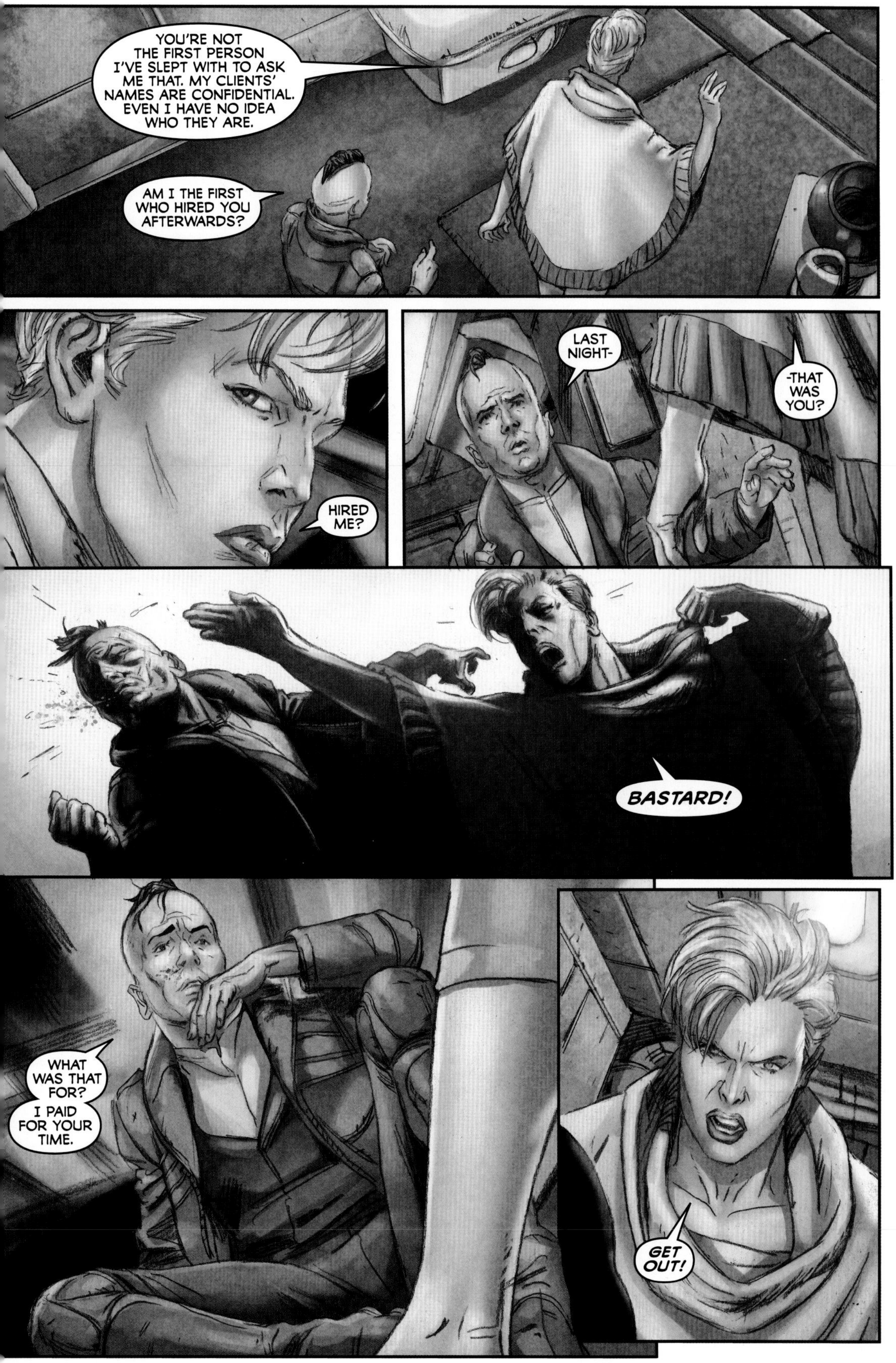
YOU'RE NOT THE FIRST PERSON I'VE SLEPT WITH TO ASK ME THAT. MY CLIENTS' NAMES ARE CONFIDENTIAL. EVEN I HAVE NO IDEA WHO THEY ARE.
AM I THE FIRST WHO HIRED YOU AFTERWARDS?
HIRED ME?
LAST NIGHT-
-THAT WAS YOU?
BASTARD!
WHAT WAS THAT FOR?
I PAID FOR YOUR TIME.
GET OUT!

YOU HAD NO RIGHT TO DO WHAT YOU DID.

I-I JUST WANTED TO KNOW WHAT IT'S LIKE TO BE YOU.

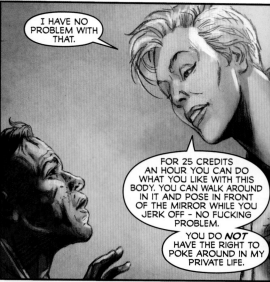

I HAVE NO PROBLEM WITH THAT.

FOR 25 CREDITS AN HOUR YOU CAN DO WHAT YOU LIKE WITH THIS BODY. YOU CAN WALK AROUND IN IT AND POSE IN FRONT OF THE MIRROR WHILE YOU JERK OFF – NO FUCKING PROBLEM.

YOU DO **NOT** HAVE THE RIGHT TO POKE AROUND IN MY PRIVATE LIFE.

I'M USED TO PERVERTS GOING THROUGH MY UNDERWEAR, BUT MY MAIL, MY PICTURES, MY *DIARIES.* WHAT MADE YOU THINK IT WAS OKAY TO DO THAT?

YOU'RE RIGHT. I'M SORRY.

PLEASE GO AWAY.

WHERE ARE THEY?

THE CHILDREN IN THE PICTURES.

YOUR CHILDREN.

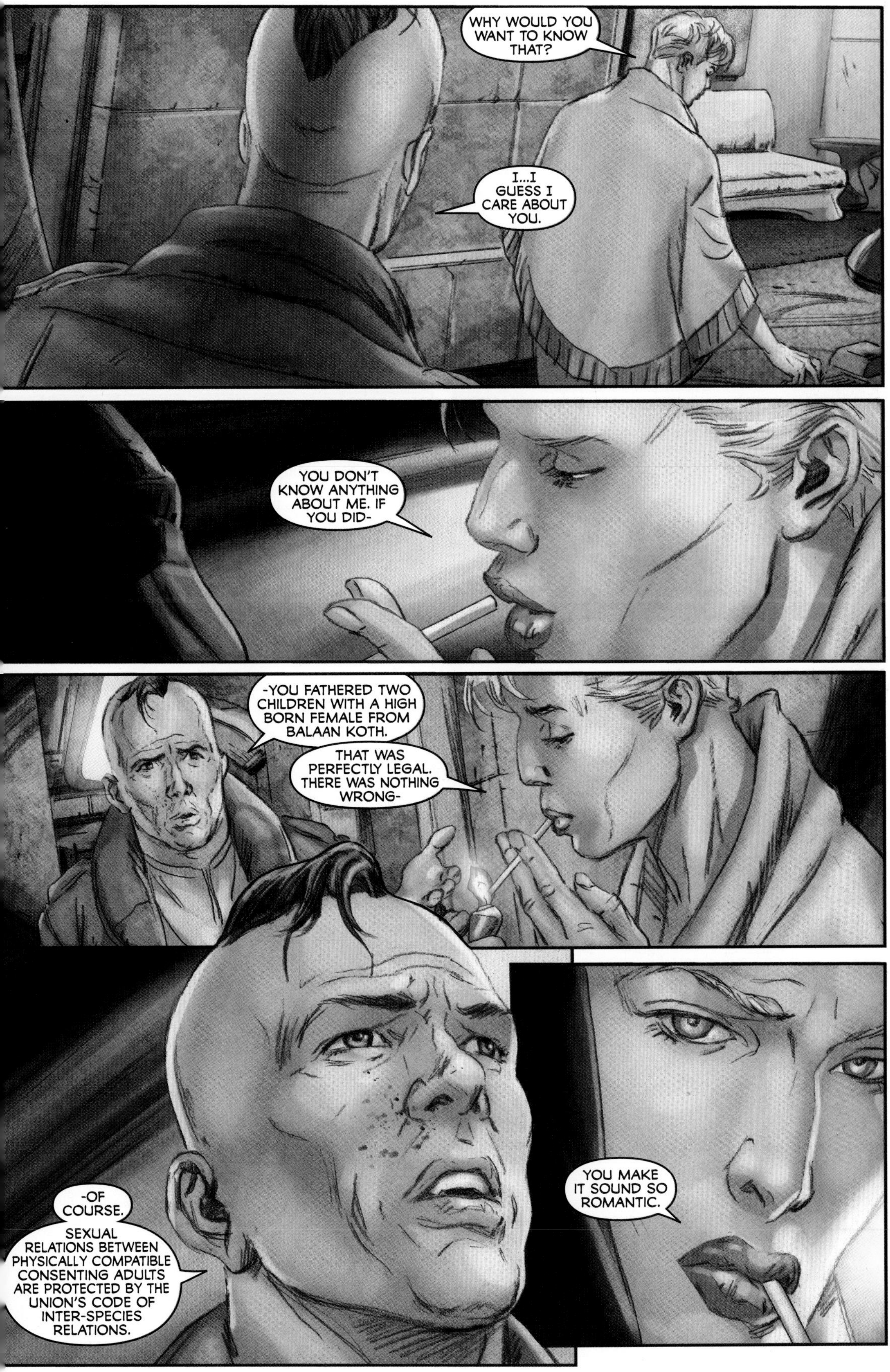
WHY WOULD YOU WANT TO KNOW THAT?
I...I GUESS I CARE ABOUT YOU.
YOU DON'T KNOW ANYTHING ABOUT ME. IF YOU DID-
-YOU FATHERED TWO CHILDREN WITH A HIGH BORN FEMALE FROM BALAAN KOTH.
THAT WAS PERFECTLY LEGAL. THERE WAS NOTHING WRONG-
-OF COURSE.
SEXUAL RELATIONS BETWEEN PHYSICALLY COMPATIBLE CONSENTING ADULTS ARE PROTECTED BY THE UNION'S CODE OF INTER-SPECIES RELATIONS.
YOU MAKE IT SOUND SO ROMANTIC.

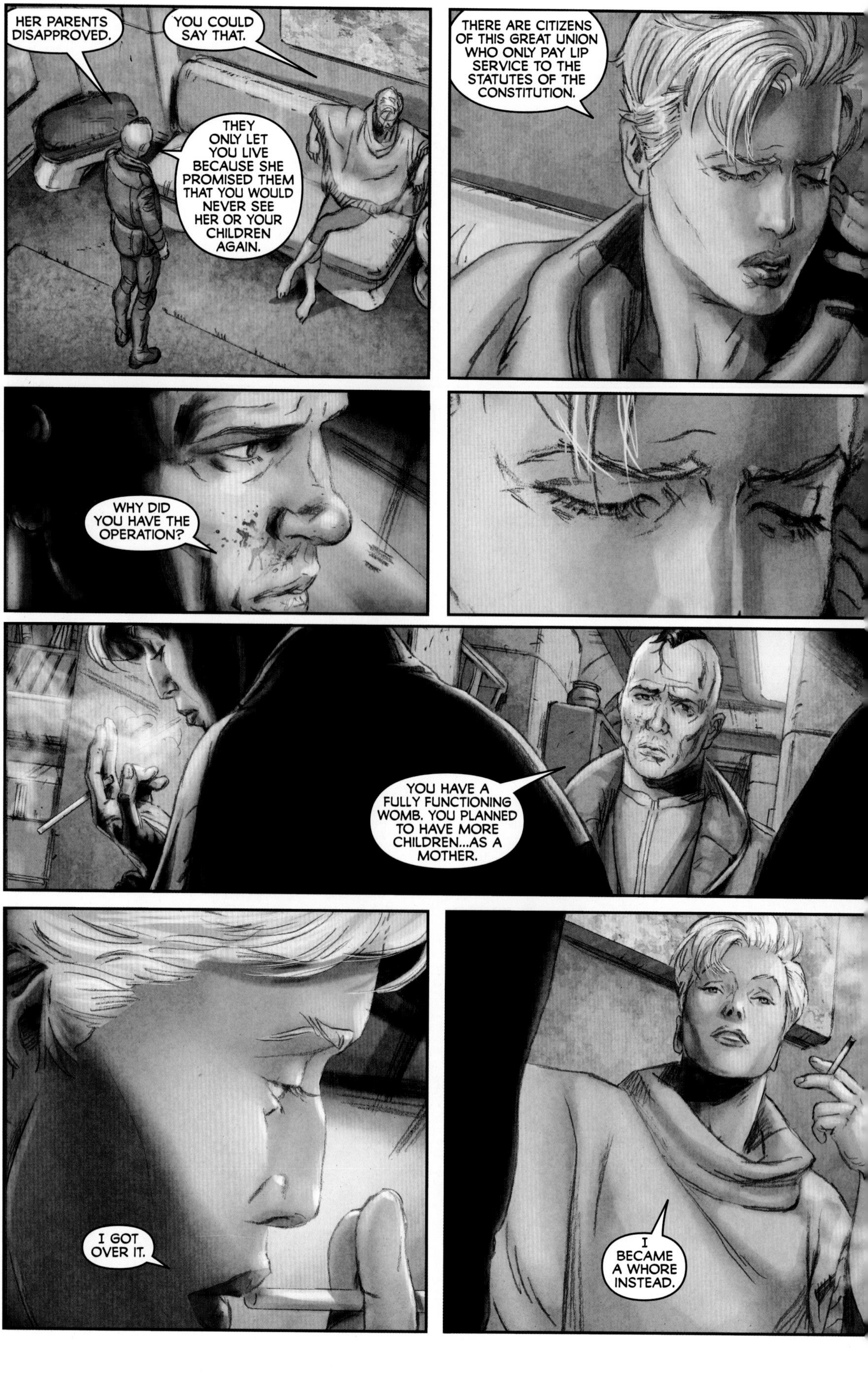
HER PARENTS DISAPPROVED.
YOU COULD SAY THAT.
THEY ONLY LET YOU LIVE BECAUSE SHE PROMISED THEM THAT YOU WOULD NEVER SEE HER OR YOUR CHILDREN AGAIN.
THERE ARE CITIZENS OF THIS GREAT UNION WHO ONLY PAY LIP SERVICE TO THE STATUTES OF THE CONSTITUTION.
WHY DID YOU HAVE THE OPERATION?
YOU HAVE A FULLY FUNCTIONING WOMB. YOU PLANNED TO HAVE MORE CHILDREN...AS A MOTHER.
I GOT OVER IT.
I BECAME A WHORE INSTEAD.

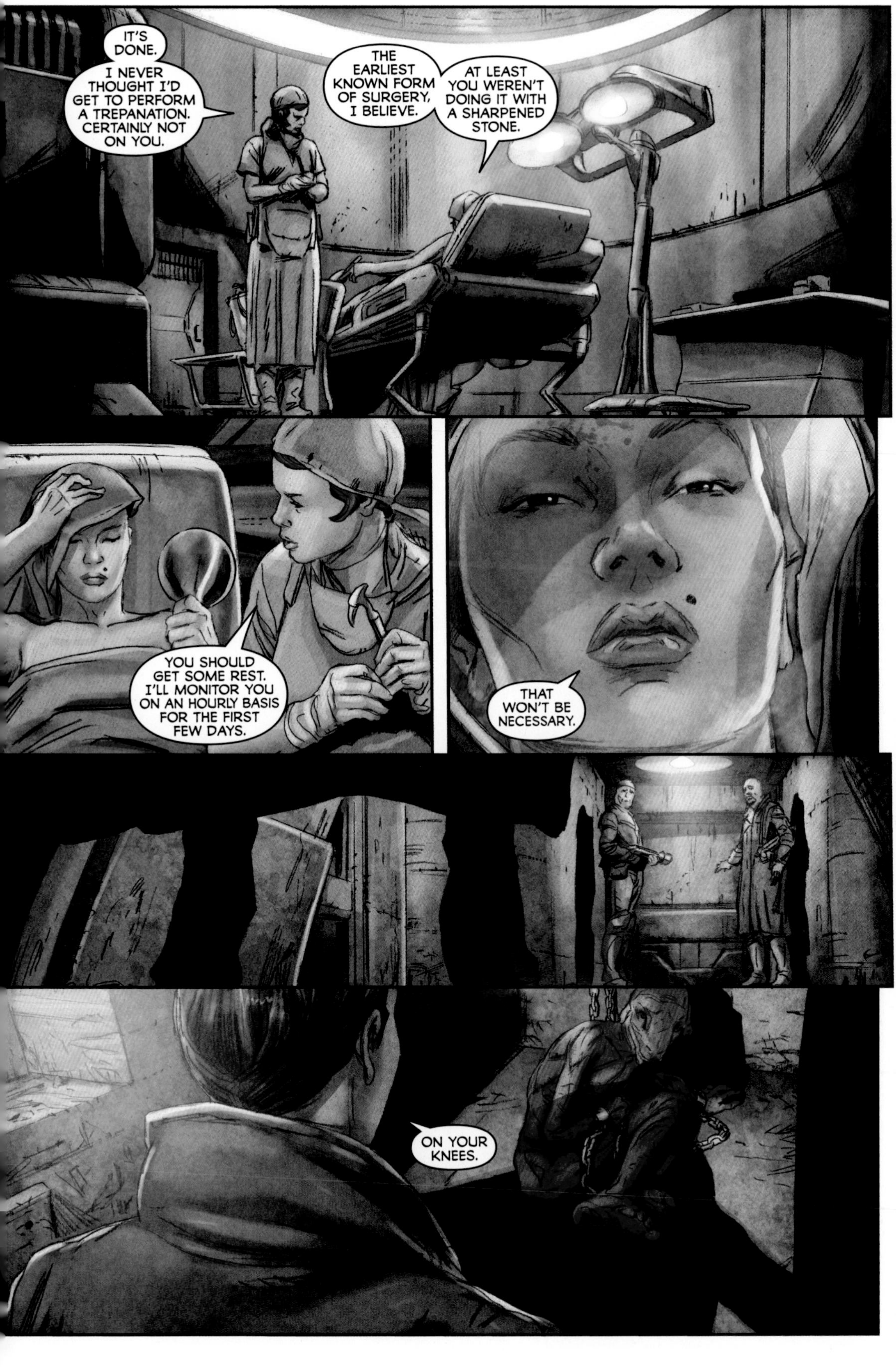
IT'S DONE.
I NEVER THOUGHT I'D GET TO PERFORM A TREPANATION. CERTAINLY NOT ON YOU.
THE EARLIEST KNOWN FORM OF SURGERY, I BELIEVE.
AT LEAST YOU WEREN'T DOING IT WITH A SHARPENED STONE.
YOU SHOULD GET SOME REST. I'LL MONITOR YOU ON AN HOURLY BASIS FOR THE FIRST FEW DAYS.
THAT WON'T BE NECESSARY.
ON YOUR KNEES.

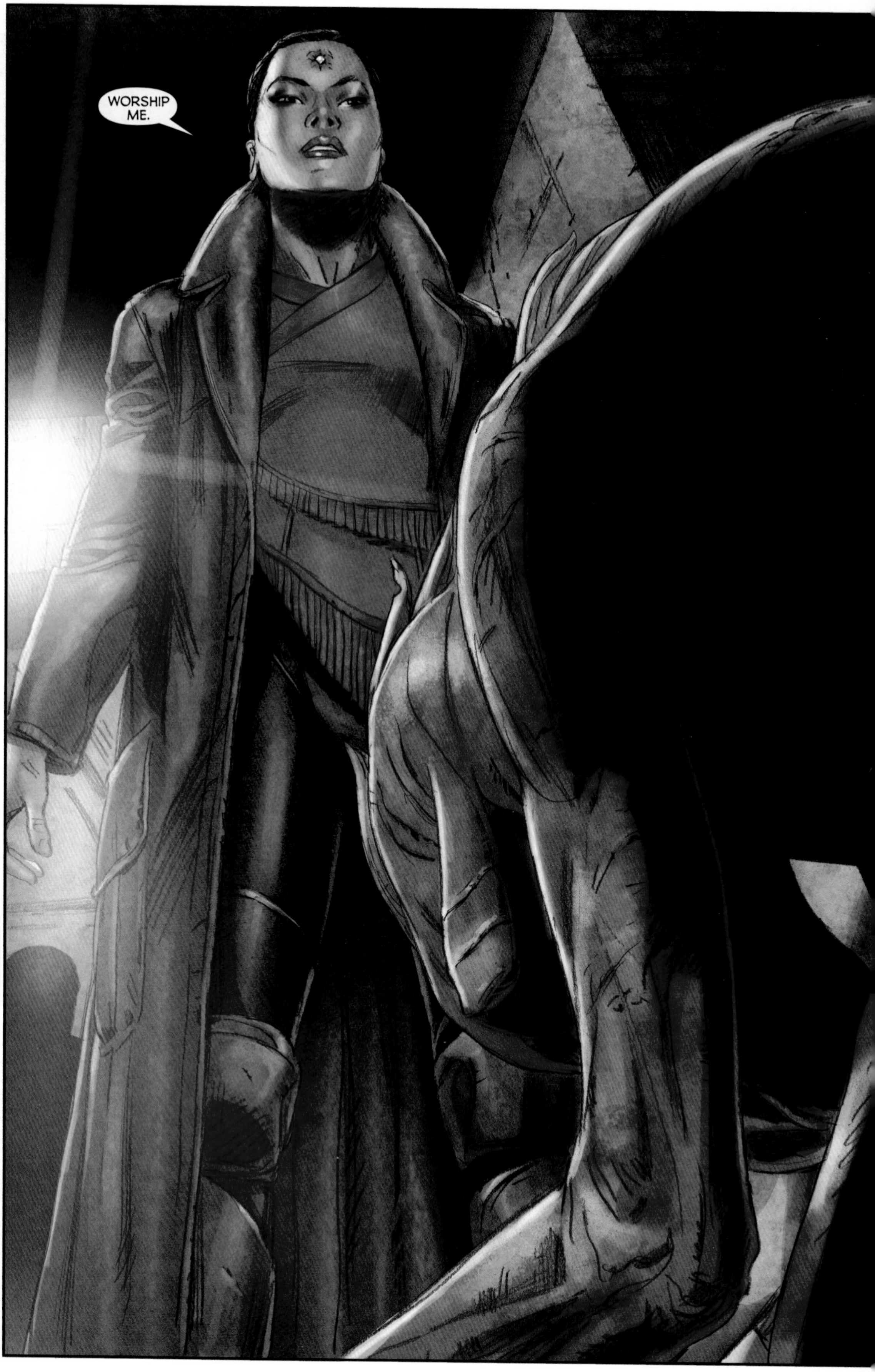

WORSHIP ME.

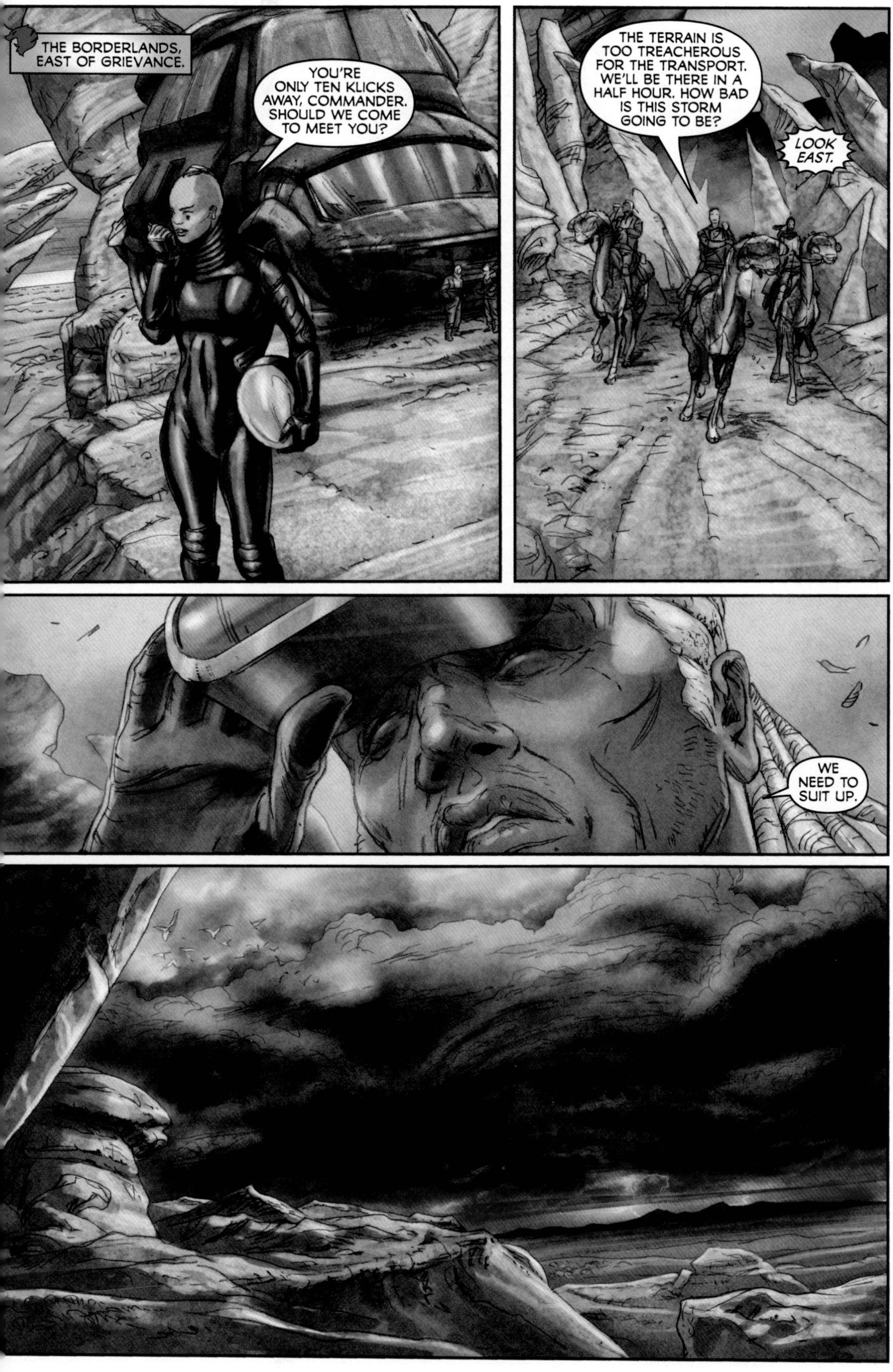

THE BORDERLANDS, EAST OF GRIEVANCE.
YOU'RE ONLY TEN KLICKS AWAY, COMMANDER. SHOULD WE COME TO MEET YOU?
THE TERRAIN IS TOO TREACHEROUS FOR THE TRANSPORT. WE'LL BE THERE IN A HALF HOUR. HOW BAD IS THIS STORM GOING TO BE?
LOOK EAST.
WE NEED TO SUIT UP.

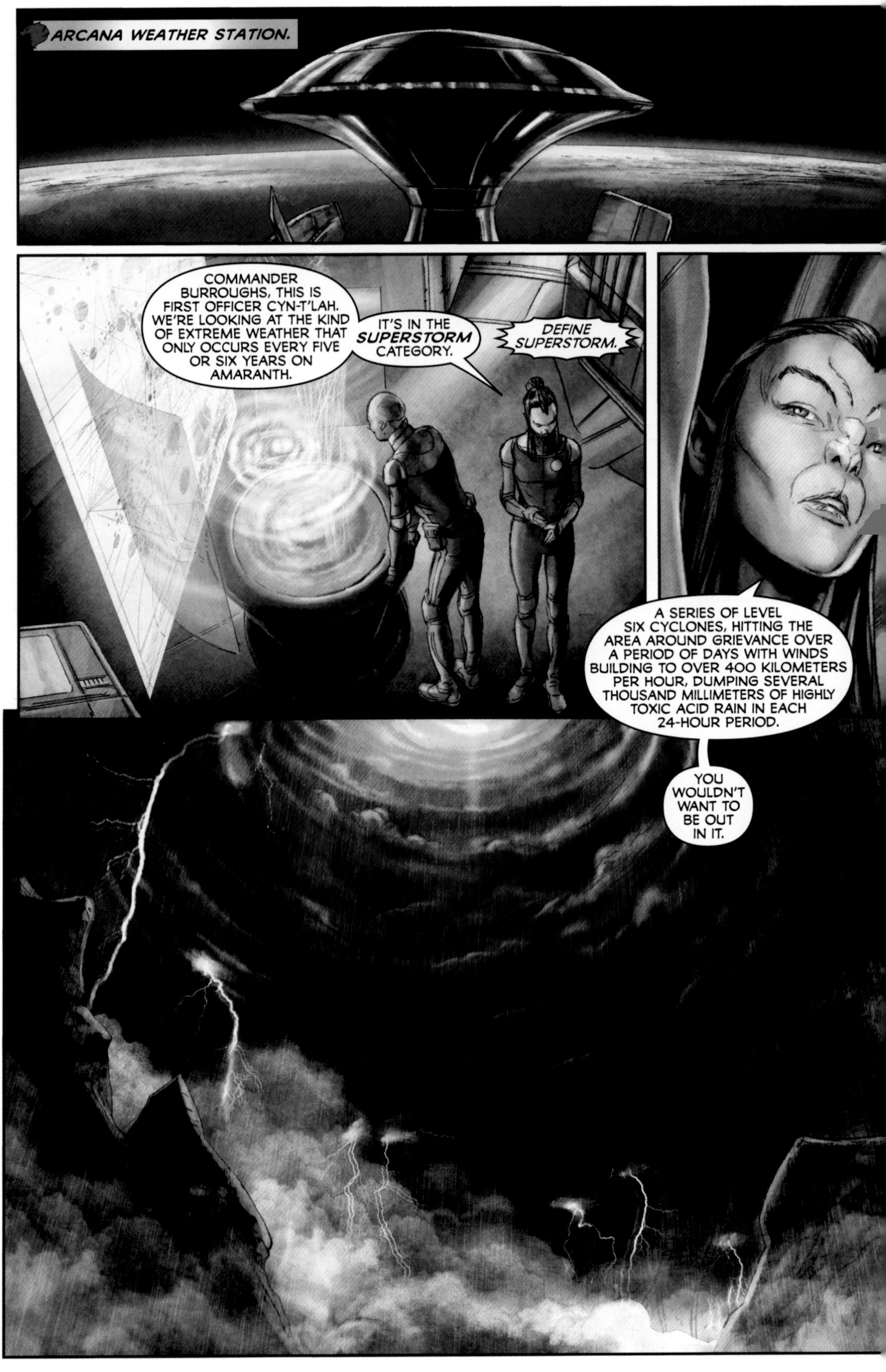
ARCANA WEATHER STATION.
COMMANDER BURROUGHS, THIS IS FIRST OFFICER CYN-T'LAH. WE'RE LOOKING AT THE KIND OF EXTREME WEATHER THAT ONLY OCCURS EVERY FIVE OR SIX YEARS ON AMARANTH.
IT'S IN THE SUPERSTORM CATEGORY.
DEFINE SUPERSTORM.
A SERIES OF LEVEL SIX CYCLONES, HITTING THE AREA AROUND GRIEVANCE OVER A PERIOD OF DAYS WITH WINDS BUILDING TO OVER 400 KILOMETERS PER HOUR, DUMPING SEVERAL THOUSAND MILLIMETERS OF HIGHLY TOXIC ACID RAIN IN EACH 24-HOUR PERIOD.
YOU WOULDN'T WANT TO BE OUT IN IT.

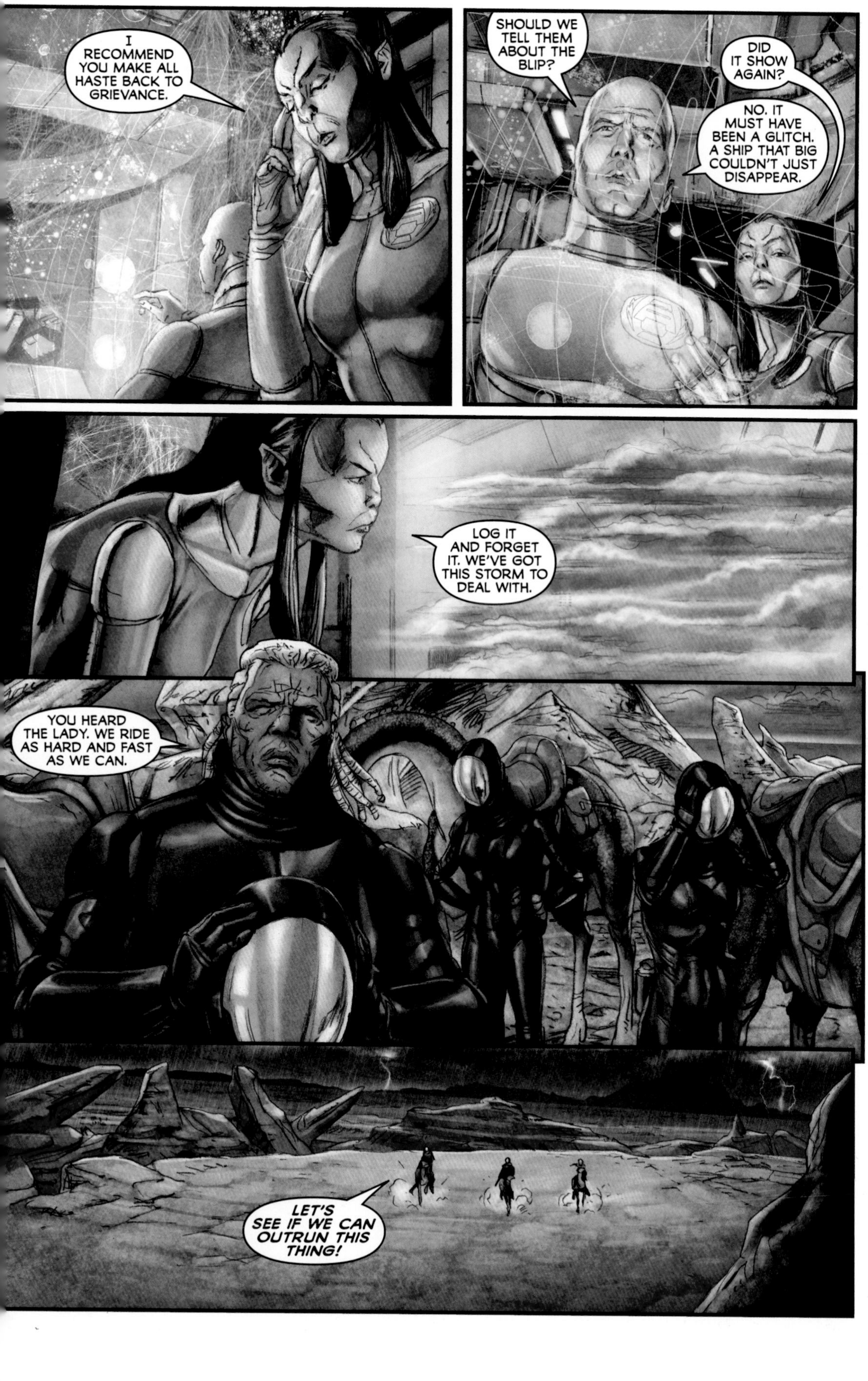

I RECOMMEND YOU MAKE ALL HASTE BACK TO GRIEVANCE.
SHOULD WE TELL THEM ABOUT THE BLIP?
DID IT SHOW AGAIN?
NO. IT MUST HAVE BEEN A GLITCH. A SHIP THAT BIG COULDN'T JUST DISAPPEAR.
LOG IT AND FORGET IT. WE'VE GOT THIS STORM TO DEAL WITH.
YOU HEARD THE LADY. WE RIDE AS HARD AND FAST AS WE CAN.
LET'S SEE IF WE CAN OUTRUN THIS THING!

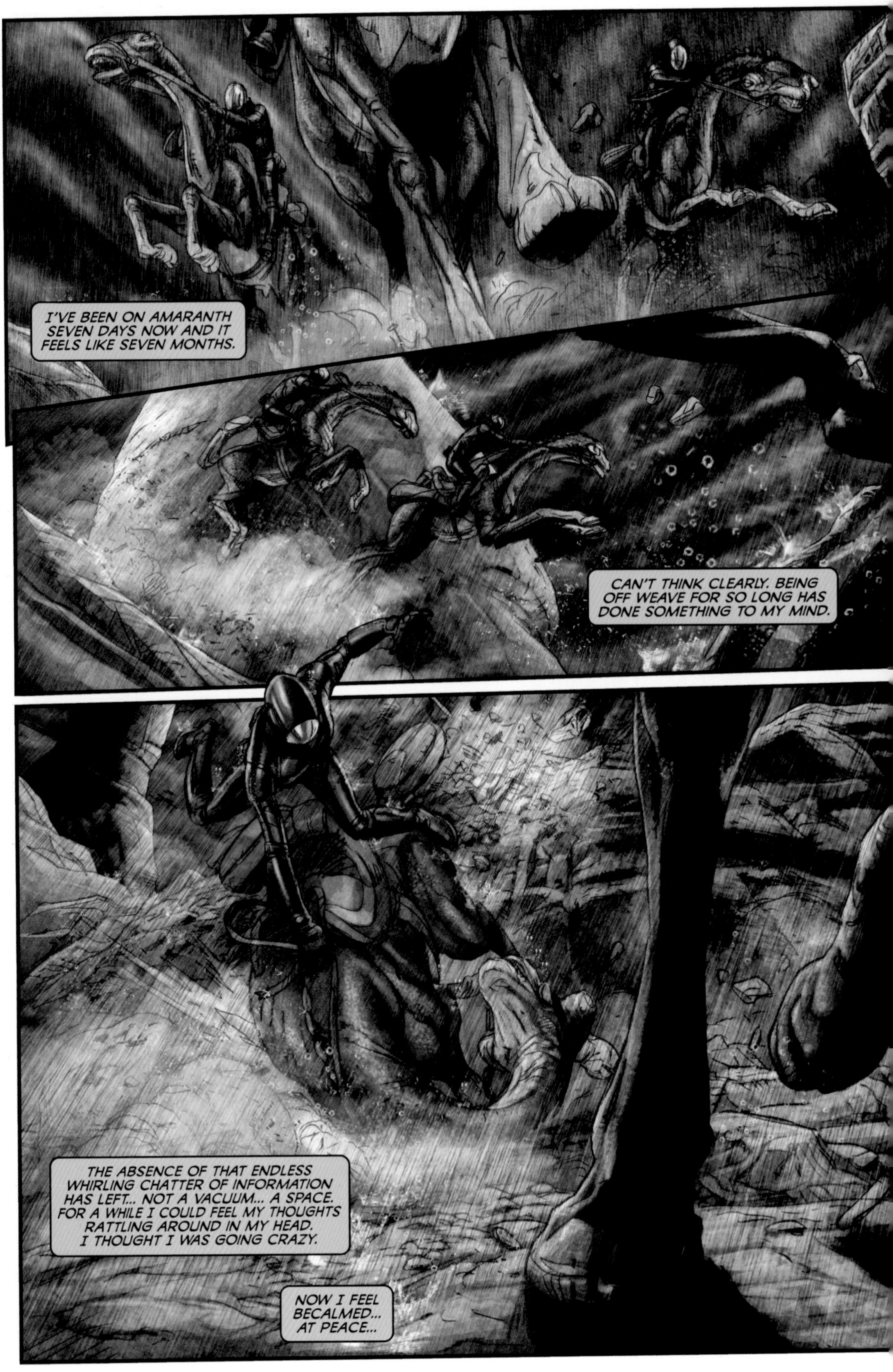
I'VE BEEN ON AMARANTH SEVEN DAYS NOW AND IT FEELS LIKE SEVEN MONTHS.
CAN'T THINK CLEARLY. BEING OFF WEAVE FOR SO LONG HAS DONE SOMETHING TO MY MIND.
THE ABSENCE OF THAT ENDLESS WHIRLING CHATTER OF INFORMATION HAS LEFT... NOT A VACUUM... A SPACE. FOR A WHILE I COULD FEEL MY THOUGHTS RATTLING AROUND IN MY HEAD. I THOUGHT I WAS GOING CRAZY.
NOW I FEEL BECALMED... AT PEACE...

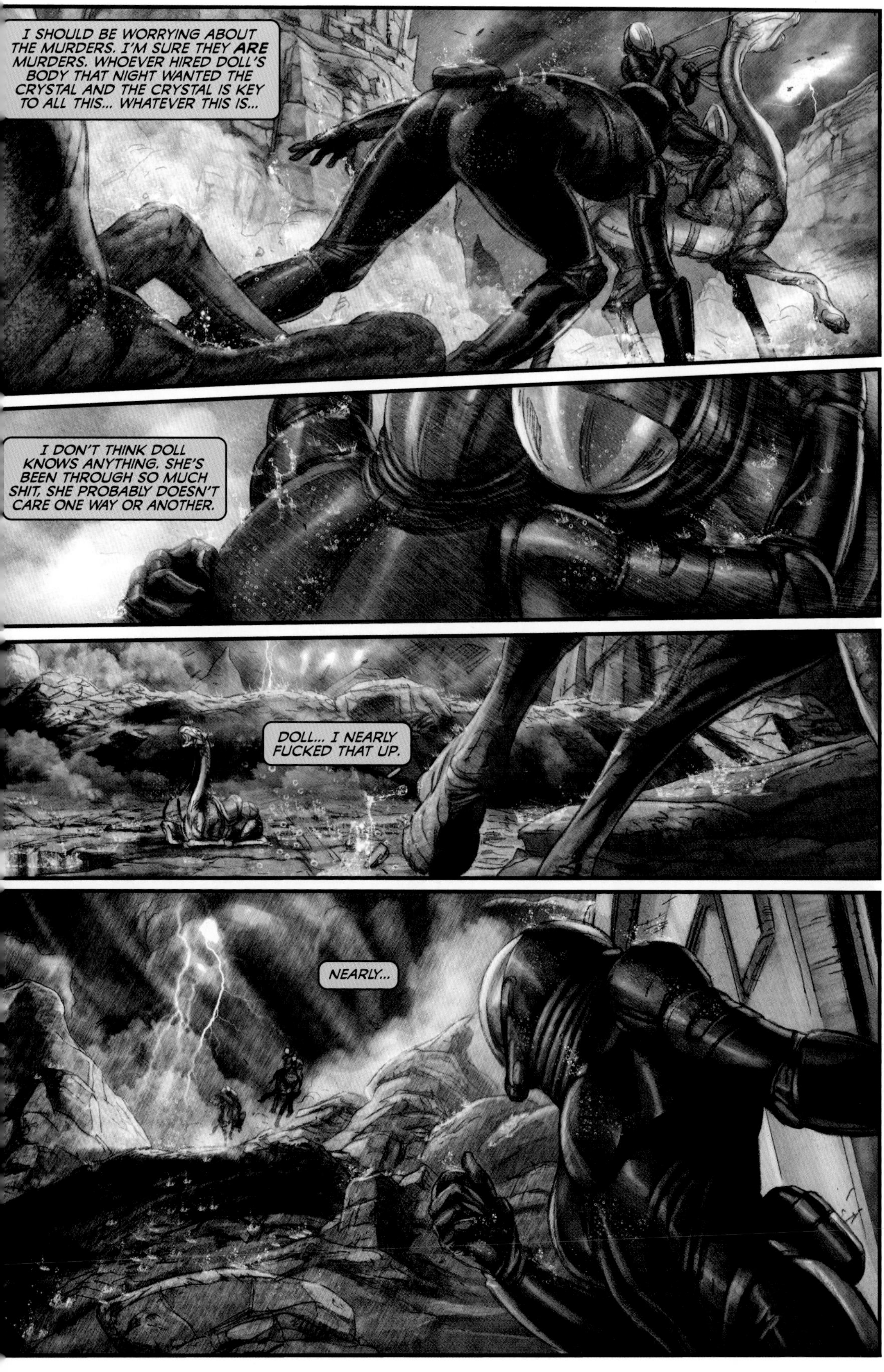
I SHOULD BE WORRYING ABOUT THE MURDERS. I'M SURE THEY ARE MURDERS. WHOEVER HIRED DOLL'S BODY THAT NIGHT WANTED THE CRYSTAL AND THE CRYSTAL IS KEY TO ALL THIS... WHATEVER THIS IS...
I DON'T THINK DOLL KNOWS ANYTHING. SHE'S BEEN THROUGH SO MUCH SHIT, SHE PROBABLY DOESN'T CARE ONE WAY OR ANOTHER.
DOLL... I NEARLY FUCKED THAT UP.
NEARLY...

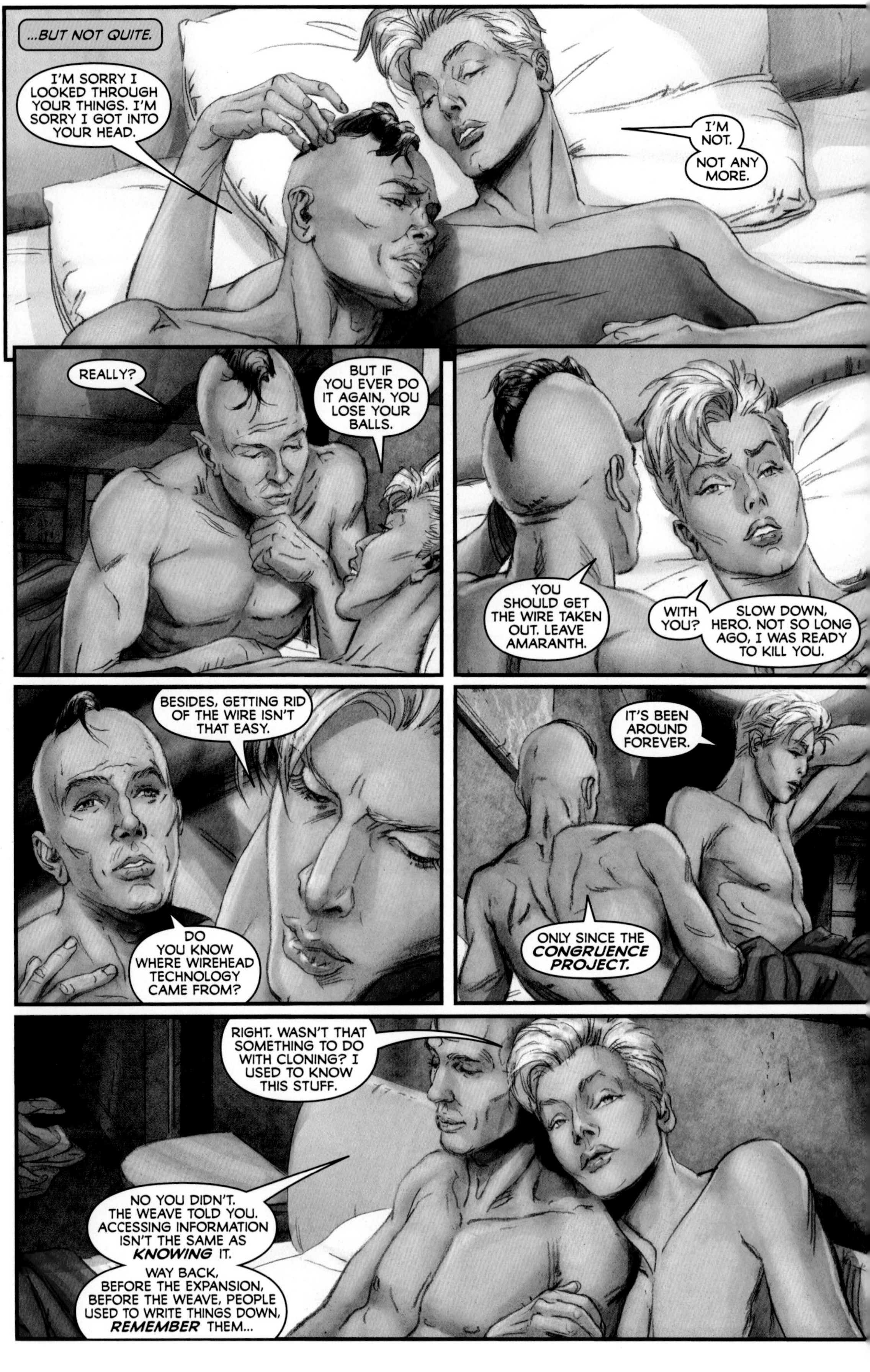
...BUT NOT QUITE.
I'M SORRY I LOOKED THROUGH YOUR THINGS. I'M SORRY I GOT INTO YOUR HEAD.
I'M NOT.
NOT ANY MORE.
REALLY?
BUT IF YOU EVER DO IT AGAIN, YOU LOSE YOUR BALLS.
YOU SHOULD GET THE WIRE TAKEN OUT. LEAVE AMARANTH.
WITH YOU?
SLOW DOWN, HERO. NOT SO LONG AGO, I WAS READY TO KILL YOU.
BESIDES, GETTING RID OF THE WIRE ISN'T THAT EASY.
DO YOU KNOW WHERE WIREHEAD TECHNOLOGY CAME FROM?
IT'S BEEN AROUND FOREVER.
ONLY SINCE THE *CONGRUENCE PROJECT.*
RIGHT. WASN'T THAT SOMETHING TO DO WITH CLONING? I USED TO KNOW THIS STUFF.
NO YOU DIDN'T. THE WEAVE TOLD YOU. ACCESSING INFORMATION ISN'T THE SAME AS ***KNOWING*** IT.
WAY BACK, BEFORE THE EXPANSION, BEFORE THE WEAVE, PEOPLE USED TO WRITE THINGS DOWN, ***REMEMBER*** THEM...

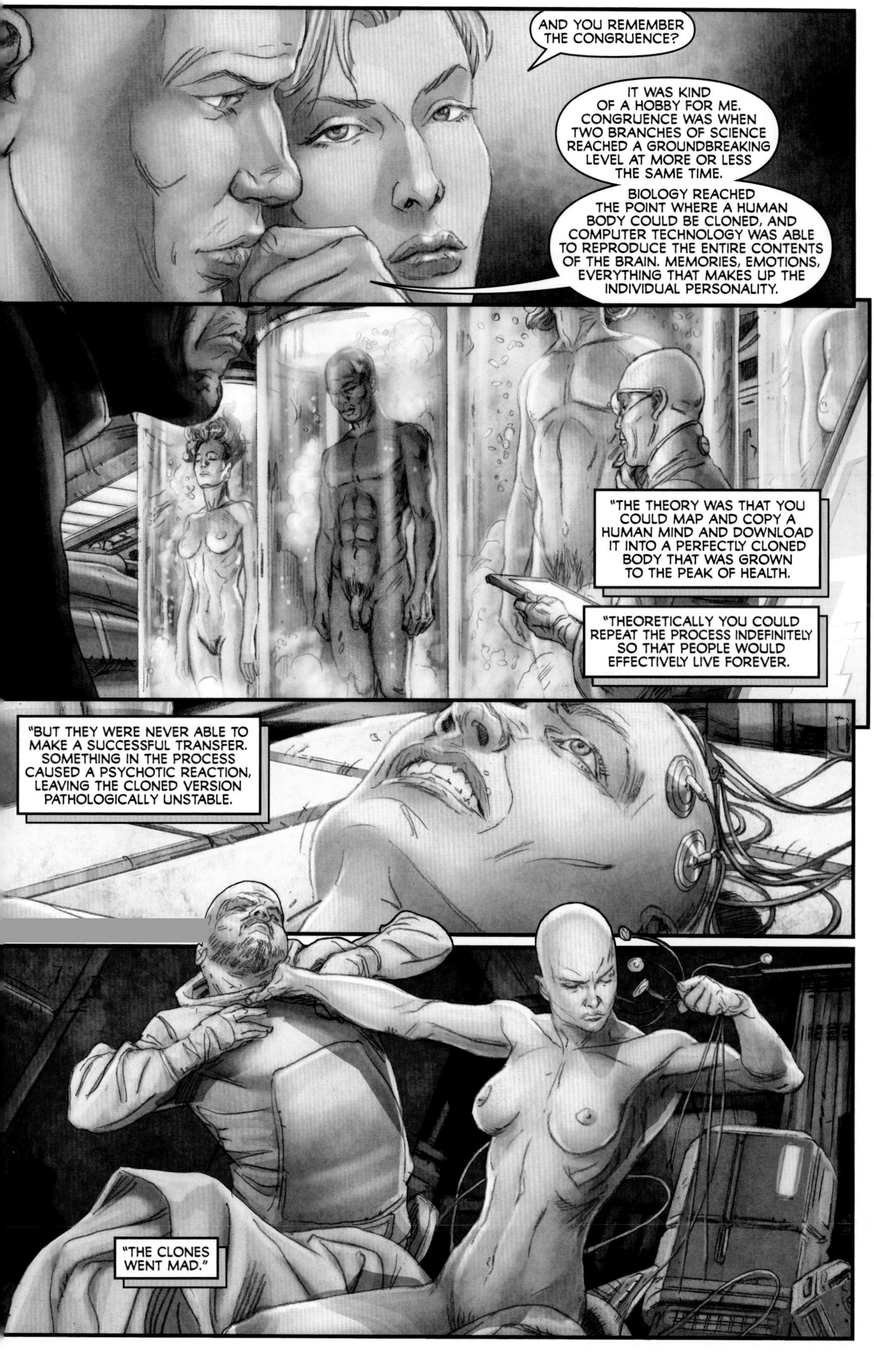
AND YOU REMEMBER THE CONGRUENCE?
IT WAS KIND OF A HOBBY FOR ME. CONGRUENCE WAS WHEN TWO BRANCHES OF SCIENCE REACHED A GROUNDBREAKING LEVEL AT MORE OR LESS THE SAME TIME.
BIOLOGY REACHED THE POINT WHERE A HUMAN BODY COULD BE CLONED, AND COMPUTER TECHNOLOGY WAS ABLE TO REPRODUCE THE ENTIRE CONTENTS OF THE BRAIN. MEMORIES, EMOTIONS, EVERYTHING THAT MAKES UP THE INDIVIDUAL PERSONALITY.
"THE THEORY WAS THAT YOU COULD MAP AND COPY A HUMAN MIND AND DOWNLOAD IT INTO A PERFECTLY CLONED BODY THAT WAS GROWN TO THE PEAK OF HEALTH.
"THEORETICALLY YOU COULD REPEAT THE PROCESS INDEFINITELY SO THAT PEOPLE WOULD EFFECTIVELY LIVE FOREVER.
"BUT THEY WERE NEVER ABLE TO MAKE A SUCCESSFUL TRANSFER. SOMETHING IN THE PROCESS CAUSED A PSYCHOTIC REACTION, LEAVING THE CLONED VERSION PATHOLOGICALLY UNSTABLE.
"THE CLONES WENT MAD."

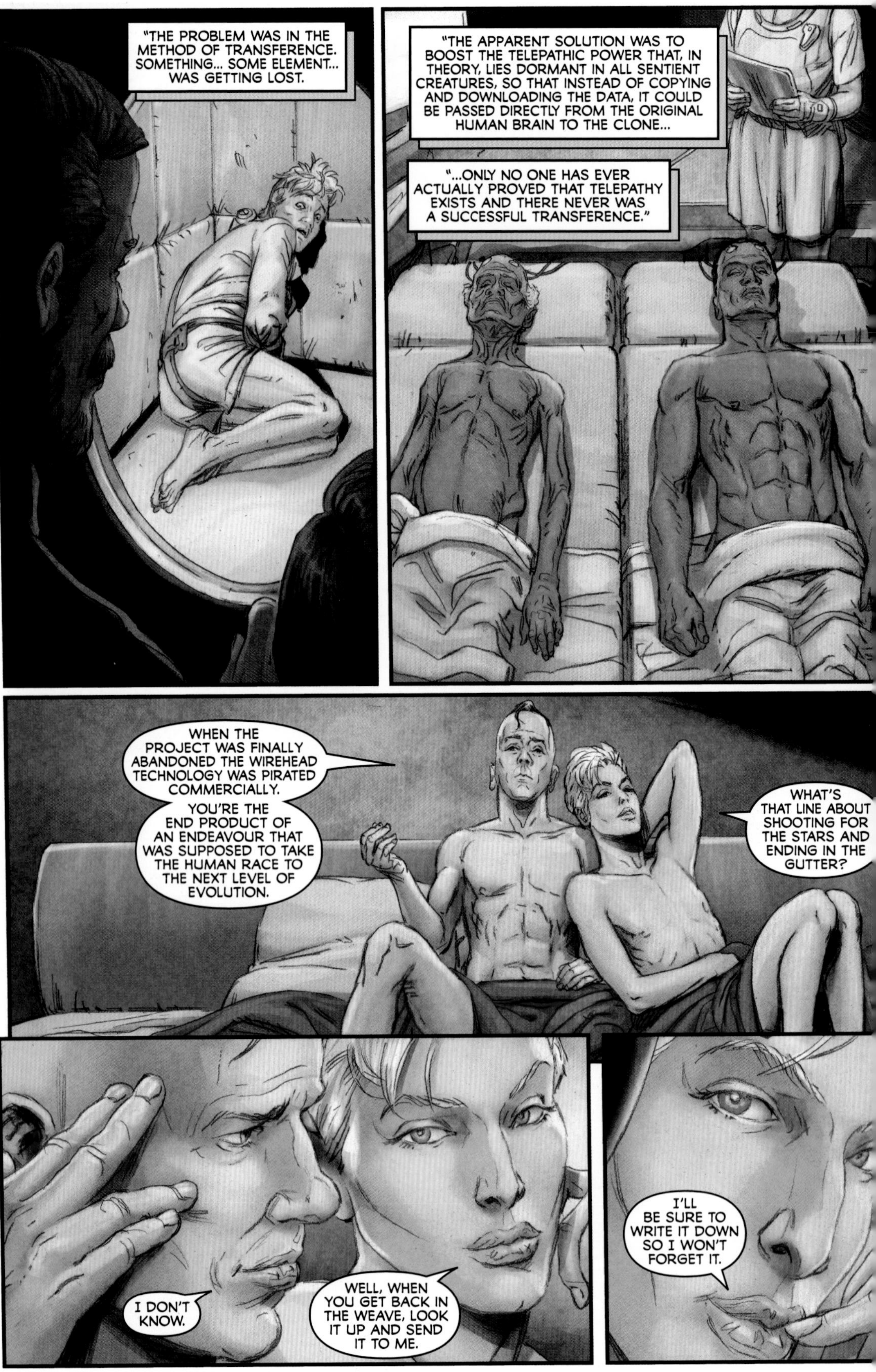

"THE PROBLEM WAS IN THE METHOD OF TRANSFERENCE. SOMETHING... SOME ELEMENT... WAS GETTING LOST.
"THE APPARENT SOLUTION WAS TO BOOST THE TELEPATHIC POWER THAT, IN THEORY, LIES DORMANT IN ALL SENTIENT CREATURES, SO THAT INSTEAD OF COPYING AND DOWNLOADING THE DATA, IT COULD BE PASSED DIRECTLY FROM THE ORIGINAL HUMAN BRAIN TO THE CLONE...
"...ONLY NO ONE HAS EVER ACTUALLY PROVED THAT TELEPATHY EXISTS AND THERE NEVER WAS A SUCCESSFUL TRANSFERENCE."
WHEN THE PROJECT WAS FINALLY ABANDONED THE WIREHEAD TECHNOLOGY WAS PIRATED COMMERCIALLY.
YOU'RE THE END PRODUCT OF AN ENDEAVOUR THAT WAS SUPPOSED TO TAKE THE HUMAN RACE TO THE NEXT LEVEL OF EVOLUTION.
WHAT'S THAT LINE ABOUT SHOOTING FOR THE STARS AND ENDING IN THE GUTTER?
I DON'T KNOW.
WELL, WHEN YOU GET BACK IN THE WEAVE, LOOK IT UP AND SEND IT TO ME.
I'LL BE SURE TO WRITE IT DOWN SO I WON'T FORGET IT.

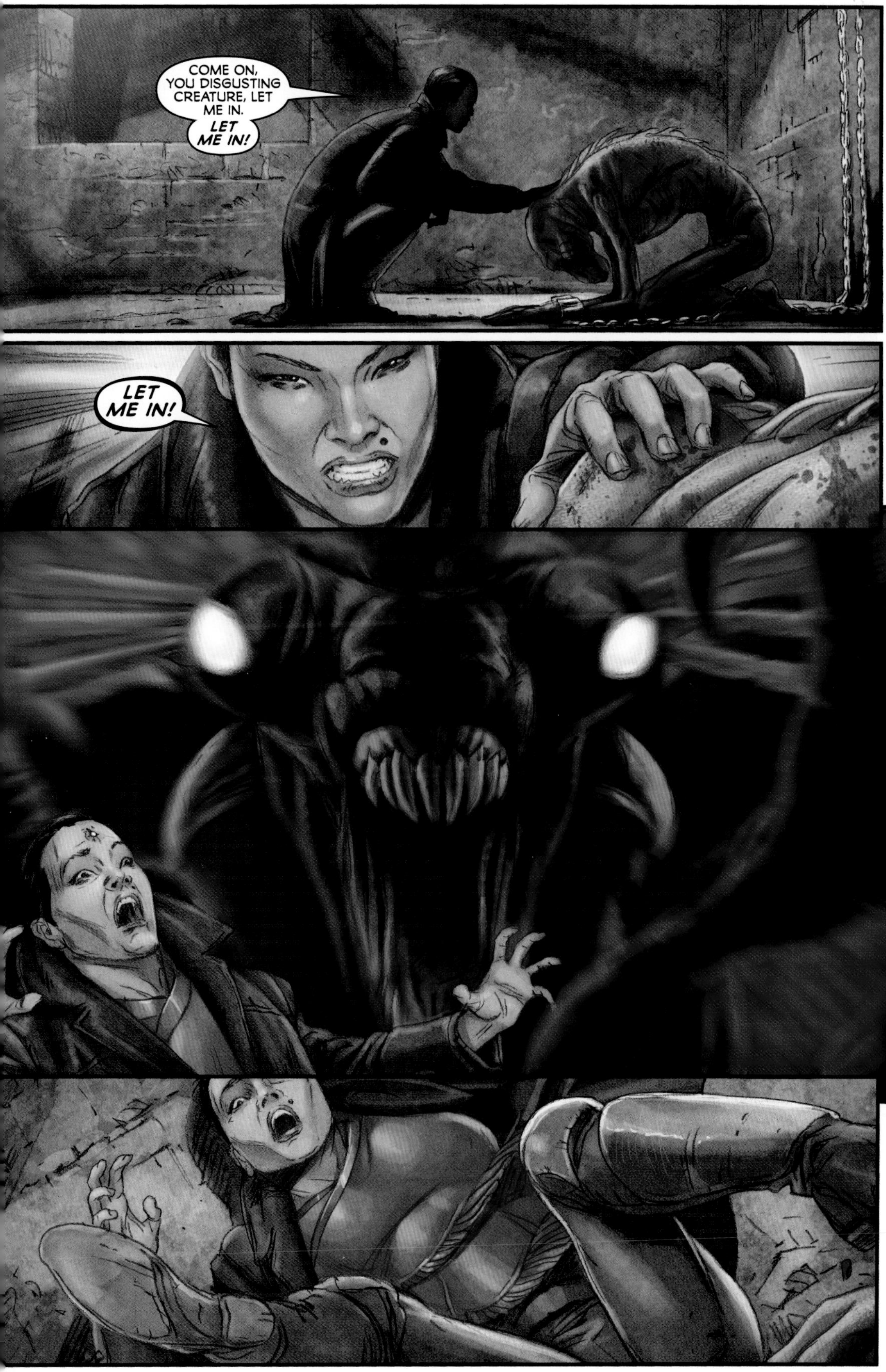
COME ON, YOU DISGUSTING CREATURE, LET ME IN.
LET ME IN!
LET ME IN!

I'M NOT GOING TO LEARN ANYTHING FROM YOU, AM I? WHATEVER THAT THING WAS, IT FRIGHTENED YOU SO MUCH...IT'S ALL YOU CAN THINK OF...

POOR THING.

KILL IT.

YES, DIRECTOR. UM...

WHAT IS HE DOING HERE?

HE'S BEEN LURKING AROUND SINCE YOU WENT IN THERE.

IT'S NOT DARK... THEY SAID IT WAS DARK. BUT IT'S NOT...IT'S LIGHT...IT ILLUMINATES... BURNS AWAY THE SHADOWS...

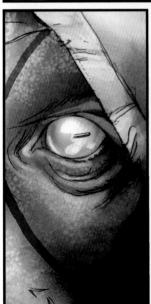

YOU HAVE IT! THERE! THERE! THE EYE! GIVE IT TO ME...

PLUCK IT OUT...

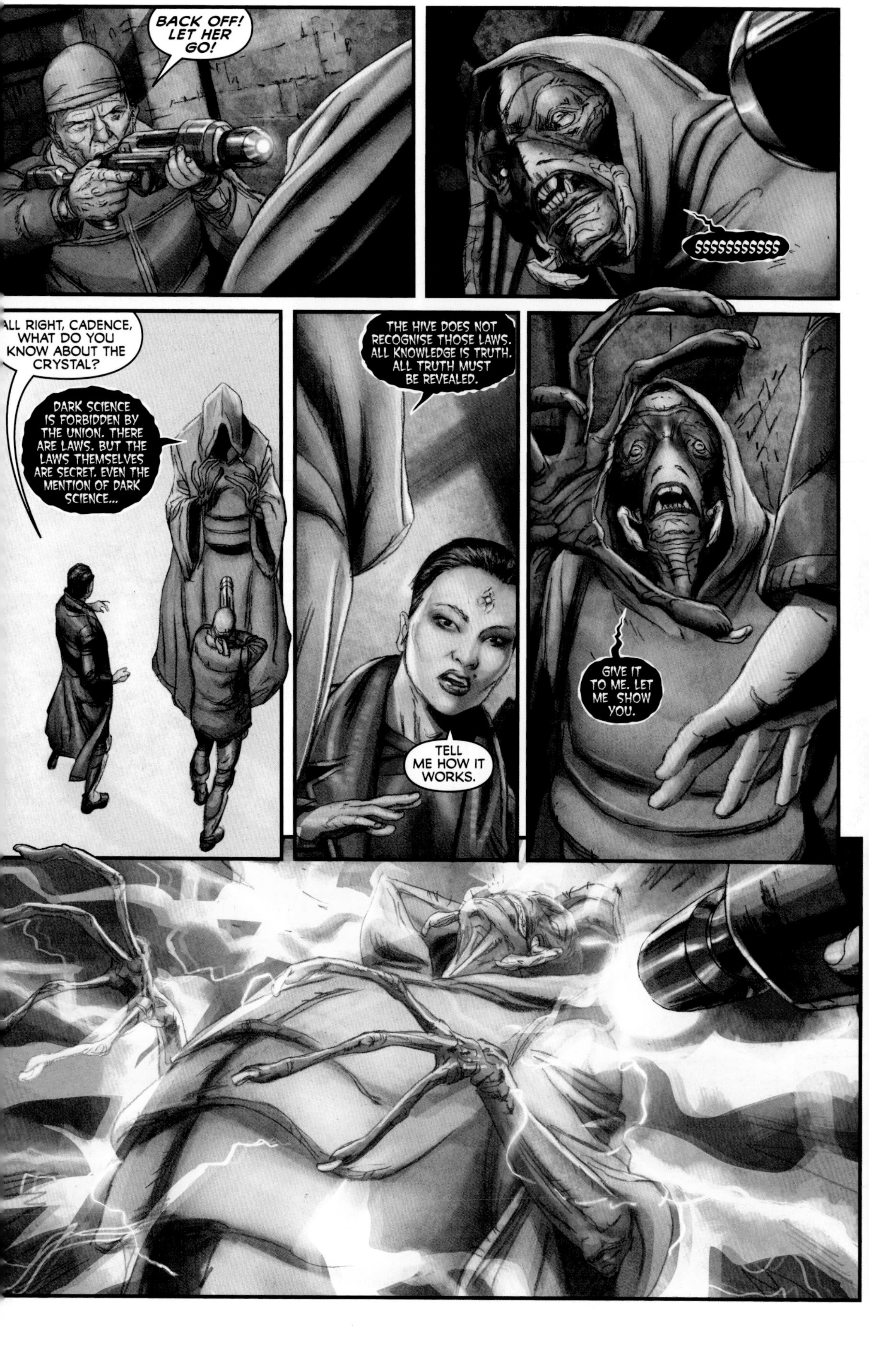
BACK OFF! LET HER GO!
SSSSSSSSSSS
ALL RIGHT, CADENCE, WHAT DO YOU KNOW ABOUT THE CRYSTAL?
DARK SCIENCE IS FORBIDDEN BY THE UNION. THERE ARE LAWS. BUT THE LAWS THEMSELVES ARE SECRET. EVEN THE MENTION OF DARK SCIENCE...
THE HIVE DOES NOT RECOGNISE THOSE LAWS. ALL KNOWLEDGE IS TRUTH. ALL TRUTH MUST BE REVEALED.
TELL ME HOW IT WORKS.
GIVE IT TO ME. LET ME SHOW YOU.

I TOLD YOU – *HANDS OFF!*

GET HIM TO MEDICAL. TELL THEM TO KEEP HIM SEDATED UNTIL I SAY OTHERWISE.

DIRECTOR, THE STORM WARNING–

DEAL WITH IT!

IDIOTS!

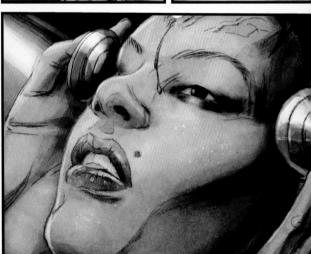

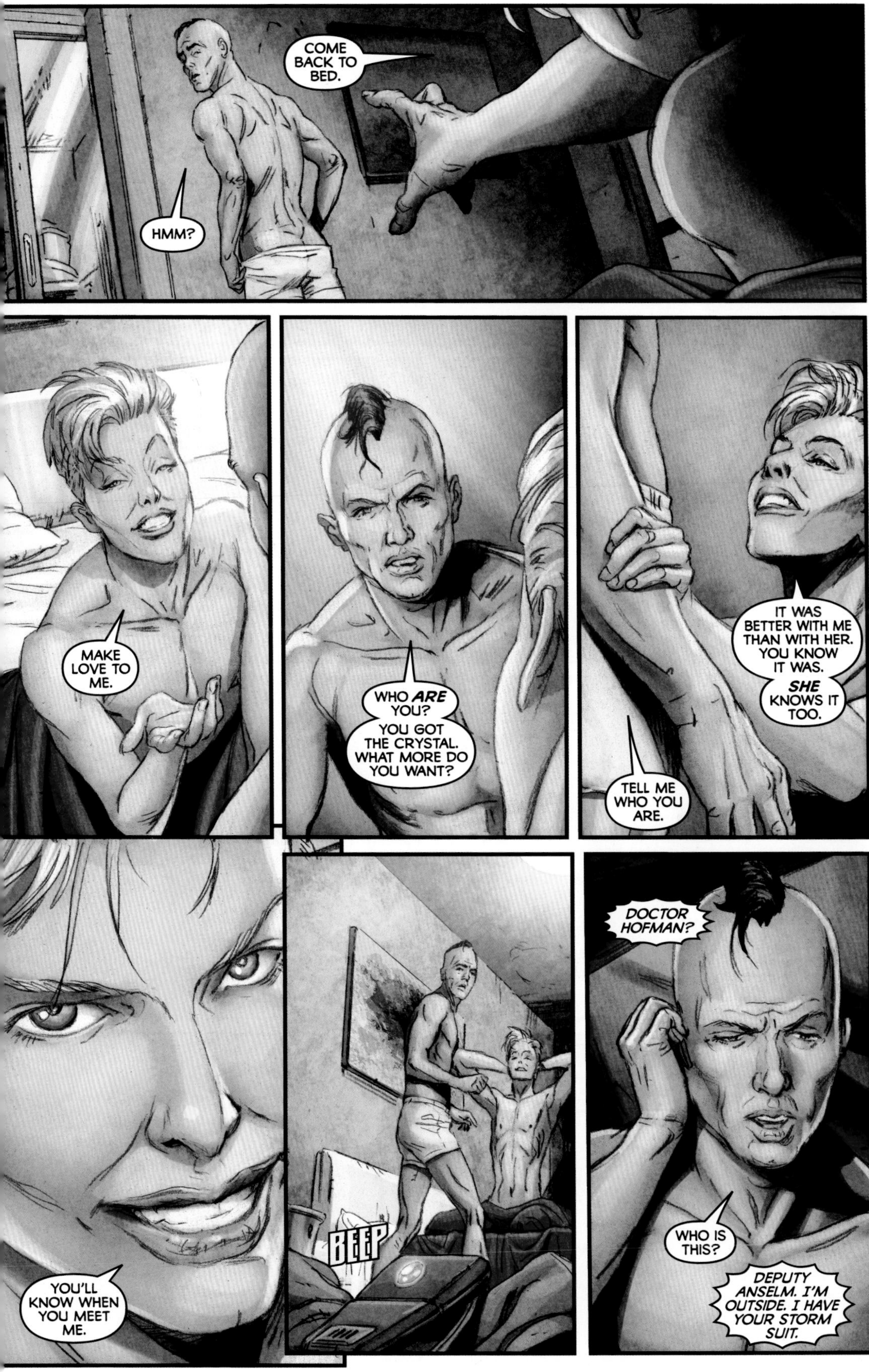
COME BACK TO BED.
HMM?
MAKE LOVE TO ME.
WHO *ARE* YOU?
YOU GOT THE CRYSTAL. WHAT MORE DO YOU WANT?
IT WAS BETTER WITH ME THAN WITH HER. YOU KNOW IT WAS.
SHE KNOWS IT TOO.
TELL ME WHO YOU ARE.
YOU'LL KNOW WHEN YOU MEET ME.
BEEP
DOCTOR HOFMAN?
WHO IS THIS?
DEPUTY ANSELM. I'M OUTSIDE. I HAVE YOUR STORM SUIT.

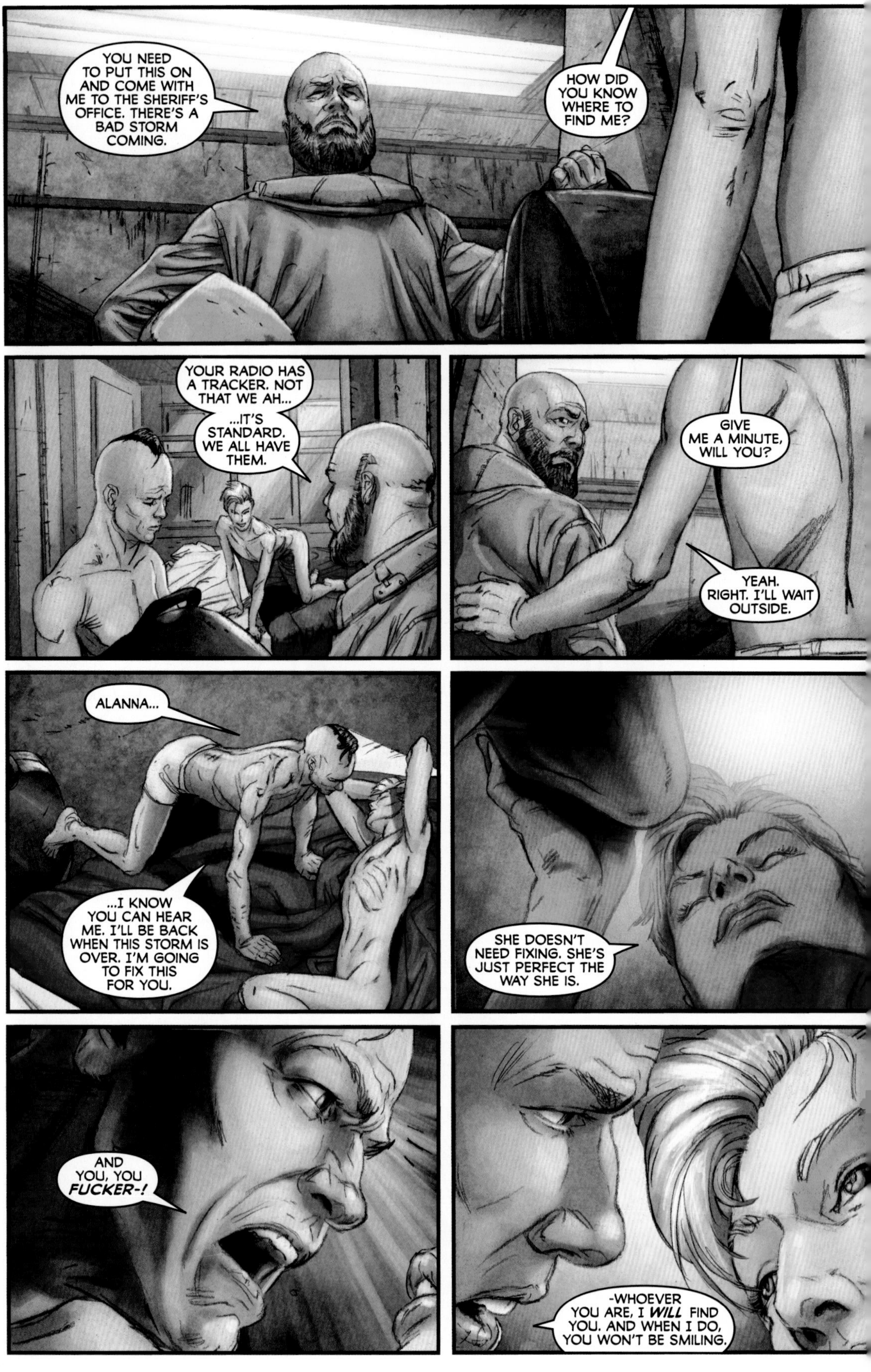

YOU NEED TO PUT THIS ON AND COME WITH ME TO THE SHERIFF'S OFFICE. THERE'S A BAD STORM COMING.
HOW DID YOU KNOW WHERE TO FIND ME?
YOUR RADIO HAS A TRACKER. NOT THAT WE AH...
...IT'S STANDARD. WE ALL HAVE THEM.
GIVE ME A MINUTE, WILL YOU?
YEAH. RIGHT. I'LL WAIT OUTSIDE.
ALANNA...
...I KNOW YOU CAN HEAR ME. I'LL BE BACK WHEN THIS STORM IS OVER. I'M GOING TO FIX THIS FOR YOU.
SHE DOESN'T NEED FIXING. SHE'S JUST PERFECT THE WAY SHE IS.
AND YOU, YOU FUCKER-!
-WHOEVER YOU ARE, I WILL FIND YOU. AND WHEN I DO, YOU WON'T BE SMILING.

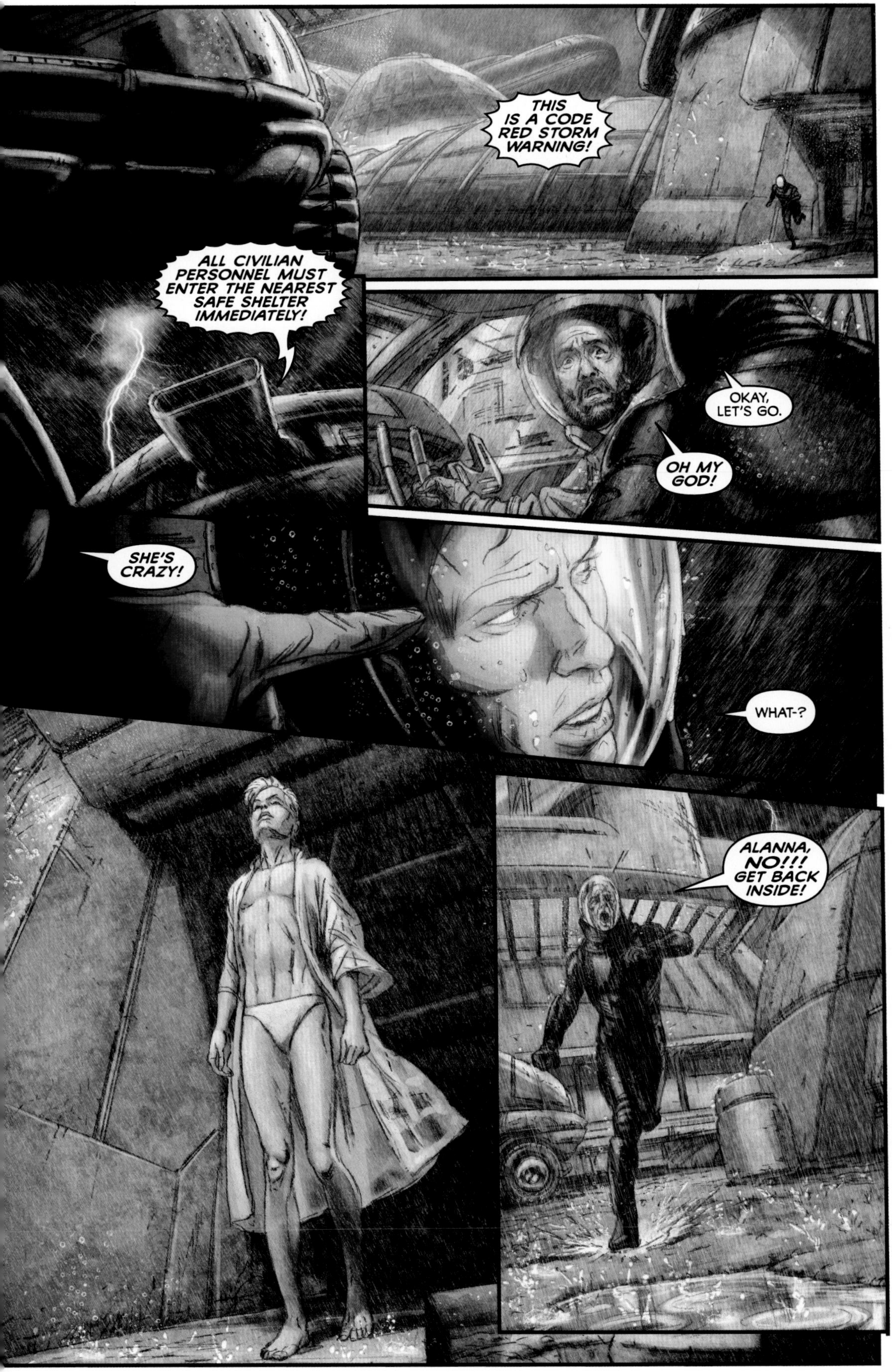
THIS IS A CODE RED STORM WARNING!
ALL CIVILIAN PERSONNEL MUST ENTER THE NEAREST SAFE SHELTER IMMEDIATELY!
OKAY, LET'S GO.
OH MY GOD!
SHE'S CRAZY!
WHAT-?
ALANNA, NO!!! GET BACK INSIDE!

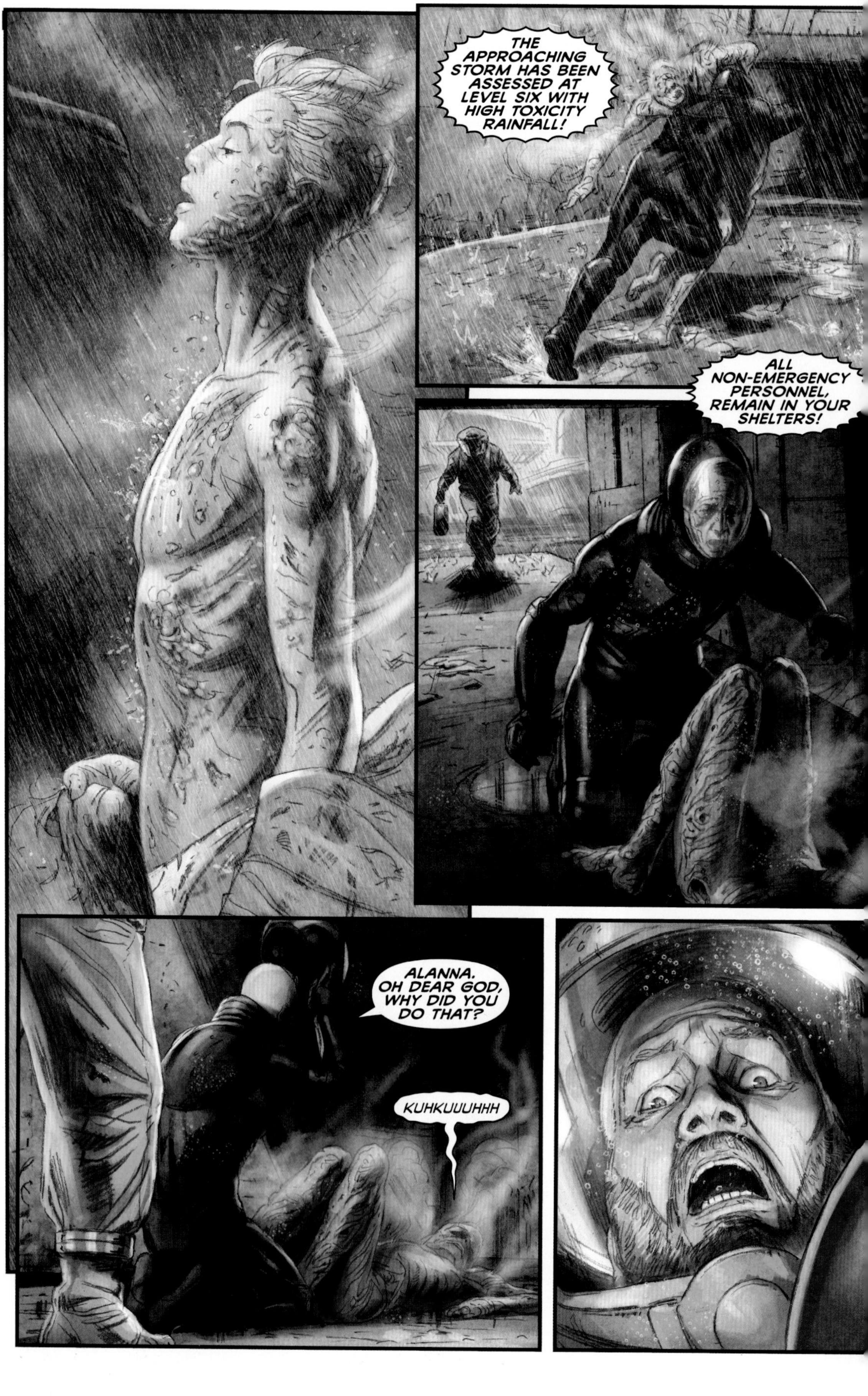
THE APPROACHING STORM HAS BEEN ASSESSED AT LEVEL SIX WITH HIGH TOXICITY RAINFALL!
ALL NON-EMERGENCY PERSONNEL, REMAIN IN YOUR SHELTERS!
ALANNA. OH DEAR GOD, WHY DID YOU DO THAT?
KUHKUUUHHH

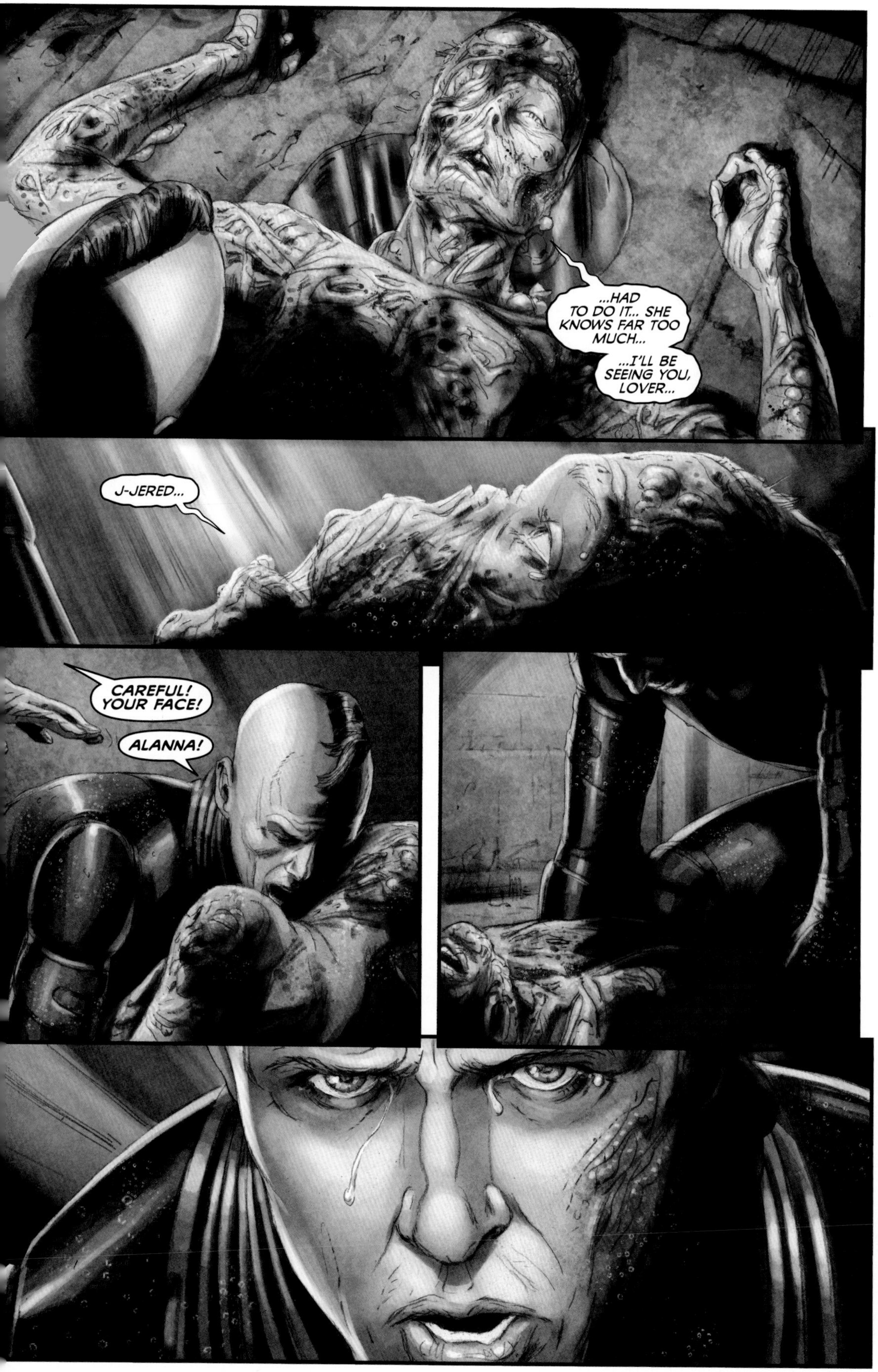
...HAD TO DO IT... SHE KNOWS FAR TOO MUCH...
...I'LL BE SEEING YOU, LOVER...
J-JERED...
CAREFUL! YOUR FACE!
ALANNA!

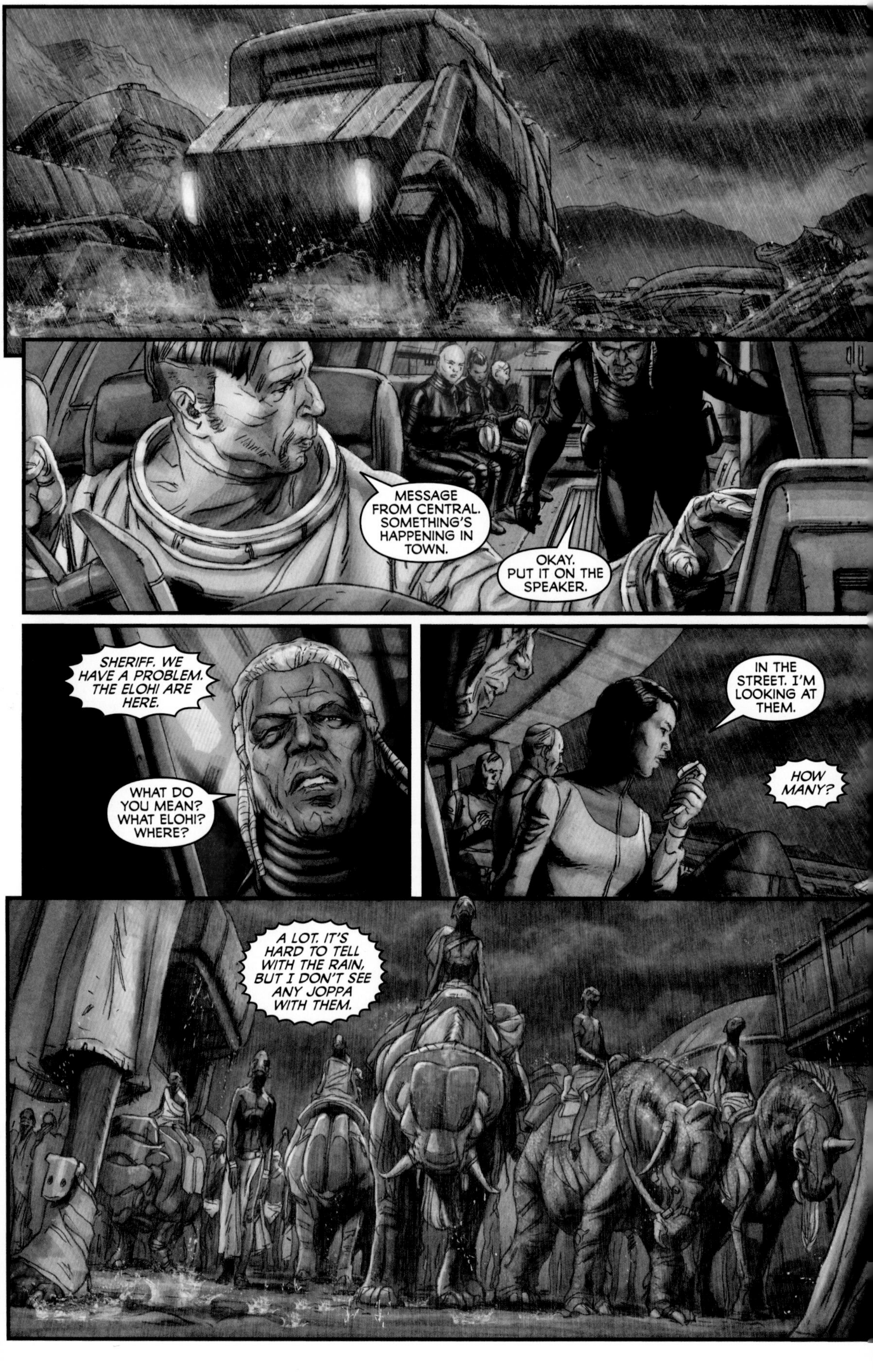
MESSAGE FROM CENTRAL. SOMETHING'S HAPPENING IN TOWN.
OKAY. PUT IT ON THE SPEAKER.
SHERIFF. WE HAVE A PROBLEM. THE ELOHI ARE HERE.
WHAT DO YOU MEAN? WHAT ELOHI? WHERE?
IN THE STREET. I'M LOOKING AT THEM.
HOW MANY?
A LOT. IT'S HARD TO TELL WITH THE RAIN, BUT I DON'T SEE ANY JOPPA WITH THEM.

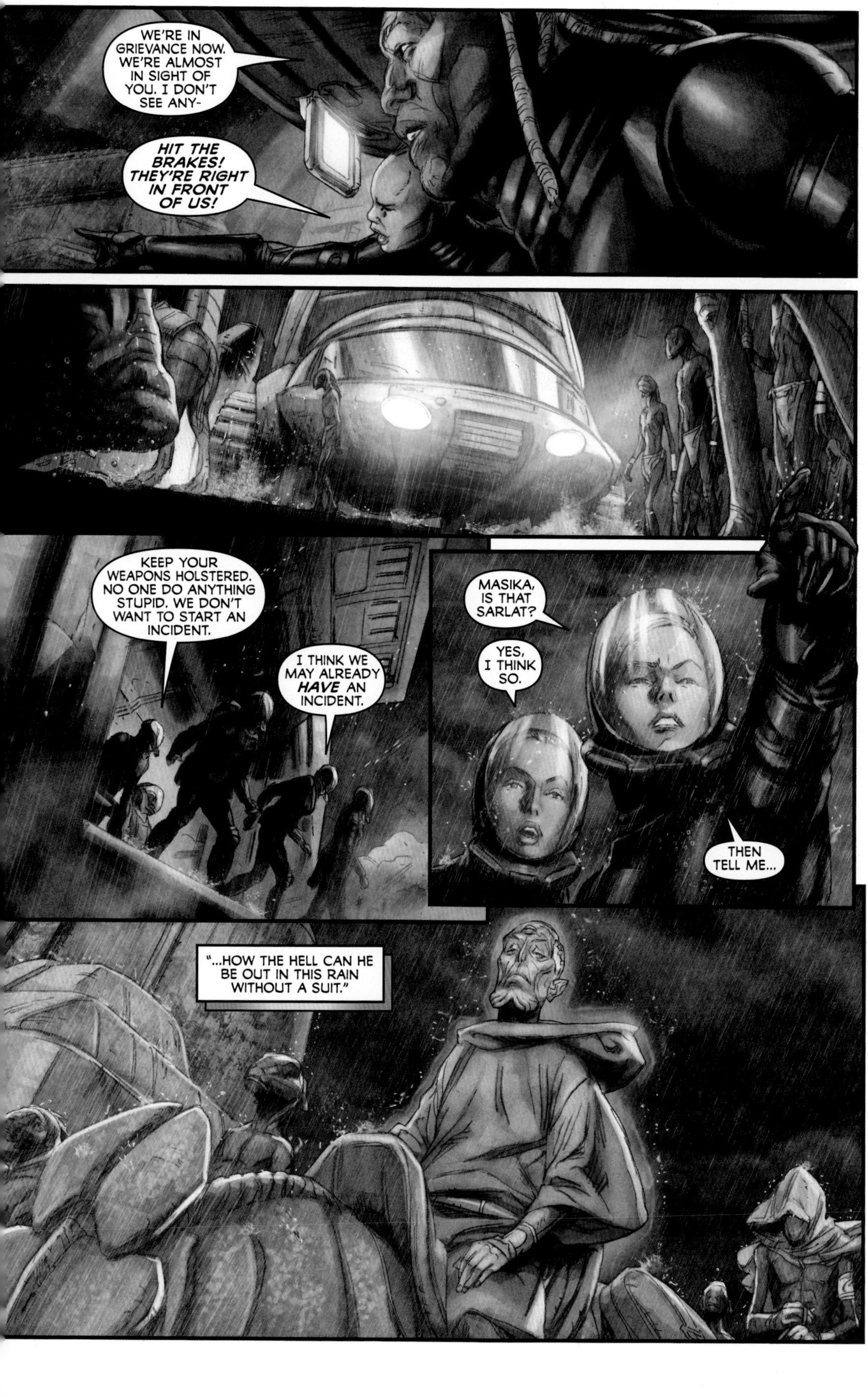
WE'RE IN GRIEVANCE NOW. WE'RE ALMOST IN SIGHT OF YOU. I DON'T SEE ANY-
HIT THE BRAKES! THEY'RE RIGHT IN FRONT OF US!
KEEP YOUR WEAPONS HOLSTERED. NO ONE DO ANYTHING STUPID. WE DON'T WANT TO START AN INCIDENT.
I THINK WE MAY ALREADY HAVE AN INCIDENT.
MASIKA, IS THAT SARLAT?
YES, I THINK SO.
THEN TELL ME...
"...HOW THE HELL CAN HE BE OUT IN THIS RAIN WITHOUT A SUIT."

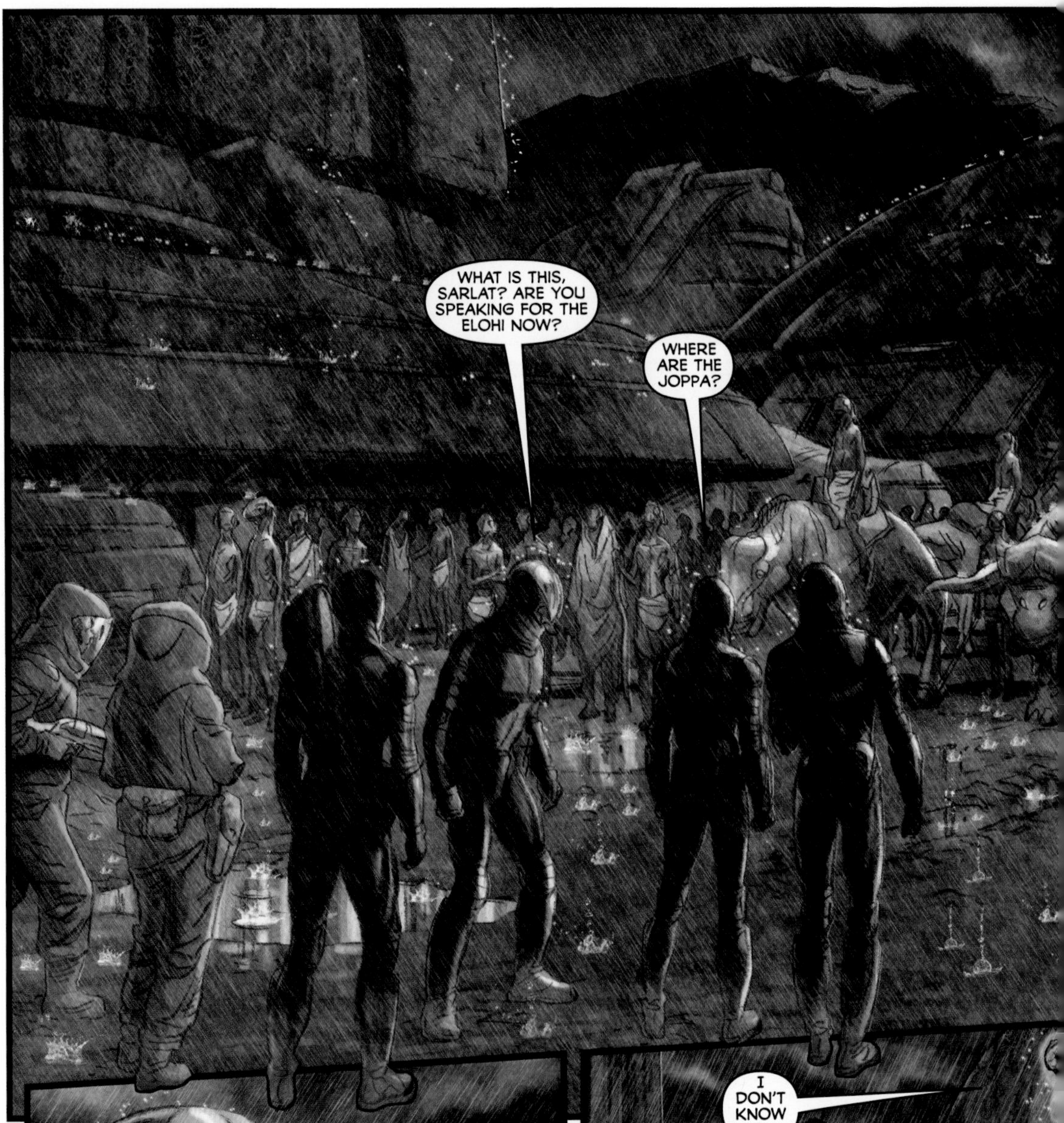
WHAT IS THIS, SARLAT? ARE YOU SPEAKING FOR THE ELOHI NOW?
WHERE ARE THE JOPPA?

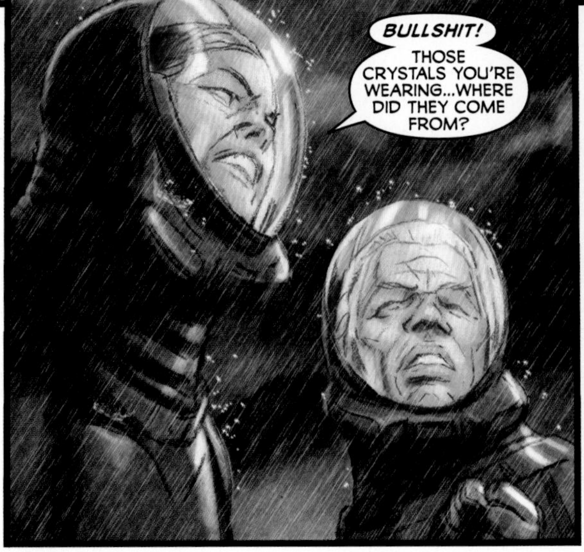
BULLSHIT!
THOSE CRYSTALS YOU'RE WEARING...WHERE DID THEY COME FROM?

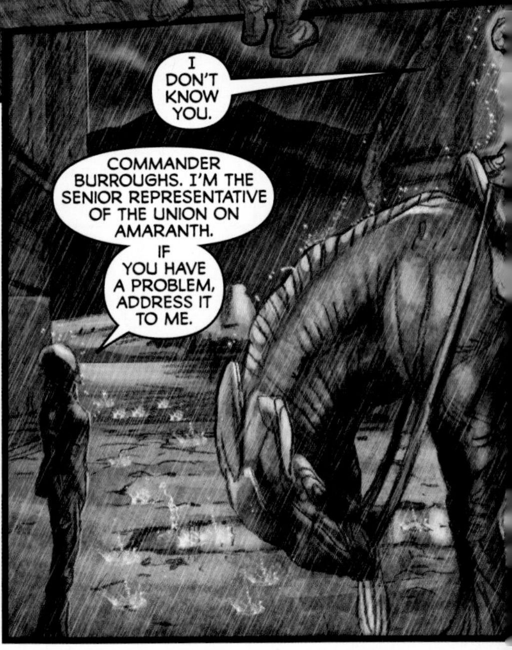
I DON'T KNOW YOU.
COMMANDER BURROUGHS. I'M THE SENIOR REPRESENTATIVE OF THE UNION ON AMARANTH.
IF YOU HAVE A PROBLEM, ADDRESS IT TO ME.

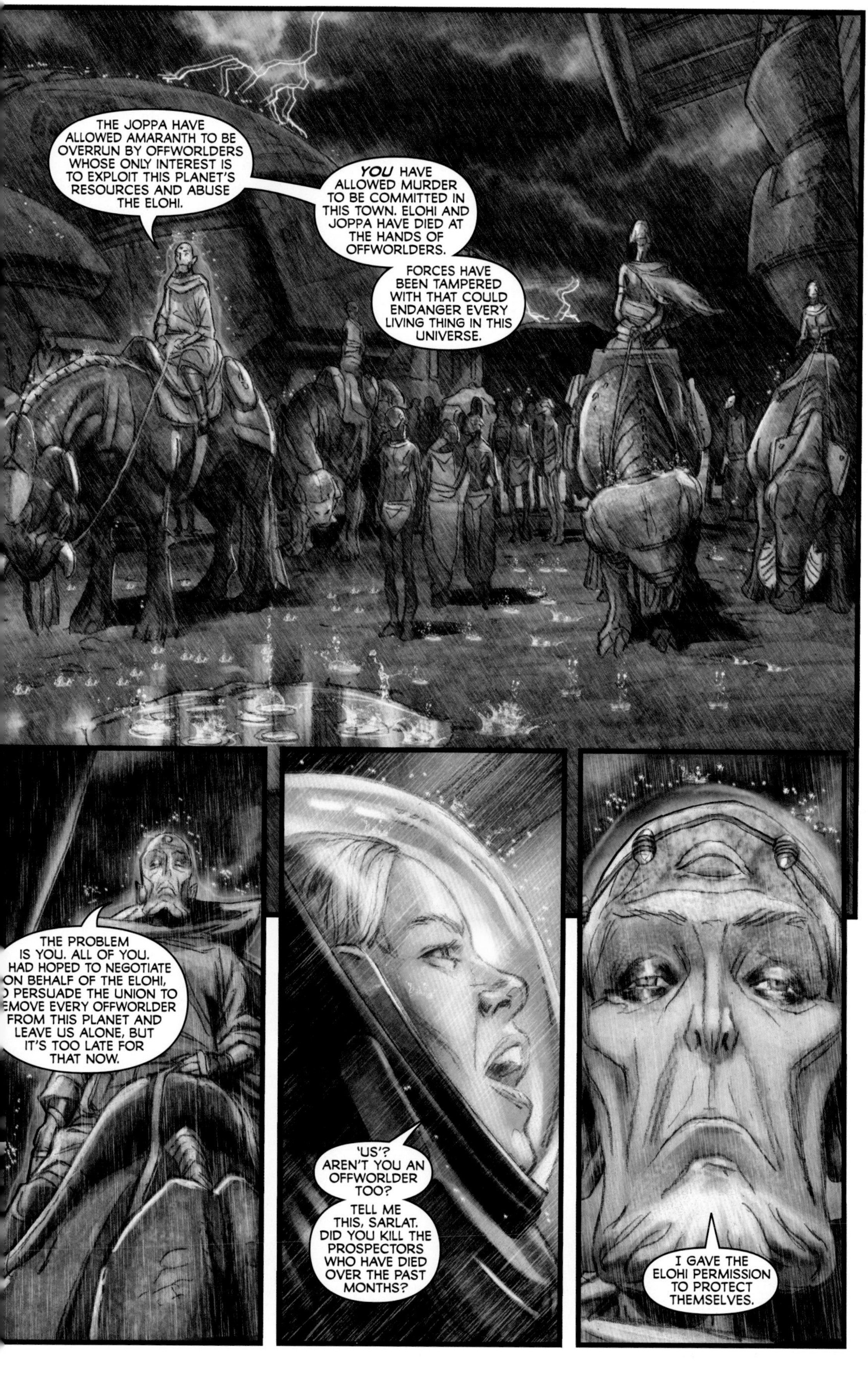
THE JOPPA HAVE ALLOWED AMARANTH TO BE OVERRUN BY OFFWORLDERS WHOSE ONLY INTEREST IS TO EXPLOIT THIS PLANET'S RESOURCES AND ABUSE THE ELOHI.
YOU HAVE ALLOWED MURDER TO BE COMMITTED IN THIS TOWN. ELOHI AND JOPPA HAVE DIED AT THE HANDS OF OFFWORLDERS.
FORCES HAVE BEEN TAMPERED WITH THAT COULD ENDANGER EVERY LIVING THING IN THIS UNIVERSE.
THE PROBLEM IS YOU. ALL OF YOU. HAD HOPED TO NEGOTIATE ON BEHALF OF THE ELOHI,) PERSUADE THE UNION TO EMOVE EVERY OFFWORLDER FROM THIS PLANET AND LEAVE US ALONE, BUT IT'S TOO LATE FOR THAT NOW.
'US'? AREN'T YOU AN OFFWORLDER TOO?
TELL ME THIS, SARLAT. DID YOU KILL THE PROSPECTORS WHO HAVE DIED OVER THE PAST MONTHS?
I GAVE THE ELOHI PERMISSION TO PROTECT THEMSELVES.

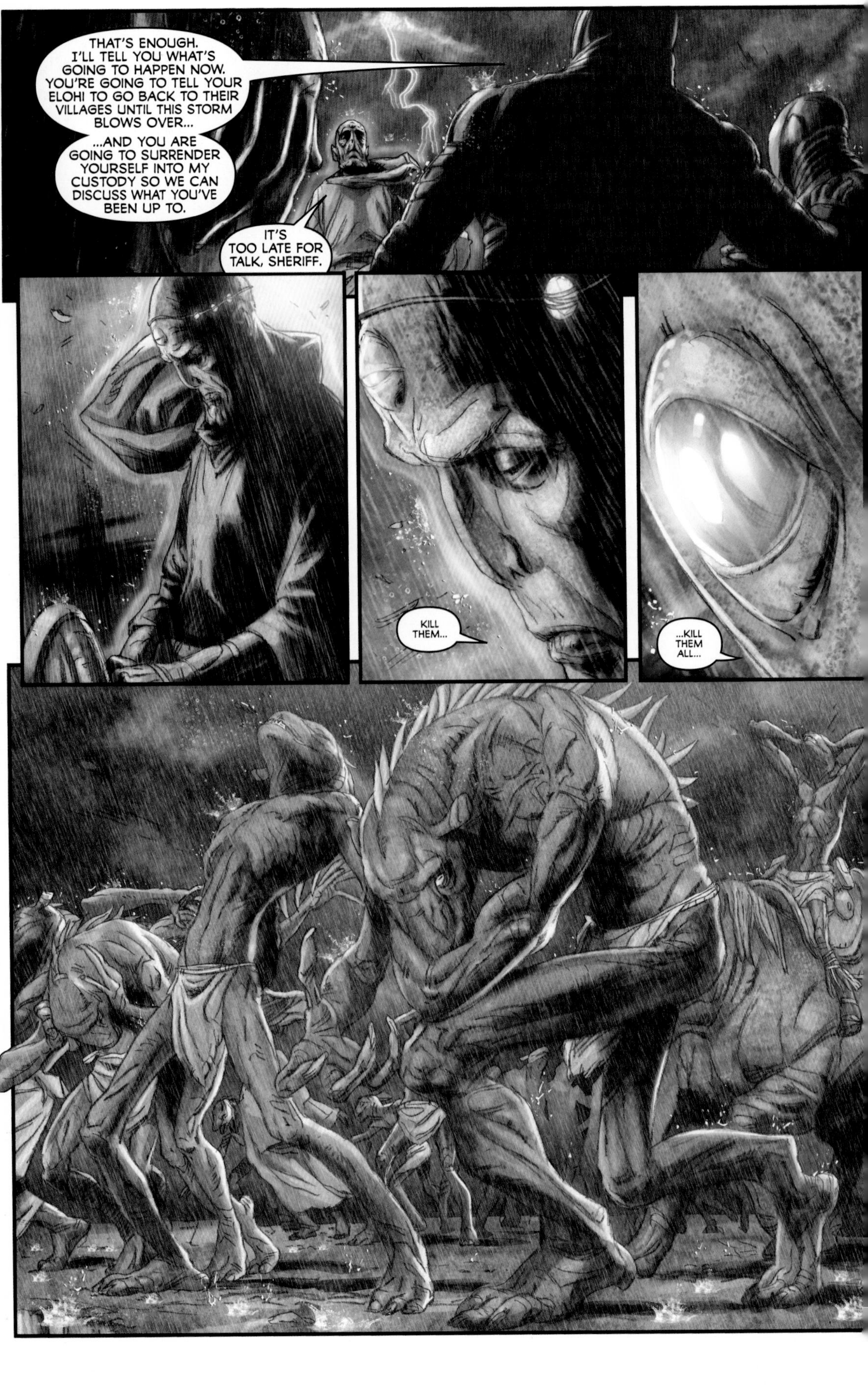

THAT'S ENOUGH. I'LL TELL YOU WHAT'S GOING TO HAPPEN NOW. YOU'RE GOING TO TELL YOUR ELOHI TO GO BACK TO THEIR VILLAGES UNTIL THIS STORM BLOWS OVER...
...AND YOU ARE GOING TO SURRENDER YOURSELF INTO MY CUSTODY SO WE CAN DISCUSS WHAT YOU'VE BEEN UP TO.
IT'S TOO LATE FOR TALK, SHERIFF.
KILL THEM...
...KILL THEM ALL...

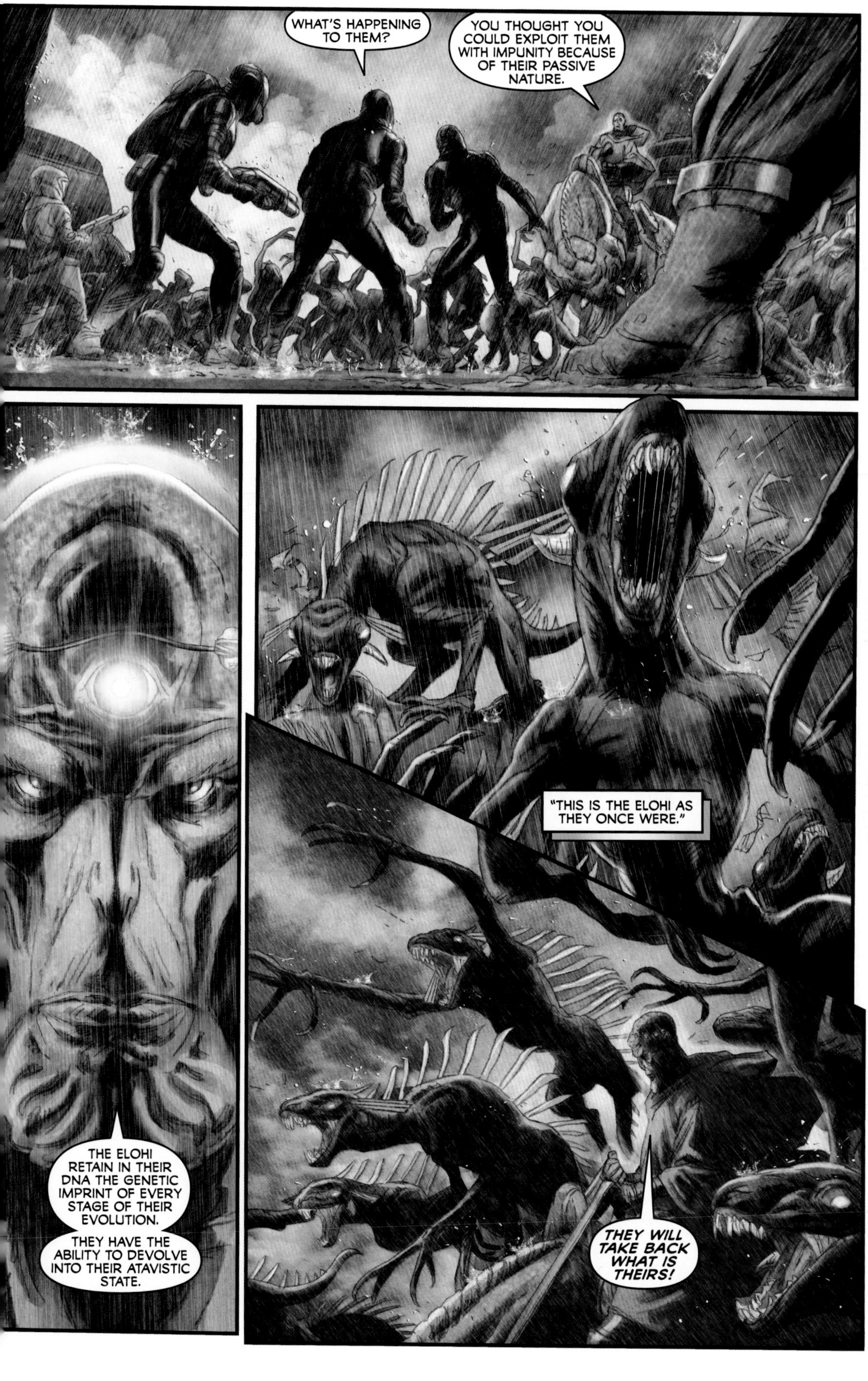
WHAT'S HAPPENING TO THEM?
YOU THOUGHT YOU COULD EXPLOIT THEM WITH IMPUNITY BECAUSE OF THEIR PASSIVE NATURE.
THE ELOHI RETAIN IN THEIR DNA THE GENETIC IMPRINT OF EVERY STAGE OF THEIR EVOLUTION.
THEY HAVE THE ABILITY TO DEVOLVE INTO THEIR ATAVISTIC STATE.
"THIS IS THE ELOHI AS THEY ONCE WERE."
THEY WILL TAKE BACK WHAT IS THEIRS!

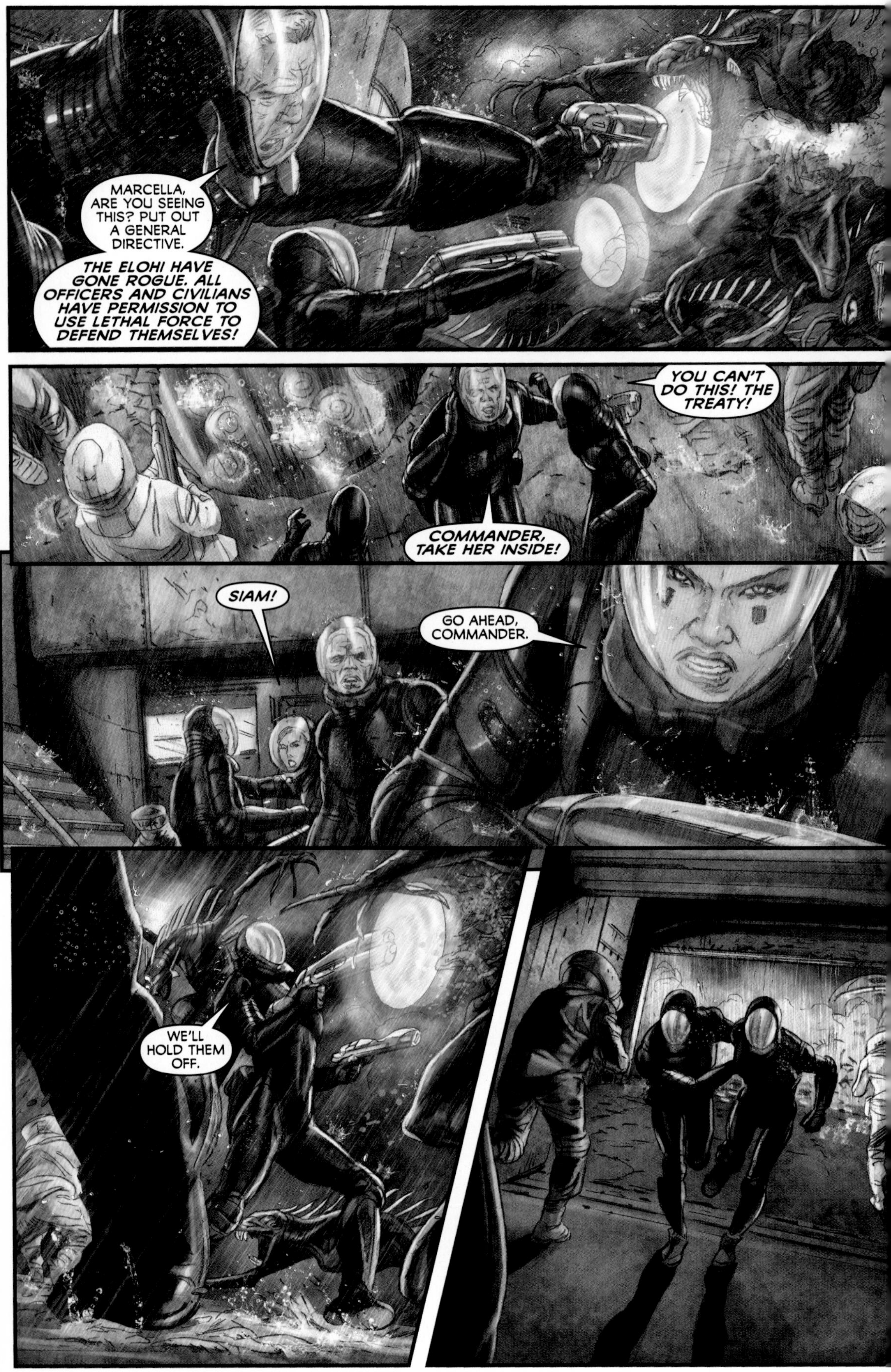
MARCELLA, ARE YOU SEEING THIS? PUT OUT A GENERAL DIRECTIVE.
THE ELOHI HAVE GONE ROGUE. ALL OFFICERS AND CIVILIANS HAVE PERMISSION TO USE LETHAL FORCE TO DEFEND THEMSELVES!
YOU CAN'T DO THIS! THE TREATY!
COMMANDER, TAKE HER INSIDE!
SIAM!
GO AHEAD, COMMANDER.
WE'LL HOLD THEM OFF.

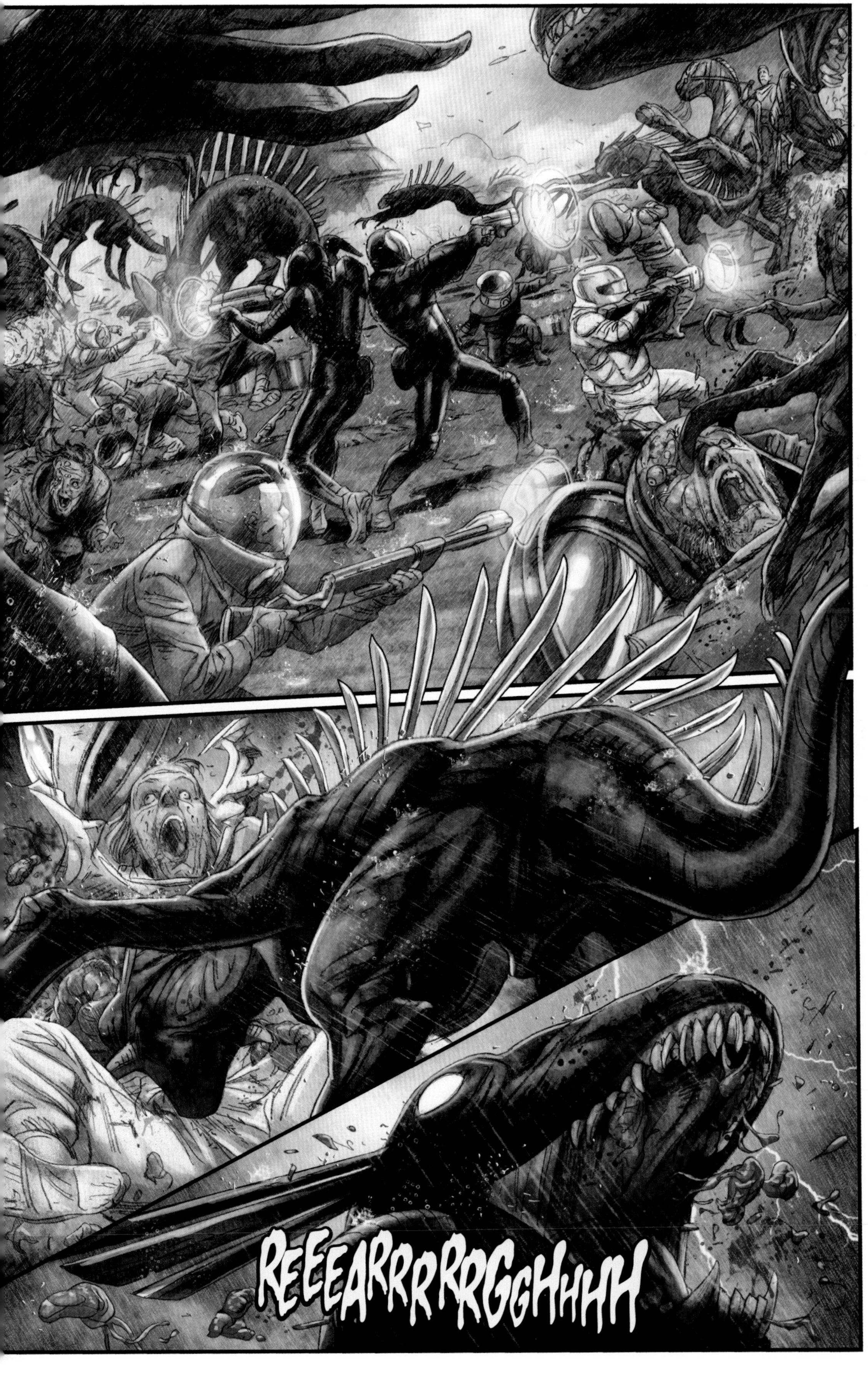
REEEARRRRRGGHHHH

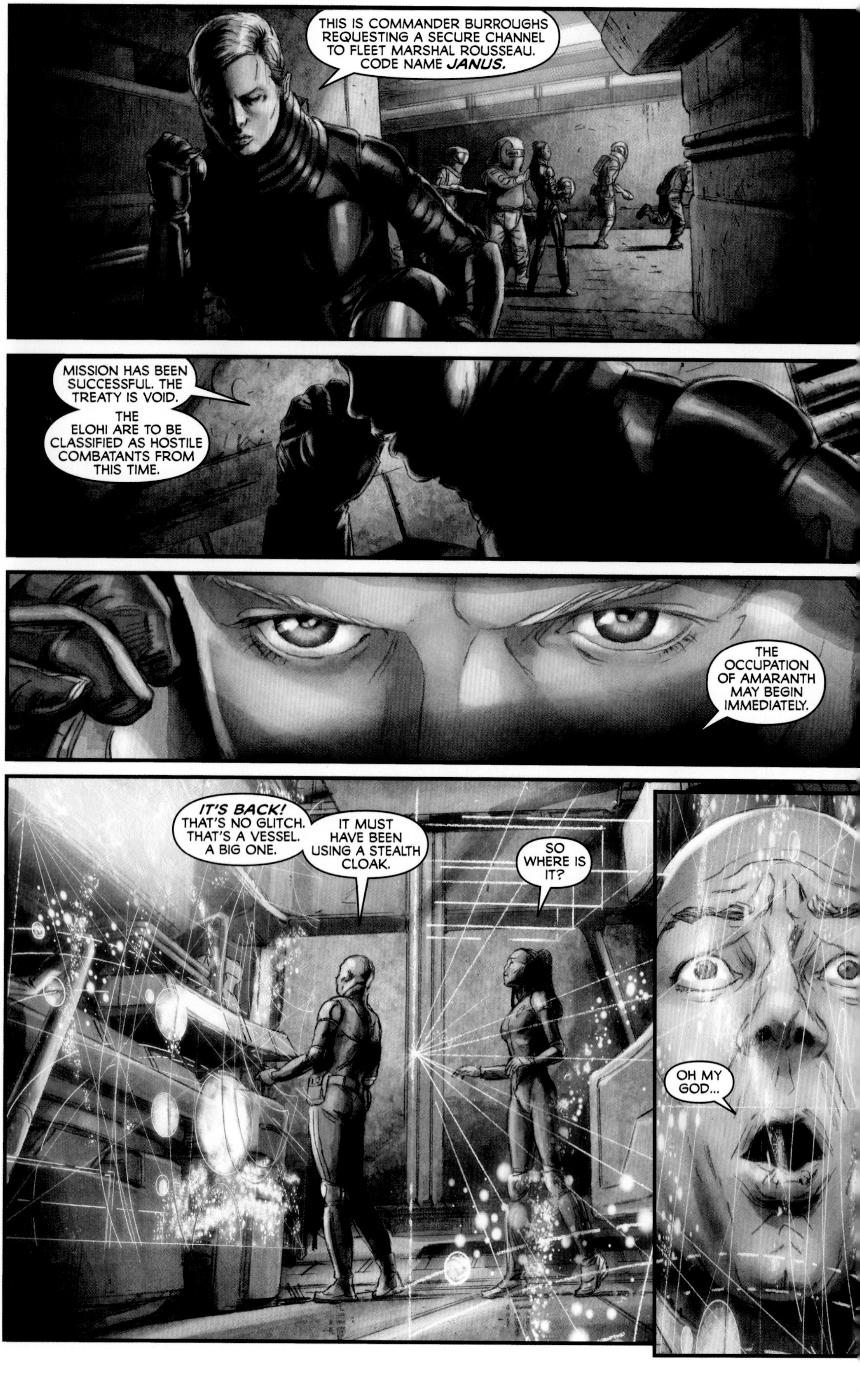
THIS IS COMMANDER BURROUGHS REQUESTING A SECURE CHANNEL TO FLEET MARSHAL ROUSSEAU. CODE NAME *JANUS.*
MISSION HAS BEEN SUCCESSFUL. THE TREATY IS VOID.
THE ELOHI ARE TO BE CLASSIFIED AS HOSTILE COMBATANTS FROM THIS TIME.
THE OCCUPATION OF AMARANTH MAY BEGIN IMMEDIATELY.
IT'S BACK! THAT'S NO GLITCH. THAT'S A VESSEL. A BIG ONE.
IT MUST HAVE BEEN USING A STEALTH CLOAK.
SO WHERE IS IT?
OH MY GOD...

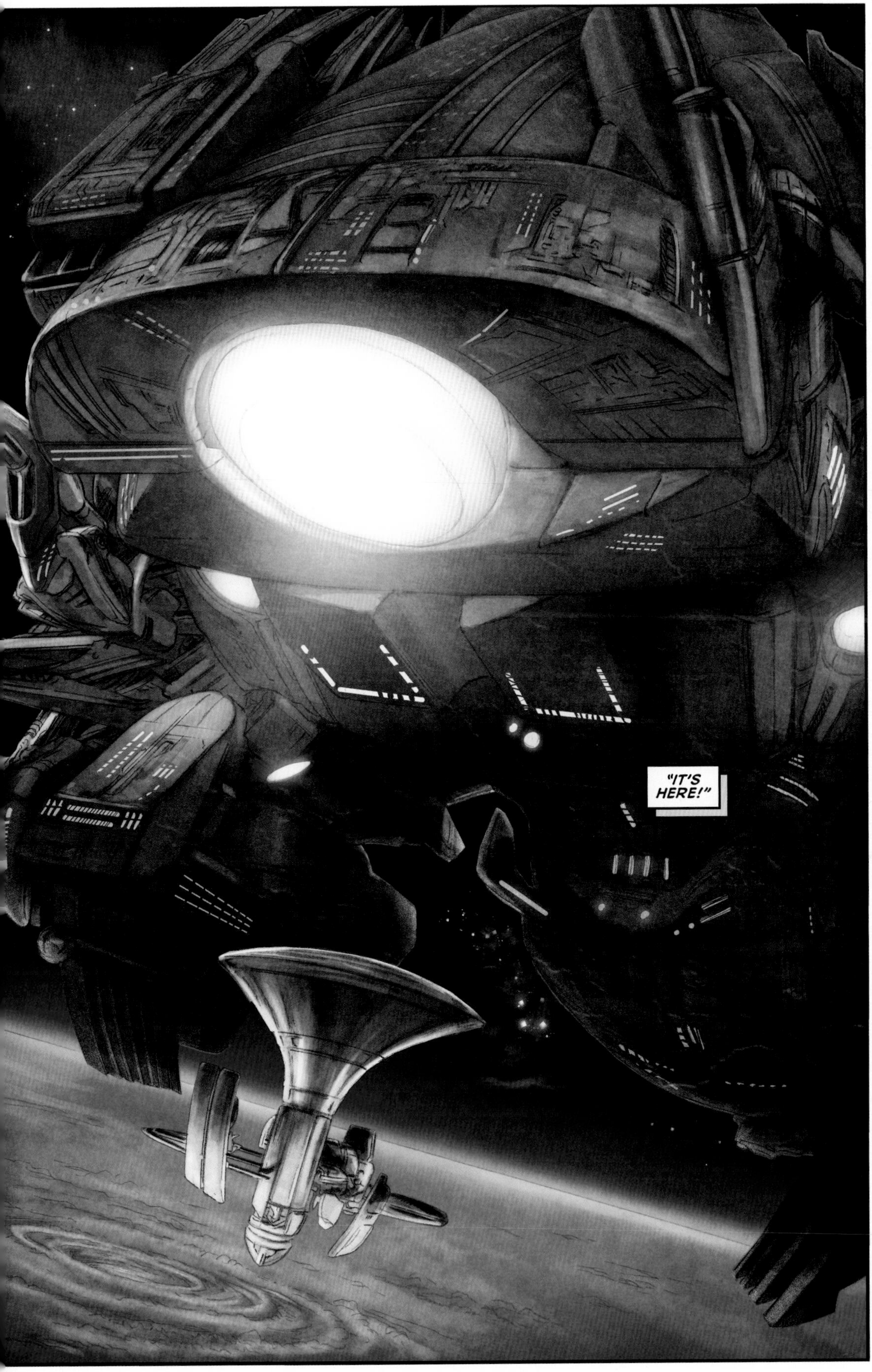
"IT'S HERE!"

"Let your plans be dark
and impenetrable as night,
and when you move,
fall like a thunderbolt."

Sun Tzu – The Art of War

CONTINUES IN

SEASON TWO

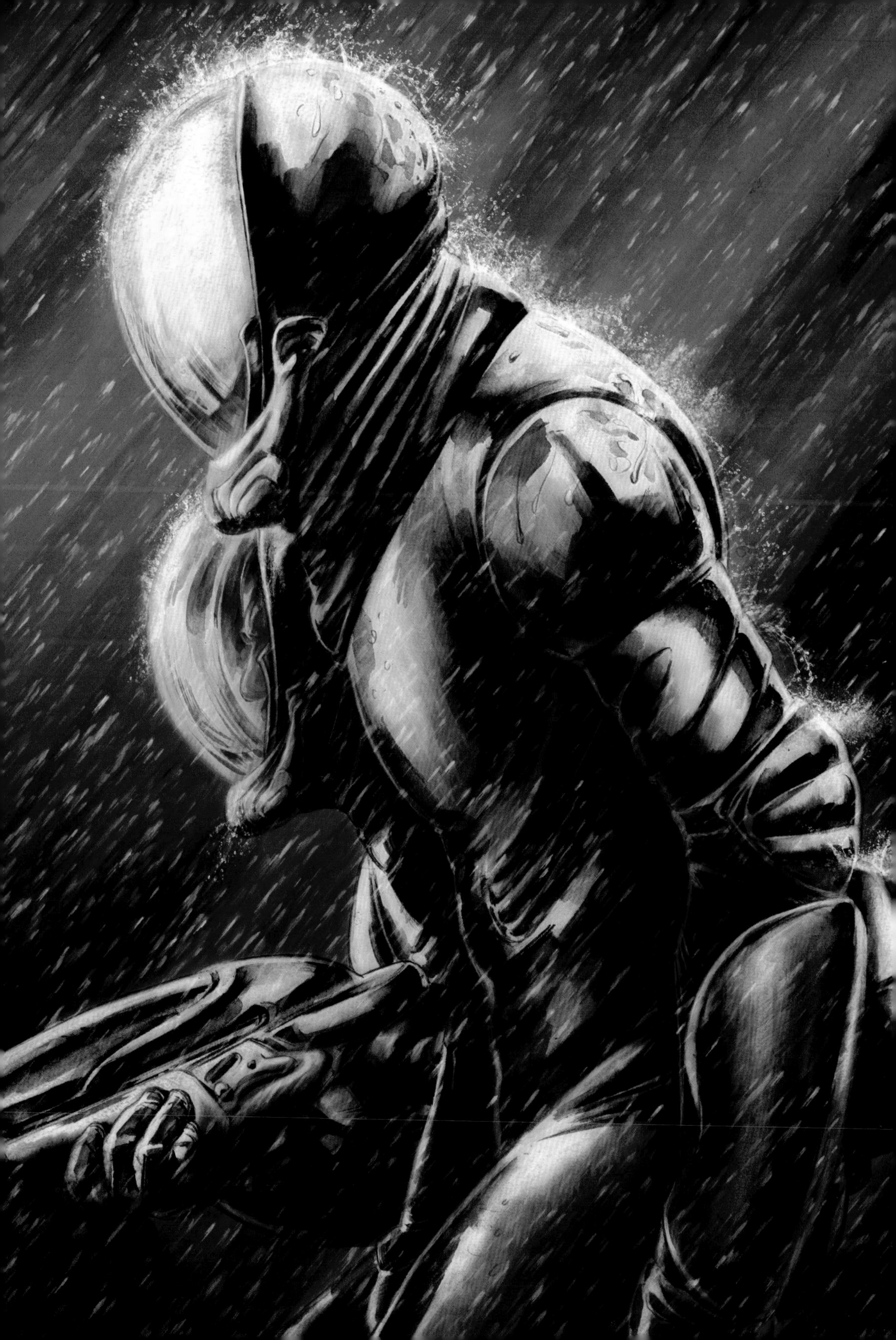

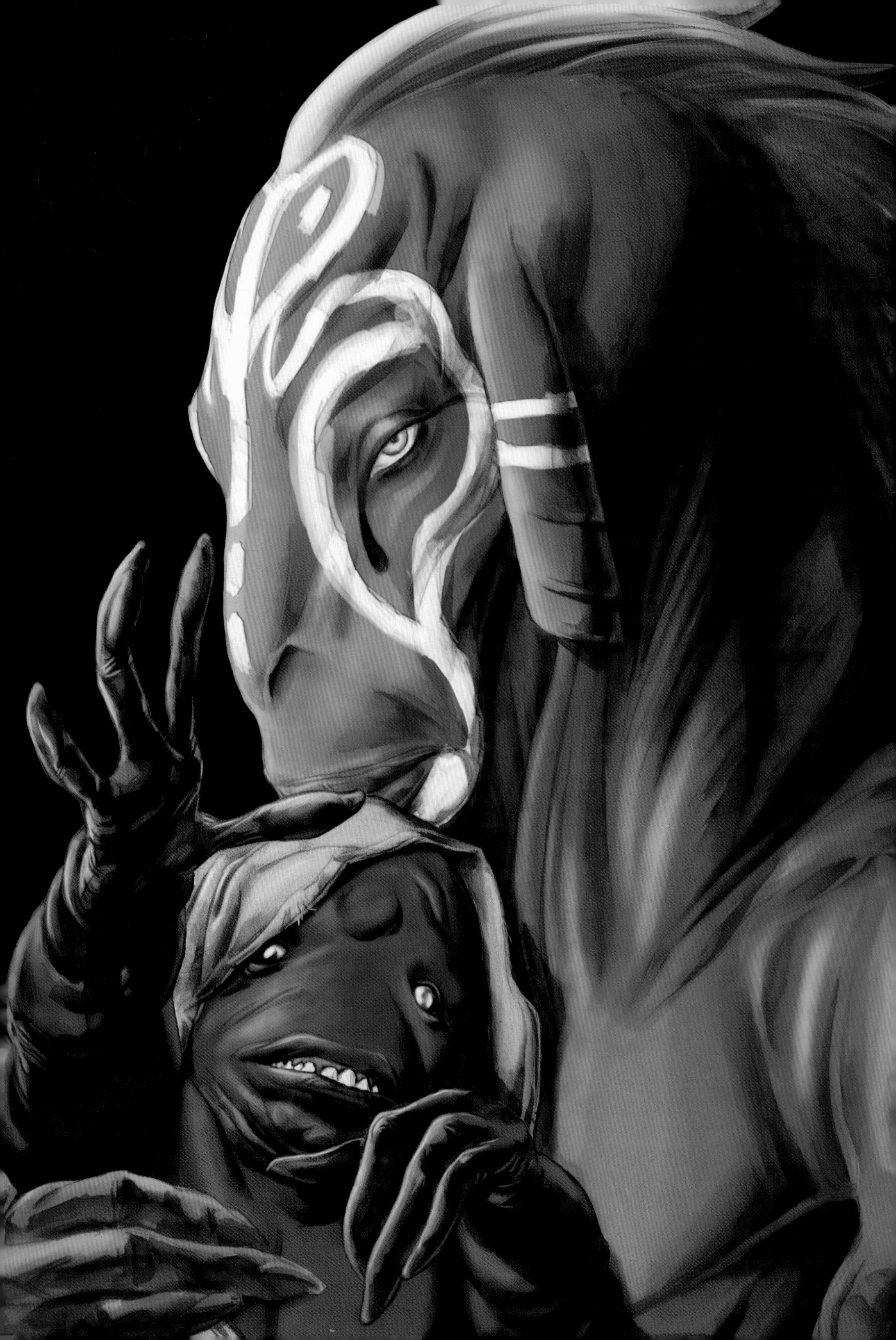

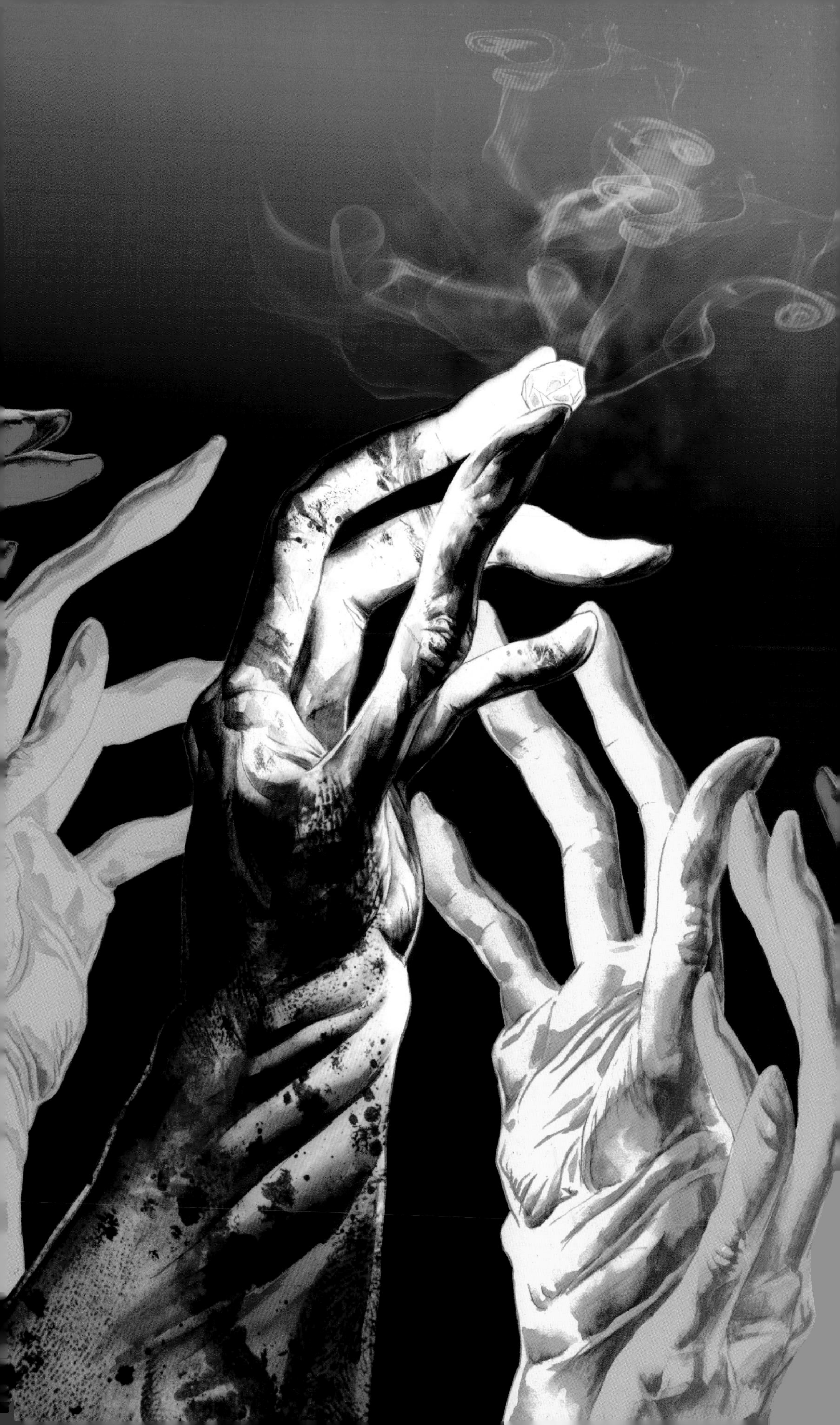

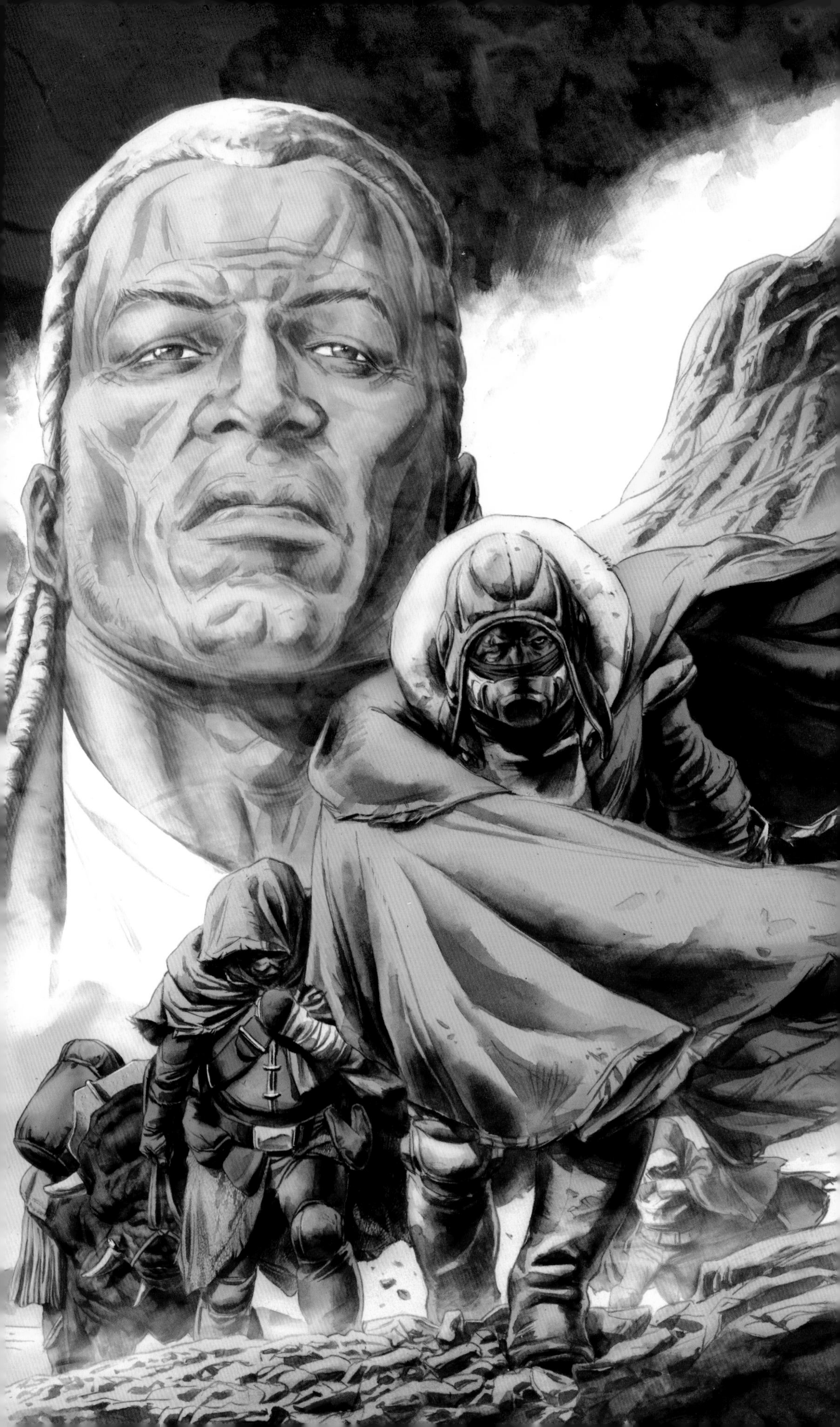

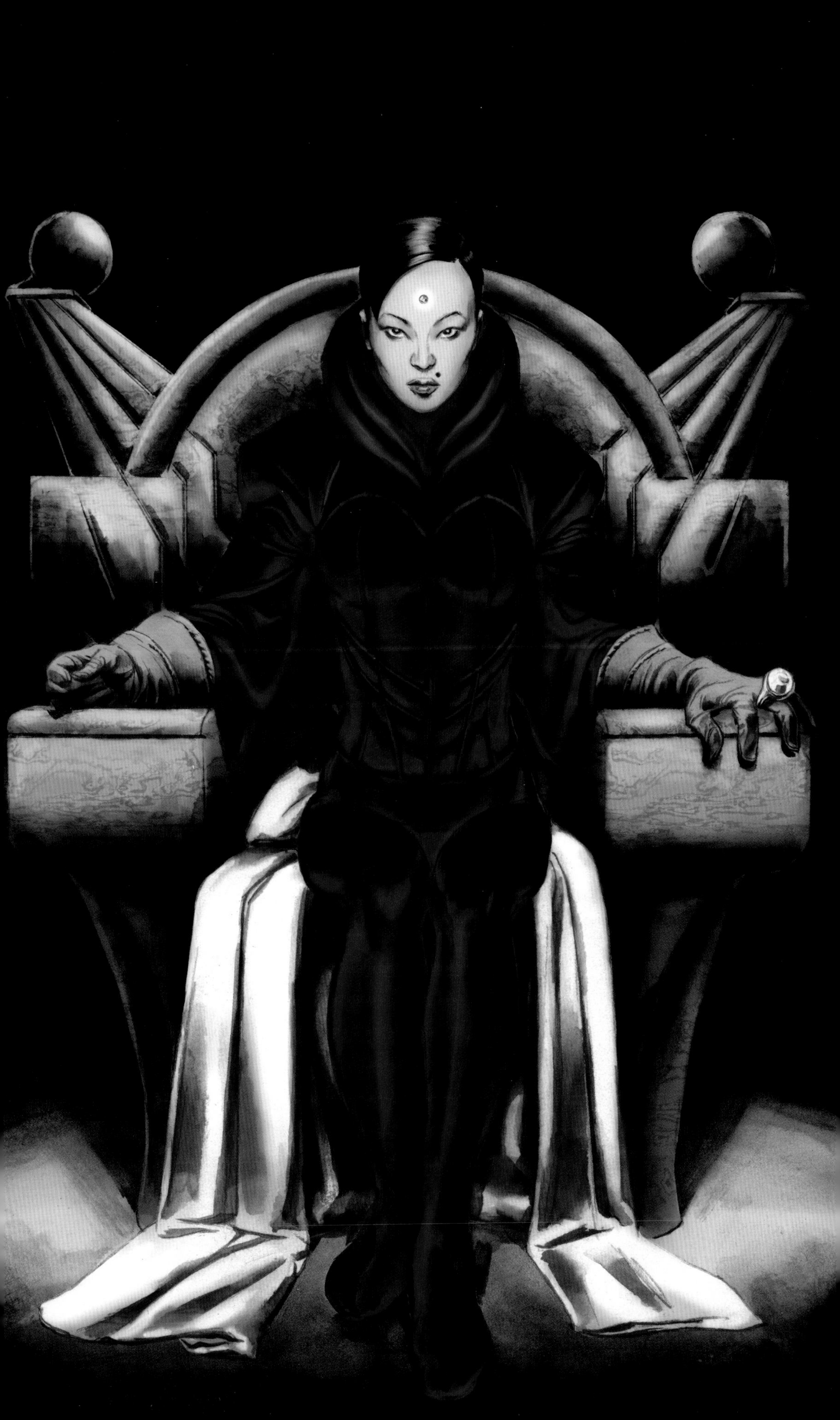

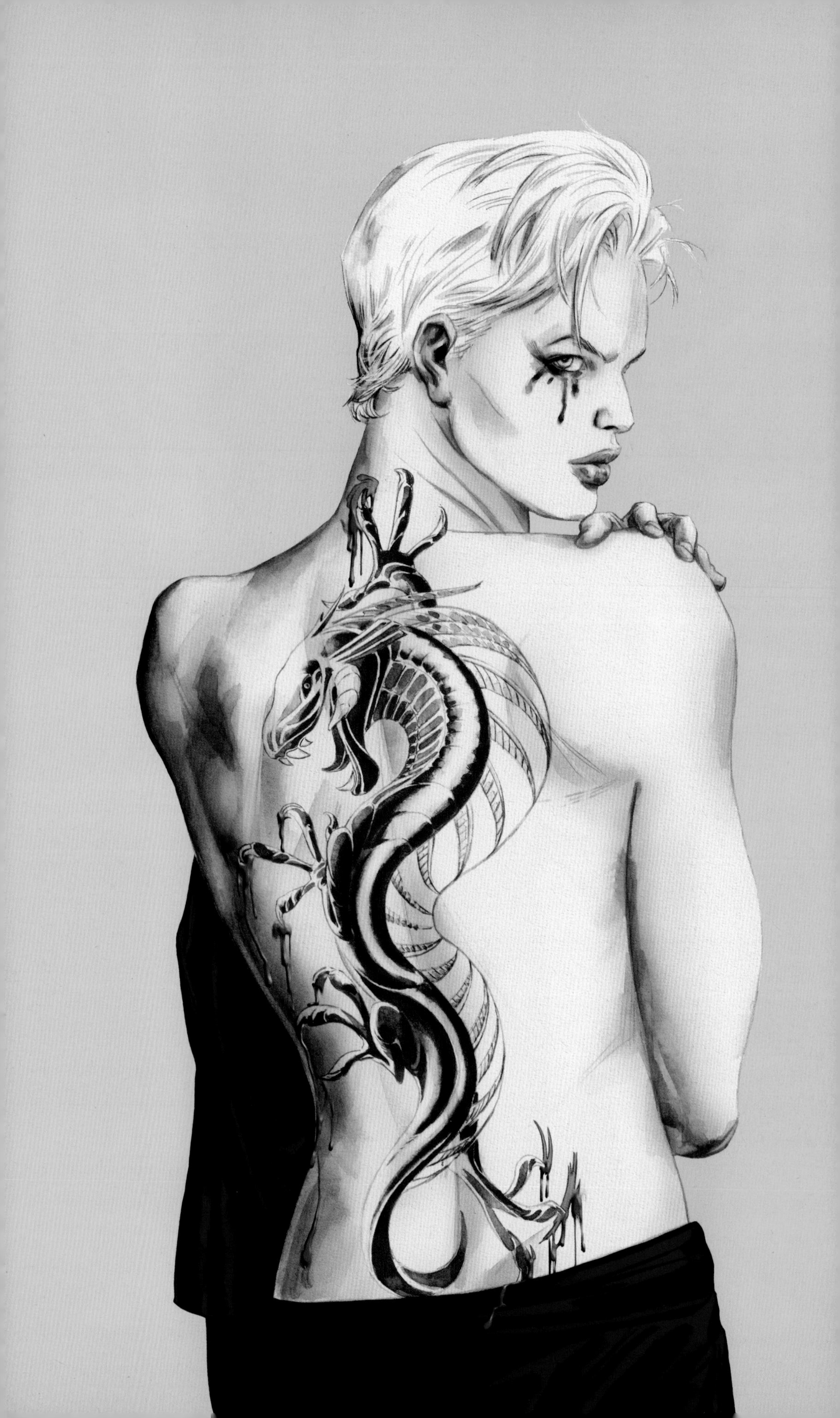

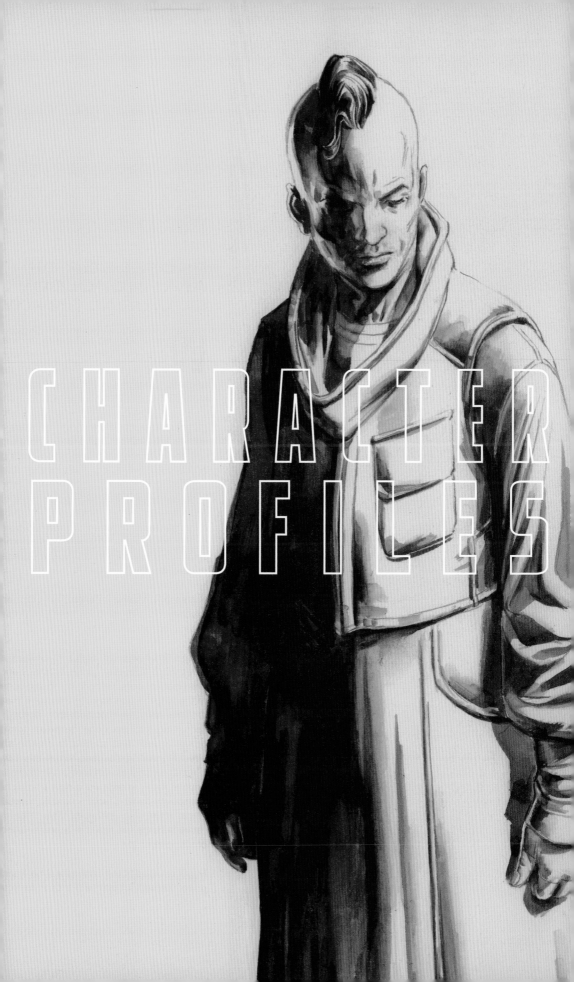

CHARACTER PROFILES

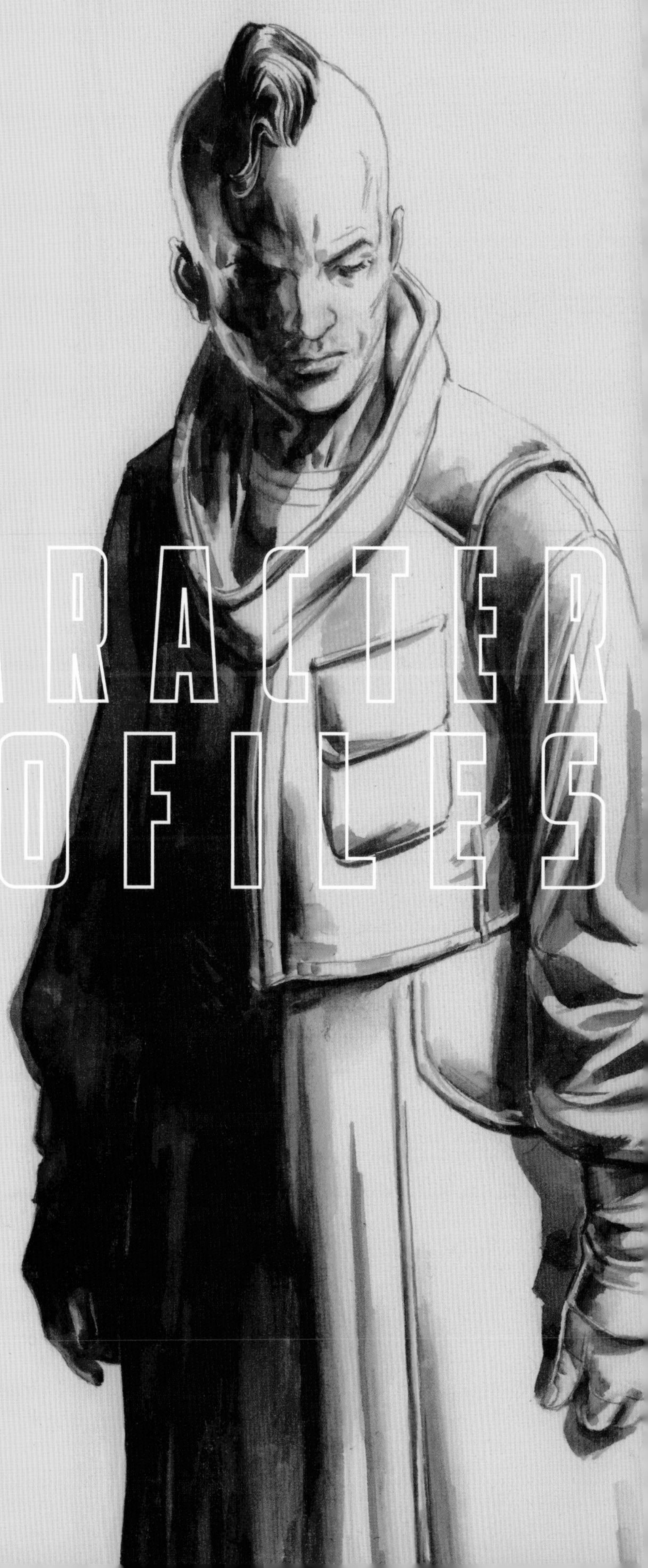

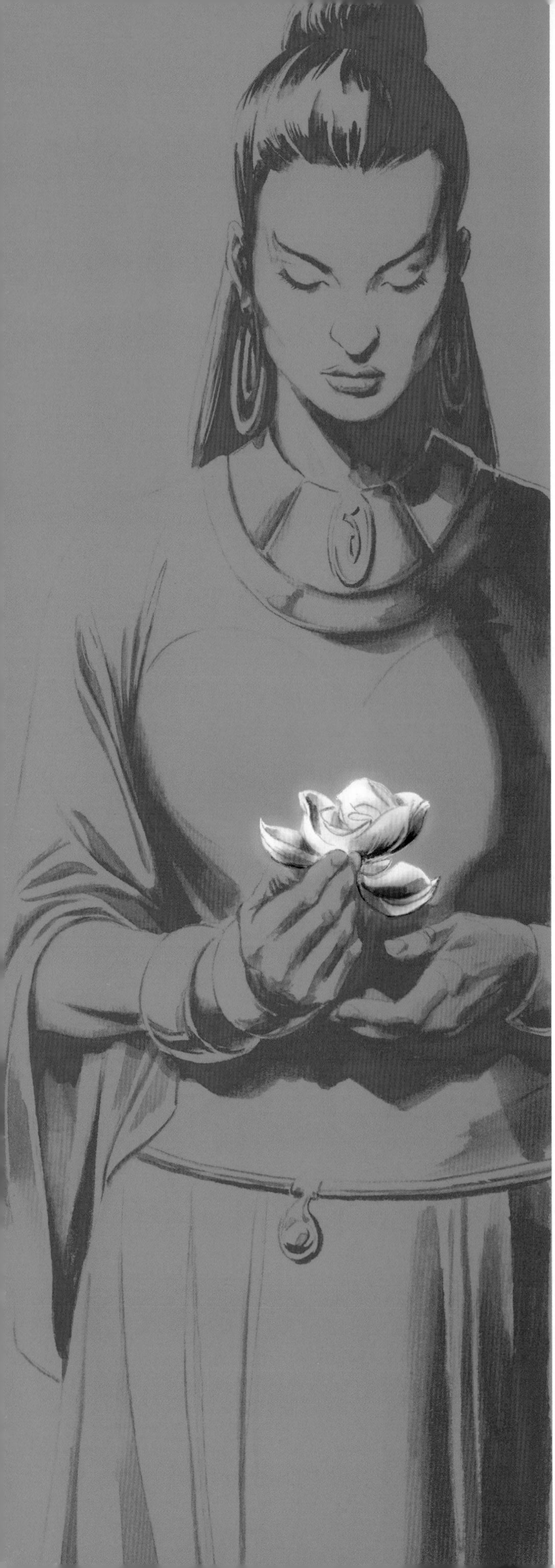

MASIKA ZENDA

PROFESSOR OF ANTHROPOLOGY CULTURAL ENVOY

When I was coming up with the line-up for the Storm Dogs team, it was clear that we needed a character who was more philosophical than might be expected on a criminal investigation team. There's a tendency to write detectives and pathologists as hard-bitten and perhaps a little cynical, their skins toughened by rubbing up against criminals and encountering death on a daily basis. I wanted to have someone who could stand back from the grim reality and see the bigger picture of how the murders on Amaranth will affect the relationship between the native culture of the planet, and the off-worlders who have come uninvited to exploit the planet's mineral wealth.

Professor Masika Zenda is not an experienced criminologist. Her expertise lies in cultural studies and language.

Doug's brief was to depict Masika in a way that reflects that gentle, scholarly and philosophical personality. In our discussions of the way the human race will evolve over the millennia, we decided that although continuing intermarriage between ethnic groups would tend to have a melting-pot effect of creating a generic human ethnicity, it is entirely conceivable that in the future, a pride in family lineage will create a trend to manipulate genetic factors so that physical ethnic traits are enhanced. This pride in racial heritage will result in a preservation of ethnic diversity.

Masika studied at the University of Kal Phan, one of the leading centres of anthropological research, where she wrote a paper on her own Earth ancestry. She has traced her heritage all the way back to the Benin of 19th Century West Africa and is one of the very few to make the trip back to the home planet of the human race. This field trip led to an almost obsessive interest in tribal cultures and the consequences of intercultural conflict.

Since graduating at the age of only eighteen years (Earth Standard), she has spent the last two decades traveling throughout the Union of Free Independent States, studying the cultures of over a dozen planetary systems at first hand. Her experience of contrasting social and belief systems has proven invaluable to the many diplomatic missions of which she has been a part.

Now, for the first time, she has been drafted into a Crime Investigation Team. The situation on Amaranth is delicate. Its culture is not technologically advanced enough to be considered for membership of the Union and that means that the local population must be treated with kid gloves. Masika's rôle is to liaise with the natives and to ensure that their rights are protected. Next issue we'll begin to see how complex and frustrating that task will turn out to be.

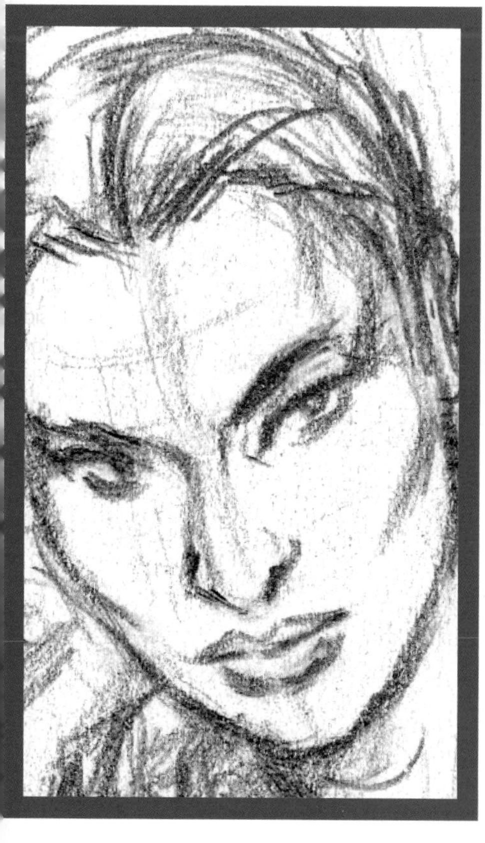

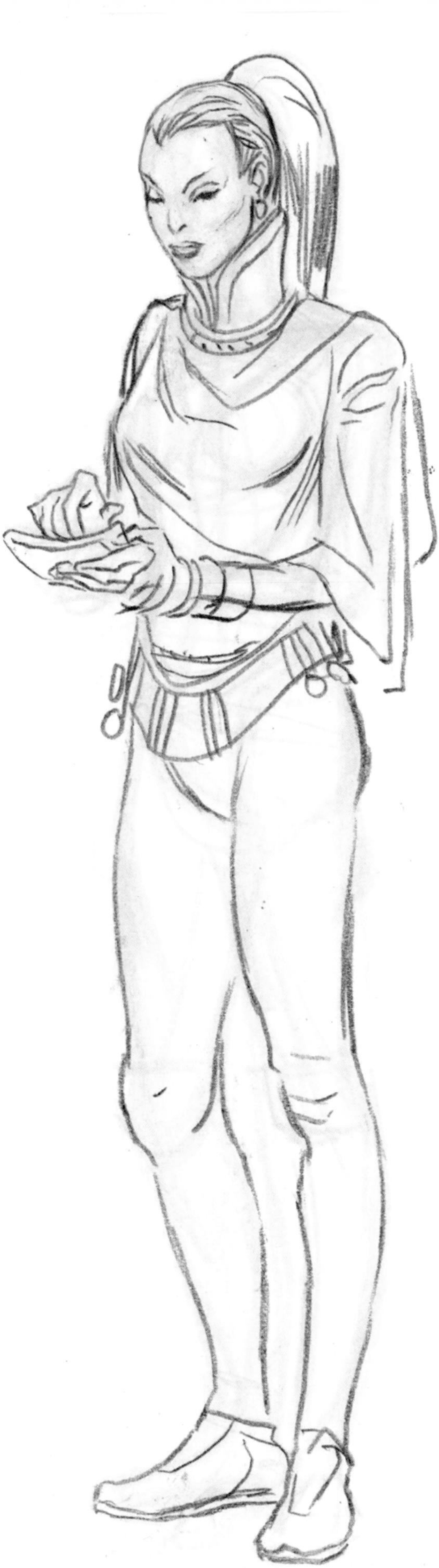

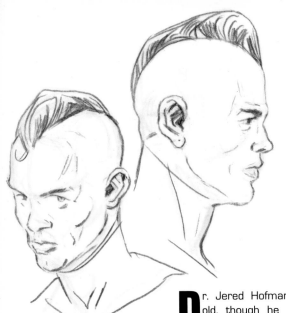

JERED HOFMAN

DOCTOR OF MEDICINE
FORENSIC PATHOLOGIST

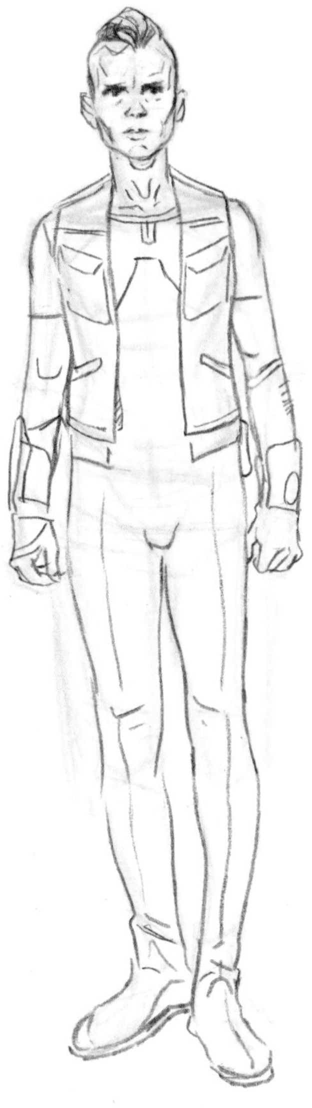

Dr. Jered Hofman is 28 years old, though he often appears younger. Precociously talented, he graduated first in his class at medical school but, unlike his peers, chose to specialise in the virtually obsolete art of physical dissection of cadavers. It is only in the context of a world like Amaranth, where the use of advanced technology is forbidden, that Jered's skills have any place.

I like Jered. I'm sure most writers have had the experience of a fictional creation taking on an autonomous existence. Jered very quickly became one of those. He developed a voice that let me know when he was acting out of character and guided the direction of his story arc. Jered is vulnerable and sensitive and above all, passionate. Passionate about life and about death. We see in this issue that the contemplation of the dead is anything but a sign of morbidity. He believes there is a pattern in the traumatized bodies and minds that will lead him to some great truth. The tragedy of a life abruptly and prematurely ended drives him to experience every moment of his own life to the fullest.

Jered is bisexual. He finds it unnatural to exclude half the human race from the role of potential lovers because of their gender. His current boyfriend dumped him in issue one as he arrived on the planet, and the implication is that he was being unfaithful to Michael. Jered's sensuous nature precludes him from remaining monogamous, but he does love. Perhaps too easily, and too often, but always with sincerity.

The comic-book form has many advantages over the novel. Ideas can be communicated with a single image that would take a chapter of prose to express. On the other hand, an episodic comic with a complex plot structure is necessarily elliptic and demands compression of both dialogue and action. A 22-page episode doesn't leave much time to spend on introspection and there are aspects of Jered's character we may never get around to exploring - Jered's relationship to his Jewish ancestry for instance. The practice of religion has all but disappeared this far into the future, replaced by rationalism and scientific enquiry, but Jered remains fascinated by the concept of faith. He's an expert on ancient theology and has explored his own family heritage back to its Jewish origins. A nostalgic affection for the idea of the Judaeo/Christian god provides him with an ethical focus and he often engages in one-sided debates with an imagined deity that the rational side of his mind knows cannot exist.

As always, the character description I gave to Doug was more about these internal conflicts than physical appearance. As a result, Doug drew Jered from the inside out and his interpretation perfectly captures the profound, caring and ultimately fragile personality of a man who believes that the uncompromising pursuit of truth and justice is a righteous goal.

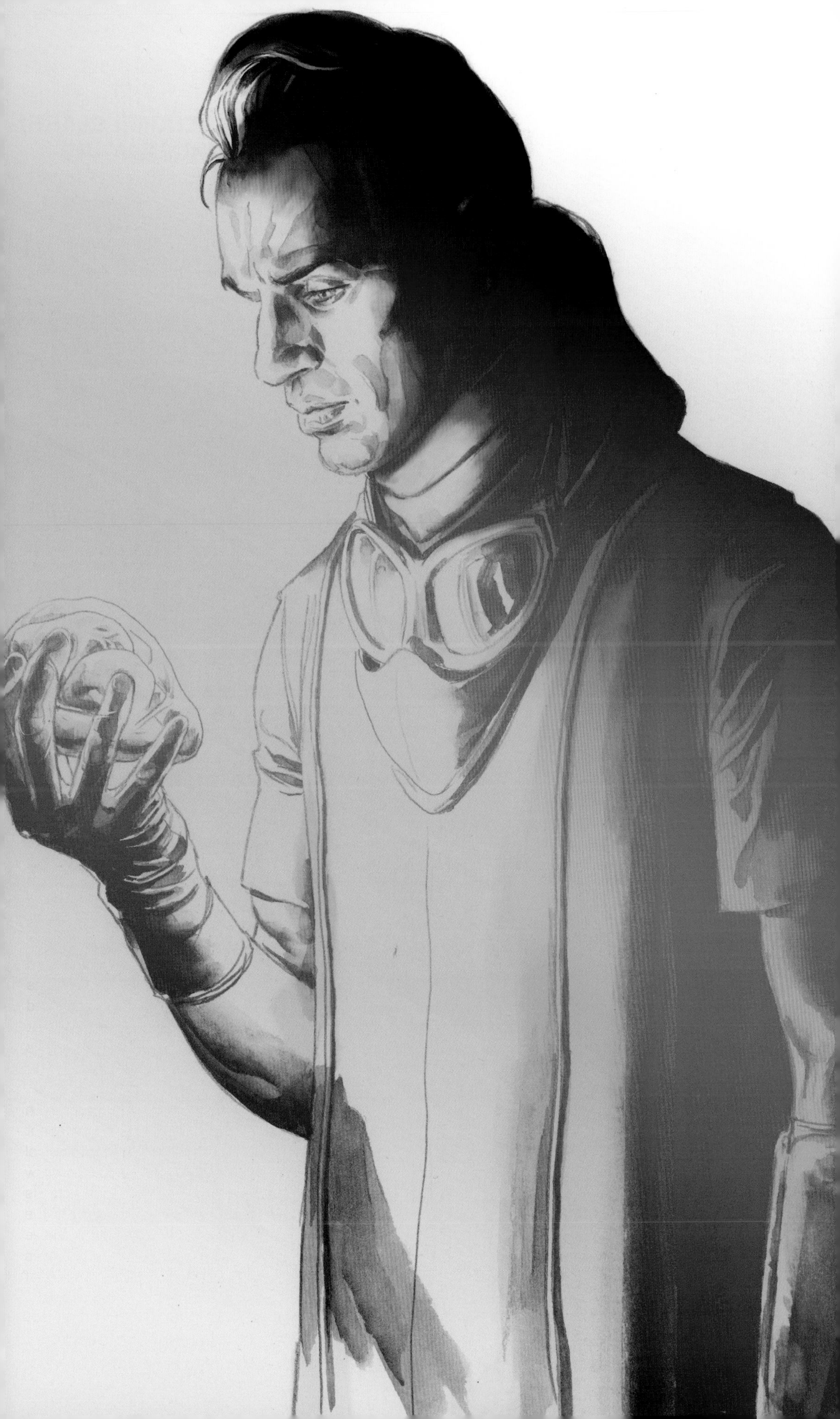

BRONSON

DEPUTY SHERIFF
FORMER TROOPER (SECOND CLASS)
VETERAN OF THE BORDER WARS

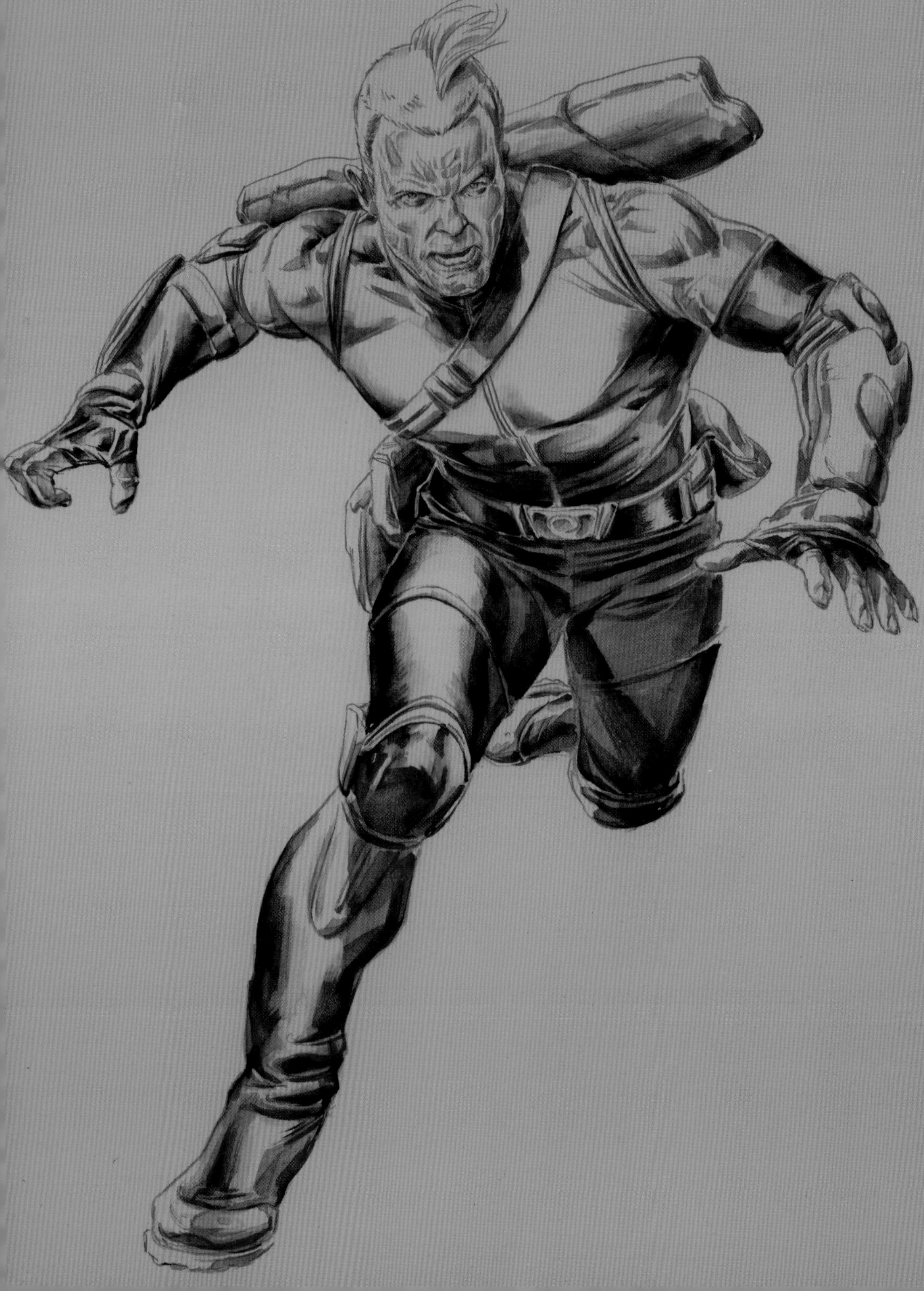

Bronson doesn't have another name, or if he does, I don't know it. Everyone has always called him Bronson. It could be a first name or a surname. I chose it, of course, because of the actor Charles Bronson. Taciturn, tough, uncompromising... the drawings that Doug came up with were probably also influenced by the name and that worked well. I have no idea if the actor will still be remembered in the time of the Storm Dogs, but if he is, Bronson would undoubtedly respect him as a role model.

At the end of this issue, we know that Bronson doesn't only model himself on an image of machismo, but he has also confirmed the hints of xenophobia and brutality we saw in the earlier episodes. He is a psychotic murderer with deep-rooted hatred of all non-human species. He has nothing but contempt for the Elohi and the Joppa – 'Drifters' and 'Slugs' as he prefers to call them. In other words he is a reprehensible, thoroughly dislikeable character - a bad guy. That isn't the whole story though. The white hat/good guys, black hat/bad guys belong to the era of Roy Rogers and The (original) Lone Ranger. Creating a well-rounded character means layering in some nuances and contradictions. The most convincing hero/ine is the one with flaws in her character. The fascinating bad guy is the one with redeeming characteristics. In Bronson's case redemption starts with a dry and witty sense of humour. He is good at sensing the weaknesses in others and can use that humour to good effect...or cruel intent... a witty sadist, then.

There's another redemptive element to the fictional villain – the history. There may be human beings who are evil by nature, but I prefer to believe that it is nurture that forms the villain. Bronson wasn't born bad. His back story reveals the origins of his xenophobia and his distrust of authority, along with his self-reliance and his volatility. I could tell you now, but that would spoil the surprises. There are hints in the story though. We know from this issue that Bronson fought in the frontier wars he refers to as 'The Troubles' and that he lost an arm, which has been replaced with a bio-mechanical prosthetic limb. That must have been traumatic in all senses of the word. Typically, Bronson's adaptability means he has made the most of it. He's all man and about 15% machine - a South Paw with a murderous left cross.

Like most of the offworlders who came to Amaranth, Bronson is an outsider and a misfit, whose military history makes him almost unemployable anywhere else. When he arrived on the planet, he was just another prospector, hoping to make a fast buck. Sheriff Starck recruited him as a deputy after Bronson took out a drunken miner on a killing spree. While everyone else ran for cover, Bronson faced down the gun-toting madman, disarmed him and knocked him senseless with a single blow from that mechanical fist. When Starck congratulated him on his sense of civic duty, Bronson looked at him as if he were crazy. His responsibility as a citizen was the last thing on his mind, he insisted. "That cocksucker spilled my drink."

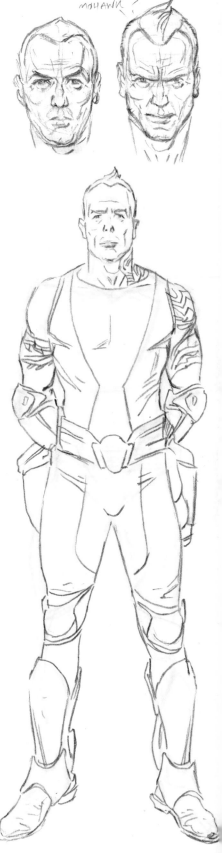

MOHAWK?

TATOOS RUN UP SIDE OF NECK(?)

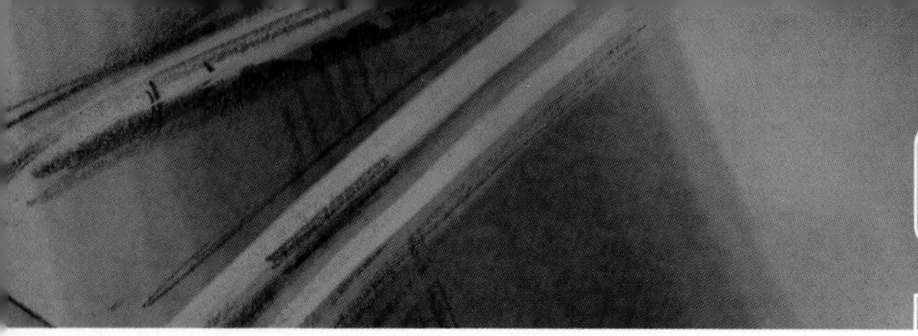

SIAM LOCKE

These sketches show the visual development of Siam Locke as Doug tried out a number of looks for the character. She was always going to have a tough physical appearance but there were a number of ways to go. Recently we have seen some great warrior women in the media. Vasquez led the way for women to have equal rights to bear heavy arms and kick ass in the movie ALIENS but at one point I thought of pursuing a Calamity Jane type of character – hard drinking and foulmouthed. In the end though, we went for the big muscular look combined with a face that suggests sensitivity and self-control.

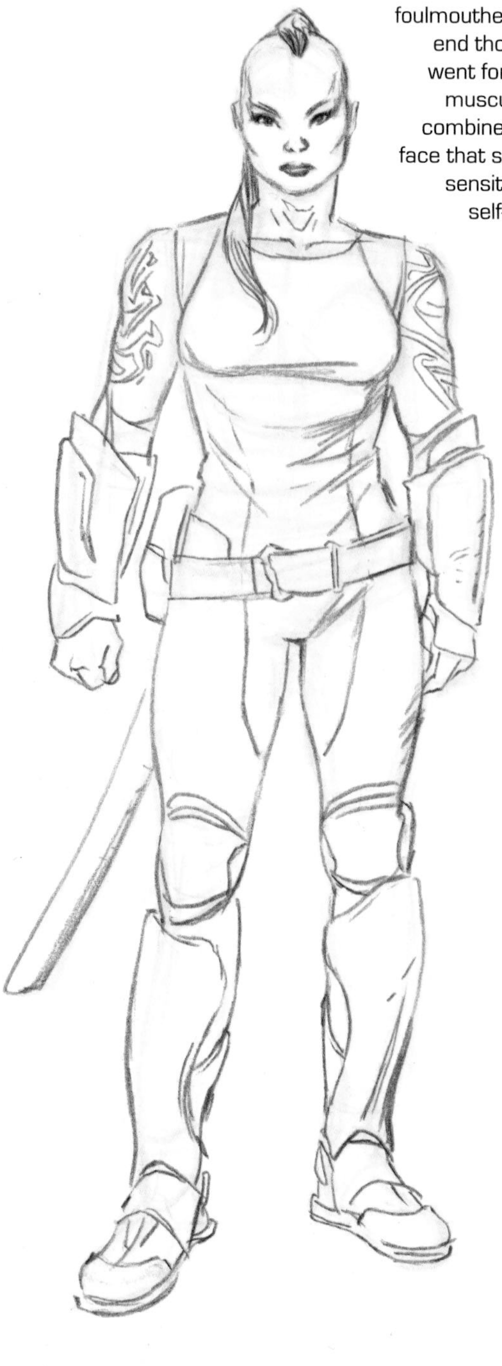

In issue #1 we observed Siam saying her farewells to her family and we saw something of the pride and expectations they have for her. Those expectations have become a real burden for her. Although the Union of Free Independent States has a constitution that enshrines equality of opportunity for all individuals, the reality is a little different. Siam was born on a colonised frontier planet a lot like Amaranth and has mixed-race parentage. Both her parents are descended from settlers who married into the indigenous species and despite the official statutes, in reality that made them second-class citizens, who have lived in relative poverty for generations. Siam's parents saved hard to pay for pre-natal genetic modifications and then all the bio-mechanical implants they could afford once she hit puberty, to give her every advantage in a military career – the only practical way to get offworld and make something of her life.

Siam has now been a trooper in the military for nearly seven years and has served in several campaigns against the warlike races that regularly challenge the authority of the Union. As human kind has expanded through space, many alien cultures have been encountered and most have been invited to join the federation. In some cases, a less-developed culture like that of the Elohi and Joppa of Amaranth, may be given protected status in order for them to develop independently until they reach a level of technological and intellectual development that will allow them entry to the Union.

In other cases, a culture may be simply too aggressive or plain xenophobic, or perhaps simply unwilling to submit to the rules and standards of the Union. At any one time the Union may be pursuing campaigns against several of these hostile cultures with a view to 'demilitarisation'. In other words, they are invaded, their weapons seized and destroyed their leaders incarcerated and an appropriate form of caretaker government installed. Siam has served with distinction, to the extent that she was selected to train for the special duties that led to her being assigned to Cassandra Burroughs' investigation team at the Commander's personal request. Her brief is to protect the team, to keep them safe for the duration of their stay on Amaranth.

Her family is proud of Siam. She knows that. She also knows that she will never be officer material. No matter how well she performs, she will never be more than front line cannon fodder – a genetically-modified fighting machine. In her own words, "I'm just the muscle here. All I have to do is keep the team alive and arrest the perps. What are they going to do? Make me a general?"

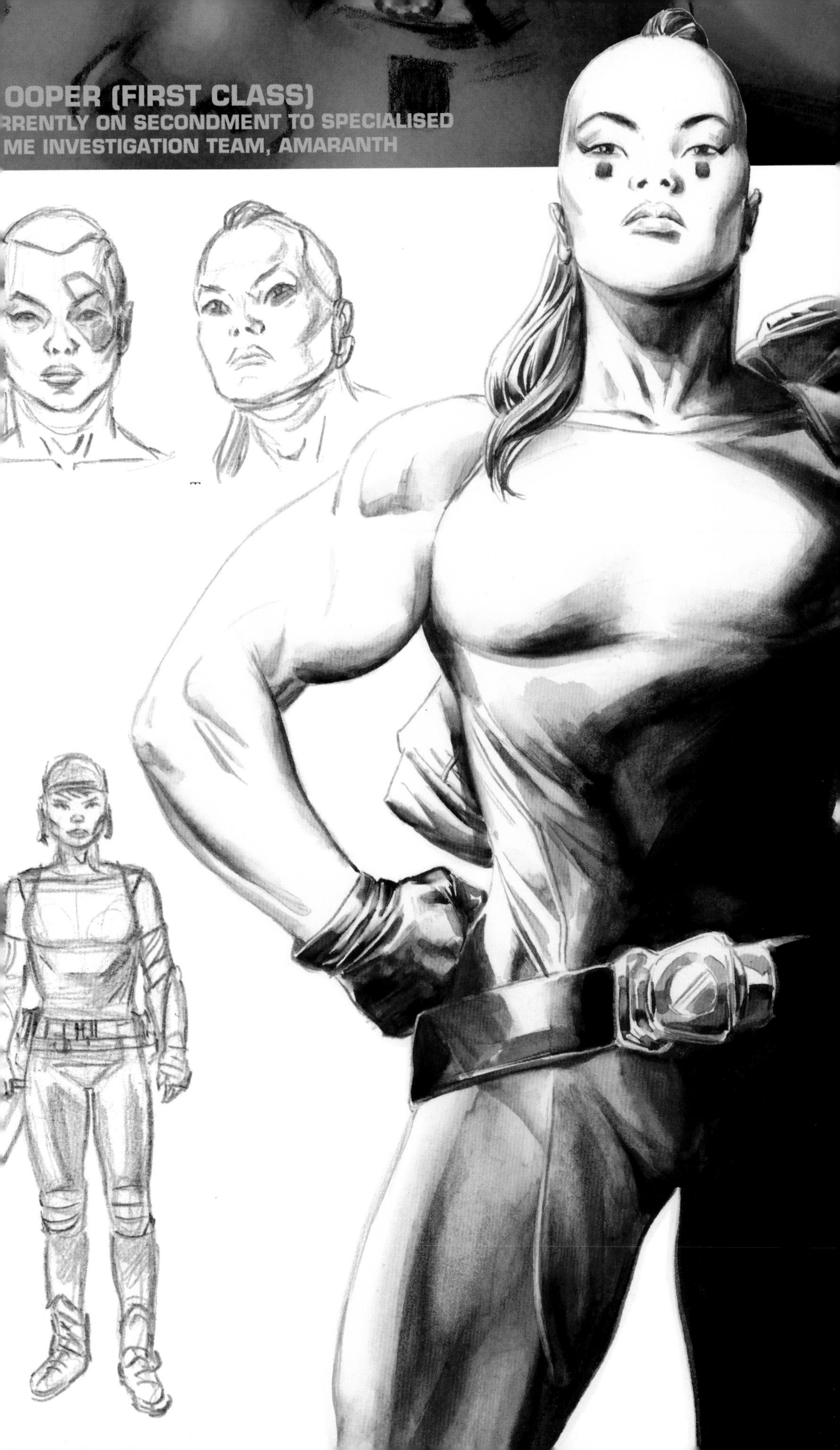
OOPER (FIRST CLASS)
RRENTLY ON SECONDMENT TO SPECIALISED
ME INVESTIGATION TEAM, AMARANTH

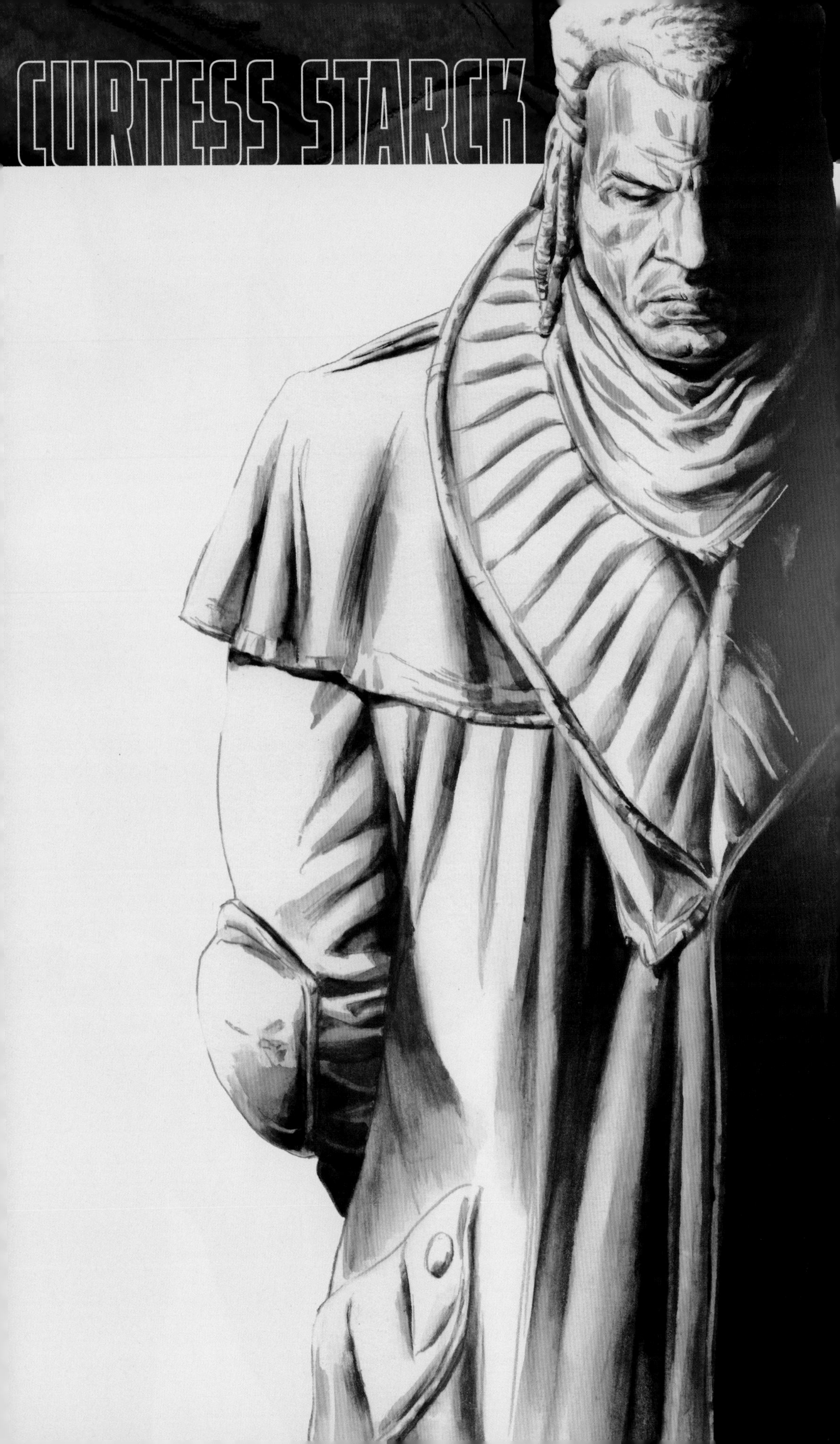
CURTESS STARCK

HERIFF AND HEAD OF LAW ENFORCEMENT
RIEVANCE, AMARANTH

52-year-old Starck is a veteran law enforcement officer whose career spans almost thirty years and a dozen different locales throughout the Union of Free Independent States. There was a time when he was in line for a prime judicial post in the Bureau of Law Enforcement Affairs, but a controversial investigation implicated him in the infamous Taal/Sandorfi corruption scandal. Although never charged, his reputation was irreparably damaged and within months he found himself despatched to Amaranth, the ultimate dead-end appointment. Starck is the kind of bluff, tight-lipped individual who doesn't give away too much about his private life and he is unlikely to be drawn on whether he was directly involved in the Sandorfi Corporation's wrongdoing. There were rumours that, to the contrary, he had acted as a whistle blower and had been falsely and deliberately implicated in order to invalidate him as a witness.

Doug has depicted him as a stoic who contains his bitterness behind that wall of silence. On Amaranth he is the quintessential pragmatist, bending or ignoring the law to keep the peace. Although appointed by the Union, he could not operate without the tacit approval of the Arcana Corporation, whose workforce he polices. He is a loner, with no real friends and no romantic relationship beyond his regular visits with the proprietor of the Sunset Club, a discretely upmarket bordello. If there is more to Starck's story then Madam Clara is the only one who knows it, and she isn't talking either.

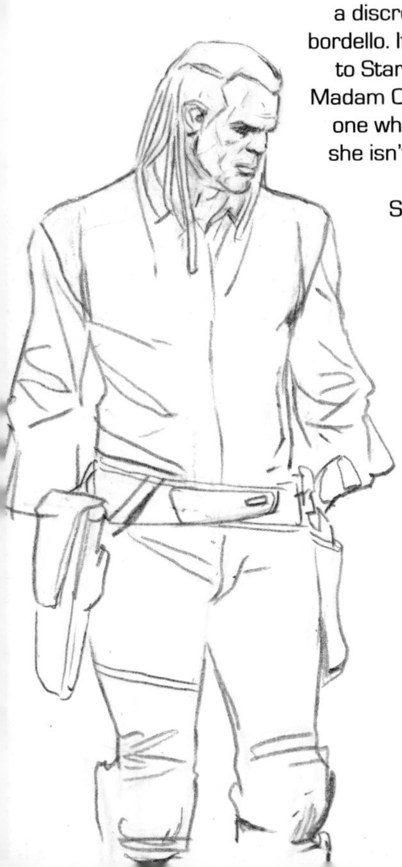

Starck senses a kindred spirit in Cassandra Burroughs. He hasn't asked but he's assuming that, like him, she must have pissed off someone with influence to be chasing down perps on a no-account planet like Amaranth. She has shown enough guts to gain his respect and based on the instinctive assessment he made, when he recognised her as a fellow Storm Dog, he'll back her up without question, even if it means taking a bullet for her.

And speaking of bullets...Starck's body bears the marks of dozens of wounds from knife thrusts, gunshots and more fists and blunt objects than he cares to remember. After last issue's knock 'em down, drag 'em out fight with Bronson, he has a few more scars, but there's a sense that the old warhorse is damned near indestructible.

He'll have to be if he's going to survive what's coming.

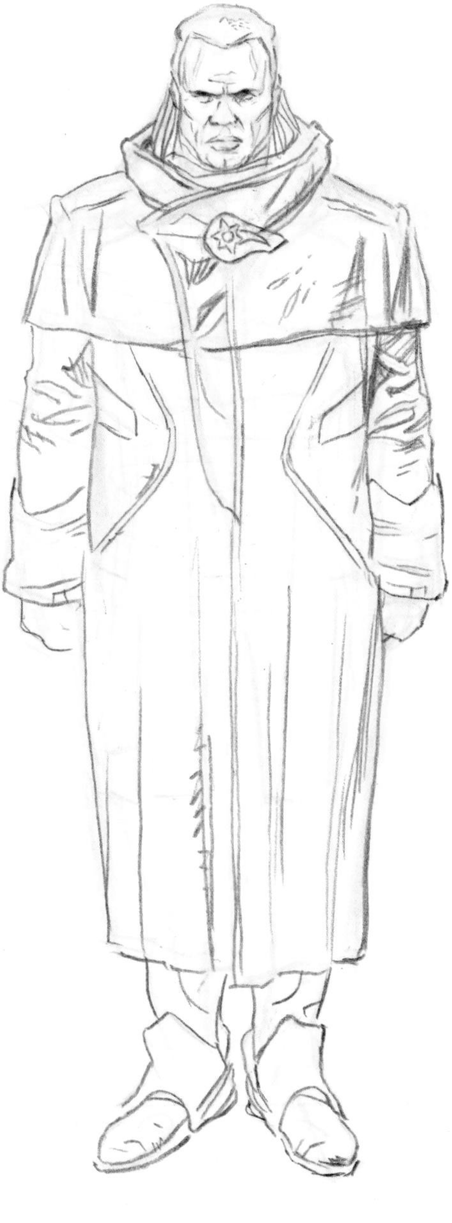

Page 20

Panel 1
Some time later. The rain has stopped and the sky is clear. Maybe a little vapour still rising from some of the remaining puddles.

Masika: WHAT HAPPENED HERE?

Panel 2
Now we have a clear view of the mayhem. The bodies of the miners – what's left of them – are lying amid the torn up wreckage of the vehicle. The team have taken off their helmets and are examining the crime scene. Cassandra is filming with a hand-held video camera. Hofman is kneeling beside the remains of one body probing the melted flesh with some kind of intrument. Bronson is heaping pulped flesh and bones into a slick black body bag. More body bags are piled up for the others.

Siam is pointing off-panel, maybe towards us. Once again, she is the first to spot the action.

Starck: THERE'S OUR PROBLEM, SAME AS THE OTHERS.

(linked balloon):   NO WITNESSES. NO SURVIVORS.

Siam (pointing):   HATE TO CONTRADICT YOU, SHERIFF--

Panel 3
A strange apparition is approaching. Diego is staggering towards them ululating in some mad inhuman tongue – a weird song of ecstasy and insanity. He is wearing his rain suit, but he has thrown off the hood so we can see his contorted features. His eyes are literally glowing as if there were some source of nuclear energy inside his head. He is seeing something so wonderful and horrible that it has driven him completely insane.

He is walking on twisted unbalanced limbs (in fact his body is virtually disintegrated inside the suit. His body is only intact above the neck, but we won't know that until the suit comes off.)

[LETTERS: DIEGO'S VOICE IS A QUAVERING SING-SONG AND THE LETTERS SHOULD REFLECT THAT, IRREGULAR AND RISING AND FALLING IN A WEIRD CHANT.]

Diego: AAAAOOOOOOOOAAAA

Panel 4
Zoom to head and shoulders. Although the rain hasn't touched his face, his features still have a ravaged look as if he is being eaten up from the inside. The glowing eyes add to this effect. [XXXXX - REMOVED FOR SPOILERS - XXXX]

His lips are drawn back in a manic grin, the glowing eyes wide and staring at some vision we can only guess at.

Diego: OOOOOOAAAAAAAAAAA

Panel 5
Diego's legs finally give out and he collapses onto his knees, reaching out to them with a twisted gloved hand. His last words are spoken clearly but quietly. A simple statement.

Diego: TOO MUCH

Panel 6
He falls forward onto his face at the feet of Siam, his arm outstretched towards her.

The rent in the back of his suit is visible now. And inside the suit, the body looks too small, as if it has collapsed in on it

[NO COPY]

LEFT: Doug's original thumbnails, actual size

BELOW: The pencilled page, with Doug's colour notes

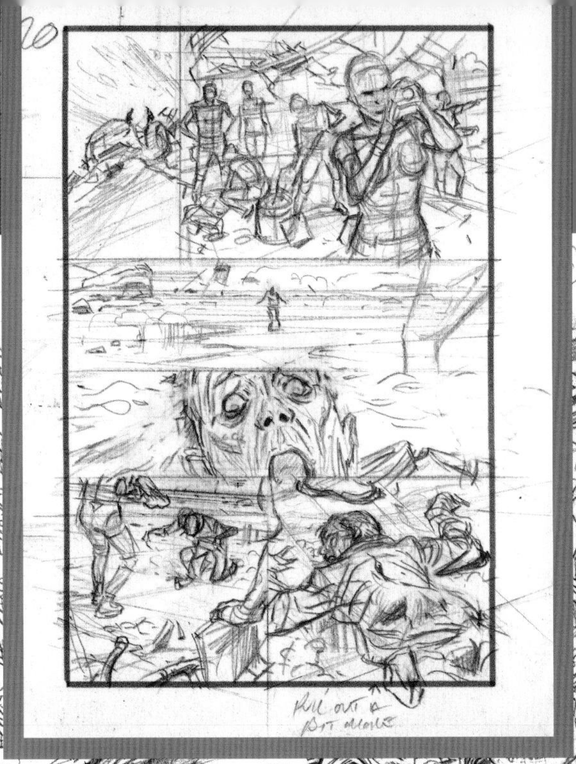
PULL OUT A BIT MORE

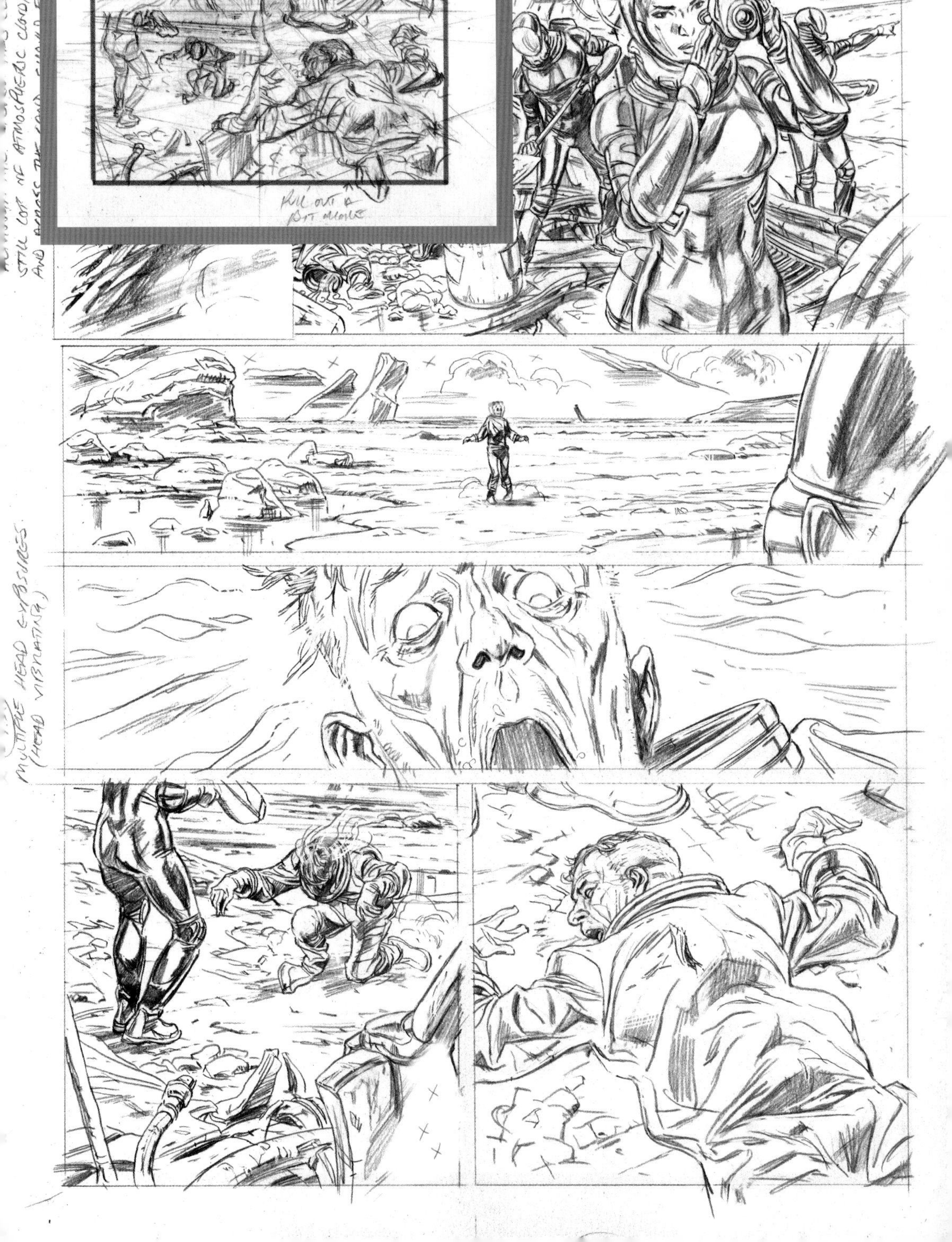
MESIKA'S VISOR REVEALS HER FACE INSIDE. IMAGINE IT UP-LIT WITH AN EERIE LIGHT (I WILL SEND YOU A GUIDE).
MULTIPLE HEAD EXPOSURES (HEAD VIBRATING)

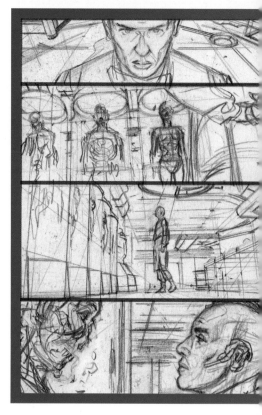

Page 1

Panel 1
Wide panel: The morgue.
Head and shoulders of Jered.

      Jered: JERED HOFMAN, FORENSIC
PATHOLOGIST. FIRST REPORT AT 27.15 HOURS,
LOCAL TIME.

      (linked balloon):   THERE ARE SEVEN
CADAVERS FROM PREVIOUS INCIDENTS.
PRELIMINARY AUTOPSIES BY RESIDENT
SURGEON INDICATE CAUSES OF DEATH AS
FOLLOWS…

      Caption (Jered):   "SURGEON!" …HIS NOTES
READ LIKE A FIRST YEAR MED STUDENT.

Panel 2
We are looking from behind Jered towards a row of transparent
cylinders, each containing the remains of a dead body. The
cylinders are upright so that what is left of the bodies look that
much more grotesque as they are in an upright position, rather
than laid out as you would expect in a morgue.

The cylinders are filled with some kind of translucent material
that holds the bodies in place, and there is some form of
lighting inside the cylinder to give an eerie glow to them. They
seem almost like some kind of religious relics. There are seven bodies – the victims of the previous unexplained deaths t
brought our team to Amaranth. One of these bodies was torn apart by wild animals, while the others were either stabb
strangled, bludgeoned or shot with the same pulse weapon we saw used in the opening scene of Part One. Several of
bodies (including the one torn to pieces by animals) have suffered extra decomposition from the effect of the acid rain.

      Jered (off):   …TWO CASES OF BLUNT FORCE TRAUMA, TWO STABBINGS, ONE
      STRANGULATION BY LIGATURE, ONE LETHAL INJURY FROM PULSE HANDGUN.

Panel 3
Switch to a side view showing Jered in profile, facing the dead bodies. This shot should establish the context of the morg
Behind Jered the five new victims (the prospectors from issue 1) are laid out in a more traditional way on gurneys, ready
Jered to perform the autopsies. We don't have to see these five bodies in detail until next page. The focus of this page is
Jered and the slightly ghostly preserved bodies from previous incidents.

Jered is wearing scrubs and surgical gloves, a transparent mask around his neck.

      Jered: THESE FINDINGS ARE INCONCLUSIVE AS ALL THE BODIES HAVE SUFFERED
      ACCELERATED DECOMPOSITION AFTER EXPOSURE TO ACID RAIN, INCLUDING THE
      EARLIEST REPORTED VICTIM, WHO WAS APPARENTLY ATTACKED BY ANIMALS.

Panel 4
Zoom to close-up of Jered face to face with one of the preserved corpses. The two profiles facing one another. One dead a
partially disintegrated by the acid rain, and Jered's melancholy features, contemplating the face of mortality.

      Caption (Jered):   WHY WOULD AN ANIMAL ATTACK BE CLASSIFIED AS A 'SUSPICIOUS
DEATH'? THERE'S SOMETHING HERE THAT STARCK HASN'T TOLD US YET. SOMETHING
THAT CONNECTS THESE DEATHS.

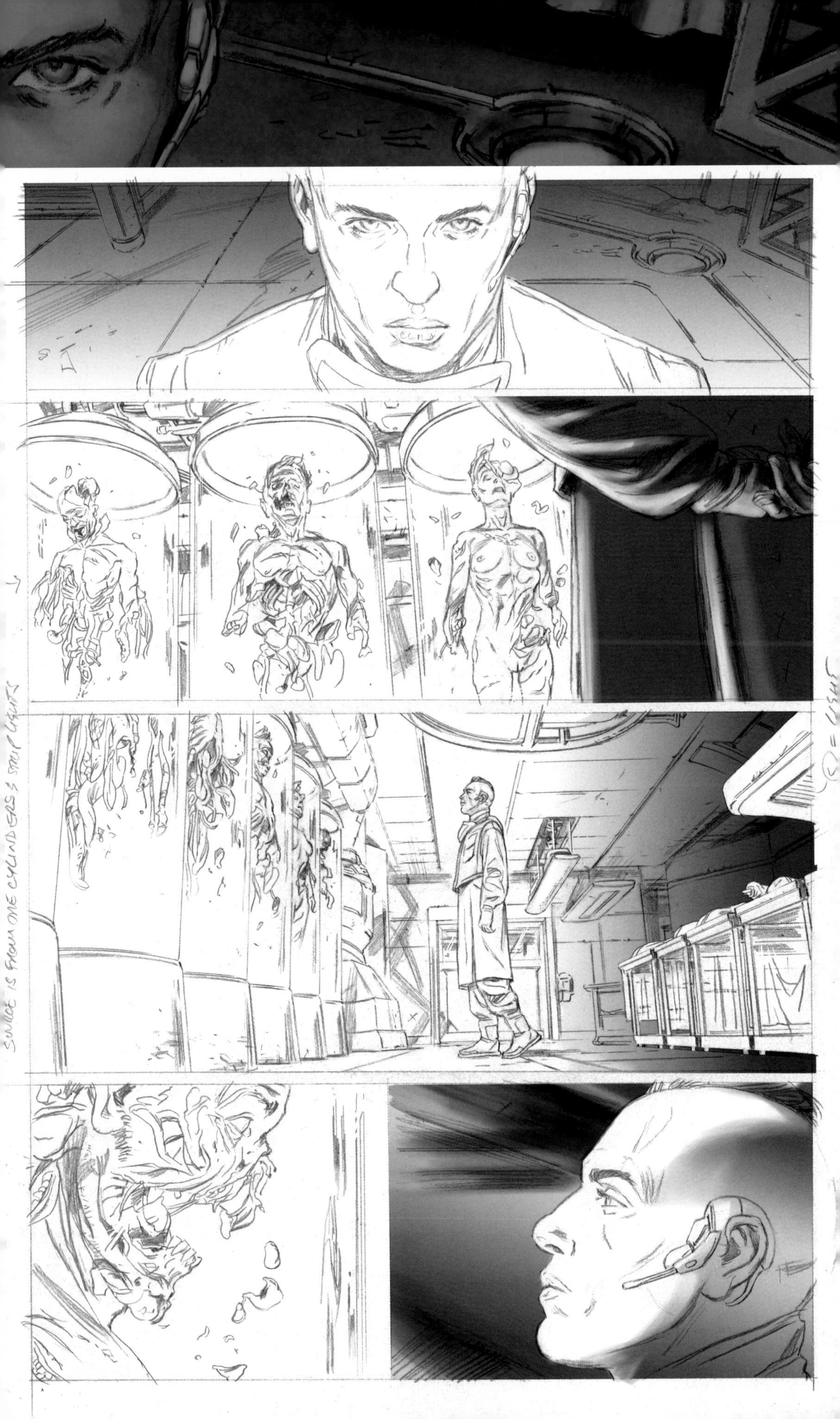
SOURCE IS FROM THE CYLINDERS & STRIP LIGHTS
(L) = LIGHTS

SCRIPT TO ART

Page 9

Panel 1
Cut to the trail where the team (Bronson, Siam, Starck and Cassandra) has to leave their vehicle and switch to riding the local version of horses – the Colanths - to ride up into the foothills. Colanths are slimmer animals than we saw the prospectors riding in Part 1. These are the animals the cops ride so they are a little more agile, adapted to narrow hill paths. They have driven out from Grievance in a large motorized vehicle – basically a big cattle truck with space for all four animals. A sleeker vehicle than the prospectors were riding in. We don't need to see too much of the vehicle, just an indication of it parked in the background. They are taking rain suits and weapons plus enough food and water for a couple of days in saddle-bags of some kind. Bronson has a pulse-rifle (similar to the pulse guns we've already seen but with longer barrels for long-distance shooting.). Cassandra, Siam and Starck just have their pistols.

It's windy and sand is blowing hard into their faces, so they wear goggles to keep the sand out of their eyes. They are also wearing cloaks (good visually in a windy setting).

Caption: THE EASTERN HILLS.

Panel 2
Bronson watches Siam swing easily onto the back of her mount.

Bronson: YOU EVER RIDE A COLANTH BEFORE?

Siam: I RODE A SANDWORM ON MESKLYN.

Panel 3
Bronson is impressed.

Bronson: NO SHIT? I SERVED THERE IN THE TROUBLES.

Siam: YOU WERE PART OF THE OCCUPATION?

Panel 4
Bronson lifts an arm.

Bronson: LEFT AN ARM THERE.

Panel 5
Siam looks at him for a moment.

[NO COPY]

Panel 6
Then she jerks on the reins of her mount and moves away uphill, as if she's been riding Colanths all her life.

[NO COPY]

Panel 7
Bronson watches her go. [Doug, Bronson and Siam have a mutual fascination. Siam is the opposite of Bronson in most ways, but their common history in the military also gives them a lot of shared experience and their relationship will be ambiguous. Bronson is certainly attracted to Siam.]

[NO COPY]

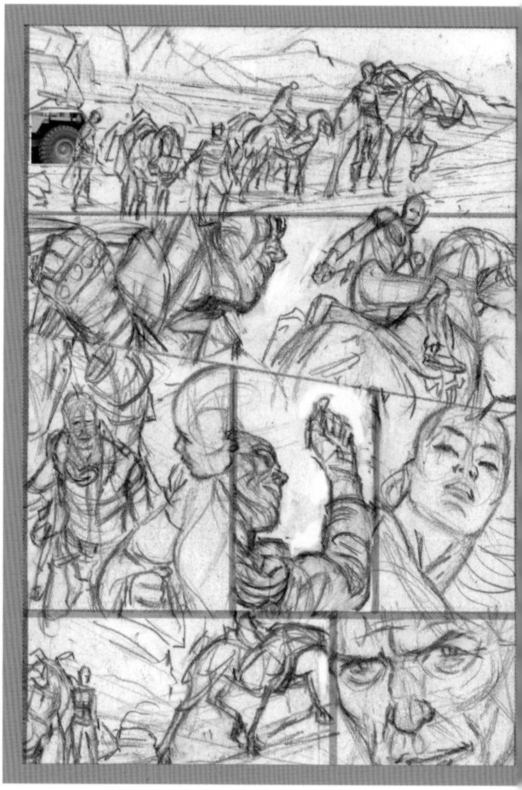

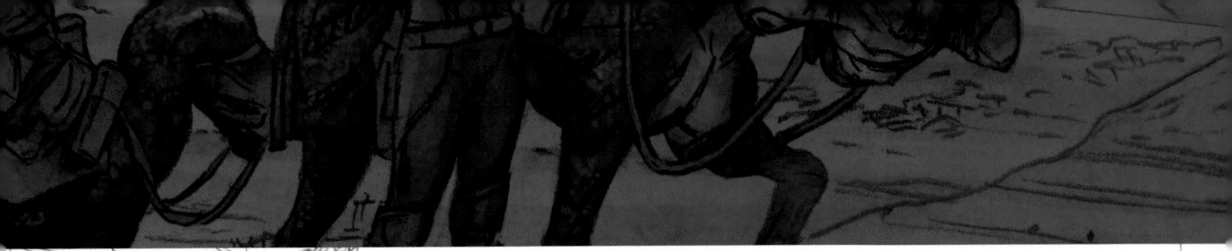

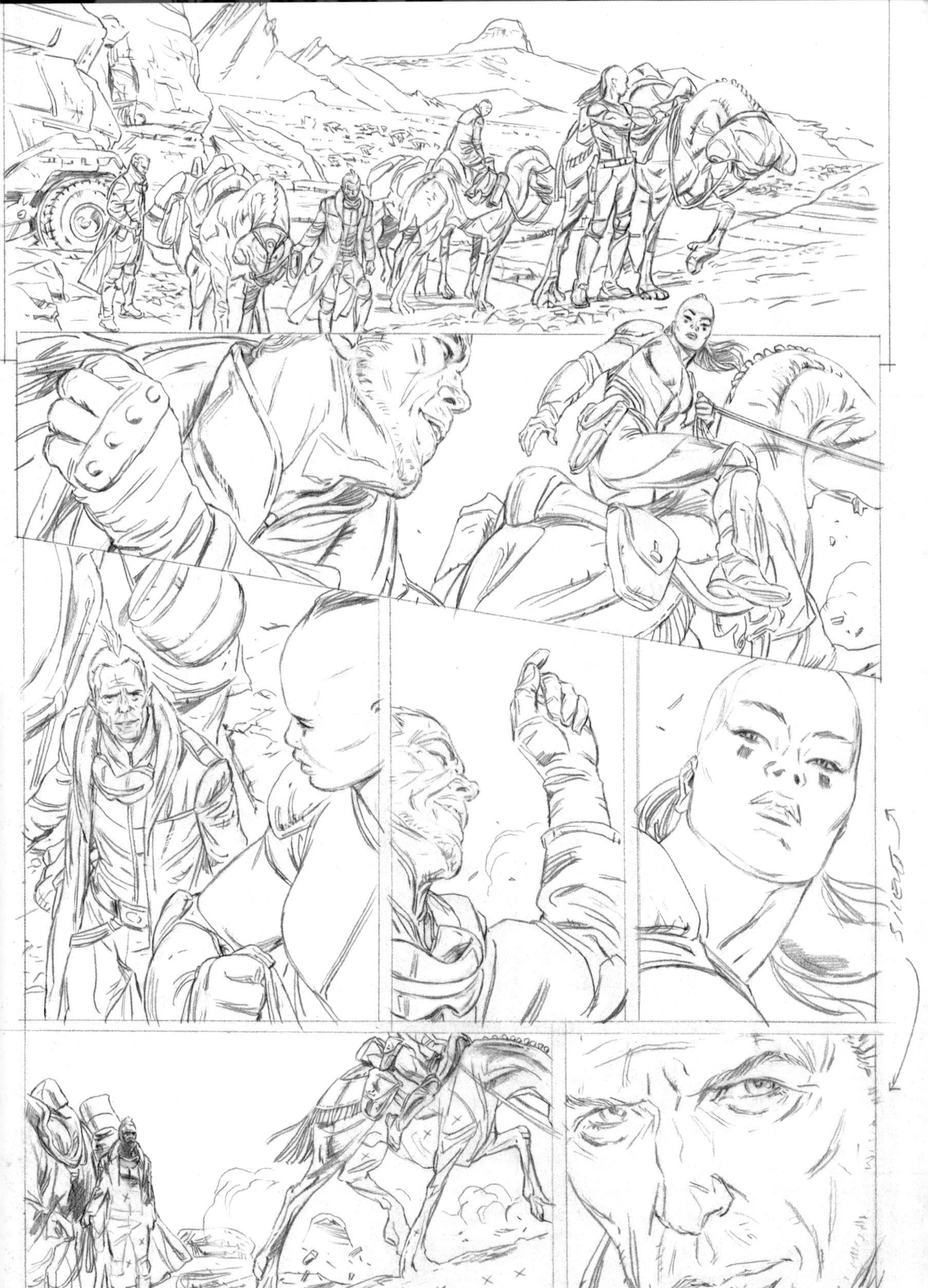
SILENT
SILENT
KICKING UP DUST AS SIAM RIDES UP AN INCLINE

SCRIPT TO ART

Page 4

Panel 1
Bronson's hand is busted up badly, the artificial fingers snapped and bent backwards. The wrist is limp and dangling as Bronson turns away from the buckled pillar, holding his forearm and cursing with rage.

Starck is still groggy but moving towards Bronson from behind.

     Bronson: SHIT!

Panel 2
Close-up on the broken wrist and the smashed fingers, showing sections of wiring and metal that have broken through the synthetic flesh.

     [NO COPY]

Panel 3
Starck grabs Bronson round the neck from behind with one arm, gripping his forearm with his other hand so he has Bronson in a hammerlock, hauling him violently backwards. As he does this, Bronson's vest splits to reveal a tattoo on his chest.

Doug: The tattoo is of a skull in the middle of a flaming sphere (representing a planet) with a dagger through the whole design. Beneath it, the number 29. Siam will know what this represents and somewhere down the line, where appropriate, we'll have her tell the story: [****** - removed for spoilers.]

Panel 4
Small close-up of the tattoo.

     [NO COPY]

Panel 5
Small close-up on Siam as she spots the tattoo.

     [NO COPY]

Panel 6
Full-length shot of Starck leaning back on the pillar, holding the struggling Bronson in the hammerlock. The fight is over and Starck snarls his last command to Bronson.

     Starck: YOU'RE FINISHED HERE BRONSON.

     (linked balloon): I WANT YOU OFF AMARANTH ON THE NEXT TRANSPORT.

This issue, you'll see the original script for Page 4 doesn't match the art. At Doug's request the opening scene was expanded and the rest of the script adjusted to give him an extra page for the action.

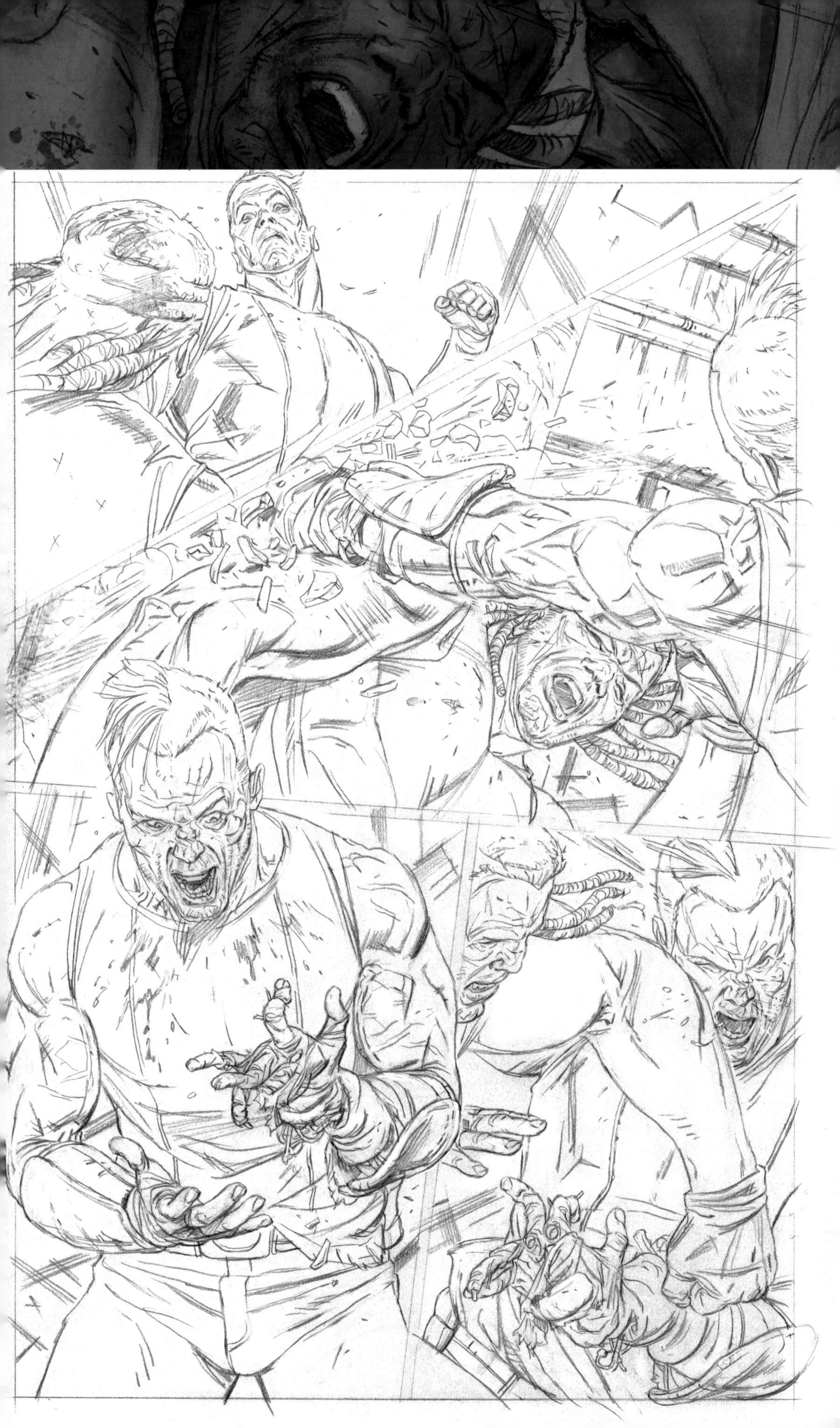

SCRIPT TO ART

Once again I've chosen a page where Dou deviated from the script on a couple c points, firstly altering the point of vie for Panel 1. The deep vertical panel works a lc better than my suggestion of an overhead vie Doug also suggested that the crystals shou be worn rather than embedded in Sarlat's hea which made more sense. One paragraph ha been removed. You'll have to wait for Season to find out what that revealed...

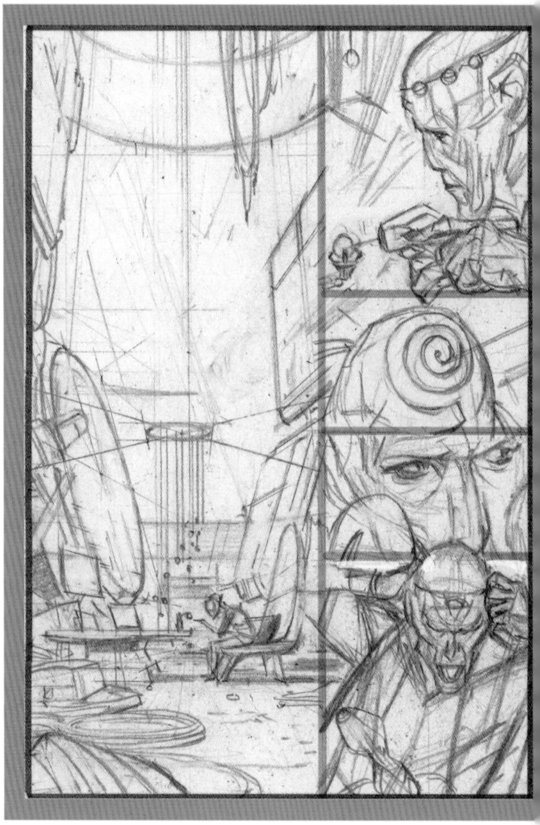

Page 5

Panel 1
Cut to: the ancient ruined Kismati city.

Doug, the back story is [XXX REMOVED FOR SPOILERS XXX] That's just for your information so you have a feel for this scene and what Sarlat is up to. No problem if the readers are still a bit mystified...

We are inside one of the ruined buildings. The architecture of the rooms is on a different scale to our own, built for a race of beings who were taller than us, and more importantly had ideas on a grander scale than us. This is a high POV, looking down towards Sarlat as he works on a crystal. Make him quite small and seen from above and behind. There are all kinds of coiled wires and cables all over the floor and hanging from the ceiling. Pieces of half-wrecked technology – machines that are long abandoned, dusty, rusty, broken – but a few of them are also plugged in and turned on, so there are glowing screens and control panels among the wreckage. Clearly Sarlat has been able to activate some parts of the machinery.

Sarlat himself is seated in a chair that is far too big for him, at a workbench covered in tools and retro/cyber-punk laptops and hand-held devices.

In front of him, in a semi-circle around the table, a large number of crystals are hanging from wires suspended from the ceiling, making a skein of glowing gems and wires. The crystals are all shapes and sizes. Sarlat is working on a single large crystal that is delicately clamped into place on the desk (not on a wire) – though at this distance we won't see it too clearly. He is working on it with a laser – a little like Dr Who's sonic screwdriver.

[NO COPY]

Panel 2
A side-view (?) of Sarlat working on the crystal. The crystal is suspended a few inches above the surface of the desk, clamped into the grip of thin adjustable metal arms that rise out of the desk and hold the crystal by the edges so that it is accessible at all angles.

Sarlat is all concentration, focusing the beam from the laser onto the crystal. The beam is incredibly narrow – the thickness of a hair. This is delicate work.

Sarlat has a whole row of crystals embedded into his forehead – half-a-dozen at least. They line up on either side of the eye in the centre of his forehead, growing progressively smaller as they follow the curve of his head all the way back to his ears.

[NO COPY]

Panel 3
Close-up of the crystal and the beam tracing a fine pattern onto its surface – it looks abstract but it means something to Sarlat.

[NO COPY]

Panel 4
Suddenly Sarlat jerks his head back, eyes wide as he feels the first pinprick of the Joppa's distress signal.

Sarlat: WHAT-?

Panel 5
Then he screams in agony, dropping the laser and clutching his head with both hands.

Sarlat: AIIEEEEE

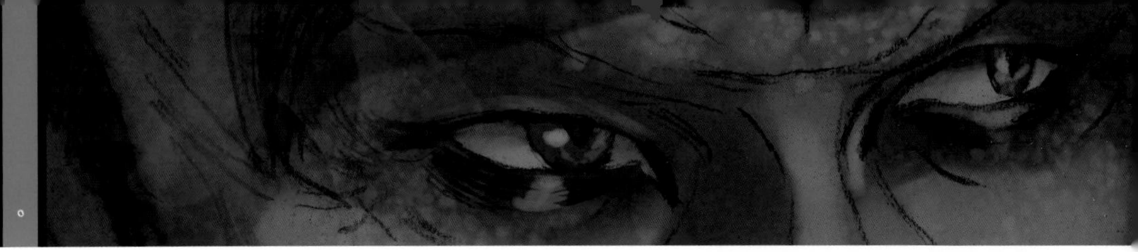

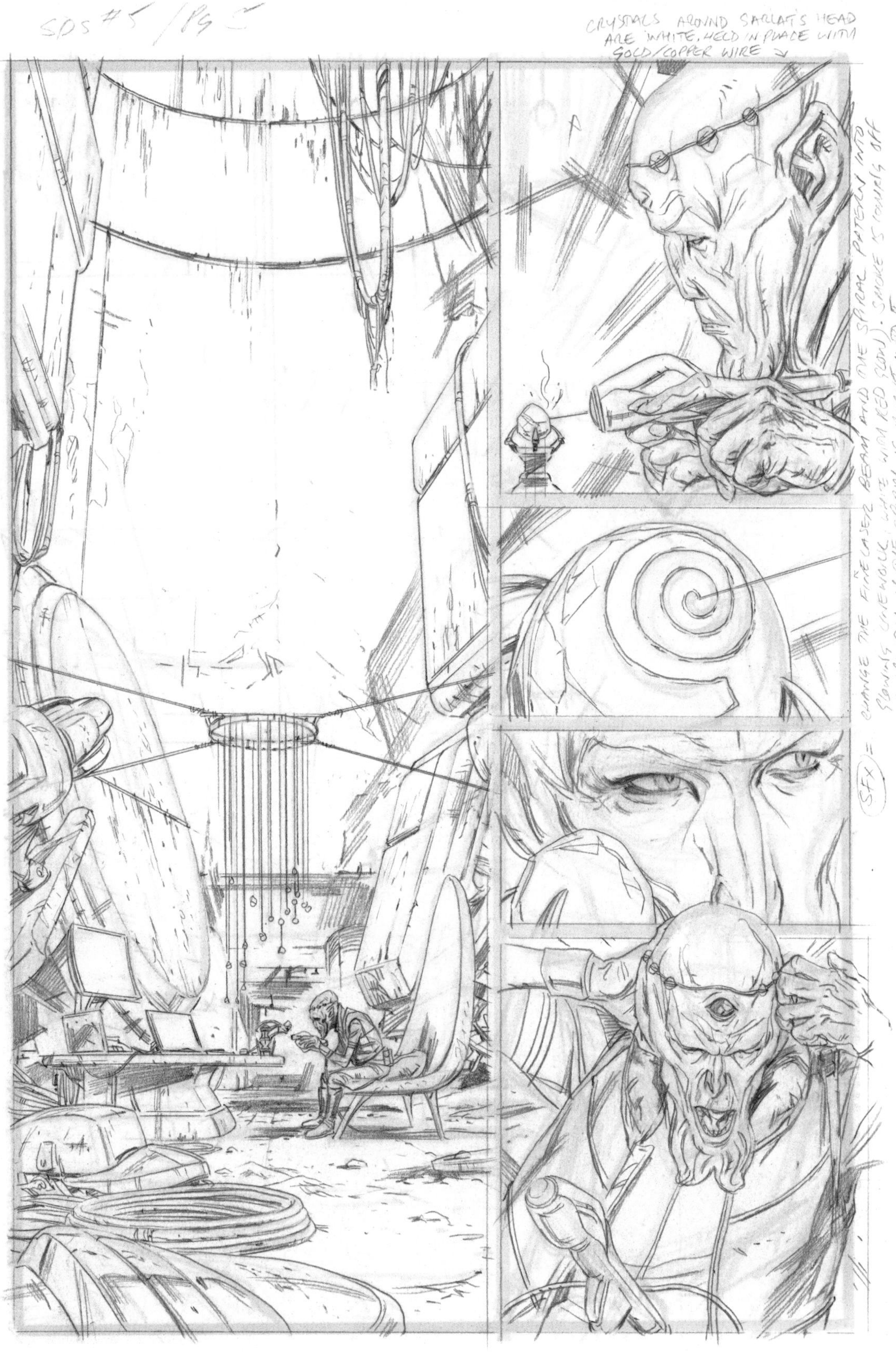
SDS #5 / Pg 5
CRYSTALS AROUND SARLAT'S HEAD ARE WHITE, HELD IN PLACE WITH GOLD/COPPER WIRE
SFX = CHANGE THE FINE LASER BEAM AND THE SPIRAL PATTERN INTO GLOWING LINEWORK (WHITE WITH RED GLOW). SMOKE IS COMING OFF THE CRYSTAL AS THE SPIRAL IS BURNT INTO IT.

DAVID HINE has been making comics professionally for 30 years. He has written scripts for SPIDER-MAN, X-MEN, THE INHUMANS, DAREDEVIL, BATMAN, GREEN LANTERN, THE SPIRIT, SPAWN, THE DARKNESS, CROSSED and ELEPHANTMEN. He is happiest working on creator owned projects like STRANGE EMBRACE, THE BULLETPROOF COFFIN with Shaky Kane and STORM DOGS with Doug Braithwaite, all published through Image comics. He has also written THE MAN WHO LAUGHS, illustrated by Mark Stafford for Selfmadehero in the UK. His preferred drink is JD and Coke, but Pepsi will do.

In a 20 + year career (he started when he was three) **DOUG BRAITHWAITE** has worked on many of the comic industry's flagship titles and has drawn just about every major character for both Marvel and DC Comics. His elegant drawing style has graced such titles as: JUSTICE, UNIVERSE X, PARADISE X, WOLVERINE: ORIGINS, JOURNEY INTO MYSTERY and his current project, STORM DOGS, with friend and co collaborator, David Hine. He has also been known to provide storyboards and concept designs for commercials, games and film. He is a native of London, England.

ULISES ARREOLA has been coloring comics for almost a decade. His main inspirations come from videogames, science-fiction art and traditional painting. He has worked at DC Comics on titles including SUPERMAN/ BATMAN, GREEN ARROW, BATGIRL and JUSTICE LEAGUE DARK. For Marvel Comics he has worked on YOUNG X-MEN, HALO: BLOOD LINE, JOHN CARTER: THE WORLD OF MARS and JOURNEY INTO MYSTERY. The latter was his first collaboration with Doug Braithwaite. Ulises is born and raised in Guadalajara, Mexico. He lives with his girlfriend Laura, Taison the dog and a cat named Cucho. He is working hard to fulfill his ambition to some day draw comics too!

JIMMY BETANCOURT has been lettering comics for the award-winning studio Comicraft for 12 years, proudly serving as part of Comicraft founder Richard Starkings' revolutionary army of fontmeisters and designers. When not showing off his skills as 'fastest letterer in the west' or watching a Lakers game, he's enjoying his time with his daughter Delaila in their home sweet home of Los Angeles.